LONG SHADOWS

Cultural Expressions of World War II

Interwar Preludes, Responses, Memory

Phyllis Lassner, Series Editor

Long Shadows

The Second World War in British Fiction and Film

Edited by Petra Rau

Northwestern University Press | Evanston, Illinois

Northwestern University Press
www.nupress.northwestern.edu

Printed in the United States of America

10 9 8 7 6 5 4 3 2 1

Library of Congress Cataloging-in-Publication Data

Names: Rau, Petra, 1969– editor.
Title: Long shadows : the Second World War in British fiction and film / edited by Petra Rau.
Other titles: Cultural expressions of World War II.
Description: Evanston, Illinois : Northwestern University Press, 2016. | Series: Cultural expressions of World War II: interwar preludes, responses, memory | "This edited collection saw its beginnings in an international conference titled "The Second World War: Popular Culture and Cultural Memory," organized in 2011 by Lucy Noakes, Juliette Pattinson, and myself at the University of Brighton"—Acknowledgments. | Includes bibliographical references and index.
Identifiers: LCCN 2015047829| ISBN 9780810133280 (pbk. : alk. paper) | ISBN 9780810133297 (cloth : alk. paper) | ISBN 9780810133358 (e-book)
Subjects: LCSH: English fiction—20th century—History and criticism. | English fiction—21st century—History and criticism. | Motion pictures—Great Britain. | World War, 1939–1945—Literature and the war. | World War, 1939–1945—Motion pictures and the war.
Classification: LCC PR888.W66 L66 2016 | DDC 823.914093584053—dc23
LC record available at http://lccn.loc.gov/2015047829

CONTENTS

ACKNOWLEDGMENTS

This edited collection saw its beginnings in an international conference titled "The Second World War: Popular Culture and Cultural Memory," organized in 2011 by Lucy Noakes, Juliette Pattinson, and myself at the University of Brighton. A huge thank-you goes to both for their enthusiasm, expertise, and hard work. Their edited collection *British Cultural Memory and the Second World War* (Bloomsbury, 2013) is an excellent and necessary companion volume to our efforts in this book. Both address the same issue from slightly different angles but attest to the cultural impact of the war in Britain and to the ongoing process of making sense of it from the early postwar years to the present day. I am very grateful to the Centre for Studies in Literature at the University of Portsmouth, which part-sponsored the event, and to my former colleagues there who supported it with good cheer.

Phyllis Lassner was an early champion of this collection. A particularly big thank-you must go to all contributors, who assisted their editor with patience and intellectual generosity. Moral support also came from Stephen Benson, Christine Berberich, Marina MacKay, and Gill Plain. Cath, Pip, and Otto don't get to choose the books they have to support, and I am therefore all the more grateful for their forbearance with yet another mentioning of the war.

A further thank-you to Rachel Goodyear, who copyedited meticulously and helped turn Anglo-Saxon prose into its Americanized version, and to the School for Literature, Drama, and Creative Writing at the University of East Anglia for financial assistance with this service.

LONG SHADOWS

PETRA RAU

Introduction
Long Shadows and Blind Spots

Few countries attribute as much importance to the Second World War and its memory as Britain; nowhere else has this conflict developed such longevity in cultural memory and retained such presence in contemporary culture. Since 1945 Britain has been involved in a range of military conflicts, yet by common consensus the phrase "the war" refers to the Second World War rather than any contemporaneous deployment of troops, say in the Middle East. The definite article is worth commenting on since its colloquial use indicates how much the 1939–45 war has shaped the generation that witnessed it. Before the war of 1914–18 assumed its status as the First World War it was called "the Great War" to distinguish its scope and impact from previous conflicts. There was nothing "great" about it other than the devastation it wreaked. The phrase "the war" suggests that the war in question is the determining conflict in the lives of those who participated in it, which would make it a temporally contingent signifier, as it were. Yet in its simplicity the phrase "the war" combines the form of the litotes with the meaning of the adynaton, the rhetorical figure Kate McLoughlin has identified as the classic gesture of unrepresentability in conjunction with war.[1] Mentioning "the war" is both an understatement and a gesture of futility, dispensing with epithets, numericals, or adjectives: does one need any more words for the scale of this catastrophe? No other war caused so many casualties and so much material damage, involved industrial genocide, impacted so many nations and their civilian populations, extended its battlefields over such a vast territory, unleashed nuclear weapons, shifted so many borders and displaced so many people, produced such mountains of bureaucratic documentation, and cast such long shadows in its aftermath, including a decades-long chillier version with proxy wars in remote places. Global statistics aside, for the British, "the war" has a status no other conflict since has overwritten, and that makes the meaning of the war in British culture different from say, its import in France or the United States. This book is primarily about how literature has helped shape this process in Britain but it also attends to other significant forms of (mass) cultural production, such as film and TV. More precisely, the essays collected here suggest that this is a continual work in progress and is subject to trans-generational revisions, political expediencies, commercial considerations, and the vicissitudes of popular taste. It would indeed be more accurate to speak of the meanings the war has been given at various moments in British cultural life. These semantic variations and fluctuations in cultural import are rooted in the specificity of the British war experience as well as the political aftermath of the war in Europe and its implications for Britain's position on the global stage. In other words, the books and visual material discussed in these essays respond to how the war has been interpreted and remembered; what is at stake is the way in which the war has been emplotted as a hegemonic cultural narrative *about* Britain.

Britain at War (and All That)

Although Britain's war spanned four continents—Europe, Africa, Asia, and Australia—and three oceans, the focus of popular memory has remained largely on mainland Britain and the theaters of war closest to home.[2] And even among the major military events here—the Battle of Britain, the evacuation from Dunkirk, the bombing raids, the D-Day landings—the Blitz has a special status. Again we note the use of a definite article. On the Continent, *Blitzkrieg* or "lightning war" was the term that summed up the speed and force with which Poland, Holland, France, and Belgium were overrun and forced to capitulate. In Britain, "the Blitz" stands for the prolonged aerial attack on cities and ports over nine months from September 1940 to May 1941; it is H. G. Wells's *The Shape of Things to Come* that is conjured up here rather than efficient military strategy. This was a relatively new experience that carried the war into the civilian sphere. The German bombing raids destroyed large areas in industrial cities (Coventry, Birmingham, Manchester, Belfast, Glasgow) and particularly targeted ports (Hull, Liverpool, Plymouth, Portsmouth, Southampton, Bristol, and Cardiff), but it is the attack on the capital that serves as the synecdoche for the experience of being bombed: London, which suffered fifty-seven consecutive nights of raids, particularly in the East End and the docklands area, saw the heaviest attacks and almost half the casualty numbers of the bombing. While the experience of the Blitz has lodged itself in popular memory for a number of reasons, statistics are perhaps least responsible.

The bombing reshaped the night life and the sleeping patterns of the inhabitants of London: underground stations became insanitary mass shelters when the air raid sirens went off; makeshift cellar bars moved from basement to basement. Street signs were taken down for fear of assisting an invading enemy, which made navigating the urban landscape harder, not least when bomb damage reshaped topography overnight. The blackout imposed a preindustrial darkness that facilitated both crime and sexual opportunism. The bombing also created a shortage of housing that opened up private spaces to strangers. Flats had to be shared. Children or entire families evacuated from imperiled or bombed urban areas found themselves "parked" with those in villages and country towns who had space but weren't always willing to accommodate evacuees.[3] There is a surreal quality to some of these experiences and images, captured in Lee Miller's photographs, Elizabeth Bowen's short stories, and Henry Moore's drawings.[4] What this surreality attempts to express is the rupture of war, its fundamental incongruity with ordinary life precisely at the moment when war has become ordinary, as in the famous photographs of gas mask containers being carried as nonchalantly as handbags, milk being delivered cheerfully across mounds of rubble, or books being perused by seemingly unperturbed readers in the bombed, roofless London Library. Those images are of course also litotes, symbols of national values (stoicism, emotional restraint, perseverance, good humor) that have since assumed mythical status: "London can take it." The Blitz on London is a narrative of resilience and sacrifice (which does not apply, for instance, to the much greater destruction of Hull and Coventry) that is core to the larger story of the People's War. The phrase itself, which forms the title of

Angus Calder's seminal 1969 social history of the war, refers to Britain's response to total war: the wide-ranging mobilization of civilians for the war effort that required unprecedented national consensus across all sections of society. The People's War, like the Blitz, was underpinned by a tremendous propaganda effort whose upper-middle-class civil servants and slogan writers initially got "the people" entirely wrong and produced posters and phrases that many citizens considered offensive and patronizing. Most notable was the them-and-us rhetoric in "*Your* courage, *your* cheerfulness, *your* resolution, will bring us victory." Indeed, as I have argued elsewhere, propaganda posters are a fairly good indication of how uncertain the political establishment was of the people's cheerfulness, resolution, and courage (in short, morale) in the early stages of the war.[5] Class divisions remained visible and palpable throughout the war, which is why propaganda worked so hard to convince everyone that they had to be overcome if the war was to be won. Propaganda films played a major part in demonstrating how national consensus and unity could be and was achieved: Noel Coward's *In Which We Serve* (1942) and Anthony Asquith's *The Way to the Stars* (1945) are master classes in arguing that "we're all in it together." As Richard Farmer demonstrates in his essay, these films were also made with an eye on how the war would be remembered.

Today, the metropolitan Blitz functions as a universal metonymy of the civilian British war experience, and to that end it is privileged and institutionalized in museums and national curricula as "a key moment in Britain's national history . . . a national history that spoke of Britain as historically and therefore 'traditionally' and 'naturally' standing for democracy, decency and freedom in a dangerous world."[6] Lucy Noakes's use of apostrophes in this quotation points to Roland Barthes's analysis of myth as a second-order semiological system that "transforms history into nature."[7] Myth should not be understood as fabrication or fiction, nor is it mendacity. Rather, it functions to disguise its own mechanics: it makes things "mean something by themselves" (Barthes, "Myth Today," 148); hence the appearance of naturalness. In the myth of the Blitz, the British "naturally" come together and put all social grievances, divisions, and self-interest aside to fight a common enemy because this is "what they are like" or "what they have always done." It "goes without saying." That this behavior was an effort (and therefore by no means a natural response), stimulated by propaganda, imposed by wartime legislation, and resented by many, is conveniently lost in this secondary semantic layer. Myth lingers because it simplifies a very complex set of circumstances into a much more straightforward and emotionally resonant *fact* that appears to need no explanation. The sanitized interpretation of the Blitz as a moment of resilience and unproblematic national unity has become a cliché of considerable political expediency since the 1980s, wheeled out by politicians and the mass media at opportune moments from the Falklands War to the terrorist attacks on London's public transport system in 2005.

Angus Calder's revisionist social history *The Myth of The Blitz* (1992) has done little to dislodge the myth in the popular memory: it has become a truism, and evidence for the way in which propaganda photography and film have won an easy victory. Calder's work was crucial for many other academic and popular historians who have given us a much more complex picture of the British home front, for instance: Sonya O. Rose's *Which People's War: National Identity and Citizenship in Wartime Britain* (2004), Juliet Gardiner's *Wartime: Britain 1939–1945* (2005), or Susan R. Grayzel's *At Home and Under Fire: Air Raids and Culture in Britain from the Great War to the Blitz* (2012). Antisemitic attitudes hardened in London; the disaster at Bethnal Green tube station where 173 people were crushed in an accident on the stairs was covered up as a direct hit; looting, striking, or black marketeering have been written out of the popular home front narrative altogether as have conscientious objectors or pacifists, many of whom did agricultural or clerical work or served in the fire or ambulance service. The presence of Allied service personnel created sexual opportunities and rivalries. Birth rates rose; so did divorce rates and crime rates. Enemy aliens were interned both in the dominions and on the Isle of Man, irrespective of whether they could prove their loyalty to the British crown or had suffered persecution under the Nazis.

Most remarkable, perhaps, is how the cultural memory of the war has overwritten the military narrative with a civilian one, and this also accounts for the greater presence of women. The British war effort called women into the factories, recruited them in so-called land armies for agricultural work, demanded their skills in offices, and put them into uniform in the women's branch of the Auxiliary Territorial Service (ATS), the Women's Auxiliary Air Force (WAAF), the Women's Royal Naval

Service (Wren), or the Women's Voluntary Service (WVS). If women's wartime service identity did not yield an acronym, it might still turn them into nurses or air raid wardens. In Britain, the war drafted women from their conventional domestic sphere into the war effort to an extent that was unique in Europe (only Soviet Russia actively trained women for frontline service, notably as women pilots). Contrary to popular belief, women in Nazi Germany escaped much of this mobilization because of the gender-specific division of labor in Nazi ideology. The Bund deutscher Mädel (League of German Girls) supported the war effort as flak helpers, searchlight operators, or signals auxiliaries during bombing raids or served as nurses' assistants at train stations and in hospitals. The femininity of the German woman was not to be compromised by the masculine business of war, and her British counterpart, newly but temporarily in trousers and overalls, was exhorted to do her best to remain feminine.[8] More important than mandatory use of lipstick and curlers were the opportunities outside the home that the war afforded this generation of women. These shifts in, or relaxations of, gender roles, did not outlast the war: the postwar era saw a return to conservative interpretations of masculinity and femininity, which is one of the reasons why many women who left the domestic sphere during the war remember this time with a certain nostalgia.

One of the reasons why the popular narrative of Britain at war could establish itself as the dominant one was that the literary representation of war in the 1940s never became mainstream or indeed entered a literary canon. (The best-known novel of the decade, Orwell's *Nineteen Eighty-Four* is not about war but about totalitarianism.) In other words, no one knew what to do with this awkward decade, pinched between late modernism, Angry Young Men, the return to realism, and early postmodern experiments. Bestselling writers in the decade often avoided the war as a straightforward topic and offered escapism in the form of crime, historical romance, or comedy of manners, as Gill Plain argues in her essay. Those who might fulfill conservative notions of canonicity—Henry Green, Elizabeth Bowen, Patrick Hamilton, Rose Macaulay, Stevie Smith—had to be rediscovered decades later and editions of their work could still be hard to come by (which in turn made them hard to include on university reading lists). For a long time, the literature of the 1940s languished without much critical attention. Its coming to renewed prominence within the academy[9] is perhaps thanks to the emergence of fields of study that are attentive to its specificity: memory studies, trauma studies, and the weakening of the boundaries between the popular and the literary, an entirely appropriate way of shaking off modernist doxas for the sake of cultural history and period study. And yet even the return of mid-century writing to the academic agenda (and publishers' back lists) has not resuscitated every writer of potential interest: a case in point is Storm Jameson, prolific and politically engaged (and discussed in this volume by her biographer, Elizabeth Maslen), whose focus on European issues and conditions might serve as a corrective to the focus on home front issues of British battlefields. She remains largely out of print.[10] Many who were popular at the time—Graham Greene, George Orwell, Nevil Shute, Alexander Baron—wrote about war in a way that counteracted the popular myths that were already shaping up during the war years. These writers were popular precisely because they did not patronize their audiences. Patrick Hamilton (who was at the time more successful as a playwright and scriptwriter) conceived of shared living space in wartime as a catalyst for psychopathological behavior, as Eluned Summers-Bremner argues in her essay on *The Slaves of Solitude*. Both Elizabeth Taylor and Elizabeth Bowen emphasized how strange it was to live in borrowed spaces. Their characters are not psychopathological but afflicted with such a sense of the provisional and contingent that this uncertainty affects their sense of identity to the extent that the reader might come to think of the conditional tense and the subjunctive mode as stylistic hallmarks of wartime fiction.

In contrast, the home front was a rather neglected space in the British war film of the 1950s and the bestselling fiction of the time. This decade was characterized by the representation of specific military battles, service groups, or localized theaters of war. Here, the war could be replayed with hindsight and with an eye on a specifically male audience.[11] The appeal lay in the focus on wartime homosociality (in contrast to the reality of postwar nuclear families): on submarines, in the merchant navy, on RAF bases or in bomber crews, in POW camps or in combat units, men fought the war as an old-fashioned test of masculinity but not without humor and not without working through anxieties about class or male authority.[12] That war remained a popular subject is borne out by paperback sales and box office figures. Indeed, many war novels became bestsellers with the help of film adaptations, such as Nicholas Monsarrat's *The Cruel Sea* (1951, filmed 1953), or Alistair MacLean's *The Guns of Navarone* (1958, filmed 1960). As Robert Murphy has argued, during a period in which the war had deepened the generation gap between parents and children, the war film was one of the few things fathers and sons could share.[13] The wide range of British military experiences covered by the decade's war films is astonishing, as is their success against competition from Hollywood. For Murphy, this success is rooted in the audience's attraction to the "myths around Britain's achievement in the Second World War" (*British Cinema in the Second World War*, 234), but as Mark Connelly has argued, not all campaigns captured the cinematic or audience's imagination: Italy and certainly Greece remained marginal and had to wait for fiction and its TV adaptations later in the century;[14] the Strategic Air Offensive and the Battle of the Atlantic were similar casualties in the popular memory, often only represented by one film.[15] The Far East did not fare much better. Nevil Shute's *A Town Like Alice* (1950) focused on the Commonwealth's experience under Japanese occupation and was adapted to film in 1956. David Lean's Oscar-winning *The Bridge on the River Kwai* (1957), based on Pierre Boulle's French novel, recalls the experience of British servicemen as Japanese POWs but it is fiercely critical of poor leadership (whether British or Japanese) and highly ambivalent about concepts such as "honor" or "heroism." If the Pacific theater of war featured at all in the popular memory of the war it is because of these iconic cinematic representations. The protracted and arduous Burmese campaign (1942–45), for instance, saw epic battles but while Stalingrad, El Alamein, or even Dunkirk resonate, hardly anyone has heard of Kohima. Nor does Singapore ring a bell. (It was not until 1978 that J. G. Farrell's *The Singapore Grip* fictionalized the fall of that city to the Japanese in 1942.) Egypt, however, is on the map because of Christopher Landon's novel *Ice Cold in Alex* (1957, filmed 1958) and a whole host of other films about Rommel, "Monty," or El Alamein as the turning point of the British war on the road to victory. In contrast, the British defeat in Southeast Asia and the Pacific focuses the representation of war here on the fate of POWs in Japanese camps. Consequently, spiritual resilience had to replace military success: just as Dunkirk became the rescue by the little boats, Singapore and Malaya could be turned into stories of stoic resilience—at a push. Yet the war in the Pacific was won by the United States, and the British defeat in this theater felt too much like a prelude to the postwar disintegration of the British Empire in Asia, and therefore another reason to keep attention firmly clamped on Europe and its fringes.

Britain's geographical position as an island nation made its war experience very different from that of continental countries. It made German invasion much harder to undertake, let alone achieve, although it was a real threat in the early stages of the war. Mainland Britain escaped occupation, but the Channel Islands, with their proximity to the French coast, were not so fortunate, and as a result their place in the British narrative of the war is complex and contentious. Occupied territories fell under Nazi German (or in the Pacific theater, Japanese) rule, which in Europe meant that public officials were forced to collaborate with the occupying army and were subject to the German requisitioning of food, weapons, horses and vehicles, natural resources, buildings and accommodation, clothes, labor, and whatever else Germany extracted for its war effort. Artworks were taken, musical instruments carried off, typewriters and radios collected, real estate expropriated—everything that was moveable was moved "heim ins Reich," from borders to bibles. Nazi rule also meant the systematic registration, persecution, rounding up, ghettoization, and deportation of Jews to concentration and extermination camps. It meant able-bodied men and women could be taken to German farms and factories as slave laborers; political dissidents and members of resistance movements, Sinti and Roma, Jehovah's Witnesses and religious opponents to Nazism, homosexuals, and the disabled were subject to the same Aryan race laws, euthanasia practices, and persecution as the citizens of the Third Reich. As the continental front line moved forwards and back in the latter stages of the war, many occupied territories became battlefields and virtual thoroughfares for armies in retreat or advance. Their landscapes may still bear the battle scars of Allied and Axis bombings, and the Channel Islands are still physically marked by bunkers, tunnels, and other vast concrete fortifications. The birth registers of many Nazi-occupied territories indicate tens of thousands of ostensibly fatherless entries, children that are the offspring of wartime unions between German soldiers and local women. Yet the events and aftermath of Nazi occupation are some of the least explored aspects of the war throughout Europe and Britain.[16]

Coming to terms with what happened under Nazi occupation continues to be a protracted and difficult process for many formerly occupied countries, and the Channel Islands are no exception. Madeleine Bunting's critical account *The Model Occupation* (1995) earned her the respect of fellow historians but her revelations (accompanied by many sources and photographic evidence) were less welcome among the Channel Islanders themselves, who did not want to be reminded of aspects of the occupation that did not cast them as unequivocal patriotic victims: the amicable relations between well-provisioned and well-mannered German soldiers and local women; the deportation of Jewish residents to Auschwitz; the virtual absence of any resistance; the appalling treatment of foreign slave laborers. Active collaboration and resistance lie at the extreme ends of a wide spectrum of behavior that for many wartime citizens might have meant some sort of accommodation: a mode of survival in which one does not actively support Nazism but manages the terminal risks of open resistance through a carefully calibrated case-by-case decision of daily muddling through, with all its attendant incremental erosion of moral integrity. The pragmatic solutions found immediately after the war often had the aim of restoring a level of cohesion and enabling a national community to leave the war behind rather than dealing with the political, ethnic, or social ruptures within communities that occupation produced or deepened. Most notoriously, in France Charles de Gaulle declared that every French citizen had resisted (presumably by dint of being French). Such resistance myths alongside representative trials of official Nazi collaborators and war criminals reestablished a sharp moral line between German guilt and the collective innocence of the occupied; the murkier the reality, the sharper the retroactive line. The ensuing collective silence also made it harder to remember, let alone commemorate, the past in its complexity. It is no coincidence that "the war" provides such a rich seam for recent European crime writing (a genre whose solutions often require an investigation into the past): Jo Nesbø, Henning Mankell, Stieg Larsson, or Carlo Lucarelli are just some of the writers whose plots revolve around the secret afterlife of occupation.

The Channel Islands occupation leads a truly shadowy existence, barely on the margins of popular memory or media representation in Britain. It does not fit into the hegemonic narrative of the resilient island race "standing alone" as the sole bastion of freedom in Europe. In this narrative of national character and moral exceptionalism, the Channel is a sort of Marianas Trench between the compromised occupied Continent and the democratic "Sceptered Isle," but it comes at the cost of ceding Guernsey, Jersey, and Alderney to France, as it were. Integrating it into the British story of the war would mean admitting that when put to the test, British behavior was neither better nor worse than that of any other nation under Nazi occupation. The fiction about the occupation—Tim Binding's *Island Madness* (1998), Guy Walters's *The Occupation* (2004), Mary Ann Shaffer and Annie Barrows's *The Guernsey Literary and Potato Peel Pie Society* (2008), Margaret Leroy's *The Collaborator* (2011), Mary Horlock's *The Book of Lies* (2012)—is part of the literary rediscovery of neglected aspects of the war and a more morally complex version of its history, as Sue Vice discusses in her chapter. Yet these British books have emerged long after revisionist literary and cinematic treatments of Continental occupation, beginning early with French existentialists' novels (de Beauvoir's *Le Sang des autres*, Camus's *L'Étranger*, Sartre's *La Mort dans l'âme*) and followed by Marcel Ophuls's documentary *Le Chagrin et le pitié* (1969) and Louis Malle's then taboo-breaking *Lacombe, Lucien* (1974). Similarly, Harry Mulisch's novel about the Dutch occupation, *De Aanslag* (1982), also long preceded Paul Verhoeven's film *Zwartboek* (2008), while the Danish occupation (generally thought to be the least ignominious) had to wait until 2008 to be filmed by Ole Christian Madsen in *Flammen & Citronen* (2008). Conversely, in Poland films such as Andrzej Wajda's *War Trilogy* (1954–58) and Andrzej Munk's chilling *Passażerka* (1963) preceded Andrzej Szczypiorski's novel *I ominęli Emaus* (1974), let alone more recent fictional treatment by contemporary Polish writers Joanna Bator and Szczepan Twardoch and director Pawel Pawlikowki's award-winning *Ida* (2014). Norway, too, took a long time to address its occupation. Escaped journalist Åke Fen published his report *Nazis in Norway* in a Penguin special in 1942, and John Steinbeck's novella *The Moon Is Down* (1942) was disseminated in occupied countries for propaganda purposes, but after the war it took the German writer Siegfried Lenz's *Stadtgespräch* (1965) before the crime writer Jo Nesbø's *Rødstrupe* (2000) tackled head-on what Per Petterson's *Til Sibir* (1996) and Gunnar Kopperund's *Lysets Tyd* (1998) only managed to approach indirectly: wartime collaboration and home-grown fascist leanings.

The fear of invasion in an island nation—and its relative rarity compared with the historical experience of countries sharing borders on a landmass—is perhaps also partly to blame for why the Channel Islands have habitually been squeezed out of the British narrative of "the war." Averting the threat of invasion had certainly heightened the reputation of the RAF fighter pilots who defended British air space against the Luftwaffe in the Battle of Britain. It featured in one of the most violent British films of the war, Cavalcanti's *Went the Day Well?* (1942), in which German paratroopers land near an English village and are killed one by one by the local population. It is a perennial trope in counterfactual fiction and film of the Second World War, from Kevin Brownlow and Andrew Mollo's *It Happened Here* (1964) to Jack Higgins's *The Eagle Has Landed* (1975), Len Deighton's *SS-GB* (1978), and, more recently, C. J. Sansom's *Dominion* (2012) and Jason Hewitt's *The Dynamite Room* (2014). This shadow of an invasion, let alone an occupation, still hangs over Britain: it is partly a coin-operated fictional fantasy in which the limits of consensus in general and fascist sympathies in particular can be explored more fully. Any present fears about Britain's security can be played out or worked through on the counterfactual stage. Invasion anxiety has borne some bizarre commercial fruits, such as the now ubiquitous "Keep Calm and Carry On" merchandise.[17] The slogan epitomizes the stiff upper lip mentality attributed to the wartime generation, but it was actually a government poster printed in huge numbers prior to the war to counteract mass panic anticipated to break out in response to aerial attacks. Part of the divisive early propaganda campaign cited above that showed so little confidence in citizens' morale, the poster was never displayed publicly and remained largely unknown until it was discovered by accident again in 2000. Since then it has been marketed on mugs, posters, towels, T-shirts, stationery, and key chains as well as parodied and co-opted for political campaigns.

The continued media presence of the war might lead any non-British visitor or resident to the conclusion that this war is actually still being fought, at least on TV and in the pages of the *Daily Mail* and *The Sun*, when in any other participating or affected country (with the exception of Germany) it has long been consigned to the historical archive. Then again, it was a war that utilized modern media in an unprecedented way and for this reason it is of course the most extensively documented war of the twentieth century; its bureaucracy alone has kept historians and archivists busy. Radio broadcasts, propaganda material, newsreels and photography, amateur films, alongside the mountains of paperwork, minutes, files, communiqués, Mass Observation reports,[18] and reminiscences constitute a near-inexhaustible if exhausting archival corpus.

Fallout

I argued above that in its mythology and media representation, "the war" developed an unprecedented longevity. Its official duration actually depended on where a person happened to be and what nation he or she belonged to. For Britain the conflict is demarcated by the declaration of war against Germany on September 3, 1939 and, at the other end, by the German signing of the surrender documents on May 8, 1945 and the Japanese signing of the surrender documents on September 2, 1945. For those Britons deployed or interned in the Pacific, this war officially lasted one day short of six long years, but it was much longer for the Chinese who had been invaded in 1937 and shorter for the Americans who joined the war in 1941. Even for the troops, war did not suddenly stop: many soldiers continued to be deployed in the administration of occupied territories, notably in the British occupation zone in Germany. British POWs had to be repatriated from German and Japanese territory, often in a very fragile state of health.

Since Homer's urtexts of warfare, the *Iliad* and the *Odyssey*, we think of the *nostos* (or homecoming) as part of the conflict rather than its aftermath. Odysseus's protracted journey back to Ithaca, with its delays and perils, is integral to the story of the Trojan War as is Agamemnon's fate at the hands of his adulterous wife and her lover. Unlike the implacable heroes of Greek myth, the war would be harder to mythologize or shake off for those who came back deeply traumatized by what they had witnessed, endured, or done, like Charley Summers in Henry Green's *Back* (1946). The point of the novel's title is of course that coming back to where one has left off (the desire for restoration and resumption) is always met with frustration because nothing ever stays the same: by definition the one who returns always lags behind, caught between desire for the past and the need to catch up with the present. Both temporal spaces are versions of "back" but they are irreconcilable. Then there were those who had no "home" to return to because it had been bombed, because the war years had estranged them from their spouses, because the territorial changes of the 1945 Potsdam Conference made it harder if not impossible for them to return to the Continent, or because they did not wish to return to countries that had deemed them nonpersons. Exiles and refugees, the Jewish children of the *Kindertransport*, Polish and Czech servicemen—many of them stayed and made Britain their home, and this often meant that energy was devoted to making a life in Britain rather than looking back: Elias Canetti, Arthur Koestler, Hilde Spiel, Gitta Sereny, H. G. Adler, Michael Hamburger, Frank Auerbach, Eric Hobsbawm, Nicolas Pevsner, and George Szirtes are among many who have made a tremendous contribution to British cultural life. It is characteristic of this group that their memoirs, if they did write them, were published decades after the war. As Lyndsey Stonebridge has recently pointed out in *The Judicial Imagination*, witnessing such dislocations and deracinations also affected postwar British fiction. Refugees and various Displaced Persons from all over Europe wander through the early fiction of Iris Murdoch (who worked at the UNRRA camps) and cast a long shadow over *Eva Trout*, the last novel of Elizabeth Bowen (who reported about the 1946 Paris Peace Conference).[19]

British soldiers, however, could come home to a country whose boundaries had not changed. This was not the case on the Continent where territorial changes reordered Europe, from 1945 to 1948, into much more ethnically homogeneous groupings; where so-called Displaced Persons waited in holding centers or reused former concentration or POW camps to return home or to be given permission to emigrate; where millions of expellees were on the move, often merely with the clothes on their backs and whatever they could carry, to find a new residence.[20] In Eastern Europe, Soviet liberation from Nazi occupation and collaboration helped set up a transition to communist rule. According to Tony Judt, the years 1945–48 saw both the beginning of Europe's reconstruction and its ideological division, and they also molded Europe's postwar memory.[21] In the Eastern bloc, the war would be remembered differently, as a fight against fascism and capitalism and for a communist future. In those countries, 1989 is a watershed that releases the Eastern bloc from decades of communist oppression that either buried the Second World War in an ideological foundation myth or emplotted it in ways that made it much harder to establish an accurate historical record, let alone remember it in all its contradictions and complexities. None of this ideological layering applies to Britain, but this is not to say that the war is not also seen as the threshold to a new era.

In spite of its official *durée*, the war also had its *longeur*. After the victory at El Alamein, and certainly after the Soviet Army's victory in the Battle of Stalingrad in 1943, it seemed clear that Nazi Germany could not win this war. It was not clear how long it would take the Allies to defeat fascism and force Germany (and Japan) into unconditional surrender. The enormous military campaigns of the invasion of Italy, the Normandy landings, and the real thrust of the bombing campaign were still to be accomplished, but with the immediate threat of invasion gone there was a sense in Britain that after the winter of 1942–43 winning the war was a matter of time. Psychologically the war and the postwar could overlap. Indeed, those six long war years took their toll emotionally and spiritually even before hostilities ceased. All-encompassing as total war must have felt at least in urban areas, it invaded the private lives of millions in ways that the previous world war never did. This was partly the result of the Emergency Powers Act of 1939, which enabled the British government to pass defense regulations that intruded into almost every aspect of daily life: it rationed food, clothing, and energy. It restricted mobility, communications, and privacy. It requisitioned property and resources. Wartime propaganda involved the most modern technologies such as radio and newsreel: frontline footage, however edited and censored, could be presented to a cinema audience and bring the battlefield into the auditorium. Newspapers did not just deliver the war to the breakfast table but incessantly instructed citizens about their do's and don'ts. Propaganda posters did the same, and were displayed in canteens, mess halls, factories, offices, underground stations, shops, on buses, and—blown up to Orwellian proportions *avant la lettre*—on billboards at the roadside.[22] The slogan "There's a war on, you know" soon mutated from a morale-building rallying call to a busybody's exhortation. Small wonder, then, that escapism became the point of popular reading and cinemagoing habits, as Gill Plain argues, hence the success of Gainsborough period dramas, crime fiction, and historical romance.[23] On the most banal level of quotidian existence the war was an intrusion into lives and minds from which many sought to escape at least temporarily. Its omnipresence was partly responsible for the eagerness with which many sought to leave it behind as soon as possible. The need for economic and urban reconstruction shifted the focus onto the present and the future, and that odd commingling of hiatus between and overlap of war and postwar in the late 1940s is perhaps best captured in the term "reconstruction fiction" that Paula Derdiger uses for her analysis of Elizabeth Taylor's novel *At Mrs Lippincote's*: much of this literature is still about the war but can reflect about it more critically in the secure knowledge of having emerged from it.

The desire to leave both the war and the prewar behind was also expressed by the electorate, who associated the Conservative Party with the policies and social attitudes of the 1930s. The man who had steered the country through the war was not deemed to be the best choice for its future course: Labour's Clement Attlee replaced the Conservative Winston Churchill as Prime Minister, and his government set up what became known as the Welfare State. Following the Beveridge report of 1942, the British government passed legislation that set up the National Health Service (NHS) throughout the United Kingdom by 1948, which made fundamental health care free at point of use. This service remains a cornerstone of postwar British social identity, proudly celebrated in the opening ceremony at the London Olympic Games of 2012. The principle underlying the NHS—that medical care is a human right and a social responsibility in a civilized society—has undoubtedly contributed to greater social equality in Britain. It is often cited as a direct achievement of the war—as if it had been a war aim—and indeed fighting for a better future became part of official propaganda in the latter stages of the war as a way of cementing the national consensus of unity. More accurately, the landslide victory of Attlee's Labour Party, which had run a campaign on the slogan "Let us face the Future" and with the Welfare State as part of its election manifesto, suggested that the electorate gave a clear majority mandate to a party that would not restore Britain to the 1930s but reward the war effort with social and economic reforms. It is astonishing, then, given this desire for change, that the most potent symbol of the future—children—do not feature more prominently in the British films and fiction of the postwar years. Allan Hepburn's essay refers to a number of infants as *minor* characters, wandering in from the fringes of the plot. These double minors appear strangely evacuated from discourses about the future as if they had to be protected from its uncertainty rather than placed squarely in its center. Humphrey Jennings's film *A Diary for Timothy* is an exception. When children are at the heart of the fictional future, as in William Golding's 1954 dystopia *Lord of the Flies*, they are ill equipped to survive.

The war had bankrupted Britain; it was seriously short of the labor force required for rebuilding the nation's economy, public services, and housing. Rationing continued until 1954. Tellingly, the titles of David Kynaston's trilogy of postwar British history (*Austerity Britain: 1945–51, Family Britain: 1951–57, and Modernity Britain: Opening the Box, 1957–59*) suggest a trajectory of slow recovery marked by economic strain and inwardness. Socioeconomic progress throughout the 1940s and 1950s was slow and social attitudes remained conservative. Unlike the United States, Britain did not descend into the peculiar combination of McCarthyite anticommunist witch hunts coupled with an increasingly consumerist society that ensured social conservatism (a milder version of which shaped the Adenauer years in West Germany). Rather, Britain's anxieties were less about the political enemy within or without than about what now constituted Britishness (*plus ça change*). In that sense, the cultural fallout from the war did not so much reveal the limits of consensus but questioned precisely what remained of it without the external stimulus of war. According to Alice Ferrebe, the literature of the 1950s was much more politically engaged than it is often given credit for.[24] Why were there "angry young men"? The campus novel and the kitchen sink drama spoke of social aspirations and domestic claustrophobia, the Wolfenden report of 1957 pointed to the dire situation of homosexual men, while the early work of Doris Lessing and Margaret Drabble showed young women despairing at the prospect of a life limited to hosting, scrubbing, suckling, dressing, and perming. And how did the new immigrants from the West Indies fit in? The popularity of TV series such as *The Hour* or *Call the Midwife* is based not just on unqualified nostalgia for mid-century chic; well-made period drama also conveys the racism, sexism, deep-rooted class prejudice, and homophobia of the postwar years. No decade was dingier than the 1950s.

Gill Plain has suggested that peace is perhaps not the right word at all for the late 1940s and early 1950s, hence the inverted commas in the subtitle of her study of the literature of the 1940s, *Literature of the 1940s: War, Postwar and the "Peace."* Indeed, the Cold War had already blossomed into existence in the final months of the Second World War and kindled anxieties of nuclear conflict (Nevil Shute's 1948 novel *On the Beach* became one of the early postwar bestsellers, and Golding's first novel was set in the aftermath of nuclear war). Totalitarianism was not vanquished but expanded its influence under Stalin to turn Eastern Europe into a communist bloc while China emerged from civil war as a communist People's Republic. George Orwell's *Nineteen Eighty-Four* was not so much a futuristic dystopia as an extrapolation from the already known (Nazism) to the yet to be fathomed (Stalinism). An early and persistent advocate of the importance of Europe (and an international outlook) for Britain was Storm Jameson, whose novels engage thoroughly with the vicissitudes of Continental politics before, during, and after the war, as Elizabeth Maslen argues. Yet much of her work remains out of print. This is not the case for much of the popular fiction that lucratively grafted itself onto the ideological divides of the Cold War in order to point to the continuities between the Second World War and its frostier cousin on the one hand, and between the modus operandi of Western democracies and Eastern dictatorships on the other. In his analysis of spy fiction Adam Piette identifies so-called emergency-state thinking that legitimizes measures against political threats in a genre that articulates uneasy ambivalences about postwar democracy.

If the war fared well at the box office in the 1950s, its legacy also continued to put young men into uniform: National Service remained in place for young men from the ages of 17 to 21, and before long, British troops were deployed again in Korea, against communist insurgents in the Malayan "Emergency," in Kenya, and in Cyprus. These conflicts were part of a painful and violent process of decolonization that would ultimately dismantle the British Empire and diminish Britain's influence on the world stage. This process began shortly after the war with the partition of British India in 1947 and continued with Palestine, Ceylon, and Burma gaining independence in 1948. It is perhaps ironic that the Prime Minister who had held the empire together during the war presided over its most violent resistance to British rule in the mid-1950s in the Mau Mau uprising in Kenya, during the Suez crisis in 1956, and until Malayan independence in 1957. All of these cessations also meant the loss of access to natural resources for British merchants and entrepreneurs, settlers and planters. The population of the United Kingdom might have felt that the effort of the war entitled them to a better future, but its government resisted precisely such concessions to its colonial subjects although it had deployed colonial troops to fight racist regimes without addressing its own racist attitudes. A long-standing critic of British hypocrisy, E. M. Forster had marveled at the inconsistencies in British foreign policy in his wartime essay "On Tolerance" (1944). According to Phyllis Lassner, a number of postwar British women writers felt similar discomfort at the persistent racial inequality that lay at the heart of imperialism.[25] The contribution of colonial troops to Allied victory remains a blind spot in popular memory, not least because many of these troops were deployed in the Asian theater of war. While they featured in propaganda posters such as in the *Together* campaign, and in war films of the 1940s and '50s (where they tend to be Canadian, Australian, or South African), their contribution deserves much more recognition. The pension rights of Gurkhas, for instance, were at the forefront of a recent celebrity campaign by the actress Joanna Lumley. Postcolonial writers such as Ngũgĩ wa Thiong'o, Thomas Keneally, Michael Ondaatje, Amitav Gosh, and Biyi Bandele have reminded their English-language audience of the contribution of nonwhite troops and non-European battlefields. Michael Perfect's timely essay on the novels of Zadie Smith and Andrea Levy analyzes the arguments between the war and Britain's postwar path to a multicultural society.

Britain's postwar diminution on the world stage—most palpable in the diplomatic and military debacle of the Suez Crisis of 1956—and the disintegration of the British Empire may well have contributed to the nostalgia with which the Second World War continues to be remembered. The wars to pacify and hold on to the empire are less morally clear-cut or justifiable, and retrospectively elevate the Second World War to the last "good" war, that is, a war fought for good causes.[26] "The war" remains an occasion for universal patriotism and pride that none of the subsequent conflicts seemed to merit. In fact, on occasions when "the war" was referenced in acts of particularly obvious grandstanding—as in Margaret Thatcher's response to the Argentine invasion of the Falkland Islands—it seemed oddly disproportionate: here was a prime minister whose foreign policy could easily tolerate a Chilean dictator but who compared Argentina's claim to the Malvinas to a German invasion; who evoked war and empire as a part of monumentalist glorious national history ("putting the great back into Great Britain") to reclaim patriotic sentiments while arguably beginning to dismantle social equality (one of the war's "rewards") at home. In the postwar political life of the United Kingdom, the narrative of the Second World War would be utilized in highly selective ways by whatever party was in government, such was and is its currency.

A turning away from "the war" was perhaps most discernible in the 1970s, at the height of antiwar sentiments in the wake of the highly televised Vietnam War. This trans-generational fatigue produced more skeptical historians (of whom Calder was only one representative) and filmmakers who veered away from the masculinity narratives of the 1950s and the grand epics of the 1960s towards the ironies and graphic violence of non-heroic war films of the 1970s and 1980s. Indeed, more ambivalent interpretations of wartime history often implied doubts about contemporary wars, as in Richard Attenborough's *A Bridge Too Far* (1977). The spectrum of representation simply widened, and it is hard to determine definite trends for specific audiences:[27] war as caper or adventure (*The Great Escape*; *Where Eagles Dare*) coexisted with antiwar film; the comedy and banter of wartime film continued alongside much more parodic send-ups in TV series such as *Dad's Army* (1968–77), about the Home Guard, or *'Allo 'Allo* (1982–92), about occupied France, but it also included drama (*A Family at War*, Granada 1970–72; *Fortunes of War*, BBC 1987), and POW adventure (*Colditz*, BBC 1972–74; *Tenko*, BBC 1981–84). The success of imported war-themed American TV series—*Hogan's Heroes; The Winds of War*—also lay in the older demographic of British TV audiences: men who had served in the war or who had grown up with war films. It is perhaps easy to forget how young some of the wartime generation were and how formative (and exciting) those war years were for them. War films remain a staple of the afternoon and weekend television schedule (again appealing to an older demographic). British-made war documentaries such as *The World at War* (1973) and *The Nazis: A Warning from History* (1997) are broadcast virtually on a loop on satellite channels such as *The History Channel*, *Yesterday*, or *Dave*; on terrestrial channels they are shown with a frequency that perhaps speaks more of the credit crunch than of audience tastes. The respectable viewing figures of dramas from *Bomber Harris* (1989) to the more recent *Foyle's War* (2002–2015) and *Bomb Girls* (2012–present) are an indication of how reliant the British have become on television as an interpretation of the past.

Where in all of this is the Holocaust? It is now educationally institutionalized (as are the Nazis) in the National Curriculum in the United Kingdom. The Imperial War Museum in London has housed a permanent Holocaust exhibit only since 2010. Fiction about the Holocaust is still a contested territory. Linda Grant's work, discussed by Margaret D. Stetz in this volume, offers a lateral and gendered approach. Anglo-Jewish writers (whether or not this term would resonate with them) have certainly approached the subject, among them Lisa Appignanesi, Jenni Diski, Howard Jacobson, Stephen Fry, and the children's fiction writer Judith Kerr. While *Hitler Stole Pink Rabbit* remains a classic, John Boyne's *The Boy in the Striped Pyjamas* (2008) is more popular with young readers than with critics. Both Martin Amis's *Time's Arrow* and D. J. Thomas's *The White Hotel* deployed postmodern devices to avoid telling a straightforward story, signaling that this is perhaps still beyond the narrative authority of non-survivors. The *Kindertransport* has produced some memoirs, but it has come to prominence in British culture as a result of Anthea Bell's translation of W. G. Sebald's hybrid prose narrative *Austerlitz* (2001). The liberation of Belsen featured in *The Rings of Saturn*, and, in the same prose work, the fate of emigrés such as the poet Michael Hamburger, or the artist Frank Auerbach (in *The Emigrants*). Sebald, who had made East Anglia his home, wrote in German, and alongside Günter Grass and Herta Müller is perhaps today the most revered contemporary German-language writer abroad, haunted by a past that we now increasingly accept as deserving transnational attention. Phyllis Lassner has suggested that refugees did not have the status of survivors and were not readily classed as Holocaust victims. Their fiction and memoirs therefore do not necessarily sit squarely in the category of Holocaust writing.[28] Here, too, we see Britain's separate status from the Continent. Tony Judt's epilogue to his magisterial *Postwar* (2005) reminds France that it still has not really tackled its involvement in the expropriation, persecution, rounding up, and deportation of Jewish citizens or refugees. Britain's record might raise questions of a different nature: why were immigration quotas not revised? What happened to the Jews on the occupied Channel Islands? Why were persecuted Jews treated, on arrival in the United Kingdom, as enemy aliens and interned? How antisemitic or racist was wartime and postwar Britain? How much resonance did the Holocaust have in this society? How helpful were the British authorities in supporting the search for war criminals? How successful in helping to reeducate fascist Germans into critical democratic citizens? These questions reach beyond the scope of this volume, but perhaps we have to turn to popular culture again to get an inkling of a response. The successful BBC TV series *Who Do You Think You Are?* (2004–present) presents ten well-known media personalities whose family history is being traced, complete with visits to archives, museums, libraries, and memorial sites, as if it were a genealogical treasure hunt. The program's producers of course carefully select the ten candidates in order to ensure a worthwhile viewing experience, but perhaps more importantly to cover a range of audiences who may have a stake in seeing *modern* Britain's family history as a heterogeneous, multicultural spectrum. By now the selection is a formula composed of the second- or third-generation immigrant (less often a white colonizer); at least one nonwhite and non-Christian person; a descendant from the aristocracy and one from the desperately impoverished, workhouse-battered masses, perhaps even with a criminal background; someone has to have a war story, and someone else is of unexpectedly "foreign" blood; one story will revolve around a gender or sexuality issue; and the Jewish person's family history, no matter when they arrived in Britain, will involve the Holocaust and a visit to the place of their presumed or recorded death. Thus the Shoah becomes part of British history while also remaining comfortably removed; it is included and excluded at the same time. It does, however, acknowledge that remembering the Holocaust is a transnational responsibility.

The narrative of the Second World War is not a static one, not even in the manner in which its myths are deployed. Its texts include literary and cinematic representations, websites, family and oral history, photography and documentaries, material artifacts and pedagogical approaches, exhibitions in museums and archives, gaming and reenactment culture, and tourist and heritage sites. The cultural memory of the war is both private and public, and it is cultivated, curated, interpreted, and contested. What is being remembered today is a bricolage of events, images, statements, and myths that has merged historical facts with interpretations and representations.[29] Since most people today were not alive at the time, they do not remember this war but recall its images and stories, or recall what they have seen or were told. Lucy Noakes has pointed out that the BBC People's War website[30] includes many narratives posted by subsequent generations (children or grandchildren, nephews and nieces) on behalf of the wartime generation;[31] they are already mediated, secondhand stories. This public way of registering family history is clearly a tribute to the achievements of a generation of whom relatively few are left; it is also a mark of anxiety over losing direct access to the past, of "the war" irrevocably drifting into a remoter category and becoming archival, textbook history rather than living memory. What would be at stake, for the British, in letting go?

What is at stake in holding on? Perhaps the most predictable answer to this question is that a more comprehensive record of the war could be reimagined: current fictions and films can address blind spots without necessarily debunking as wholesale fiction the hegemonic narrative of "the war," which of course includes much that is true and verifiable. Historical fiction and period drama are often commercial products, but they also offer the opportunity to make an intervention in cultural memory. In her recent analysis of contemporary fiction, Victoria Stewart has pointed to the role of wartime secrecy in shaping the selectivity of the British war story. Almost seventy years later, some of these secrets can be lifted. Disclosure does not necessarily (just) establish a fuller record but reveals how difficult it is to arrive at a record in the first place. For instance, in the metafictional closure of Ian McEwan's *Atonement* (2001), his protagonist-narrator concedes to having shaped the narrative to satisfy the desires of the implied reader: factual truth and emotional truth have different narrative value; the latter simply makes for a better story. (Precisely *how* to tell the story of the war is already a major concern in 1940s fiction about the war, as the work of Stevie Smith, Elizabeth Bowen, Graham Greene, or Henry Green attests to, but that *a* story would come to be told even if it was going to be a series of facts garnished with holes, misdirections, and rhetorical maneuvers was never in doubt.) More than just a challenge to predominant perceptions of the war, contemporary reimaginings may also express what Stewart astutely suggests is a degree of ambivalent nostalgia for an apparently more comprehensible form of warfare.[32] Or perhaps even a past that seemed more straightforward. As Natasha Alden has demonstrated, the manner in which fiction "uses" the past tells us as much about the contemporary historical novel as it does about the nature of some writers' preoccupation with a war they feel they've missed out on and by which they remain "demonstrably obsessed."[33]

Previously underdiscussed, obscured, or little-known aspects of the war have been illuminated since the end of the Cold War: the work at Bletchley Park, where the code of the Enigma machines was broken (Robert Harris, *Enigma*; Ian McEwan, *The Imitation Game*); Britain's secret missions in France (Sebastian Faulks's *Charlotte Gray*); British involvement in Greece (Louis de Bernière's *Captain Corelli's Mandolin*); alien internment (David Baddiel's *The Secret Purposes*); the regional experience of war (Peter Ho Davies's *The Welsh Girl*; Robert Edric's *Peacetime*); nor is the Channel Island occupation a fictional secret any more, as I argued above. The bombing campaign over Germany also moved from the shadows into award-winning limelight (A. L. Kennedy's *Day*; Michael Frayn's *Spies*). Prisoners of war are not necessarily the plucky heroes of *The Colditz Story* or *The Captive Heart* but are allowed hunger, trauma, boredom, and sexuality (J. G. Ballard's *Empire of the Sun*; Gerard Woodward's *Nourishment*). Victoria Stewart's essay discusses a tremendously important aspect of wartime communication: letter writing and what this censored mode could and could not reveal. Darker aspects of the home front—looting, black marketeering, strikes, low morale, sex crime—are often accommodated in crime fiction (as in the work of Laura Wilson or Barbara Nadel). Sarah Waters's *The Nightwatch* has also provided a bleaker version of the Blitz narrative in the near-subterranean lives of gay characters and conscientious objectors. Children's fiction also plays a very large part in transmitting the wartime generation's experiences such as evacuation and family separation. The treatment of war, then, reaches across the boundaries of the so-called literary and the so-called popular, which is one of the reasons why this volume does not go to great lengths to distinguish carefully between these categories.[34]

The Asian theater of war has been brought to attention again in English-language fiction, even if it did not always include British characters, by Tan Twan Eng's *The Gift of Rain*, Kazuo Ishiguro's *A Pale View of Hills*, and Tash Aw's *The Harmony Silk Factory*. Translations into English have enriched the British readership's opportunities of finding out about others' fictional wartime experiences, from Vasily Grossman's *Life and Fate* to Gert Ledig's *Payback*, from Elsa Morante's *History* to Steve Sem Sandberg's *The Emperor of Lies*. Much fascinating work is still awaiting translation into English. British writers have also invested a great deal of imagination (and research) into fictionalizing other nationals' war: Helen Dunmore has written on the siege of Leningrad and Rhidian Brook about the occupation of Germany. Nazis, unfortunately, have never been *démodé* and have provided an apparently untiring market with every variety of black-booted and uniform-clad nasties, live or undead, male or female, in crime fiction or pornography, factual or counterfactual, in art installations or museum exhibits, in adapted LEGO versions and with unfortunate haircuts.

In a country where the past enjoys both considerable cultural cachet and a high economic turnover, the Second World War forms an important and lucrative part of Britain's ample History & Heritage portfolio: its study has produced some of the most engaging and incisive academic historians who have become global authorities on the conflict; its TV versions have shaped the viewing habits and perceptions of generations, and the reruns of these documentaries and series are staples of the weekly TV diet; its material remnants furnish the tourist industry with museums, bunkers, warships, war cabinet rooms, and Bletchley Park; its fictionalization has won national and international prizes; its representation in visual and plastic art often courts controversy and astronomical sums. World War II is of course also "consumable history" in the commercial sense:[35] it reliably stocks the shelves of museum gift shops with replica ration books, jigsaw puzzles, postcards of propaganda posters, paperback copies of standard works of history, children's books on the Blitz and evacuation, and DVD documentaries in thematically arranged box sets. Its artifacts clutter the display cabinets of every junk shop and militaria dealer on the high street (including the more dubious Nazi souvenirs in back rooms). It also provides a whole industry with a subgenre of (more or less) historically motivated combat video games: from the tremendously successful shooters *Call of Duty* and *Medal of Honor* series to strategy games in which gamers can replay historical campaigns as in *Battlefield 1942*. Historical reenactment, a popular pastime in Britain, ensures that replica uniforms and militaria artifacts command respectable prices on eBay. World War II reenactment societies provide eager cameo actors for yet another BBC, ITV, or Channel 5 documentary. Reenactment (or historical interactivity) is now also considered a pedagogical tool for elementary school pupils (5–11 years). Museums provide children with period costumes to get a feel for history, and schools, too, choose evacuation as a civilian World War II experience with which children are encouraged to empathize by coming to class with a suitcase, period clothes, and a cardboard label round their neck.

In Britain, then, the Second World War remains a cornerstone of the cultural memory of the twentieth century, but neither the content of that memory nor its mediation is utterly fixed.[36] Subsequent political agendas have shaped it as much as the technology used to frame and transmit it. It has long stopped being uncontested ground. The myths of "the war" tell us as much as the challenges to it do about what lies at the heart of any British war story: what does it mean, at any particular moment, to be British? How is this story of national values, character, and identity written through the stories of the British at war? If we treat the Second World War as a theme rather than an event, we can trace how this story and its characters reflect the strategies of making sense of both the conflict and the changing nature of Britain. What this volume of essays demonstrates in this reading is that Britain continues to be a work in progress, deeply committed and nostalgically attached to the war story, but willing to revise it and test it, expand it and qualify it. Above all, there is a persistent sense that the known past (as in the received tradition) is by no means the whole story; that its margins, blind spots, codes, and clichés, its hyperbole and omissions, are of an unplumbed complexity that might help make sense of where Britons think they are today.

Notes

1. Kate McLoughlin, "War and Words," in *The Cambridge Companion to War Writing*, ed. Kate McLoughlin (Cambridge: Cambridge University Press, 2009), 15–25, at 20.

2. The BBC's public Internet archive of personal World War II recollections, the People's War, may serve as a fair indicator of popular memory. Of the 47,000 entries, just over 15,000 are "set" in the United Kingdom; about 5,000 entries concern Europe and just under 1,000 each deal with the war in Asia and Africa respectively. By far the largest number within the "location" category are entries on London. See http://www.bbc.co.uk/history/ww2peopleswar/.

3. Country mansions and grand houses had to open up entire wings and accommodate boarding schools, hospitals and convalescent centers, house the nation's art treasures or a zoo, or turn themselves into soldiers' billets. Traces of such spatial requisitioning can still be seen in Eltham Palace (Greenwich), Croome (Worcestershire), Blickling (Norfolk), Chatsworth (Derbyshire), Hatfield House (Hertfordshire), Carlton Towers (Yorkshire), Muncaster Castle (Cumbria), or Kimmel (North Wales). See John Martin Robinson, *The Country House at War* (London: Bodley Head, 1989). Some estates were so roughly treated by billeted soldiers that their owners never returned. The wartime billeting was often a sign of the owner's loosening hold on family property

(rather than a concession to the national consensus that both gentry and "people" were "in it" together).

4. For a recent analysis of the surreal in metropolitan ruins, see Leo Mellor's *Reading the Ruins* (Cambridge: Cambridge University Press, 2012), particularly ch. 3.

5. Petra Rau, *English Modernism, National Identity and the Germans, 1890–1945* (Farnham, Eng.: Ashgate, 2009), 186–96.

6. See Lucy Noakes, *War and the British: Gender and National Identity* (London: I.B. Tauris, 1998), 45.

7. Roland Barthes, "Myth Today," in *Mythologies* (London: Vintage, 2009), 109–59, at 129.

8. See, for instance, the chapter "Sex and The Third Reich" in Dagmar Herzog's *Sex after Fascism: Memory and Morality in Twentieth-Century Germany* (Princeton, N.J.: Princeton University Press, 2007), 10–64, as well as the chapter "'Be Truly Feminine': Contradictory Obligations and Ambivalent Representations" in Sonya O. Rose's *Which People's War? National Identity and Citizenship in Wartime Britain, 1939–1945* (Oxford: Oxford University Press, 2004), 107–51.

9. The field picks up shortly before the turn of the millennium: see, for instance, Gill Plain, *Women's Fiction of the Second World War: Gender, Power and Resistance* (Edinburgh: Edinburgh University Press, 1996); Jenny Hartley, *Millions Like Us: British Women's Fiction of the Second World War* (London: Virago, 1997); Phyllis Lassner, *British Women Writers of World War II: Battlegrounds of Their Own* (Basingstoke, Eng.: Macmillan, 1997); Mark Rawlinson, *British Writing of the Second World War* (Oxford: Oxford University Press, 2000); Rod Mengham and N. H. Reeve. eds., *The Fiction of the 1940s* (London: Palgrave, 2001); Victoria Stewart, *Narratives of Memory: British Writing of the 1940s* (Basingstoke, Eng.: Palgrave, 2006); Lyndsey Stonebridge, *The Writing of Anxiety: Imagining Wartime in Mid-Century British Culture* (Basingstoke, Eng.: Palgrave, 2007); Marina MacKay, *Modernism and World War II* (Cambridge: Cambridge University Press, 2009) and *The Cambridge Companion to the Literature of the Second World War* (Cambridge: Cambridge University Press, 2009); Kristine A. Miller, *British Literature of the Blitz: Fighting the People's War* (Basingstoke, Eng.: Palgrave, 2009); Sara Wasson, *Urban Gothic of the Second World War* (Basingstoke, Eng.: Palgrave, 2010); Leo Mellor, *Reading the Ruins: Modernism, Bombsites and British Culture* (Cambridge: Cambridge University Press, 2011); and Gill Plain, *Literature of the 1940s: War, Postwar and "Peace"* (Edinburgh: Edinburgh University Press, 2013).

10. Phyllis Bottome is another writer whose antifascist novels were so successful at the time that they were adapted into Hollywood films. And while some of her work has recently been reissued as well as critically discussed, she remains a casualty of reading lists that often eschew the middlebrow in favor of aesthetically more consistent and complex prose. See, for instance, Judy Suh, *Fascism and Anti-Fascism in Twentieth-Century British Fiction* (Basingstoke, Eng.: Palgrave, 2009); and Pam Hirsch, *The Constant Liberal: The Life and Work of Phyllis Bottome* (London: Quartet Books, 2010).

11. Sue Harper and Vincent Porter, "Cinema Audience Tastes in 1950s Britain," *Journal of Popular British Cinema* 2 (1999): 66–82, at 77.

12. See Christine Geraghty, *British Cinema in the Fifties: Gender, Genre and the "New Look"* (London: Routledge, 2000), 175–96.

13. Robert Murphy, *British Cinema in the Second World War* (London: Continuum, 2000), 205.

14. Alexander Baron's *There's No Home* (1950) and Norman Lewis's evocative *Naples '44* (1978) put the invasion of Italy on the literary map, but Greece had to wait for Evelyn Waugh's *Sword of Honour* trilogy (1965) and Olivia Manning's final volume in the *Balkan Trilogy* (1987), *Friends and Heroes* (both the Balkan and the Levant trilogy were made into a very popular BBC television adaptation under the title of *Fortunes of War* [1987]). A British soldier in Greece also featured on the wider canvas of Greek's mid-century political landscape in Louis de Bernières' *Captain Corelli's Mandolin* (1994), and by then the tone had become rather uneven.

15. Mark Connelly, *We Can Take It! Britain and the Memory of the Second World War* (Harlow, Eng.: Pearson, 2004), 248–66.

16. For an overview of the occupation on the Continent, see Mark Mazower, *Hitler's Empire: Nazi Rule in Occupied Europe* (London: Allen Lane, 2008). The often decades-long delay in exploring the histories of occupation may be indicative of the moral complexities and the painful memories involved. The first full-scale history of occupied Poland, Halik Kochanski's *The Eagle Unbowed: Poland and the Poles in the Second World War*, only appeared in 2012 (London: Penguin).

17. A copy of the poster is available, unsurprisingly, in the shop of the Imperial War Museum, London. See http://www.iwmshop.org.uk/product/19919/Keep_Calm_and_Carry_On_Poster.

18. See Nick Hubble, *Mass Observation and Everyday Life: Culture, History, Theory* (Houndmills, Eng.: Palgrave, 2006).

19. See Lyndsey Stonebridge, *The Judicial Imagination: Writing after Nuremberg* (Edinburgh: Edinburgh University Press, 2011), particularly 118–66.

20. For this aftermath see Ben Shepherd, *The Long Road Home: The Aftermath of the Second World War* (London: Bodley Head, 2010); Sarif Gemie, Fiona Reid, and Laure Humbert, *Outcast Europe: Refugees and Relief Workers in an Era of Total War, 1936–1948* (London: Continuum, 2011); R. M. Douglas, *Orderly and Humane: The Expulsion of the Germans after the Second World War* (New Haven, Conn.: Yale University Press, 2012); and Keith Lowe, *Savage Continent: Europe in the Aftermath of World War II* (London: Viking, 2012).

21. Tony Judt, "The Past Is Another Country: Myth and Memory in Postwar Europe," in *The Politics of Retribution in Europe: World War II and Its Aftermath*, ed. István Deák, Jan T. Gross, and Tony Judt (Princeton, N.J.: Princeton University Press, 2000), 293–323, at 296.

22. See, for instance, the display in *War Posters: Weapons of Mass Communication*, ed. Jim Aulich (London: Imperial War Museum, 2010), 166–68.

23. See also Plain, *Literature of the 1940s*.

24. See Alice Ferrebe's *Literature of the 1950s: Good, Brave Causes* (Edinburgh: Edinburgh University Press, 2012).

25. See Phyllis Lassner, *Colonial Strangers: Women Writing the End of the British Empire* (New Brunswick, N.J.: Rutgers University Press, 2004).

26. See Michael Burleigh, *Small Wars, Far Away Places: The Genesis of the Modern World* (London: Macmillan, 2013).

27. See Murphy, *British Cinema in the Second World War*, 239–68; and the introduc-

tion to Michael Paris, ed., *Repicturing the Second World War: Representations in Film and Television* (Basingstoke, Eng.: Palgrave, 2007).

28. See also Phyllis Lassner, *Anglo-Jewish Women Writing the Holocaust: Displaced Witnesses* (Basingstoke, Eng.: Palgrave, 2008), 3.

29. See Geoff Eley, "Framing the People's War: Film, British Collective Memory, and World War II," *American Historical Review* 106, no. 3 (2001): 818–38, at 819.

30. See WW2 People's War website, http://www.bbc.co.uk/history/ww2peopleswar/.

31. Lucy Noakes and Juliette Pattinson, eds., "War on the Web: The BBC's People's War Website and Memories of Fear in Wartime in 21st-Century Britain," in *British Cultural Memory and the Second World War* (London: Bloomsbury, 2013).

32. Victoria Stewart, *The Second World War in Contemporary British Fiction: Secret Histories* (Edinburgh: Edinburgh University Press, 2011), 8.

33. See Natasha Alden, *Reading behind the Lines: Postmemory in Contemporary British War Fiction* (Manchester: Manchester University Press, 2014), 15.

34. In *The Historical Novel*, Jerome de Groot distinguishes between genre fiction focusing on male agency, heroism, and adventure and (presumably postmodern) literary war novels that foreground the difficulty of writing oneself "into" that period (London: Routledge, 2009), 102–9. Not all literary historical fiction is necessarily postmodern or interested in perforating realist conventions. Similarly, not all genre fiction (or popular fiction) about war is by or about men. For a summary of *popular* war writing see Petra Rau's "Violent Pleasures: War as Entertainment" in *The Bloomsbury Introduction to Popular Fiction*, ed. Christine Berberich (London: Bloomsbury, 2014), 254–67.

35. See Jerome de Groot, *Consuming History: Historians and Heritage in Contemporary Popular Culture* (London: Routledge, 2009).

36. See also the essays in Gill Plain and Danielle Hipkins, eds., *War-Torn Tales: Literature, Film and Gender in the Aftermath of World War II* (Oxford: Peter Lang, 2007).

GILL PLAIN

Escaping 1945

Popular Fiction and the End of the War

The declaration of war in September 1939 had a profound silencing effect on writers. Stephen Spender's "Autumn Journal," for example, opens with an assertion of verbal impotence, "I am going to keep a journal because I cannot accept the fact that I feel so shattered that I cannot write at all. . . . Words seem to break in my mind like sticks when I put them down on paper."[1] Less commonly noted, though, has been a parallel absence of writing about the war's end. Here, reluctance as much as impotence was the problem: after six long years of conflict, writers and readers were increasingly seeking distraction rather than engagement. As a Mass Observation respondent noted in 1944, "I like light fiction best . . . and I prefer them to have a happy ending, even if it is highly improbable." This respondent, like many others, was looking for escape, concluding that there was "enough tragedy in real life to want to read about it." However, escape and escapism are far from straightforward categories, and the "light fiction" that emerged at war's end might more appropriately be described as a "literature of exhaustion," articulating the anxieties of 1945 at the same time as it sought vigorously to deny their power. These anxieties were complex and multifaceted: the nation that in July 1945 voted overwhelmingly for the radical change of a Labour government was equally—and paradoxically—yearning for a return to "normality," which "in essence meant life before the war."[2] These two contrasting desires for change, however, were subsumed by an awful continuity. The end of war brought frustration at ongoing rationing and unresolved housing shortages, international uncertainty, the atomic bomb, and a scarcely articulable narrative of loss. For many, the process of grieving was subsumed by the mundane difficulty of reconfiguring a domestic life radically undermined by the enforced separations and communal structures of wartime life. By 1945 Britain was tired, and it sought distraction from its exhaustion in the pleasures of popular film and fiction.

The Beginning of the End: War in Transition

To borrow a well-worn phrase from Virginia Woolf, in or around 1943, something changed. As the war progressed towards its end, the preoccupations of British writers, filmmakers, readers, and spectators underwent a significant transformation. There was good reason for this transition: 1942's decisive victories in North Africa suggested that the Nazis could, and eventually would, be beaten. Inevitably this resulted in a shift in public attitudes to the conflict, and imminent threat mutated into a concept of duration: a sentence to be endured as much as a conflict to be won. In the words of Patrick Hamilton, the war, "which had begun by making dramatic and drastic demands, which had held up the public in style like a highwayman, had now developed into a petty pilferer."[3] The miserable attrition of the spirit that Hamilton locates in the dark "muffled" December of 1943, and the nation's increasing disaffection with both war and war news, was obviously not universal: soldiers preparing for D-Day undoubtedly perceived the war as far from already over. But even for those in very real danger, there is a limit to how long body and mind can exist in a state of emergency. The abnormal becomes normal, and people adapt.[4] In cultural terms, cinema historians have long regarded the box-office triumph of the Gainsborough melodramas, beginning in 1943 with *The Man in Grey*, as evidence of this transition in public taste, away from documentary realism and towards a cinema of pleasurable excess that Michael Balcon would later dub "tinsel."[5] This change in appetite was recognized, and catered for, by *Picturegoer* magazine, the popular mouthpiece of 1940s film fandom. In the editorial for October 14, 1944 the magazine made its position emphatically clear:

As we recorded some time ago the Swastika is doing a disappearing act.

So too are stories allied to Nazi brutality, or to grim aspects of the war.

The time will come when great war stories will be screened again.

. . .

And those pictures will be welcome.

But at the moment the immediate feeling is: "Let's get away from the Nazis."[6]

The serious intent behind this statement is evident from the content of the magazine. Aside from the attention lavished on the Gainsborough melodramas and the dedicated coverage of Hollywood stars, considerable space was given to the production of quality costume dramas such as Laurence Olivier's *Henry V* and David Lean's *Great Expectations*. By contrast, the popular and star-studded RAF "war story" *The Way to the Stars*, in spite of being entirely devoid of Nazis, or even enemy aircraft, scarcely merited a mention.[7]

The apparent war weariness that drove cinemagoers into the arms of the Gainsborough stars was equally evident in reading habits. David Kynaston records that Penguin "Specials," designed to inform and educate, reached a peak of popularity in 1942. By 1945 there had been a massive slump in sales, and the series was temporarily abandoned (*Austerity Britain*, 55). Mass Observation's *Books and the Public* (1944) suggests that most readers had little energy for self-improvement and no appetite for war, and this pattern was replicated by writers, many of whom were unable or unwilling to maintain a state of emergency after the immediate threat of invasion had passed. The popular crime novelist Margery Allingham is a case in point. Her 1941 novel *Traitor's Purse* sees detective Albert Campion struggling to save the nation from a fiendish fifth column conspiracy. The tone of the novel is deadly serious, its language rich with somewhat lurid expressions of national jeopardy: "England was such a little place. It would take so short a time to fan the poison out all over her lovely petite body."[8] With Nazi agents poised to destroy the war economy, the end of the world is nigh—but, fortunately, the cooperative efforts of Campion, his plucky girl assistant, Amanda, and the loyal working-class Lugg combine to save the day. The next Campion adventure, however, presents a very different picture. In *Coroner's Pidgin* (1945), the war-weary detective comes home from battle to find himself in the midst of a farce. With a corpse in his bed and a dowager determined to take the law into her own hands, the obligatory Nazi conspirators can hardly get a look in. Spy fiction is replaced by a comedy of manners in which the detective spends much of the novel as a bemused bystander.[9]

Yet the questions remains: why—when American and Russian involvement had made the end of the war a realistic prospect—did people want to escape even from good news about the conflict? Britain was about to win, but diaries of this final year suggest that hope was hard to come by—as were potatoes and coal.[10] The return of blitzkrieg in the form of rocket attacks was similarly dispiriting, as is evident from the diary of Vere Hodgson. Hodgson, a teacher and welfare worker who wrote throughout the war years, attempts to engage with the impact of "Doodle Bugs" and the moral issues of an uncertain future, but her entry for August 20, 1944, collapses from the abstract to the personal, embracing a fantasy built around visual and tactile pleasure:[11]

> We discussed the fate of civilization over tea, and were not too happy. These robots have changed everything. The Germans can in the future, in complete secrecy underground, prepare in the years to come, more of such things, and launch them on an unprepared world. We shall be caught on the wrong foot again, given no time to recover, and then darkness will close down on us. I am sorry to be so gloomy, but really life is so different now that all earthly possessions seem to be of little importance. The treasures of the Past have been saved this time, but I feel it is the beginning of the Gotterdammerung [*sic*]. . . .
>
> Got the *Face Without a Frown*—Georgiana, Duchess of Devonshire by Iris Leveson Gower. This is the one with the magnificent hats. The author has made such a splendid story out of it, though one would like to know much more. She was one of those charming good-natured people who come to a bad end through their own good qualities and trust in others. She had

> a good brain, and in modern times would have had a chance to use it. But in the 18th C. and born to great wealth she just wasted her time in aimless gambling and extravagant dress.
>
> The luxury of life and the profusion of money is hard to imagine in these impecunious days. Hundreds of servants they had at every one of their big estates. . . . Half the lackeys slept on a pallet under the stairs. But there was plenty of food, rough comfort and good comradeship among themselves. (Hodgson, *Few Eggs and No Oranges*, 517–18)

This is, in many respects, an exemplary late-war statement, combining deep-seated anxieties about the future, the consolations of fiction, and an emergent nostalgia—not just for magnificent hats, but for a sense of certainty, order, and community. Here, in Hodgson's transition from present anxiety to past security, lies the growing awareness that peace would be much more complex than anticipated.

"The Return of Old Evils": Postwar and Peace

The end of war meant the return of choice and responsibility, and the beginning of reconstruction. It meant looking at, and doing something about, a world radically changed by six years of war, and there was much here that did not bear scrutiny. Even before Hiroshima, area bombing had represented a phenomenal advance in man's capacity for destruction. The dawning of the atomic era would confirm that power and generate considerable, intense anxiety. Among the more extreme reactions listed by *Peace and the Public*, a Mass Observation study published in 1947, are the cases of children chalking up "shoot all scientists" on walls across London, and a woman who, after Hiroshima, "retired to bed for a fortnight feeling that nothing was worthwhile anymore."[12] More common, however, were doubts, uncertainty and cynicism. For the majority, irrespective of the optimism embodied in the Labour election victory, expectations of peace and postwar reconstruction seemed to have been managed down, and the study quotes an anonymous mother, speaking in terms that evoke the same nostalgia for community expressed by Vere Hodgson: "Worst of all, the friendly spirit of common burdens and real goodwill has vanished in a flash. We are now neck and neck again after money, job, power, favour . . . Peace means to me the return of old evils" (*Peace and the Public*, 10).

The emerging details of the full extent of the Holocaust similarly resisted assimilation. Frances Partridge—Bloomsbury group writer, translator, committed pacifist, and prolific diarist—writes that on seeing the images of liberated camps, she felt "as though the world's sanity had received a fatal blow," but Partridge's shock is counterpointed by her observation that for Mrs. C. in the kitchen it was easier to assimilate the individual tragedy of a German mother's suicide.[13] Other diarists seemed to share Mrs. C's inability to absorb or analyze the concentration camp revelations. In the case of George Beardmore, exhaustedly attending the funerals of rocket attack victims and overseeing the rehousing of survivors, the news is distanced—a report of a report—he writes simply that "the full horror of the Concentration Camps at Belsen and Buchenwald was the chief topic in press and radio" (April 26, 1945; Beardmore, *Civilians at War*, 193). Vere Hodgson's diary, meanwhile, reveals a disturbing schism between reaction and understanding. On April 20 she writes "we are stricken with horror at the awful revelations from the Concentration Camps" (Hodgson, *Few Eggs and No Oranges*, 580). Three days later the impossibility of comprehending the camps leaks through in a thoughtless aside: "There are no soap flakes. I suppose they are all being sent to swab down those awful Concentration Camps" (April 23, 1945; Hodgson, *Few Eggs and No Oranges*, 582).[14] The end of war exposes the means of war, something that many found themselves unable or unwilling to contemplate.

On a more quotidian level, but closer to home and more immediate in its pressure, was the need to escape from J. B. Priestley and the planners. A set of instructions from *Three Men in New Suits* (1945) explains the problem:

> We stop trying for some easy money. We do an honest job of work for the community for what the community thinks we're worth. We stop being lazy and stupid, greedy and callous. We try to remember that it's much more important—and much more fun—to create than to possess. It's also much better to live uncomfortably, on short rations, as the Russians did, in a society that knows what it's doing and where it's going, than it is to lead a luxurious existence—for a little while—in a society that's wob-

> bling from one disaster to the next. Instead of guessing and grabbing, we plan. Instead of competing, we co-operate. We come out of the nursery—and begin to grow up.[15]

Without wishing to dismiss Priestley, or suggest that he was not popular, this is an exhausting manifesto. It is an iteration of the cost of change that forgets, or asks its readership to forget, that this price has already been paid in the suffering of war.[16] It is hard not to feel that Priestley is moving the goalposts, and even if this was necessary, it was not what people wanted to hear. There was a perception that the nation deserved some reward, and in turning away from the rhetoric of planning towards a past imagined as "a site of physical pleasure," cultural preference becomes a means of expressing both dissatisfaction and desire (*Picturing the Past*, 129). It offers a space of excess and rebellion in which it becomes possible not to take things entirely seriously.

This is particularly the case in relation to the more nebulous, intangible fears of 1945, chief among which were women and heterosexuality. The difficulty of getting back to some imagined ideal of gender "normality" is evident from the explosion of divorces in 1946. Alan Allport's study of demobilization records an astonishing 60,300 decrees granted in 1946, up from 15,600 in 1945, and a miserly 4,100 in 1935.[17] He also reports a rise in the number of sexual assaults, and an alarming number of women murdered by their returning spouses. Significantly, in cases of the wife's infidelity, many of these soldiers escaped with manslaughter convictions, as if murder was an entirely reasonable response to sexual betrayal in wartime—or, perhaps, an unfortunate but unsurprising side effect of training husbands to kill (Allport, *Demobbed*, 3, 85, 163–64). Further evidence of anxiety regarding women's increased visibility and mobility can be found in the disappearance of uniformed women from the screen. In Humphrey Jennings's *A Diary for Timothy*—an account of the first six months of a child's life spanning autumn 1944 to spring 1945—women's roles are those of wife, nurse, and mother. The same is true of Anthony Asquith's *The Way to the Stars* (1945). The WAAFs reputed to inhabit the air force base never make an appearance on screen. Rather, the narrative is one that stresses the importance of reconstituting the heterosexual family—both through its representation of Toddy (Rosamund John) as an exemplary wife, mother, and widow, and through the plot trajectory that insists that Pilot Officer Penrose (John Mills) must grow up, abandon his homosocial attachment to the military community, and accept the risk of love, marriage, and domestic responsibility.[18]

The anxieties embedded in these reconstitutions of maternal femininity should not be underestimated. Alongside fears about what war had done to men, lay a potent concern about the conflict's impact on children. Dorothy Burlingham and Anna Freud's study of young children in wartime stresses that exposure to war's destruction may excite primitive destructive impulses in the child—attracting, rather than horrifying or traumatizing it:

> War conditions, through the inevitable breaking-up of family life, deprive children of the natural background for their emotional and mental development. The present generation of children have therefore little chance to build up their future psychological health and normality which will be needed for the reconstruction of the world after the war.[19]

A number of postwar films, from the anarchic but ultimately reassuring *Hue and Cry* (1947) to the more disturbing crime dramas *The Blue Lamp* (1950) and *Cosh Boy* (1952) foreground the impact of war on youth culture. In the crime films, the adolescent can arguably be read as a casualty of war: out of control and running wild, their moral sense arrested by the conditions of their upbringing. But cinema did not confine itself to diagnosing crisis, and—through the repeated presentation of conventional heteronormativity—it contributed to the growing cultural pressure to undo the damage of wartime segregation and restore the family unit. Yet this normalizing process was far from stable. As demonstrated by films such as *The Wicked Lady* (1945)—in which Barbara (Margaret Lockwood) cheats, schemes, and murders her way to an early death at the hands of her highwayman lover, leaving her virtuous and domesticated friend Caroline to inherit husband and happiness—punishment for the damned does not erase the spectacle of female agency, or effectively rebut the arguments in favor of selfishness, pleasure, and vice. Lockwood's character, frustrated by the limitations and propriety of domesticity, strives throughout the film to achieve a "masculine" agency imagined through sexual liberation (she takes a lover), employment (she becomes a highwayman), and violence (she kills those who threaten her). Her refusal to acknowledge patriarchal authority can be read as an extreme manifestation of the liberation experienced by women working in the Second World War. As Sonya Rose has demonstrated, the economic emancipation attendant on wartime employment changed women's relationship to the public sphere: it also brought considerable opprobrium, especially towards those women identified as "good time girls" (*Which People's War*, 71–92). Such undercurrents of gender anxiety invest even the most frivolous of melodramas with transgressive potential, and—given the immense popularity of Lockwood—the postwar female spectator was as likely to leave the cinema remembering the pleasures of vice as the rewards of virtue.[20]

Popular cinema at the end of the war, then, tended to look backwards, either to a nebulous historical past, characterized by sadomasochistic passions and magnificent frocks or—as in the case of Noel Coward's *Brief Encounter* (1945)—to a newly valorized 1930s, rendered desirable by a potent nostalgia for the known and familiar. Popular fiction also encompassed the historical, embracing both the distant and recent past as a means simultaneously of escaping and negotiating the contemporary anxieties raised by the war, and the equally unsettling prospect of peace. The parallel process of escaping and confronting 1945 can be traced through the "postwar" fictions of two enormously successful writers, Georgette Heyer and Nancy Mitford.[21] The ostensibly frivolous fictions of these two women, published in the critical postwar years of 1944–46, occupy a complex double space: both of their time and resistant to it, escapist and critically engaged. The one voice lures the reader with its exotic otherness, the other reassures with its recognition of proximity. As Diana Wallace has argued, while readers might be attracted to the richness of a past world, "any historical novel always has as much, or perhaps more, to say about the time in which it is written."[22]

Shopping and Submission: Georgette Heyer's "Good Escapist Literature"

Wallace's study of women's historical fiction also observes that novels of the 1940s exhibited "an almost obsessive concern with transgressive and subversive femininities in the form of wicked ladies and wilful or wayward women" (Wallace, *The Woman's Historical Novel*, 80), but not all costume novels found their focus in explicit transgression. Some spoke directly to the postwar moment, articulating a set of desires that resonated powerfully with the conflicted position of women at the end of the war. The beginning of Heyer's *The Reluctant Widow* (1946) typifies this tension:

> Although she would not for any consideration have acknowledged it, the prospect of being able to cast her burdens on his shoulders could not but attract her. . . . The disagreeable necessity of confronting an irate employer no longer loomed before her; and it was fatally easy to allow herself to be carried into a fantastic dream wherein she was only expected to do as she was bid.[23]

Elinor Rochdale's fantasy of submission is presented as the logical desire of a woman who has, like the wartime nation, experienced six years of disagreeable hardship. Reduced to penury by her father's ruin, Elinor's desire for security is understandable, but it coexists with an equally contemporary desire for independence. Indeed, she begins the book by asserting that she would rather receive a wage for her labor than be dependent on the charity of her relatives (*Reluctant Widow*, 23). Her narrative thus becomes a search for acceptable terms through which a woman can reconcile her desire for agency with the limited possibilities offered by her society.

In her heroine's dilemma, Heyer acknowledges the contradictory pressures placed on women in wartime—the demand that they contribute to the war effort, often through the adoption of male roles, while yet maintaining their traditional femininity. Margaret Higonnet observes that propaganda "reminded female defense workers that they were not themselves—that is, not 'natural'—but behaving temporarily *like men*," and the expectation that women maintain this double consciousness permeated the culture of the 1940s.[24] Sonya Rose confirms the emphasis on a temporary transformation:

> Representations . . . were designed to instil patriotic commitment while at the same time reassuring both women *and* men

> that, regardless of what it was women were doing during the war, their femininity would survive.
>
> Drawing upon a familiar melodramatic narrative, one frequently deployed theme promised that love and marriage would follow wartime service and sacrifice. (*Which People's War*, 128)

At the end of the war, attitudes towards working women hardened further. John Bowlby's work on adolescent criminality, published in 1946, identified separation from their mothers as a common denominator among delinquent youth, while women's magazines were wholeheartedly propounding a pro-natalist, domestic agenda (*Austerity Britain*, 98). In this normalizing context, the "rescue" of Elinor from a life of drudgery as a working woman places *The Reluctant Widow* firmly in line with contemporary propaganda. Yet it would be a mistake to assume Heyer's total allegiance to the postwar cult of the housewife: even without the conservative gender pressures of 1946, the conventions of genre insist that Elinor's narrative could only end in marriage. This is the shape of the formula, and the space of transgression lies not in the ending, but in the narrative crises that beset the heroine en route to her eventual happiness. *The Reluctant Widow* pushes few boundaries in this respect: the novel is an exciting combination of detective story and gothic romance, with echoes of *Pride and Prejudice*. Indeed, in its concern with international intrigue the book looks back to an earlier phase of the conflict, and might be seen as an early manifestation of a rapidly emerging nostalgia for the war itself, hinted at in Vere Hodgson's diary when she imagines the pleasures of "rough comfort and good comradeship." Far more troubling, in terms of the "subversive femininities" discussed by Wallace, and the particular tensions of the postwar period, are the trials and tribulations that beset Hero Wantage, the protagonist of Heyer's *Friday's Child* (1944).

Friday's Child is a Cinderella narrative that takes an oblique and witty approach to social criticism. The book is based on the premise of a woman so naive that she takes everything her husband says *literally*, thereby getting into great trouble, and at the same time exposing the folly, hypocrisy, and double standards of fashionable male society.[25] Hero Wantage is not an entirely typical Heyer heroine, being utterly besotted with her husband and childhood friend, Lord Sheringham, who has married her in a fit of pique after being turned down by the "incomparable" Isabella Milborne.

Hero's conviction that her husband can do no wrong is presented as laudable loyalty, and the book demands that "Sherry" grow up and become worthy of his teenage bride.[26] The presentation of Hero, though, is more complex than this summary might suggest. Moving immediately from the school room to the private house of marriage, and spending most of her time with Sherry's male friends, Hero learns the language of male banter rather than that of female propriety; and in consequence, many of her problems arise from her inappropriate linguistic register. As Kathleen Bell has noted, Heyer often makes use of cross-dressing heroines,[27] but Hero represents a subtly different manifestation of this trope. She is, in effect, a linguistic cross-dresser—able to perform polite femininity when required, but much more at home in homosocial environments.

Hero's problems, which largely stem from her behaving like a man when she should be acting as a woman, emphasize the extent to which femininity is a learned condition. Hero exists outside the social codes that police polite behavior, and her innocence enables Heyer comically to expose the cynical double standards of both Regency and contemporary society:

> "It isn't Sherry's fault!" Hero said, firing up in defence of her free-spoken husband. "He is forever telling me what I must not say! The thing is that I don't perfectly remember what I may say, and what I may not. I dare say I ought not to call that dancer a fancy-piece either?"
>
> "Upon no account in the world!" Mr Ringwood said emphatically.
>
> "Well, I must say I think it's very hard. What may I call her, Gil?"
>
> "Nothing at all! Ladies know nothing of such things."
>
> (*Friday's Child*, 124–25)

Hero's confusion throws into sharp relief the impossible demands of performing femininity in the 1940s, and in other respects too the book offers insight into the preoccupations of wartime culture. The crises of the plot include the machinations of the unpleasant Lord Revesby, who has fathered an illegitimate child for which he will take no responsibility, and the question of whether the novel's secondary heroine, Isabella, will put passion over status in her choice of husband. While Revesby's behavior is another instance of the double standards surrounding sexual encounters, Isabella's choice of husband speaks to the anti-elitist attitudes emerging from wartime social change. This being a Regency romance, her choice is between two aristocrats, but she finds herself repulsed by the chill decorum of her most wealthy suitor and opts instead for the warm-blooded "people's" aristocrat, Lord Wrotham. In *Friday's Child*, as in the later *The Reluctant Widow*, Heyer stresses the value of the social contract. A capacity for cross-class respect is a sign of virtue in a character, and it is to Sherry's credit that he is "always very easy with his fellow-men" (*Friday's Child*, 136).

Yet perhaps the novel is most manifestly a "postwar" text in its extensive fantasies of conspicuous consumption (*Friday's Child*, 44). Hero spends fortunes and, after years of living Cinderella-like with her ugly cousins, has more frocks than she can wear. Heyer's novels of the mid-1940s thus seem to present a twin fantasy of shopping and submission. Unlike Elinor Rochdale, who puts up a fight, Hero has no problem submitting to her husband, and in many ways seems to be living out the reward-contract described by Sonya Rose. Yet Hero is uncomfortable with the hyperbolic femininity of the fashionable set, and finds it difficult to let go of the language she shares with her male friends. The parallel is clear, as are the fears felt by the men in the novel. Hero's marriage is thus an act of reassurance in which a boyish, energetic woman is infantilized, not least through her husband's claim that "Hero is a nonsensical name for a girl" (*Friday's Child*, 40). Society sees heroism as the preserve of men, and in renaming his wife "Kitten," Sherry grants her a position closer to that of a pet than an adult woman.

Somehow, the Regency woman, like her Second World War compatriot, must navigate a path rigidly policed by the gender norms of a culture that prioritizes a decorative role for women. Not for nothing did wartime advertisements announce that "beauty is your duty!" and women's magazines insist that relaxing standards of appearance was not an option.[28] As Ursula Bloom warned in *Woman's Own*, "if you let go now, you may not get the chance to pull up afterwards. Stay lovely" (February 8, 1941). The world created by Heyer thus offers the pleasures of familiarity and easy identification, while simultaneously transporting its readers to a richer and happier time in which adventures are played out in a world of plentiful food, spacious houses, and fantastic outfits. Beauty was still a duty but, in contrast to the world of the 1940s, the rewards were plentiful and guaranteed.

Heyer dismissed *Friday's Child* as escapism: "I think myself I ought to be shot for writing such nonsense, but it's unquestionably good escapist literature, and I think I should rather like it if I were sitting in an air-raid shelter, or recovering from flu."[29] However, as the terms of her self-criticism imply, the novel has a distinctly contemporary appeal, both as a source of pleasure and as a site for the mediation of postwar anxieties. A similar consolatory combination is achieved in one of the best-selling books of the following year, Nancy Mitford's *The Pursuit of Love* (1945). Beneath a frivolous surface, *The Pursuit of Love* uses the recent past to articulate and understand present needs. That its diagnosis was effective is evident from its "instant and phenomenal success."[30] The book hit the spot—it was perfectly judged for 1945—but the reasons for this success, and indeed the complexity of the novel, risk being lost in the biographical fascination that predominates in much writing about the Mitford family. In treating *The Pursuit of Love* solely as a roman à clef, Nancy Mitford's skill as a writer of fiction is obscured, as is the novel's critical engagement with the desires and pressures of war's end.

A Fantasy of Plenty: Nancy Mitford and the "People's War"

Victoria Stewart has suggested that "a memory plot can provide an element of escape tempered by a return to the present," and this formulation seems highly appropriate for *The Pursuit of Love*, which begins with a nostalgic revisitation of the past and ends with shocking finality in the traumatic reality of the present.[31] This duality is crucial: *The Pursuit of Love* offers an uninhibited, almost joyful, evocation of a lost world, but the richness of this fantasy coexists with the depiction of a changing society. Linda's story, the distorted bildungsroman at the center of the narrative, is shaped by the diffident background figure of her cousin Fanny, and from the intersecting lives of these two women there emerges an unresolved textual tension between a celebrated romanticism and a validated modernity. The book, then, is knowingly nostalgic, and while it permits the reader a frivolous escape to the past, it never suggests they would actually be better off living there.

At the heart of the novel is the Radlett family who live "in a world of superlatives," utterly at odds with the encouraged wartime attitude of muted understatement.[32] Those who inhabit this world are expected to be robust enough to survive a landscape—both physical and emotional—of extremes (Mitford, *The Pursuit of Love,* 17). Fanny, the narrator, tells us that she spent her holidays at Alconleigh, the Radlett family home, and "while some of them slipped by with nothing much to remember, others were distinguished by violent occurrences and had a definite character of their own" (*The Pursuit of Love,* 9). This statement is followed by a comic catalog of excessive incidents, from her cousin Linda's attempted suicide over the death of her dog, to the tormenting of neighboring children with the facts of life. In establishing the parameters of "violence" through the tribulations of childhood, the book immediately achieves a fantastical sleight of hand. Memory brings back into focus not simply prewar events, but also a prewar frame of reference. "Violent occurrences," a term that for the past six years can only have connoted the horrors of wartime, slides effortlessly back to an earlier, more innocent set of meanings. Time, and the calm control of Fanny's distancing narration, softens the impact. Violence becomes fun again.

Fanny's narration is crucial to the operation of *The Pursuit of Love.* Even as she speaks with warmth of the eternal verities of Alconleigh, her voice and point of view remain remorselessly modern. She is a pragmatist, not a romantic, and her tone is very much that of the "modern age." This is a novel, then, in which an adult voice remembers the romantic ideals of childhood—but it is noticeable that these are ideals which Fanny herself never fully shared. While her cousins declare how lucky she is to have "wicked parents" (*The Pursuit of Love,* 11), and yearn themselves to be "total orphans" (*The Pursuit of Love,* 10), Fanny remains profoundly grateful for her surrogate mother, the unglamorous Aunt Emily, and the solid upper-middle-class education she provided. To her, the world of the Radletts is somewhere for a holiday—not for "real" everyday life. Yet even as her distance implicitly criticizes the past as child's play, her indulgence of the Radletts encourages a nostalgia for a mode of living that cannot be recovered, and this is central to the book's appeal. In its double-voiced discourse the book delights in the Radletts, while simultaneously celebrating the values of Aunt Emily. Yet here perhaps lies the real veneration of the past, for Emily's modernity is, paradoxically, a traditional one. Although far from middle class, she qualifies as an icon of what Alison Light has termed "conservative modernity," an embodiment of traditional values within a newly "feminine" form. In Light's definition, conservative modernity "could simultaneously look backwards and forwards; it could accommodate the past in the new forms of the present," respecting long-established national modes of being, such as self-control, reticence, and stoicism, but deploying them within a newly domestic context.[33] This is a crucial shift in perspective, and one that is central to a novel that is, above all, about women's experiences and choices in the twentieth century.

The narrative drive of the novel comes from Linda and Fanny's negotiation of public and private worlds and, although focused on the "story" of Linda, it draws ongoing contrasts between the two women's lives based upon their education, upbringing, and engagement with the ideological force of romance. *The Pursuit of Love* is a fairy tale, but it is also a female bildungsroman, with all the limitations that implies (*The Pursuit of Love*, 69). From the outset Linda is depicted as being "paralysed by her longing for love" (*The Pursuit of Love*, 32), and while Fanny grows out of her adolescent fantasies, Linda is so permeated by the ideology of heterosexual romance that she can conceive of no other mode of being (*The Pursuit of Love*, 44–45). The contrast with Fanny is clear: not only does her commonsense distanced perspective control the narrative, making the painful obsessions of childhood seem distant and comical, but her fantasies diverge from those of Linda. While Linda's imagination constructs a version of "some day my prince will come," Fanny's more prosaically focuses on a local farmer (*The Pursuit of Love*, 34). Immediately, then, the cousins are distinguished by a contrasting relationship to the real, and by Fanny's yearning for an independence that will be embodied in her "companionate" marriage to the scholarly Alfred.

The two women also act as representatives of a generation. Almost at the end of the novel, in an uncharacteristic moment of reflection, a sense of obsolescence is articulated by Linda:

> "It's rather sad," she said one day, "to belong, as we do, to a lost generation. I'm sure in history the two wars will count as one war and that we shall be squashed out of it altogether, and people will

> forget that we ever existed. We might just as well never have lived at all, I do think it's a shame." (*The Pursuit of Love*, 147)

While it is odd that these words should be given to a character repeatedly depicted as living in a sort of eternal present (*The Pursuit of Love*, 107, 113, 123), it is important to note Mitford's construction of the interwar years as a liminal space—a site of uncertainty and flux in which an entire generation feels itself in limbo. Not for nothing does Linda marry a crypto-fascist and a communist and fail to make sense of both relationships before finding happiness in a relationship outside time, as the mistress of Fabrice, a French aristocrat. The past is unresolved, the future uncertain, and the dominant political ideologies work only to negate each other. Linda's retreat from the contemporary moment seems, in one sense, an admirably lucid response to this social and political impasse. And yet it is also, of course, deeply problematic. Linda's retreat into a nineteenth-century fantasy of decorative, sensual femininity (*The Pursuit of Love*, 114–15) is one of the many events of the novel that exposes the limitations of Alconleigh as a fantastical space. With its fairy tale ogres and medieval chaperonage (*The Pursuit of Love*, 49), it facilitates the development of a mindset that imprisons Linda, limits her horizons, and roots her in an ultimately destructive gender binary. After her sojourn in Paris with Fabrice, we learn that Linda is finally "fulfilling the promise of her childhood, and [becoming] a beauty" (*The Pursuit of Love*, 125). The cost of this entirely passive becoming is a life without resources beyond the realm of fairy tale, and a subjectivity that functions only in relation to a male other (*The Pursuit of Love*, 145).

Yet Linda, for all her romantic ahistoricism, is also a significantly national figure. Described as "instinctively and unreasonably English" (*The Pursuit of Love*, 73), she and her family function as hyperbolic embodiments of national resistance. In its representation of peace, the novel quietly critiques the rampant jingoism of Uncle Matthew, preferring the calm understatement of Emily's conservative modernity. In its depiction of war, by contrast, it wholeheartedly endorses the roaring excesses of the Radletts, turning them into another manifestation of the people's aristocracy. From the outset of the novel, the aristocratic world has been one in which hardships are endured in an uncomplaining and stoical manner, and the book implies that the life of the landed gentry ideally prepares you to be part of the "people's war."[34] With Matthew's schemes for resisting invasion, and Linda's stoical response to bombing, the family comically enact the resilience demanded by prevalent propagandist myths of Englishness. Arguably, Mitford's depiction of the "sacred" relationship between Matthew, his tenants, and his land (Mitford, *The Pursuit of Love*, 64) turns the book into an apology for a way of life on the verge of redundancy, but it is an apology that feeds into cherished national ideas of eccentricity and community. Matthew would not dream of abandoning England in its hour of need, and his xenophobic prejudices are rewritten as a laudable loyalty, particularly in comparison with the villains of the novel, the complacent and inauthentic Kroesigs.

As his name suggests, Sir Leicester Kroesig is capitalism incarnate and the antithesis of people's war ideology. His mindset is "utterly commercial" (Mitford, *The Pursuit of Love*, 63–64), he is a great admirer of Hitler, and his "general attitude to what he called the man in the street was that he ought constantly to be covered by machine-guns" (Mitford, *The Pursuit of Love*, 73). Crucially, he is fundamentally opposed to war with Germany on the grounds that war "brings people together and opens their eyes" (Mitford, *The Pursuit of Love*, 73), presumably to the reality of their exploitation by an international capitalist elite. The Kroesigs are performing an Englishness that means nothing to them: concerned only with their own welfare and obsessed by the appearance of rectitude, they are uncanny precursors of Elizabeth Bowen's chilling Kelway family in *The Heat of the Day* (1948). Both books suggest that the suffocating repressiveness of middle-class life does not uphold moral principles, but rather evacuates them: while the life-denying Kelway household breeds a Nazi spy, the Kroesigs, to Mitford, are simply Nazis.

Mitford, then, is ruthless in her condemnation of those who do not endorse a traditional mode of instinctive patriotism, but the book is far from a straightforward piece of flag-waving propaganda. Indeed, the novel's Englishness resides as much in its refusal of seriousness as in its active assertion of national values. *The Pursuit of Love* is a novel of escape not simply in its deployment of nostalgia, but also in its gleeful assault on the shibboleths of war. Seriousness is evoked, and almost immediately banished, for example in the novel's account of Dunkirk. In an unusually bleak paragraph, Mitford reports that "London people cried openly in the buses, in the streets, for the English army which was lost" (*The Pursuit of Love*, 124), before turning sharply around to announce that "suddenly one day, the English army turned up again" (*The Pursuit of Love*, 125). The juxtaposition represents a comic refusal to mourn that evokes the post-traumatic reactions of the 1920s. Alison Light's work on the interwar period suggests that the rise of the detective story is symptomatic of "a loss of appetite for melodrama" (Light, *Forever England*, 70–71). These are books in which "nothing is sacred," and they work "more to relieve generalized anxiety than to generate strong emotion" (*Forever England*, 67, 71). Much the same could be said of *The Pursuit of Love*, and the novel utilizes a characteristically British understatement—Alfred has had a "fascinating time" at Dunkirk—to translate the horrific into something manageable. This bantering tone is an intensely English response to crisis and its aftermath, and it sets *The Pursuit of Love* alongside the cinema of the period in its use of litotes, euphemism, and humor as modes of reassurance. But the novel also offers escape in a fantasy of plenty. Just as Georgette Heyer's heroines enjoyed a rich world of Georgian luxury, *The Pursuit of Love* revels in Linda's lavish lifestyle as Fabrice's mistress: "the floor of her bedroom was covered with waves of tissue paper through which, like wrecks and monsters half submerged beneath a shallow sea, appeared fur coats, hats, real mimosa, artificial flowers, feathers, scent, gloves, stockings, underclothes and a bulldog puppy" (*The Pursuit of Love*, 122–23). Here is everything absent from the shops of austerity Britain, a frivolous celebration of a scarcely recognizable mode of femininity.

Even more fantastical to a half-starved nation, though, is the magical appearance of Juan, the Spanish refugee. In a pantomime transformation he is revealed to be a remarkable cook, turning the inhospitable Alconleigh larder into an "Aladdin's cave" (*The Pursuit of Love*, 138), filled with the forbidden delights of black-market produce. In the pleasure of illicit consumption, the final chapters of *The Pursuit of Love* construct a comic nostalgia, conjuring up "succulent birds, beasts, and crustaceans" for the vicarious delight of its readership (*The Pursuit of Love*, 138).[35] Yet crucially, this is a fantasy of plenty in the here and now: a vision of loaves and fishes for all the inhabitants of the little Britain that is Alconleigh at war—and this conservative modernity, while a long way from documentary realism, nonetheless sets the book apart from its more celebrated contemporary, Evelyn Waugh's *Brideshead Revisited* (1945). Here the strawberries and champagne of memory are precisely that: something that can never be recovered, and certainly never shared with the debased community of postwar Britain.

Waugh's negotiation of the postwar moment would need another essay, so I would like to conclude with a more unlikely juxtaposition. With the notable exception of Linda's death which is, on first reading, genuinely shocking, the final section of *The Pursuit of Love* bears comparison with Ealing's *Passport to Pimlico* (1949). In both film and novel, a community becoming dispersed and fragmented is brought together in adversity, and in both cases, their reward for togetherness is the bountiful provision of food. When the British government closes the border with the Burgundian state of Pimlico, the residents of London flock to support the cause of the underdog, throwing food over the barricades and, in one gloriously absurd shot, parachuting in a pig. Here, as in Alconleigh's Aladdin's cave, the deprivations of war mutate into reward, and nostalgia is mobilized not for a prewar "normality" but for a wartime community. This nostalgia for a semi-mythical finest hour would fairly swiftly become commonplace, but in the context of the immediate postwar, its embryonic emergence can be read as an indication not of past greatness, but of a terrifyingly uncertain present.

Notes

1. Stephen Spender, "Autumn Journal," *Horizon* 1, no. 2 (1940): 102.
2. David Kynaston, *Austerity Britain 1945–51* (London: Bloomsbury, 2007), 49.
3. Patrick Hamilton, *The Slaves of Solitude* (London: Constable, [1947] 2006), 134–35.
4. The capacity for adjustment is evident from the early years of the war. Vera Brittain, for example, recalls London's "half-amused indifference to raiders" (*England's Hour* [London: Macmillan, 1941], 151), while diarist Vere Hodgson describes people calmly continuing to eat their meals as bombs shake the world around them (January 31, 1941). Vere Hodgson, *Few Eggs and No Oranges: The Diaries of Vere Hodgson 1940–45* (London: Persephone, 1999), 119.
5. Michael Balcon, *Realism or Tinsel* (London: Worker's Film Association, 1944). See Robert Murphy, *British Cinema and the Second World War* (London: Continuum, 2000), 5. This transition is also discussed in Murphy's earlier *Realism and Tinsel: Cinema and Society in Britain 1939–1948* (London: Routledge, 1989). See also Sue Harper, *Picturing the Past: The Rise and Fall of the British Costume Film* (London: BFI, 1994); Gill Plain, *John Mills and British Cinema: Masculinity, Identity and Nation* (Edinburgh: Edinburgh University Press, 2006); and Jeffrey Richards, *Films and British National Identity: From Dickens to Dad's Army* (Manchester: Manchester University Press, 1997).

6. *Picturegoer* (October 14, 1944), 3.

7. *Picturegoer* presents a complex amalgam of loyalties, yearning for British cinema success, while admiring the power of Hollywood. It was also a site of gender normalization. In what would seem like a contradiction of stated policy, the editorial quoted above is followed by a picture spread about the documentary drama film *Western Approaches* (dir. Pat Jackson, 1944). However, this proves to be an excuse for a celebration of something Britain does well (documentary filmmaking) and a women's interest story. The article focuses on production manager Dora Wright, "the first woman to hold such a job in this country." Describing the difficulties of shooting at sea, the article is quick to reassure its readership regarding Dora's femininity: "The voyage, though fair at first, had its share of foggy weather when cameras ceased to turn and Dora took to housework and polishing the smoke-room panelling" (*Picturegoer*, October 14, 1944), 6.

8. Margery Allingham, *Traitor's Purse* (London: Penguin, 1954), 168. Allingham, recognized alongside her contemporaries Agatha Christie, Dorothy L. Sayers, and Ngaio Marsh as one of the preeminent writers of interwar clue-puzzle detective fiction, first introduced her popular detective, Albert Campion, in *The Crime at Black Dudley* (1929). Allingham's novels (the last of which, *Cargo of Eagles*, was published posthumously in 1968) vary considerably in tone, and in their engagement with the changing anxieties of mid-twentieth-century Britain.

9. More detailed analysis of wartime trends in detective fiction can be found in Phyllis Lassner, "Under Suspicion: The Plotting of Britain in World War II Detective Spy Fiction," in *Intermodernism: Literary Culture in Mid-Twentieth-Century Britain,* ed. Kristin Bluemel (Edinburgh University Press, 2009); and Gill Plain, "'A Stiff Is Still a Stiff in This Country': The Problem of Murder in Wartime" in *Conflict, Nationhood and Corporeality in Modern Literature: Bodies-at-War*, ed. Petra Rau (Basingstoke, Eng.: Palgrave, 2010).

10. George Beardmore, *Civilians at War: Journals 1938–1946* (Oxford: Oxford University Press, 1986), 187. In terms of understanding the public's response to war events, historians from Angus Calder (1969) to Juliet Gardiner (2004) take their cue from Elizabeth Bowen's *The Heat of the Day* (1948): "It was now, when you no longer saw, heard, smelled war, that a deadening acclimatization to it began to set in. . . . every day the news hammered one more nail into a consciousness which no longer resounded. . . . This was the lightless middle of the tunnel" (Harmondsworth, Eng.: Penguin, [1948] 1962, 92–93); Angus Calder, *The People's War: Britain 1939–1945* (London: Pimlico, [1969] 2008); Juliet Gardiner, *Wartime: Britain 1939–1946* (London: Headline, 2004). By late 1942 the question was not if the war would be won, but when; however, the sheer number of setbacks and disasters that would intervene between Pearl Harbor in December 1941 and V. E. Day in May 1945 was a contributing factor in the early emergence of a psychological exhaustion often termed war weariness (Calder, *The People's War*, 260–66; 304–5). For those not too tired to read, an active engagement with war news was replaced by a psychological investment in postwar reconstruction—a transition attested to by the astonishing popularity of the Beveridge Report. Published in December 1942, the combined sales of the 300-page report and its official summary numbered 635,000 copies (Calder, *The People's War*, 528). Both these elements are integral to what I term a "postwar" sensibility, a state of mind evident from at least 1943. More detailed accounts of home front disaffection and disunity can be found in Sonya Rose, *Which People's War?: National Identity and*

Citizenship in Wartime Britain 1939–1945 (Oxford: Oxford University Press, 2003) and Robert MacKay, *Half the Battle: Civilian Morale in Britain during the Second World War* (Manchester: Manchester University Press, 2002).

11. Hodgson's massive diary, first published in 1971, has a full title that neatly explains its focus and significance: *Few Eggs and No Oranges: A Diary Showing How Unimportant People in London and Birmingham Lived Through the War Years 1940–45, Written in the Notting Hill Area of London by Vere Hodgson*. Introducing the new Persephone edition (1999), Jenny Hartley observes that the diary's "emphasis on the ordinary is characteristic of the time," and notes its place within the documentary ethos of the period: "it is also a positive celebration of the nation at war, and of the recorder's place and role in it" (Hodgson, *Few Eggs and No Oranges*, v).

12. Mass Observation, *Peace and the Public* (London: Longmans, Green, 1947), 8.

13. Frances Partridge, *A Pacifist's War* (London: Phoenix, 1996), 211–12.

14. By contrast, Naomi Mitchison records an agonized family debate about the German soul, prompted by a radio broadcast about the camps (April 15, 1945). She goes on to note that, after endless frustration about her local community's political apathy, the news of the camps "seems to have got under the skin of even Carradale" (April 23, 1945). Naomi Mitchison, *Among You Taking Notes . . . The Wartime Diary of Naomi Mitchison* (Oxford: Oxford University Press, 1985), 319.

15. J. B. Priestley, *Three Men in New Suits* (London: Heinemann, 1945), 167–69.

16. For a lively account of ongoing hardship and the frustration it gave rise to, see Susan Cooper, "Snoek Piquante," in *Age of Austerity*, ed. Michael Sissons and Philip French (Oxford: Oxford University Press, 1963).

17. Alan Allport, *Demobbed: Coming Home after the Second World War* (New Haven, Conn.: Yale University Press, 2009). Allport cautions that a number of additional factors contributed to the postwar "divorce spike," including the 1937 Divorce Reform Act and the greater affordability of separation following the introduction of legal-aid schemes within the armed services (87–88).

18. As Tony Williams has noted, "Cinematic representations never reflect social problems directly. They rather focus indirectly on contemporary issues. Various British contemporary genres such as costume melodrama, *film noir*, social melodrama, and crime thriller echoed the uneasy situation of a society in which things were felt to be changing" (Williams, *Structures of Desire: British Cinema 1939–1955* [Albany: SUNY Press, 2000], 97). This is equally pertinent to the war film genre, the temporary domestication of which can be read as indicative of profound social unease. For a fuller discussion of *The Way to the Stars*, see Plain, *John Mills*, 72–81; and Anthony Aldgate and Jeffrey Richards, *Britain Can Take It: The British Cinema in the Second World War* (Edinburgh: Edinburgh University Press, [1986] 1994).

19. Dorothy Burlingham and Anna Freud, *Young Children in War-Time in a Residential War Nursery* (London: George Allen and Unwin, 1942), 29–31, 11.

20. For an account of Lockwood's immense popularity in the 1940s, see Bruce Babington, "'Queen of British Hearts': Margaret Lockwood Revisited," in *British Stars and Stardom*, ed. Bruce Babington (Manchester: Manchester University Press, 2001), 94–107.

21. Heyer's writing career began in 1921 with *The Black Moth*, and embraced mystery novels, thrillers, and historical fiction. Her fame rests most securely on her phenomenally successful, and thoroughly researched, Regency romances, which she

continued to produce until her death in 1974. Mitford's first novel, *Highland Fling*, was published in 1931, but it was not until *The Pursuit of Love* (1945) that she would enjoy significant critical and popular success. She would go on to produce a series of popular novels and several well-received biographies of figures including Madame de Pompadour and Louis XIV. My concern here, however, is with the two writers' popular and successful "postwar" fictions. The term "postwar," as described in note 10 above, is used to describe a period extending from approximately 1943 to the early 1950s. This liminal state was a time of psychological and cultural indeterminacy, a period of conflicting desires and fragmenting consensus, when people simultaneously desired radical change and the restoration of a "conservative" normality. For a more comprehensive discussion of postwar culture see Gill Plain, *Literature of the 1940s: War, Postwar and "Peace"* (Edinburgh: Edinburgh University Press, 2013).

22. Diana Wallace, *The Woman's Historical Novel: British Women Writers, 1900–2000* (Basingstoke, Eng.: Macmillan, 2005), 4.

23. Georgette Heyer, *The Reluctant Widow* (London: Arrow, [1946] 2004), 35–36.

24. Margaret Randolph Higonnet, Jane Jenson, Sonya Michel, and Margaret Collins Weitz, *Behind the Lines: Gender and the Two World Wars* (New Haven, Conn.: Yale University Press, 1987), 7.

25. Georgette Heyer, *Friday's Child* (London: Arrow, [1944] 2004), 228–29.

26. I am grateful to Petra Rau for the perceptive observation that my examples repeatedly draw on a narrative of development in which the nation (or fictional characters) must grow up to face the future—a scenario which, by implication, figures the war as a childish episode, or a precursor to the real work of reshaping the nation. For Priestley, the concept of war as a route to social maturity is undoubtedly plausible; for Heyer, it is rather part of a familiar romance narrative that fantasizes the taming, or domestication, of the hero. In the cinema, however, war and social reconstruction fairly swiftly become uncoupled. In the 1950s, the generic British war film "regressed" to childhood, increasingly choosing to retell the Second World War as a heroic individual adventure, as for example, in *Above Us the Waves* (1955), or *I Was Monty's Double* (1958); the ghost of J. B. Priestley's insistence on "coming out of the nursery" might perhaps be detected, though, in "social problem" films such as *Violent Playground* (1958) and *Sapphire* (1959), which take a "commonsense" approach to postwar issues of delinquency and racism.

27. Kathleen Bell, "Cross-Dressing in Wartime: Georgette Heyer's *The Corinthian* in Its 1940 Context," in *War Culture: Social Change and Changing Experience in World War Two*, ed. Pat Kirkham and David Thoms (London: Lawrence and Wishart, 1995), 151–59.

28. "Beauty is your duty" was the slogan used by Icilma Beauty Aids, while Yardley offered a similar sentiment in their "No Surrender" campaign: "Let us face the future bravely and honour the subtle bond between good looks and good morale." Jane Waller and Michael Vaughan-Rees, *Women in Wartime: The Role of Women's Magazines 1939–1945* (London: Macdonald Optima, 1987), 100, 104.

29. Heyer in 1943, quoted in Jane Aiken Hodge, *The Private World of Georgette Heyer* (London: Arrow, 1984), xii.

30. Selina Hastings, *Nancy Mitford, A Biography* (London: Hamish Hamilton, 1985), 165. Hastings records that *The Pursuit of Love* was the Book Society Choice for December 1945. A total of 200,000 copies were sold in the first twelve months, and it

made Mitford more money than anything else she had previously written: £798 in the first three weeks, over £7,000 after six months (Hastings, *Nancy Mitford*, 168).

31. Victoria Stewart, *Narratives of Memory: British Writing of the 1940s* (London: Palgrave, 2006), 17.

32. Nancy Mitford, *The Pursuit of Love* (Harmondsworth, Eng.: Penguin, [1945] 1986), 15.

33. Alison Light, *Forever England: Femininity, Literature and Conservatism between the Wars* (London: Routledge, 1991), 10. Light's focus is on the complex and mutable mass that comprises the English middle class, but the comparison is not inappropriate for Aunt Emily. Uncle Matthew—the embodiment of Victorian patriarchy—rages against her education of Fanny on the grounds that this project reduces his niece to middle-class mediocrity (Mitford, *Pursuit of Love*, 28–29). While Linda and her father continue to inhabit what Light would term romantic and imperial modes of Englishness, Fanny is constructed in alignment with an "inward-looking notion of the English as a nice, decent, essentially private people" (Light, *Forever England*, 8, 11).

34. For example, "no evacuees had been billeted [at Alconleigh . . .] it was felt that nobody who had not been brought up to such rigours could stand the cold of that house" (Mitford, *The Pursuit of Love*, 133).

35. The wartime national preoccupation with food should not be underestimated. Hodgson and Beardmore both list available and unavailable foods; while Hastings's biography of Mitford tells of an old friend, Mark Ogilvie-Grant, who spent his years as a POW dreaming almost constantly of food (Hastings, *Nancy Mitford*, 160).

RICHARD FARMER

"Remember the *Torrin*"
Positioning In Which We Serve

On the evening of October 23, 1942, Winston Churchill dined at Buckingham Palace. Among his royal hosts' other guests were Vice-Admiral Lord Louis Mountbatten and his wife Edwina, the South African Prime Minister Field-Marshall Jan Smuts, and Eleanor Roosevelt, wife of the American president. Despite being in such glittering and politically important company, Churchill appears to have found it difficult to focus on either his meal or his companions; General Bernard Montgomery's Eighth Army was poised to attack at El Alamein, and the war in North Africa was set to enter a potentially decisive phase.[1] After dinner, the party was treated to a screening of *In Which We Serve*, a British feature film that had premiered in London the previous month and which told the story of the fictional HMS *Torrin* from its construction to the aftermath of its sinking during the Battle of Crete in May 1941. Eleanor Roosevelt appears to have engaged with the film. Watching it alongside the nation's premier naval family was, she said, "an extraordinary experience," but she also noted the "exceptional poignancy" that the film would hold for the British more generally as "a people whose life is so tied up with the navy."[2] Churchill, though, remained distracted. He had already seen *In Which We Serve* at least once, and would be moved to tears by it on more than one occasion, but in this instance he was unable to give it his full attention. Indeed, a few days later he would write to Mountbatten to suggest that the film's flashback structure made it difficult to place the events it described in a precise chronological order. Churchill's confusion might have arisen from the fact that at what Mountbatten believed to be a "crucial point in the story," the prime minister left the screening to place a telephone call to Downing Street, nervous about how Monty's initial attack was faring.[3] The news he received was evidently positive: as he made his way back to the film, Churchill's fellow guests heard him belting out a lusty rendition of "Roll Out the Barrel."[4] Was it simply a coincidence that this song also features in *In Which We Serve*? Or had the tune lodged in Churchill's mind as he stared listlessly at the screen, only for it to reemerge a short time later by way of celebration? Given that *In Which We Serve* uses "Roll Out the Barrel" both as a sound bridge to link present and past and, later, at the moment when survivors from the *Torrin* are rescued from a life raft, there is a pleasing symmetry that Churchill was singing the tune at the moment that he saw the future and the prospect of national salvation loom into view.

In Which We Serve, therefore, was present at the very moment that Churchill first began to feel "the hinge of fate" turning in Britain's favor: "It may almost be said," Churchill later wrote, "'before Alamein we never had a victory. After Alamein we never had a defeat.'"[5] And just as Churchill's mood was transformed by news of events in North Africa, so British cinemagoers' understanding of and relationship with *In Which We Serve* was transformed by their knowledge of Montgomery's success in the desert. For until news of the Eighth Army's triumph was made public on the BBC on November 4, 1942—"at midnight we are giving the best news we have had for years"[6]—it is fair to say that the previous twelve months had not been good for Britain. Although British spirits had been lifted by American entry into the war after the attack on Pearl Harbor in December 1941—as they had by the formation of an alliance with the Soviet Union in June that year—they had been swiftly dashed by the subsequent Japanese advances in Southeast Asia, the sinking of the *Prince of Wales* and *Repulse*, the escape of the *Scharnhorst* and *Gneisenau*, the surrender of the British garrisons at Hong Kong and Singapore, and a string of reverses in North Africa which concluded with the fall of Tobruk in June 1942. In the wake of this last event, only 35 percent of people polled by Mass Observation were satisfied with the government's conduct of the war.[7] With German U-boats now able to operate in American waters, 4.5 million tons of Allied shipping was sunk during 1942, and food imports to Britain declined to less than 25 million tons (Mackay, 93; Calder,

265). Civilian morale was at a low ebb.[8] Victory at Alamein was therefore hailed not only as an important military success, but also as something like a moment of deliverance. Church bells that had been all but silent since June 1940 were rung in a noisy outpouring of emotion comprised of relief and joy in fairly equal measure.[9]

I will in this chapter assess the ways in which knowledge of British success at Alamein might have allowed for fresh interpretations of *In Which We Serve*. In so doing, I will also suggest that the prevalent conditions during a film's consumption need to be considered alongside conditions during its production when it comes to developing a comprehensive understanding of how cinematic texts generate meanings and how they function at specific times within particular societies. I will also explore the way in which self-conscious nods in the direction of a documentary aesthetic permitted *In Which We Serve* to be discussed and interpreted as a realist film, and how encouraging viewers to see the film through a realist lens helped obscure some of its more obvious propagandistic intentions and so made it easier for cinemagoers to understand it in the light of their own immediate circumstances.

As a film that contemplated the British experience of the war by way of a series of flashbacks describing events from September 1939 to the Battle of Crete, the meaning of *In Which We Serve*'s meditation on the history and nature of the conflict mutated in response to the specific cultural climate in which it was consumed. During the period of its conception, production, and early exhibition, that is, *before* Alamein, the film functioned very effectively as an emotionally stirring hymn to Britain's bloody-minded resolve, its ability to survive even the most serious of setbacks and keep fighting—history is invoked as parallels are drawn between the past and the present: lessons are there to be learned. Before Alamein, *In Which We Serve* was, as Adrian Smith has observed, a film that sought to sustain morale "at a time when Britain had little to celebrate and much to mourn."[10] Most viewers, though, saw the film only after it went on general release in January 1943, that is, *after* Alamein, and in this context the trials and torments of the war appear as the basis for a more confident assessment of Britain's military prowess and a more concretely optimistic vision of the war's future progress. History here becomes commemorative, with *In Which We Serve* functioning as a eulogy for the sacrifices that the country had made: Britain bent but did not break, and thanks should now be given for the nation's passage through a challenging period that can be considered from the relative safety of a post-Alamein present.

"This Is the Story of a Ship!"

Because *In Which We Serve* was already in cinemas at the time of Montgomery's victory, it was ideally placed to ride the wave of patriotic sentiment that surged in late 1942 and early 1943. By contrast, the Army Film Unit's *Desert Victory*—the "official" cinematic account of events at Alamein—was not completed until February 1943, and was not released theatrically until the following month. This is not to suggest that there was room for only one of these films, for, after all, *Desert Victory* earned more than £75,000 for the Exchequer and Churchill sent prints of it to Stalin and Roosevelt.[11] Rather, as a result of its serendipitous timeliness, *In Which We Serve* was able to wave the flag for the culture and society that produced and, as importantly, consumed it.

As an exquisitely crafted feature film, and as a noteworthy example of a more confident and critically acclaimed national cinema, it is hardly surprising that *In Which We Serve* garnered such lavish and widespread praise: "Nothing but 'great picture' and 'finest film of the war,'" Noel Coward, writer, actor, and codirector of the film noted with great satisfaction in his diary.[12] Yet the public's willingness to embrace *In Which We Serve*, said by trade paper *Kinematograph Weekly* to be the highest-grossing British film of 1943,[13] might also be regarded as a product of the optimism generated by British military prowess, which created an environment in which British cultural achievements were viewed all the more positively.

Consequently, *In Which We Serve* didn't have to be about the war in the desert for the war in the desert to influence public understanding of the film. Films are consumed in specific historical and cultural moments, just as they are produced in them. In many cases, these moments are deeply personal, and influence cinemagoing in very private ways; individual knowledge and experience mediates understanding of and reaction to particular films. In other cases, though, what might be thought of as the national cultural zeitgeist can create a prevalent atmosphere capable of guiding cinemagoers toward a specific reading of a film. As this zeitgeist changes, so does the range of possible—and even likely—meanings that the film generates. It would, of course, be reductive to suggest that *In Which We Serve* was productive only of a single meaning, that all cinemagoers approached the film in the same way and took the same things from it. Cinemagoing was an activity in which all could—and did—participate, and in so doing brought their extra-cinematic experiences and attitudes with them into the auditorium. The popularity of the cinema in Britain during the war was not limited to the poor, the urban, or the youthful (although these groups did account for a high proportion of ticket sales),[14] and recent work by Mark Glancy, Sue Harper, and Julian Poole has demonstrated the lack of homogeneity in film tastes across the United Kingdom.[15] So although it is not difficult to find dissenters voicing critical, ambivalent, or hostile opinions about *In Which We Serve*,[16] it is worth noting that the vast majority of comment passed about the film was positive, both in terms of the people who went to see it—no matter what their background—and the critics who sat in judgment of it, regardless of their expected readership.

As the making of meaning is contingent upon a process of dialogue between film and viewer, it is clear that the societal and cultural concerns present in a cinemagoer's life at the moment of consumption will be a contributing factor in determining the course of the dialogue that shapes understanding of a film. *In Which We Serve* was particularly sensitive to changes in how the British public thought about the war because it is so profoundly interested in telling the story of how the British experienced the war. Much of the film is presented as a series of flashbacks, from the diegetic present (that is, the sinking of the *Torrin* and the time spent by survivors on a lifeboat) to the past. These flashbacks reference a range of wartime events and present them in differing degrees of detail:

Commissioning of the *Torrin* and the final, rushed preparations for war (1939)
Declaration of war (September 1939)
The *Altmark* incident—and so indirectly the Norwegian campaign (February 1940)
Dunkirk (May–June 1940)
The Battle of Britain (Summer 1940)
The Blitz (September 1940–May 1941)

The flashbacks have been criticized for being inconsistent, for starting with the memories of one character and then switching to another, before sometimes returning to the present via a third, but this seems to miss the point.[17] By interweaving these flashbacks, and, further, by introducing into them characters who never set foot on the *Torrin*, a community of common feeling is established in which civilian lives and experiences are closely aligned with those of the uniformed crew. This allows the nation to become emotionally invested in the fate of the *Torrin* and for "the story of a ship," as the opening narration describes the film, to become the story of the nation.

However, for the ship to become an effective synecdoche for the nation, certain tensions are glossed over. *In Which We Serve*'s desire to replicate what Captain Edward Kinross (Coward) describes as the "happy and efficient" *Torrin* at the national level comes at the expense of any attempt to reflect with any degree of precision the antagonism that the social, economic, and political—not to mention national or religious—diversity of the country could generate, even in wartime.[18] So, while it is true that three families, one each from the working, middle, and upper classes, provide much of the emotional and domestic ballast in the film—and thus allow the "ordinary" and domestic to counterbalance the international—*In Which We Serve* has "no qualms whatever as accepting as normal and natural" the class structure that kept each of these families securely in their place: now was not the time to rock the boat.[19] Not that Coward would have wanted to, of course; in his autobiography he declared that "the levelling of class boundaries and rank distinctions, and the contemptuous dismissal of breeding as an important factor in life" would bring nothing but "dismal mediocrity."[20] Elsewhere he anticipated that the wartime "mania for Russia" that characterized public sympathy for the Soviet Union following the German invasion would bring "inevitable class ructions."[21] Such ructions, and indeed the mania for Russia, are entirely absent from the film, not least because its narrative concludes shortly before the onset of Operation Barbarossa, Hitler's invasion of the Soviet Union. Although the film is careful to distinguish between the different classes in the film, both formally and in terms of characterization and diction,[22] it is also assumed that each has a telling contribution to make to the war effort. As such, as Dilys Powell insisted, "but nobody felt he had a stake" in the film and its characters.[23] Or, as one cinemagoer later recalled, "these people were us . . . and the troubles and trials were what we have had to endure."[24]

I would also suggest, though, that the emotional investment that *In Which We Serve* invites its viewers to make in the fate of the *Torrin* is extended to incorporate, and, indeed, is underpinned by, the real-world events that are alluded to or re-created in the film. Because, say, Dunkirk or the Blitz are integral to both the film's narrative and affective structures *and* the cinemagoer's own experience and memories of the war, representations of these events serve to more fully align the viewer with the film and its vision of a coherent and resolute Britain. Yet as Britain's wartime story unfolded, as the grim desperation of summer 1942 gave way to the triumphal feelings of winter 1942–43, those chapters already written were either revised or reappraised so as to better reflect the position in which the country now found itself: history is a living thing, told in the present about the past, with knowledge of today's events constructing anew an understanding of yesterday's. Popular interaction with *In Which We Serve*'s representation of British wartime history underwent a similar process of transformation; the film might have remained the same, but British cinemagoers approached it in a different way, remaking it in the light of their own recent experiences. And because the film presented a coherent and consensual picture of Britain with which audiences might associate, it lost none of its power as a consequence of this process of remaking—the new history had the potential to be every bit as inclusive as that which had gone before.

Propaganda, Documentary, Reality

Although *In Which We Serve* had an obvious propagandistic intent, it sought to distract attention away from this purpose by integrating it within a quasi-documentary aesthetic and by seeking to align the film with the widespread patriotic sentiment seen at many points of the war. At a time of heightened national awareness, when questions of what it meant to be British were especially important (even if answers tended to be nebulous and clichéd), a film that made great play of being grounded in the reality of British military and civilian life could attempt to disavow its propagandistic content by reference to its supposed truthfulness. During the war, the BBC promoted a policy of "propaganda with truth," understanding that the more accurate (though not necessarily complete) the information it provided, especially in relation to bad news, the more convincing its interpretation of this information would be.[25] *In Which We Serve* is not dissimilar, using an ostensibly documentary or realist style, recognizable to contemporary cinemagoers as a result of the money that the government spent producing nonfiction films for exhibition in British cinemas and non-theatrical venues,[26] to obscure and legitimize its more insistent tugs at the nation's heartstrings and its particular vision of Britain's wartime experience.

Simultaneously, *In Which We Serve* uses these same quasi-documentary techniques to foreground its credentials as a British product by using a form and style that were coming to be regarded in some quarters as distinctly local.[27] This is not to claim that *In Which We Serve* is a documentary film, for it is clearly a fiction and owes much to the conventions and practices of the commercial cinema. Rather, it is to propose that it presents its fictions in a manner that is influenced by the realist and documentary tendencies then visible in an increasing number of British cinema programs. So while the film's fragmented temporal structure draws attention to its fictional status, not least in terms of the visual representation of the transition between time frames, the naturalistic style of many of the main performances and the banality of much of the mise-en-scène go some way towards masking the conceits and coincidences on which the narrative rests. And although the film is not averse to the inclusion of the odd reflexively "cinematic" shot (witness, for example, the high-angle pan of a dramatically backlit Richard Attenborough walking alone through the docks), there is little by way of obtrusive camerawork or editing: much of the film is shot in an artfully simplistic, semi-observational manner that allows the characters and their experiences to take center stage.

Upon its release, *In Which We Serve* was, in Angus Calder's words, "probably given more fulsome critical praise than any other British film either before or since" (Calder, 369). The panegyrics the film received were based not simply on its considerable technical, narrative, or emotional accomplishments, but also, and perhaps more importantly, on its status as a *British* film that was at once artistically credible and commercially successful. In this regard, *In Which We Serve* built on the foundations laid by well-regarded British features such as *One of Our Aircraft*

Is Missing and *The First of the Few*, both of which were released in the preceding six months. Despite the success enjoyed by these other films, *In Which We Serve* was, more than any other British film of the period, positioned as a standard bearer for British culture more generally. It was, said the *Daily Mirror*'s Reg Whiteley, a "British film to be proud of,"[28] whilst in the *Observer*, C. A. Lejeune described it as

> a work which presents the case for our native cinema more persuasively than could any theoretical apologist, being not only one of the best films ever made in this country, but one of the most sensible and sensitive films made at any time anywhere.[29]

Reviewers from the exhibition industry, where attitudes were formed with at least one eye on box-office appeal, were just as enthusiastic: *Today's Cinema* praised "a memorable British achievement" and *Kinematograph Weekly* proclaimed *In Which We Serve* "the greatest achievement in the annals of the British screen."[30] Similar sentiments were expressed by British cinemagoers, with a contributor to Mass Observation claiming that the film was "the best piece of work to come out of a British studio for a long time past" (male, 23 years old, in Richards and Sheridan, *Mass-Observation at the Movies*, 223). The emphasis that was placed on *In Which We Serve*'s status as a British product sought to differentiate it from the American films that continued to dominate British cinema screens, and in places an explicit comparison was drawn. In *The Sunday Times*, for example, Dilys Powell declared *In Which We Serve* to be "the best film about the war yet made in this country or America," whereas one wartime cinemagoer declared a preference for "English" films such as *In Which We Serve* because "the restraint and good taste of English films are superior to most of the American" (male, 35 years old, in Richards and Sheridan, *Mass-Observation at the Movies*, 226).

Even though it bore more than a passing structural resemblance to *Citizen Kane* (1941), *In Which We Serve* was celebrated as a cultural achievement that proved that British culture could stand up to, and operate independently of, American culture.[31] At the time of its premiere, a time when many Britons' feelings about the future were decidedly uncertain, *In Which We Serve* was welcomed as a film that demonstrated the continued viability, relevance, and existence of the values arising from a distinctly British culture popularly if reductively discussed in terms of stoicism, restraint, bravery, decency, and resilience. This was no less true after Alamein, when the film's confident style and explicit promotion of the British perspective allowed it to capitalize on a surge of patriotic sentiment. In both of these moments of consumption, what the *Manchester Guardian*'s reviewer called *In Which We Serve*'s "complete and devastating realism" helped associate viewers with the heavily fictionalized Britain that the film presents.[32]

Geoffrey Nowell-Smith has described the cinema as a "picturing and narrating mechanism capable of imposing on its spectators belief in the reality of what they are being shown or told." Thus, because all cinematic images contain elements of the real, and as such contain the potential for lesser or greater degrees of realism, "there is in fact no clear border at which cinematic representations pass unequivocally from the attested real to the avowedly fictional."[33] The cinema's capacity for realism therefore dresses fictionalized, part-fictionalized, and carefully edited visions of the past in the mantle of real: the historical stories told by the cinema are able to convince because they make use of a technology that presents itself as having a mimetic relationship with the real world.

In Which We Serve's temporal structure and occasional descent into melodrama militate against it being thought of as unproblematically realist, but it does attempt to harness realist and semi-documentary elements in its desire to lend authority and authenticity to its recounting of Britain's wartime story. The film begins with a montage showing the construction of the *Torrin*, with the shape of the keel as witnessed in the first shot of the montage functioning as a subtle yet evocative nod to the Ministry of Information's "V for Victory" campaign, initiated in 1941 and still running during much of the film's production.[34] James Chapman has described this montage, with its "crisp images of construction work and close-ups of hot rivets and sweating workers' faces," as "pure documentary" and, indeed, as something of an homage to prewar documentaries such as John Grierson's *Industrial Britain* (1931) (Chapman, 185). Although the documentary sequence is relatively brief, lasting only a couple of minutes, it is nonetheless important to *In Which We Serve*'s insistence that the fictional tale it presents corresponds closely enough with real-world events to act as a reliable guide to them. Few would argue that documentary filmmaking is actually any more dispassionate or objective than fictional filmmaking,[35] yet the idea that documentary films deal in facts (and their interpretation) whereas feature films deal in stories (and their telling) persists. Starting with a documentary-style montage affords the possibility that the story that follows is, as one viewer had it, a piece of "dramatic reportage" rather than a purely fictional film set against a backdrop of key dates in Britain's recent past (male, 18 years old, in Richards and Sheridan, *Mass-Observation at the Movies*, 239). By presenting its initial images in an inclusive, quasi-documentary style, *In Which We Serve* affords itself the opportunity to position its carefully constructed vignettes of "the war so far" in a similar light. So, for example, the small army of shipbuilders and riveters seen in the opening montage demonstrates how much effort the British nation as a whole put into constructing and maintaining the navy, and in doing so links the community in and out of uniform, the documentary aesthetic of the sequence grounding the message in social reality. Indeed, the focus on the "ordinary" (i.e., non-upper-class) Briton, both aboard the *Torrin* and on land, is one of those characteristics of documentary cinema that came to influence commercial cinema in Britain after 1939. It would be hard to align the politics of *In Which We Serve* with the largely left-wing sympathies of the documentary movement as a whole, yet even *Documentary News Letter*, a publication not always noted for its enthusiasm for the commercial cinema, praised the film for "put[ting] across with truth and realism the character and behaviour of three different income groups." The problem, according to *Documentary News Letter*, was that these newly three-dimensional characters were not used to make a more progressive statement about the social and political possibilities brought into play by the war (not, it was noted generously, that this meant that the film was "consciously or unconsciously fascist in intention").[36]

The process of authentication is reinforced by other factors, the most important of which is the tone and style of the remainder of the film. *In Which We Serve* is, even during its most harrowing moments, almost continually understated, and there is little of the emotional or narrative histrionics or overblown heroism that viewers had come to expect from (and enjoy in) conventional melodramas and war films such as *Gone with the Wind* (1939) or *Ships with Wings* (1941).[37] Not that this stops *In Which We Serve* from being emotionally engaging, though, for in many ways its lack of ostentatious emotionalism makes it all the more affecting; "documentary, convincing, moving" wrote one Mass Observer in a brilliantly succinct review that leaves an unwritten "therefore" between each adjective (female, 55 years old, in Richards and Sheridan, *Mass-Observation at the Movies*, 269). Although to twenty-first-century viewers this "stiff upper-lip" approach seems even more caricatured and clichéd—and hence *un*real—than films produced in other modes during the 1940s, the style was positively received by contemporary critics and viewers alike. The *Daily Film Renter* felt that *In Which We Serve*'s "simplicity and naturalness" resulted in it packing an "overwhelming emotional and patriotic punch,"[38] while in *Sight and Sound*, Evelyn Russell praised the lack of "screen heroics."[39] The *Daily Herald*, meanwhile, welcomed *In Which We Serve* as "sincere . . . and free from any 'phoney' false sentiment."[40] Indeed, emotional restraint was perhaps the most commented-upon element of the film, and many of those who wrote about *In Which We Serve* understood its low-key emotional register to constitute a core component of its appeal: "There is pathos, tragedy, strong emotion in it, but no exaggerated sentiment, and no 'glamorous' film stars stepping out of its story and showing off their 'charms'" (female, 52 years old, in Richards and Sheridan, *Mass-Observation at the Movies*, 271). The absent presence in many of these reviews was, of course, Hollywood; the integration of formal documentary qualities into narrative features was felt to represent the foundation of a uniquely British school of filmmaking. Defining British films against their American rivals—which continued to enjoy the lion's share of British screen time, much to the obvious pleasure of the vast majority of British cinemagoers—such reviews seek to codify "quality" British cinema in terms of authenticity, sincerity, and restraint (Ellis, 66–93).

Of the other factors that help to give *In Which We Serve* its veneer of realism, two are particularly important. First is a credit which reads: "This film would not have been possible without the help, guidance and co-operation of the following—the Royal Navy, the Royal Air Force, the 5th Battalion Coldstream Guards." Such an acknowledgment was not particularly unusual, as many wartime British productions received assistance from the military, but it works to remind viewers that the same organizations that were fighting the war were involved in the production of the war on screen, so collapsing some of the distance between actuality and artifice. There are two further credits that perform a similar function: one a dedication to the Royal Navy, the other listing the names of the three naval personnel who acted as advisors during production. These three credits are interspersed with the conventional credits, no fewer than seven of which—out of a total of twelve—feature the words "Noel" and/or "Coward." Coward's virtual omnipresence in the credits is unsurprising, given that he wrote, scored, produced, codirected, and starred in the film, yet at the moment of *In Which We Serve*'s release, his work was noted neither for its restraint, nor for its sincerity. Although his patriotic play *Cavalcade* enjoyed great success, Coward was best known as a writer of comedies, the most recent and most successful of which, *Blithe Spirit*, was still attracting large audiences in London at the time of *In Which We Serve*'s release.[41] By so insistently flagging the navy's contribution to the film, these credits go some way towards countering the potential that Coward's glib persona had to damage the reputation for authenticity that *In Which We Serve* was so keen to establish. It is worth noting, though, that this tactic was not entirely successful and that much of the criticism that the film attracted focused on Coward's performance as Kinross. Indeed, it might be suggested that the naturalism that characterized the remainder of the production provided too strong a contrast to the "class-conscious acting" of a leading man who was "a little too much to the fore" for some viewers' tastes (female, 42 years old, and male, 26 years old, in Richards and Sheridan, *Mass-Observation at the Movies*, 258, 228).

Second, although Lord Louis Mountbatten's name does not appear at any point—to his relief and Coward's probable disappointment—the story told in *In Which We Serve* is closely enough aligned with Mountbatten's own adventures on the HMS *Kelly* to ground the film in the real world.[42] Coward was careful to ensure that the details of life aboard ship were all correct ("astonishingly accurate," according to men who had served with Mountbatten), and the importance of his desire for authenticity was underpinned by the public's awareness that the film's narrative paralleled an actual career (cited in Smith, 414, n. 55). During production this had proved to be something of an albatross around the film's neck, not least because Coward was deemed to be granting himself airs by masquerading not simply as a high-ranking naval officer, but the king's cousin at that.[43] Mountbatten's specter haunted *In Which We Serve*'s production; his personal friendship with Coward and his personal commitment to the film ensured its completion in the face of opposition from those in the press who detested Coward and those in the government who questioned the wisdom of making a propaganda feature that showed the *sinking* of a British ship.[44] Yet the figure of Mountbatten might also be understood to have animated *In Which We Serve*'s reception, not simply by bestowing it with the royal seal of approval, but also by adding an additional layer of realism: Mountbatten was not an anonymous naval careerist, but a public figure, a man who liked to be seen to be acting heroically, and consequently someone whose exploits were known to a great many British cinemagoers.

In Which We Serve's self-conscious commitment to both formal restraint and visual and military accuracy allows the film to proffer its take on the recent past as being equally accurate. And the outcome of its handling of immediate British history is, as Ian Aitken has noted, "mainly to reassert officially sanctioned, consensual, conceptions of national identity": realist influences here lend weight to the notion of duty and common sacrifice rather than, as was the case with much European realist cinema, challenging normative tendencies.[45] And these same realist influences also allow the film to suggest, quite disingenuously, that it is presenting historical events in a dispassionate, almost objective manner. And while such objectivity is little more than a skillful fabrication, it goes some way towards obscuring *In Which We Serve*'s propagandistic purpose. For by using history—real events presented realistically—and by foregrounding its muted emotional tenor, the film presented a stirring and affecting take on the national story that could be interpreted afresh as that story continued.

Past, Present, Future

In Which We Serve presents British triumphs in far less detail than British setbacks. So while the Battle of Britain is dealt with, in just a few shots, as the backdrop to an idyllic country picnic, the Blitz is much more extensively chronicled; whilst the *Altmark* incident is referenced via a newspaper headline glimpsed in a train's dining car, the retreat from Dunkirk is the subject of a lengthy and very moving sequence. What the film shows is how to cope with reverses, how to handle loss, how to keep spirits up in the face of a torrent of bad news and keep going against seemingly desperate odds. Yet *In Which We Serve* is not a defeatist film so much as a film that sets out how the British people might use the experience of defeat in individual battles as motivation to redouble its efforts and so demonstrate its resolve and worthiness to win the war. Further, the pride generated by sequences detailing Britain's dogged determination to fight, its capacity to sacrifice and its willingness to persevere, even in the aftermath of loss and tragedy, is paralleled by the hope generated by those moments that detail British military prowess. There is just enough evidence of British success to offer an effective counterpoint to the film's dominant theme of Britain's ability to endure, and in the combination of these two motifs lies concrete and substantive evidence of the nation's capacity to win final victory.

Indeed, the Dunkirk sequence, which shows the *Torrin* assisting in the evacuation of British troops from France, gives the clearest demonstration of how *In Which We Serve* structures the events of the recent past so as to formulate a particular understanding of the present and the likely course of the future. The sequence starts with a shot of the front page of the *News Chronicle* dated May 30, 1940, and so immediately presents the events subsequently shown as a "dispassionate" account of recorded fact. The subheading—"Dunkirk is a Fortified Camp"—leaves the viewer in little doubt as to the story that is to be told, but the main headline provides the context of how this story is to be interpreted, reading as it does "B.E.F. [British Expeditionary Force] Fight Down Wedge to the Sea." Of course, it would be naive to expect a film with propagandistic intent to detail the reasons for the evacuation, but there is no suggestion in the sequence of German military and, perhaps, tactical superiority. The evacuation is what matters, not the reasons for it, and in this sense *In Which We Serve* contributes to the creation and consolidation of the myth of Dunkirk as it was coming to exist in the popular memory.[46]

The film dissolves from the shot of the newspaper to one of Kinross addressing his crew as they sail across the Channel towards France. Having reiterated that the B.E.F. is moving towards Dunkirk—"falling back," not retreating—Kinross advises his crew to treat the soldiers as "guests":

> In peacetime, as you know, there is a lot of leg-pulling between the services. But the soldiers are our brothers-in-arms, and it's up to us to get them off so that they can live to fight again. Let them

> see how much we admire the way they've fought. And don't forget, the success of our evacuation is measured by the smallness of the military casualties, not the naval ones.

This proclamation of equality between the services brings to mind an earlier, and somewhat rancorous, exchange between Able Seaman "Shorty" Blake (John Mills) and his brother-in-law concerning the rival merits of the Royal Navy and the Royal Marines. In that instance, which took place over a Christmas dinner, the argument was settled with toasts of mutual respect. There is a further echo as the *Torrin* sails back from Dunkirk, when Shorty and some of his crewmates move through the wounded and exhausted soldiers dispensing hot cocoa, biscuits, and an unceasing torrent of cheery banter. The hot cocoa might not be as celebratory as the port with which the glasses were charged in the Christmas sequence—although it might have been more appealing than the "Bovril rather heavily laced with sherry" consumed by Kinross and the army brass hats—but it binds the sailors and the soldiers together in comradeship, especially as Shorty has to raise a cup to the lips of a man whose hand has "gone wonky" during the evacuation.

By showing the navy and the army working together as equals, *In Which We Serve* establishes parity between these two services. The Royal Navy was the source of no little degree of national pride, and Clive Coultass has suggested that one reason for *In Which We Serve*'s popular acclaim was its ability to embody "British pride in the Royal Navy."[47] Indeed, one viewer noted that the film made her feel that she "would die for the Senior Service" (female, 45 years old, in Richards and Sheridan, *Mass-Observation at the Movies*, 276). Public faith in the overwhelming superiority of the navy, the body that had (in the popular imagination, at least) kept Britain's enemies at bay for several centuries, was commonplace: showing British sailors commending their khaki-clad "brothers-in-arms" was a way of investing the latter with some of the (supposed) virtues and popularity of the former. Further, the success of the evacuation from Dunkirk—and it was presented almost as a victory, even as Churchill, amidst his generally upbeat assessment of the retreat from France, cautioned at the time that "wars are not won by evacuations"[48]—presented a model of interservice cooperation that might be used not simply to avoid defeat, but to actually win victory.[49]

The second half of the Dunkirk sequence begins after the *Torrin* has reached port in Britain. There follows a succession of lengthy shots of soldiers disembarking; some under their own steam, but with a large number of wounded personnel either walking down the gangplank into the arms of waiting nurses (whose clean, bright uniforms offer an arresting visual contrast to the dirty and disheveled fatigues worn by the soldiers), or lifted off by crane while they lie inert on pallets. Throughout these shots, there is no music; the dominant sound is army boots on gangplanks and quayside. Both the duration of these lingering shots and the sound of tramping feet point to the number of men brought back safely. There follows a tracking shot that moves at head height along a line of soldiers standing on the quay, giving the viewer the chance to appreciate the toll that the fighting in France has taken on these men, offering gratitude on behalf of the viewer. Although the tracking shot moves from one vacant or tired face to the next, accompanied by an upbeat military march that swells slowly on the soundtrack, the three ranks of soldiers come smartly to attention when the command is issued, and then march off in disciplined formation, wheeling to the left before passing through an arch and out of shot. They are watched and admired by those members of the *Torrin*'s crew who stand on the deck—"If I wasn't so tired, I'd give 'em a cheer, and that's no error," says Blake, quietly. It is not too much to suggest that they might also provide inspiration for British cinemagoers. The B.E.F. might have "fallen back" from Dunkirk, but it was ready to fight on; the "grim tableau" of weary and disheveled soldiers painted by the camera is animated by a snapped command once more into a fighting force, a source of pride and, as importantly, hope.[50]

In this moment, the film finds inspiration in its carefully constructed vision of British history, informing viewers that Britain will endure, that although it has suffered it has also survived to fight on: all this we have done, all this we have the strength to do again. This message was potentially a very valuable one, especially in the context of *In Which We Serve*'s production during late 1941 and 1942—a period that Elizabeth Bowen has famously described as the "lightless middle of the tunnel."[51] In the wake of Alamein, and with Operation Torch another Allied beacon blazing bright in North Africa, the gloom was no longer so pervasive; Britons were less interested in inspiration than they were in celebration, and *In Which We Serve* offers an appreciation of the foundations on which victory was laid. Further, the sense of commemoration evident in the Dunkirk sequence became stronger; with a victory now achieved—even though the end of the war was understood to still be some way off—it was possible to contemplate the nature of and need for sacrifice, both military and civilian, and offer thanks to those who had given so much to the nation's cause.

The main narrative of *In Which We Serve* concludes in Alexandria, and the final sequence begins with a high-angle shot of the survivors of the *Torrin* standing in a group in a large warehouse. When Kinross arrives, the order is given, and the sailors all come smartly to attention. Kinross addresses those members of the ship's company that have survived—more than half, he states, have been lost—and gives a speech that is at once a moving acknowledgment of collective sacrifice and a signal lesson in how the memory of such sacrifice might be used to motivate future endeavors:

> There may be less than half the *Torrin* left, but I feel that we all take up the battle with even stronger heart. Each of us knows twice as much about fighting, and each of us has twice as good a reason to fight. You will all be sent to replace men who have been killed in other ships, and the next time you're in action, remember the *Torrin*!

After Kinross's speech, the survivors take their leave of their erstwhile captain, lining up to shake his hand: "each conducts himself as though he were like no one but himself, and yet at the same time all are like each other."[52]

There follows a montage of ships at sea and marching sailors, with commentary by Leslie Howard, in which it is explained that while "here ends the story of a ship . . . there will always be other ships and men to sail in them." The final shots, echoing those seen at the beginning of the film, show the launch of a new ship. And just as we are introduced to Kinross as he orders his gunners to "Open fire!" so this command is on his lips, and a vision of a salvo being fired on the screen, as we take our leave of him. The film has come full circle, but rather than suggesting that Britain is doomed to repeat its cycle of mistakes and reverses, the final shot of naval guns being fired suggests a more positive future, of

British servicemen putting their painfully acquired knowledge of combat and their increased desire for victory to good effect.

The Alexandria sequence itself ends with the men filing out into the Egyptian sunshine to face the future. However, visions of the future were altered by the events of October 1942 and whereas previously the survivors of the *Torrin* walked resolutely towards a future where triumph was assumed even if the methods by which it might be achieved were vague and founded on presumption rather than experience, after Monty's victory, these same men, standing here for the British military as a whole, marched straight to the glorious reality of success at Alamein.

Conclusion

In late December 1942, Mollie Panter-Downes informed readers of her regular letter to the *New Yorker* that "this fourth Christmas of the war may be remembered as the one which brought the phrase 'after the war' back into active circulation."[53] Mass Observation noted greater optimism, a higher degree of public engagement with the war, and growth in production at British factories, while a Gallup poll in December 1942 found that Churchill's personal approval rating had risen to 93 percent, up from just 66 percent following the fall of Rangoon in March the same year (Mackay, 94–95). The release of the Beveridge Report at the start of December 1942 also helped train British minds on a future that it now "made sense" to plan for; the debates about postwar reconstruction that followed on from the publication of the report could, after Alamein, anticipate victory with a far greater degree of confidence.[54]

With the end of the war now seemingly "a matter-of-fact objective on the horizon" rather than simply a "pipe dream,"[55] a film such as *In Which We Serve* that detailed Britain's ability to endure in anticipation of eventual triumph found itself bound up in the cultural moment that followed on from Alamein. Marrying an emotional celebration of what had gone before with a resolute determination to face the future and achieve victory, the film acknowledges the trials of the past, but looked forward to the future from a present that had, as a result of the Eighth Army's victory, become a much less depressing place for most Britons.

As 1943 progressed, and as the news from the front—in Europe at least—got better, *In Which We Serve* provided effective testimony for the sacrifices that had been made so that Britain might survive and triumph. Readers of the fan magazine *Picturegoer* insisted that *In Which We Serve*'s screening of the "true British spirit" made viewers "feel strong and proud" (female, sixteen years old, and anonymous respondent in Mayer, 175, 195), while one respondent to a Mass Observation survey admitted to finding the film "inspiring" because it presented a picture of Britain free from "eyewash or false notes or 'heartiness'" (female, 62 years old, in Richards and Sheridan, *Mass-Observation at the Movies*, 265). The combination of sincerity, patriotism, and timeliness helped the film find a vast and largely appreciative audience. Reactions to *In Which We Serve* were, of course, shaped by a range of factors, including publicity, newspaper reviews, and personal preferences regarding types of film and individual stars. But we might also include the historical moment in which the viewer watched the film, for cinemagoers understood it in the light of their own experiences. Just as some viewers' interactions with *In Which We Serve* were colored by their preexisting and extra-cinematic hostility to Noel Coward, so others interpreted the film in the light of events then transpiring in the real world.

The war would prove to be a long time dying, and there would be many false dawns on the road to VE Day, but Montgomery's victory brought about a shift in public perceptions of the war. Britain's war story could be and was retold, remade by the Eighth Army's success; attention was trained on the future and how to achieve it, rather than the present and how to survive it. Time, memory, and individual and collective experience were of paramount concern to wartime Britons, just as they were thematically central to *In Which We Serve*. The film encouraged cinemagoers to interweave past and present, their own lives and those of the fictional characters who populated its narrative. When Kinross demands that the ship's company "remember the *Torrin*" he makes the same demand of those watching the film. But memories are not formed in closed systems, they are malleable, and their shape is determined by the moment in which the act of remembering occurs. It was not just *In Which We Serve* that could be interpreted anew after Alamein: the *Torrin*, the war, the prospects of the United Kingdom itself—all looked very different when viewed in the light now visible at the end of the tunnel. Viewers have been heeding Kinross's exhortation for very nearly seventy years and, because the Second World War remains such a frequently referenced component of the British popular historical imaginary, will continue to do so for some time yet. However, *how* the *Torrin* will be remembered will evolve as attitudes to and interpretations of the Second World War respond to changing social, political, and cultural circumstances. Films are fully realized only at the moment of consumption; future audiences, influenced by factors as yet unknown, have the opportunity to remake *In Which We Serve* in their own image, adding a new chapter to the ongoing saga of Coward's "story of a ship."

Notes

1. Montgomery's attack initiated the second, and in the British imaginary more consequential and memorable, Battle of El Alamein, which lasted until November 4. The first Battle of El Alamein had taken place in July 1942, when a German advance towards Alexandria was halted by British and Imperial troops.

2. Eleanor Roosevelt, "My Day," *Manchester Guardian*, October 26, 1942, 5.

3. Anthony Aldgate and Jeffrey Richards, *Britain Can Take It: British Cinema in the Second World War*, new ed. (London: I. B. Tauris, 2007), 205–6; Mountbatten, quoted in Charles Barr, "'Much Pleasure and Relaxation in These Hard Times': Churchill and Cinema in the Second World War," *Historical Journal of Film, Radio and Television* 31, no. 4 (2011): 572.

4. Angus Calder, *The People's War: Britain 1939–1945* (London: Pimlico, 1992), 304.

5. Winston Churchill, *The Second World War*, vol. 4: *The Hinge of Fate* (New York: Mariner, 1985), 541.

6. Quoted in Norman Longmate, *How We Lived Then: A History of Everyday Life during the Second World War* (London: Pimlico, 2002), 484.

7. Robert Mackay, *Half the Battle: Civilian Morale in Britain during the Second World War* (Manchester: Manchester University Press, 2003), 94.

8. See the endpapers of Ian McLaine's *Ministry of Morale: Home Front Morale and the Ministry of Information in World War II* (London: George Allen and Unwin, 1979).

9. For some children, this was the first time that they could remember hearing the bells, and one was reported as saying, "Daddy, that ought to frighten the Germans away." Quoted in Anon., "All Europe Heard the Bells," *Daily Mirror*, November 16, 1942, 5.

10. Adrian Smith, "Mountbatten Goes to the Movies: Promoting the Heroic Myth Through Cinema," *Historical Journal of Film, Radio and Television* 26, no. 3 (2006): 406.

11. The National Archives (TNA) INF 1/199: "Receipts from Commercial Distribution of Films," May 1944; Jo Fox, *Film Propaganda in Britain and Nazi Germany: World War II Cinema* (Oxford: Berg, 2007), 216.

12. Noel Coward, diary entry, September 25, 1942, in *The Noel Coward Diaries*, ed. Graham Payn and Sheridan Morley (London: Weidenfeld and Nicholson, 1982), 18.

13. R. H. "Josh" Billings, "The 1943 Box-Office Results," *Kinematograph Weekly* (January 13, 1944): 51–52. *In Which We Serve* was second only to the American *Mrs. Miniver* (1942). *In Which We Serve* was the most commonly named film by Mass Observation respondents asked in November 1943 to list their favorite six films of the

preceding year. Jeffrey Richards and Dorothy Sheridan, eds., *Mass-Observation at the Movies* (London: Routledge and Kegan Paul, 1987), 220.

14. TNA: RG 23/44: "The Wartime Cinema Audience," Louis Moss and Kathleen Box, June-July 1943.

15. Mark Glancy, "*Picturegoer*: The Fan Magazine and Popular Film Culture in Britain During the Second World War," *Historical Journal of Film Radio and Television*, 31, no. 4 (2011): 453–78; Sue Harper, "Fragmentation and Crisis: 1940s Admissions Figures at the Regent Cinema, Portsmouth, UK," *Historical Journal of Film Radio and Television*, 26, no. 3 (2006): 361–94; Julian Poole, "British Cinema Attendance in Wartime: Audience Preference at the Majestic, Macclesfield, 1939–1946," *Historical Journal of Film Radio and Television*, 7, no. 1 (1987): 15–34.

16. See, for example, William Whitebait's review in the *New Statesman*, which criticized *In Which We Serve* for being both too sentimental and too stoical, or the cinemagoer who, while loyally admitting to enjoying *In Which We Serve*, found it somewhat "foreign to my nature" and "too sleek and sophisticated for my liking." William Whitebait, "The Movies," *New Statesman and Nation* (September 26, 1942): 204–5; male, 19 years old in J. P. Mayer, *British Cinemas and Their Audiences* (London: Dennis Dobson, 1947), 193.

17. Alain Silver and James Ursini, *David Lean and His Films* (London: Leslie Frewin, 1974), 17.

18. On the limits of consensus see, for example, Donald Thomas, *An Underworld at War: Spivs, Deserters, Racketeers and Civilians in the Second World War* (London: John Murray, 2003).

19. Neil Rattigan, *This Is England: British Film and the People's War, 1939–1945* (Cranbury, N.J.: Associated University Press, 2001), 92.

20. Noel Coward, *Autobiography: Consisting of Present Indicative, Future Indefinite and the Uncompleted Past Conditional* (London: Mandarin, 1992), 310. Coward was a self-made man whose own origins lay in the genteel poverty of the lower middle class.

21. Noel Coward, diary entry, July 28, 1942. In Payn and Morley, *Noel Coward Diaries*, 16. It was not only Coward who was concerned about the popularity of the Soviet Union: the British Ministry of Information ran a campaign which sought to "steal the thunder of the left." See McLaine, *Ministry of Morale*, 186–216.

22. See Jo Fox, "Millions Like Us? Accented Language and the 'Ordinary' in British Films of the Second World War," *Journal of British Studies* 45, no. 4 (2006): 839–42.

23. Dilys Powell, *Films Since 1939* (London: Longman/British Council, 1947): 25–26.

24. Female, 24 years old and anonymous respondent, in Mayer, *British Cinemas and Their Audiences*, 214.

25. Nicholas Thorpe and Frances Pronay, *British Official Films in the Second World War: A Descriptive Catalogue* (Oxford: Clio, 1980), 7.

26. Documents prepared by the Ministry of Information for the Public Accounts Committee in May 1944 show that in the previous financial year, £209,744 had been spent on the "Production of documentary films and studio shorts" and a further £150,021 had been spent on exhibition in domestic theatrical and non-theatrical venues. TNA INF 1/74: "Ministry of Information—Public Accounts Committee: Section IV: Production, Distribution and Exhibition of Films," May 23, 1944, 1–3. On government-sponsored documentaries in wartime, see James Chapman, *The British at*

War: Cinema, State and Propaganda, 1939–1945 (London: I. B. Tauris, 2008), 86–158; Thorpe and Pronay, *British Official Films in the Second World War*, 14–44.

27. On the importance of the documentary aesthetic to conceptualizations of British cinema in the 1940s, see John Ellis, "The Quality Film Adventure: British Critics and the Cinema, 1942–1948," in *Dissolving Views: Key Writings on British Cinema*, ed. Andrew Higson (London: Cassell, 1996); Aldgate and Richards, *Britain Can Take It*, 218–45; Andrew Higson, "'Britain's Outstanding Contribution to the Film': The Documentary-Realist Tradition," in *All Our Yesterdays: 90 Years of British Cinema*, ed. Charles Barr (London: British Film Institute, 1986), 72–97.

28. Reg Whiteley, "A Striking Tribute to the Navy—and a Good Film . . . ," *Daily Mirror*, September 25, 1942, 7.

29. C. A. Lejeune, "The Films," *The Observer*, October 4, 1942, 2.

30. *Today's Cinema*, *Kinematograph Weekly*, and the *Sunday Times* reviews all taken from Aldgate and Richards, *Britain Can Take It*, 205.

31. David Lean made Coward watch *Citizen Kane* in the hope of demonstrating how a flashback structure could condense a lengthy narrative into a viable running time. Kevin Brownlow, *David Lean: A Biography* (London: Richard Cohen, 1996): 153–54.

32. Anon., "*In Which We Serve*," *Manchester Guardian*, September 24, 1942, 3.

33. Geoffrey Nowell-Smith, "On History and the Cinema," *Screen* 31, no. 2 (1990): 163.

34. Examples of "V for Victory"'s cultural prominence might include Churchill's two-fingered salute, the presence of a "V" on the shield of the *Daily Express*'s masthead crusader, and the Ministry of Food's decision to promote meals that did not make use of imported foods as "Victory dishes," and to denote these on menus with a prominent "V." "V for Victory" radio broadcasts are discussed in Asa Briggs, *The History of Broadcasting in the United Kingdom*, vol. 3, *The War of Words* (London: Oxford University Press, 1970), 365–84; on British features inspired by the campaign, see Wendy Webster, "'Europe Against the Germans': The British Resistance Narrative, 1940–1950," *Journal of British Studies* 48 (2009): 959–60.

35. We should not, perhaps, be surprised that the commercial cinema was able to incorporate elements of the documentary, for, as Susan Kerrigan and Phillip McIntyre have suggested, these two modes of film practice are not as far removed from each other, let alone oppositional, as some accounts might suggest. Kerrigan and McIntyre, "The 'Creative Treatment of Actuality': Rationalizing and Reconceptualizing the Notion of Creativity for Documentary Practice," *Journal of Media Practice*, 11, no. 2 (2010): 117.

36. Anon., "Film of the Month: *In Which We Serve*," *Documentary News Letter*, 3, no. 10 (October 1942): 143–44. On the political attitudes of the documentary movement, see, for example, Fox, *Film Propaganda in Britain and Nazi Germany*, 279–89.

37. Although *Ships With Wings*'s melodramatic plot and almost comically poor, model-based special effects were lambasted by some critics, Jeffrey Richards has shown that the film was very popular with British audiences, who enjoyed its full-blooded heroism and breathless narrative pace. Richards, "Wartime British Cinema Audiences and the Class System: The Case of *Ships With Wings* (1941)," *Historical Journal of Film, Radio and Television* 7, no. 2 (1987): 129–41.

38. Anon., "Screenings," *Daily Film Renter*, September 24, 1942, 15.

39. Evelyn Russell, "The Quarter's Films," *Sight and Sound* 11, no. 43 (Winter 1942): 68.

40. P. L. Mannock, "Noel Coward Makes Best Navy Film," *Daily Herald*, September 24, 1942, 3.

41. *Blithe Spirit* opened in London in July 1941, and ran for a then record 1,997 performances.

42. S. P. MacKenzie, *British War Films, 1939–45* (London: Hambledon, 2001), 81.

43. See, for instance, Jonah Barrington, "The Battle of Noel," *Daily Express*, September 17, 1941, 7. Coward's reputation for glib cynicism did not help him, nor did the fact that he had spent much of the first two years of the war making enemies in Fleet Street, first for his largely ineffectual efforts for the Ministry of Information in France and subsequently for his work as an informal propagandist and Briton-at-large in America.

44. Coward paraphrased the Ministry of Information's response as "Here's a ship that doesn't achieve anything very much, doesn't sink any great ships and gets mined and bombed and torpedoed and finally sunk. Very bad propaganda." Quoted in Charles Castle, *Noel* (London: Doubleday, 1973), 174.

45. Ian Aitken, *European Film Theory and Cinema: A Critical Introduction* (Edinburgh: Edinburgh University Press, 2006), 213.

46. It is interesting to note, however, that *In Which We Serve* does not make reference to the flotilla of "small boats" that has come to form a central part of the Dunkirk myth; in 1942, there was no doubt that the evacuation from Dunkirk was a heroic act, but the terms of reference had yet to be clearly established. See Penny Summerfield, "Dunkirk and the Popular Memory of Britain at War, 1940–58," *Journal of Contemporary History* 45, no. 4 (2010): 794–95.

47. Clive Coultass, "British Feature Films and the Second World War," *Journal of Contemporary History* 19, no. 1 (1984): 17.

48. Winston Churchill, June 4, 1940, *Parliamentary Debates: House of Commons*, vol. 361, col. 791.

49. By the time of *In Which We Serve*'s release Mountbatten was chief of Combined Operations, and in August 1942 oversaw a raid on Dieppe that descended into a bloody debacle. Brian Loring Villa has suggested that Mountbatten's interest in Coward's film might have distracted him during preparations for the Dieppe raid. On this controversy see Smith, 405.

50. Gene D. Phillips, *Beyond the Epic: The Life and Films of David Lean* (Lexington: University Press of Kentucky, 2006), 59.

51. Elizabeth Bowen, *The Heat of the Day* (London: Vintage, 1998), 93.

52. V. I. Pudovkin, letter to *Documentary News Letter* 5, no. 1 (January/February 1944): 2.

53. Mollie Panter-Downes, letter to the *New Yorker* (December 27, 1942), in *London War Notes: 1939–1945*, ed. William Shawn (London: Longman, 1971), 256.

54. Paul Addison, *The Road to 1945: British Politics and the Second World War* (London: Pimlico, 1994), 17.

55. Mollie Panter-Downes, letter to the *New Yorker* (December 27, 1942), in Shawn, *London War Notes*, 256.

ELUNED SUMMERS-BREMNER

"Drinking and Drinking and Screaming"
Wartime Sociality in Patrick Hamilton's The Slaves of Solitude

War Begins at Home, the Mass Observation report on Britons' perceptions of the first four months of the war, closes with a chapter on morale which includes the following statement:

> However much the more logical persons may hate being at war, it is difficult to avoid the conclusion that it is essential (in wartime) to canalise anxiety and other feelings into aggressiveness. For war is not logical, in the sense of the word as we use it in this democracy. It is illogical. It represents the failure of our whole civilised ethic. In order to conduct a war thoroughly, we must . . . turn passive feelings into active feelings, and externalise violent hatreds which are ordinarily turned inwards within civilised individuals in this country. Similarly, personal, private ethics and desires have to be transformed, elevated and merged into a general pattern of the whole community.[1]

Two distinct processes are referenced here, making one's personal "ethics and desires" available to be channeled towards the common good, and a more complex psychological procedure: "turn[ing] passive feelings into active feelings" by "externalis[ing] violent hatreds." The point is that in wartime people may have to see, and experience, these two operations as being connected. To be united in a "general pattern" means allowing the process of the repression of violent hatreds to be rerouted into a more public form. This is quite a remarkable statement, because it takes as a given that in civilized Britons "violent hatreds" are "ordinarily turned inwards," that is, everyone is actively repressing violent feelings—presumably unconsciously—on an everyday basis. In wartime people will have to give up some privacy in order to express and acknowledge violent hatreds they normally more successfully repress.

Theorizing in advance of events that would occur later that year—the Battle of Britain, the fall of France, and the concerted bombing of British cities—the writers voice the fear that anxiety, if not redirected outwards, will hamper the nation's progress in the conflict. Anxiety was a pressing issue in this period, the months of tension without bombs and thus without clear focus we know as the "Phoney War." As Lyndsey Stonebridge shows, anxiety in this period is, as it was for Freud, both the means by which people manage their fears, but also a response that can exacerbate fear, since it does not need an object in order to function.[2] And Madge and Harrisson are particularly concerned that, should the usual methods of rationalizing, denying, or numbing oneself to anxiety fail, "the further phase may be either to retreat entirely into oneself or . . . to explode into violent aggressiveness" (*War Begins at Home*, 424). Of these two possibilities, the former is said to be that to which leaders should be alert.

Why should retreating entirely into oneself be the greater danger to morale? And what happens when we try to "canalise anxiety" into aggressiveness? In "total war" such transformations are difficult to track. Most civilian workers were not engaged in direct enemy combat. And if war represents the failure of Britons' "whole civilised ethic," then how could these civilians be sure their anxieties—and, indeed, an unconscious process such as the repression of violent hatreds—*were* being turned into enemy aggression? It is not as though the procedure can be clearly effected, or tested, by an act of will. The British should turn their aggression and hatred outward upon the enemy, and in doing so find new common cause as citizens of a democracy. They must become uncivilized, but in a focused, managed way so as not to produce at home a breakdown in civic behavior. What is problematic, though, is that the war's impact on the home front can make people not only different from how they were in peacetime, but also different from how they think or assume they are from day to day, as they reliably encounter and respond to the unexpected. And it is a short step from this to offering unexpected reasons for self-interested actions, or, since the war is its own reason for all kinds of unpalatable events, no reason at all. If a feeling—anxiety—that needs no object is to be transformed, in wartime, into enemy aggression without the physical presence of an enemy, it should not perhaps be surprising if this formerly internalized feeling, and, by extension, some of those unnamed "other feelings" mentioned above, found targets closer to home.

Patrick Hamilton's novel *The Slaves of Solitude* (1947) features a group of people brought together by the conflict, from late 1943 to late 1944, in a boarding house in Thames Lockdon (a version of Henley-on-Thames) on the outskirts of London. It explores the question of how British civilians managed, or failed to manage, their negative or unwelcome feelings about the war while living in temporary, wartime domestic arrangements. Thirty-nine-year-old publisher's assistant Miss Roach, bombed out of her London flat, joins others in the former Rosamund Tea Rooms. Her fellow boarders include a number of single women who, unlike herself, do not have jobs, a man of retirement age named Mr. Prest—the house's "black sheep" or unknown element—and the elderly, odious Mr. Thwaites, fittingly described, after a year in the house, as "president in hell."[3] Mr. Thwaites's bullying is primarily targeted at Miss Roach, the only member of the house who, at least when the story begins, goes up to work in London. The residents are later joined by Vicki Kugelmann, a German woman of about Miss Roach's age, who appears at first to be an ally but who quickly forms an alliance with the house's resident torturer and makes life more difficult for Miss Roach than it had previously been.

The novel is not primarily focused on the kinds of wartime hating and stereotyping with which we are familiar from accounts by evacuees of their hosts and by hosts of their evacuees, which often seem to be versions of class hatred.[4] National and gender stereotyping do frequently appear in the brutal mealtime "conversations," or harangues, orchestrated by Mr. Thwaites. But Hamilton seems less interested in merely showcasing the content of expressions of wartime domestic hatred than he is in larger, structural questions about how latent tendencies towards aggression and self-aggrandizement, anxiety and victimization can become exacerbated in the war's makeshift domestic contexts. Since "war is a violation of the whole of our idea of civilisation," and since "the business of killing and being killed violently goes down to the deepest wells of 'unrespectable' feelings" (Madge and Harrisson, *War Begins at Home*, 415), the home front can, and perhaps must, become alien, unknown territory in wartime, as people practice allowing their inward-turning hatreds a more communal form.

The question of whether the war exacerbates, rather than transforms, home front anxiety is accompanied, as the novel draws to its close, by another question regarding the extent to which such intensifications might, at times, be reconfigured. By the end of the novel, the much put-upon Miss Roach is no longer a victim. The bully who has caused her so much suffering is dead, just possibly—we cannot be sure—through her actions, and his accomplice, who depended upon his presence to set herself up as superior to the other women, has lost her power and glamor. Miss Roach thus embodies the idea that, in wartime, those who do not wish to be violent may need to become so, since searching for the cause of others' aggression in herself not only provides her with no answers but seems to incite her enemies to further provocative extremes.

One of the difficulties faced by Miss Roach, until this point, is the peculiar nature of the situations in which she is bullied. The war repeatedly put people into haphazard social groupings which many had not been in before. In air raid shelters and tube stations, on trains with groups of children moving to, or away from, towns or cities, in a range of committees and war work environments, people from different classes and communities met and modified, or confirmed, their views of each other. Mealtimes at the Rosamund Tea Rooms and the time spent communally after supper in the lounge, in particular, are unsettling to Miss Roach because, like shelters, they are not quite private yet not quite public scenarios. The rules and expectations regarding acceptable behavior are correspondingly not always clear. It is as though the fact of the war that has brought these people together remains between them in the form of a strange pressure to appear—before each other as the only audience—to get on well, for the sake of morale. At the same time, because the people are strangers to each other, it is difficult for any one of them to fully discern his or her fellow boarders' feelings on the basis of the things they do and say. More interestingly and problematically, it also becomes difficult for Miss Roach, in particular, to be certain how she herself feels, or should feel, about Mr. Thwaites and Vicki Kugelmann's sustained assaults on her composure.

A revealing finding in Mass Observation wartime diaries by civilians that we can use to contextualize the novel is the extent to which a considerable number of home front Britons, in going about their wartime lives, also began to lose touch with how they might be feeling. The methods on which they had formerly relied for gauging equanimity of mood, not only in social situations but also in time spent alone, were not always available to them in the newly pressured private as well as public environments of wartime. A number of diarists and respondents remark on their efforts to avoid thinking and feeling things about the war, or about encountering such strategies in others.[5] These efforts are largely made to avoid unwelcome feelings such as fear and anxiety, which can weaken morale and create a feeling that the enemy is winning. One of the effects of deliberately not thinking about the war, however, is that people can lose touch with their own views and feelings about wartime events. This can make them, at a later point, curious about themselves and their opinions, rather as though they were literary characters to whose views they have only partial access.[6]

Some diarists and respondents remark on the war's ability to kill connective and purposeful thought in ways they have *not* courted. One respondent says of herself and a friend that both had felt they were going mad because "the routine of life had a nightmare quality," so that "the strangeness of existence [itself] terrified [her]." Her mother's mind, too, would "keep going blank." Another who feels unhappy says she is "tired of feeling that [she] must be indulging in self pity," but is unable to find a way out.[7] Here, the displacement indicated by not knowing how what one is feeling should be described ("I *must be* indulging in self pity") could ensure the mood's continuity, since this is the effect gestures of the "I shouldn't be feeling this way" variety tend to have. This respondent also notes an inability to gauge her role in social interactions: "When I go away for weekends I either carry the silence"—of what we would now call depression—"with me or feel I am 'chattering' too much."[8]

In wartime people do live lives largely not of their own making, and in this sense might be said to participate in a story they did not create, a story of whose exact parameters and nature they remain uncertain. Not knowing where one will spend the night after one's house has been bombed is a not uncommon, and obviously distressing, example. Additionally, people "do not want to feel or think," writes one diarist in 1939, "because they do not know how much they are suffering"—in war there is no universal measure—even while the war has not yet brought "the worst pangs of personal feelings to us [in London]."[9] People's reactions to the Phoney War showed that fear *of* fear could be more mentally taxing, in some cases, than the arrival of bombs. This was demonstrated by the fact that outbreaks of mass neurosis did not, as had been predicted, occur once bombs began falling in urban centers such as London (Stonebridge, *The Writing of Anxiety*, 16–17). In response to bombing people could at least take collective actions and express collective responses, rather than remaining locked, as many were before these events, in their own private anxieties about how they would hold up under fire.

When bombs caused trauma, as they seem to have done in some cases, the symptoms were often, unsurprisingly, those now well recognized in post-traumatic stress disorder terms—numbness, shock, delayed and sometimes illogical seeming reactions and repetitions.[10] And given that people were often, on the evidence of the diaries, feeling numb and "saving up" the power of feeling for a time when less would be required of them on the level of day-to-day endurance, some conscious efforts to "not feel or think" could be hard to disentangle, for civilians, from what we would now recognize as traumatically generated behaviors.[11] As in Hamilton's novel, one of the war's legacies could be the inability to feel that one knew oneself, as well as a difficulty identifying the cause of one's state of mind, even if one was able—as many were not able—to find the requisite quiet or stress-free moments to reflect upon it.

Intriguingly, *The Slaves of Solitude* seems to showcase this phenomenon of ordinary people encountering themselves in "artificial" or socially overdetermined terms, as though they were characters in scenes written by another and did not know what they were going to do or say next. Of course, the characters in the novel *are* written by another, that is, by Hamilton, the author. Here, however, Hamilton creates theatricalized set pieces in which the reader encounters characters encountering them*selves* as players who, manipulated into acts of silent, would-be assent by one of their number who is a master of verbal tyranny, are repeatedly forced into positions of alienation from themselves and from what, it is suggested, would normally be their own thoughts, words, acts, and intentions. This effect is achieved primarily through the ways in which charged conversations drive narrative action forward,[12] and through the ways in which uncertainties and moments of opacity at certain points in those conversations cause negative affects to become attached to them. Later, these negatively charged moments become occasions on which Miss Roach, in particular, will dwell, subjecting herself to merciless self-questioning, self-doubt, and self-recrimination as to their probable meanings and implications.

And while the reader learns that it has been clear to Miss Roach's fellow boarders for some time that Mr. Thwaites "has it in for her" (*Slaves of Solitude*, 214, 279–80), Miss Roach herself is not so certain, until quite late in the story, of the extent to which the others notice or care about the fact that she is being targeted. Mr. Thwaites has "resounded through boarding-houses and hotels all his life," since they, "with the timid old women they contained, were hunting-grounds for his temperament," his "peculiar brand of loquacity and malevolence" (15). An admirer of Hitler, he associates Miss Roach with "the Russians" whom he calls her "friends," and, later in the narrative, egged on by Vicki Kugelmann, makes more directly aggressive insinuations about the protagonist's age and sexual attractiveness.

However, Mr. Thwaites's speech is oppressive not only because of its content but, more problematically, its register, through which is added to his statements an element of coercive force which is clearly felt by the other residents. But because this force is joined to archaisms that are made to seem innocuous, or, to put it another way, because the manifest content of the bully's speech acts seems to invite the listeners to laugh at or mock the speaker, it is not possible for listeners to respond to the more obvious aim—intimidation—with either the requisite mockery and light-heartedness *or* a direct challenge to the plainly cruel intent. Mr. Thwaites pushes beyond the limit of expectations regarding polite behavior for such semi-public, semi-private contexts as the predominantly female, wartime boarding house's dining room. And he does so in the knowledge that a public-spirited citizen like Miss Roach will feel she must push beyond her own efforts to be tolerant—still, in this era, a role expected of women in domestic contexts—in turn.

Mr. Thwaites is said to be "never out, never off duty" (*Slaves of Solitude*, 32) from the boarding house. He typically delivers cryptic phrases in an arch theatrical manner, in a fake Scottish (or American) accent, in the third person, or in some obviously antiquarian form. He is also fond of repetition. In the first dining room scene we witness, when Mrs. Barratt, another resident, comes to Miss Roach's aid by remarking that Mr. Thwaites does not realize how much the Russians are doing for the British side in the war, he runs through several of these, including: "Maybe I thinks more than I says," "Like the Wise Old Owl, I Sits and Keeps my Counsel," and "I Hay ma Doots, as the Scotchman said—of Yore" (20–22). The second and third phrases are each preceded by Miss Roach bracing herself for just such a phrase, and in one particular silence, "broken only by the scraping of soup-spoons on plates, the whole room, with its occupants, seemed to have to tremble in hushed reverence before the totally unforeseen and awful Bird which had materialised in its midst" (21).

The unnecessary, largely contentless additions—repetitions, accents, odd constructions and phrasings—this boarding-house bully makes to his speech also seem to replicate some of the war's other, civic home front effects. The war, as "petty pilferer," insinuates itself into people's lives through strictures and shortages (*Slaves of Solitude*, 80), despite the fact that its main theaters of action are removed from Thames Lockdon. And while Mr. Thwaites's words themselves are annoying—as well as, like the war, gesturing unreliably towards distant times and places (Scotland, America)—his tyrannical qualities are revealed not only by his words. He controls and manipulates silences so that his listeners must cringe in expectation of his words and communally register their impact, while trying simultaneously to ignore them, once they are said. And if the war itself seems "unending" (*Slaves of Solitude*, 158–59) as Miss Roach thinks of it, Mr. Thwaites's speech is its boarding-house correlative, because no one seems able to intervene to stop it.

In his reading of the novel's many displacements, Thierry Labica compares the verbal behavior of Mr. Thwaites and Vicki Kugelmann with some of the responses noted by Mass Observation in people who survived a near hit from a bomb (Labica, "War, Conversation and Context," 77). The first minutes after the blast usually produced "repetitive talking" and the "giving of inappropriate orders" which later gave way to an "uncontrollable flood of communication," "repetitiveness," and "excitement," sometimes "manic." After the event had passed, individuals often emerged with "a sense of intense pride, or enhanced personal worth" (Harrisson, *Living Through the Blitz*, 85). Here, citizens' responses are both publicly expressed and indirect, excitement and self-importance being at odds with the blast's likely primary affect of unmasterable terror. Having survived, people also frequently made the blast—in itself not fully graspable—a central feature of their war experience (*Living Through the Blitz*, 76–84). In telling of the event years later they moved themselves closer to the center of remembered action.[13]

In the novel, Mr. Thwaites and Vicki, too, each demonstrate a sense of self-importance seemingly justified by the war, and express aggressive feelings—to Miss Roach—indirectly. As Labica notes, in the novel, Blitz-related behaviors are reinserted "within linguistic activity *away* from the Blitz," making *The Slaves of Solitude* a novel "*of* this very displacement" (Labica, "War, Conversation and Context," 77, emphasis added). Feelings appropriate to the more dramatic events of wartime (bombing, fires, sudden evacuations) appear in the nondramatic context of the Rosamund Tea Rooms, where it is more difficult—for Miss Roach, at least—to see how they might be resolved. The mealtime instances of concentrated indirection of strong affect noted above, where the bully makes people feel things they would not normally feel and cannot say, may also help explain why the novel has been, until recently, so little read, and why it has not endured as an imagined record of wartime civilian behavior. The "myth" or national story of the Blitz[14] seems to have functioned so that, when people such as the Mass Observers quoted earlier could not grasp their own feelings about the war, this internal opacity need not always have mattered since a larger narrative was able to stand in for the momentary incoherence of private feelings. As a screen memory—and a screen always conceals, we should remember, as well as reveals—the narrative of Blitz communality served as a mediatory mesh or filter for the disconcerting feeling of not always knowing what one was feeling, or of not knowing whether what one was feeling was shared by anyone else.[15]

Despite how home front Britons felt or did not feel during the war, most of them seem to have borne up fairly well and to have conducted themselves in a neighborly fashion.[16] And it seems clear that a story—the Blitz narrative—simple yet capacious enough to contain elements that could be positively connected to some small part of most people's experience would help enable such behavior. As Malcolm Smith writes, after the danger of invasion felt in 1940, home front Britons' experience "became easy to mythicize" not only because it was "unfamiliar, but also because it was generally so positive and involving. It virtually demanded over-arching explanation" (Smith, *Britain and 1940*, 60). But instead of a communally agreeable slice of history, the novel gives us something else, something that is, I suggest, intrinsically difficult to recognize. In the conversations that serve as set pieces in the novel and which drive the narrative action forward we find something like a direct rendition of the affective charge those Mass Observers quoted above *might have been feeling*, if they had been able to access what they *were* feeling at the time at which they record *not* knowing what they were feeling because of the war.

Mr. Thwaites requires his fellow boarders to respond—by not feeling able to respond, which is what he desires—to his domestic performances, as though these harangues are the only available form in which to convey an outlook on the war (hence his tendency to extrapolate from personal, domestic behaviors to larger political and geographical ones; Hamilton, *Slaves of Solitude*, 17–20, 26–27, 187–88). And in this way, Hamilton usefully locates and presents for our investigation an aspect of wartime behavior that may have been more common than the historical record suggests. These are occasions in which speech does not primarily work to convey meaning, but, in the absence of felt communal meaning, to foster aggressive and inchoate feelings instead. The quotidian obliqueness of such scenes as we witness in the conversational spaces of *The Slaves of Solitude*, where what is being said is merely the means to make other people feel things they cannot say, or which they may doubt they are even feeling at all, makes them fitting material for a novel, but not so easy to render in other, more overtly documentary forms.

It is worth pointing out, as well, that this combination—intense feeling, combined with not knowing what one is feeling—also describes the symptomatology of trauma, whether experienced in or out of wartime. The shock of an unprecedented event may cause an inrush of affect which may, in turn, quickly register to the mind and nervous system as protective numbness or the desensitization of feeling (Caruth, *Trauma*, 4, 6–7). It may, in turn, produce the effects noted by Harrisson above and referred to by Labica: a rush of inappropriate speech, a tendency to make the shocking event central, even if, or perhaps because, its impact cannot be adequately recalled. Not everyone who experiences such events needs to revisit the original shock in memory or through speech or appropriate action, although those who develop debilitating symptoms, we now know, may find relief if they are able to do so in a supportive environment.

To translate this insight back into the terms of the novel, we might note that when the war, which is the source of a number of possible traumas, stops people knowing what they are feeling, this may also be because what they might otherwise be feeling no longer has a context. When the routines of daily life are disrupted by wartime, feelings that might have been dealt with through reliance on habits associated with particular times and places, or on the basis of past experience, may lose their habitual form of expression and achieve a new kind of force or density. Having one's dwelling bombed, as has happened to Miss Roach, means that feelings about that event may no longer seem viable, but might still be being belatedly processed. Conversations in the uncertain, temporary, not quite private and not quite public context of the boarding house might seem surreal to Miss Roach precisely because they are the product of displacement.

Miss Roach certainly has difficulty recalling the exact import of Vicki Kugelmann's contributions to boarding and public house conversation, as is demonstrated by the protagonist's anxious, nightly replaying of many of these scenes. Vicki's speech, like that of Mr. Thwaites, is also mannered, delivering an affective charge additional to sense that can be read as animosity, a kind of patronizing, ersatz pity towards the English woman, an open challenge to respond in kind, or a combination of all these things. The effect is to throw into question everything Miss Roach feels, thinks, says, and does. Like Mr. Thwaites's speech, Vicki's is accretive in impact. When Mr. Thwaites makes a remark that he realizes is "Thwaitesian, he is unable to resist repeating it" (*Slaves of Solitude*, 21). Vicki, too, seems impelled to make increasingly brazen verbal assaults upon Miss Roach's composure and good will towards her when her initial attempts have little noticeable effect.

Vicki, of course, is German, and so we might expect her to express herself in English in unidiomatic ways. Miss Roach is sure, however, that Vicki's affectedness is not thc simple result of having to speak in a language not her own. Rather, it is implied by the narrator, who at this point offers Miss Roach's view, that Vicki uses her foreignness as an excuse to cultivate an additional affectedness of gesture and speech that marks her out from the other women in their circle. Thus Vicki speaks with an "arch, suggestive . . . old-fashioned air" (*Slaves of Solitude*, 66), wears her hair in the style of the 1920s, and, when powdering her nose or smoking a cigarette, does these things with "more fuss, precision, and ceremony than was usual, as if these things were novelties to which she had been lately introduced and by which she was still fascinated" (67). While Vicki has the second-language speaker's tendency to express herself, in English, in ways that are "a little too excellently polished" (68), the effect is to unsettle Miss Roach, because this means she cannot be sure of the extent to which some of Vicki's actions and turns of phrase might be accidental, which, in turn, increases her own anxiety about whether she is being fair to the other woman. Yet Vicki's actions, coupled with her speech, seem to be reliably ambiguous on this question. At the point at which Miss Roach notices Vicki's precision of speech, for instance, she also observes Vicki repeatedly "tapp[ing] her cigarette over an ash-tray" when there is hardly any ash on it at all (68).

The war, and Vicki's presence in Thames Lockdon and at the Rosamund Tea Rooms, opens a space within Miss Roach's experience and environment that floods her with uncontrollable feelings, as though the uncertainties the protagonist quite naturally has about her life, her job, and about "hiding out" from the bombs of London in Thames Lockdon (*Slaves of Solitude*, 34) are being perpetually relit and inflamed. The effect would not be possible, of course, if Miss Roach did not have her own anxieties, but anxieties existing just beneath the radar of one's consciousness can be a common citizen's response to war on the home front. Faced with hatred that seems to have no cause, for most of the novel Miss Roach undergoes a process which is the reverse of Madge and Harrisson's recommendation to turn passive feelings into active feelings by externalizing violent hatreds. Instead, she deals with the fact that she is targeted by Vicki and Mr. Thwaites by trying to find a cause for their behavior in herself. This causes increased uncertainty. So when Vicki calls Miss Roach a "fast worker" for having "adopted [a] pet American already" (69), a reference to the Lieutenant Miss Roach has been going out with, the effect is to make the protagonist's feelings about the Lieutenant less clear to her than they were previously (119–20, 124–26, 147–48). This is partly because Vicki has drawn attention to a relationship the English woman has her own doubts about, and partly because the relationship has been misrepresented as something Miss Roach has sought, instead of, as is the case, a situation to which she has merely responded.

A strong measure of shock or other unnamed, difficult-to-interpret affect repeatedly arrives with each new outrageous turn in Vicki's behavior towards the protagonist. The effect is not only to alienate Miss Roach from her own experience, as she asks herself whether Vicki has really said or done what she appears to have said or done, but to place between herself and her experience inchoate feelings, among them rage, that, despite her attempts to express them rationally, seem unable to be expressed. This is partly because Vicki's responses are designed to simultaneously refuse and refuel these feelings. For instance, she perpetually places Miss Roach in the role of the jealous, less attractive rival for the Lieutenant's attentions, interpreting all of the English woman's responses as though they issue from this source. When the Lieutenant telephones Miss Roach at the boarding house one evening and asks to speak to Vicki after Miss Roach has declined to go out with him, Vicki responds to the other woman's query about their conversation by patting her shoulder and saying: "'No, my dear . . . Have no fear . . . I do not Snatch the Men'" (*Slaves of Solitude*, 204), thereby imputing to Miss Roach a desire Miss Roach has herself just actively negated.

When, on a further occasion, Miss Roach tries to indicate that she is not unduly attached to the Lieutenant, Vicki's face registers the "charmed incredulity with which one hears a child's story . . . a look of infinite benevolence, combined somehow with a look of infinite spite." This time, she pats Miss Roach's cheek and says, in her most guttural accent: "'Really! . . . You are rather A dear, aren't you? . . . Yes. You are rather A dear!'" (*Slaves of Solitude*, 208). The German woman's overplaying of her foreignness by capitalizing the indefinite article in this way ("Now, I think I will take A walk," "I have what you call A hunch!" [197]), being meaningless and so impossible to respond to, is an equally maddening affectation for this reason. Yet Vicki is also more difficult for the protagonist to deal with than Mr. Thwaites, because the effects of her manner of speaking and behaving are not uniformly felt by others. The American servicemen, for instance, seem not to notice its strangeness, perhaps because they too are strangers in England. Miss Roach is also hampered by her desire to be fair, to be a good citizen (294), even while her habits as a good citizen—to avoid getting so drunk, for instance, as to inconvenience others—are behaviors that come in for particular derision by Vicki. And of course, if Miss Roach is the only person to notice Vicki's taunting of her, she cannot finally be certain whether she is not imagining some, or all, of its effects.

The effect Vicki has on Miss Roach is inseparable from the war, just as the German woman seems to be the war's creation (ordinarily she "would not be noticed in the street as attractive or otherwise," in Miss Roach's opinion [*Slaves of Solitude*, 67]). While Vicki deftly plies her trade of disarrangement, ousting Miss Roach from the position of agent of her own feelings, the war is the larger agent of inconsequence, of actions divorced from intentions, of enjoyment not allowed but randomly, because usually drunkenly, imposed. On an evening's outing to the Dragon, a nearby restaurant, Miss Roach is made to drink a good deal more than she wants to but still does not escape being called a "silly old Roach," a "spoil-sport," and enjoined to "be *sporty!*" (163, 166). The latter injunction refers to her unwillingness to be kissed by Lieutenant Pike, who is also, at the time, kissing Vicki, on the same seat where he has formerly kissed the English woman alone. It is on this outing that Miss Roach recognizes that the war is the chief source of an acute, widespread, and unavoidable disorientation:

> No imaginable combination of peace-time circumstances could have brought about such a composition of characters as now filled the car and sat on each other's knees—the ill-looking driver, the German woman, her lonely self, and the three Americans, of presumably different classes in civil life, and presumably going to their deaths when the second front began. And yet, she was aware, all over the countryside around, all over the country, cars were racing along with just such noisy loads to just such destinations. (*Slaves of Solitude*, 158)

The travelers' nationalities are interchangeable, as are their activities: "if it wasn't sitting on each other's knees it was singing, and if it wasn't singing it was sitting on each other's knees," thinks Miss Roach, "and whatever it was it was drinking and drinking and screaming and desperate." The war, she perceives, among its "innumerable other guises," "had taken on the character of the inventor and proprietor of some awful low, cosmopolitan night-club" (*Slaves of Solitude*, 158). Far from coming together to support each other in the face of danger, these strangers seem, to Miss Roach, to have come together for no reason at all.

While the drunken outing to the restaurant is a communal instance of an excess of feeling—or so it feels to our protagonist—arising from a group of strangers who would not have been brought together were it not for the war, Miss Roach perhaps represents a peculiarly English response to this situation. Since Vicki and the Americans are foreigners, it naturally falls to Miss Roach to consider the effect their behavior will have on the much put-upon (and, we assume, English) publicans, waiting staff, chauffeurs, and fellow lodgers who face the holiday-like liberties the visitors take with expectations of politeness and neighborly consideration. Labica also observes that, instead of displaying "cooperative individuals entering into interpersonal and local rapports," as might be seen to have occurred in an earlier phase of the war in London, *The Slaves of Solitude* shows a "global historical rapport"—that constituted by the Allied war effort, presumably—constituting and "enter[ing] into individuals" in a more random fashion, and "turning them into . . . demented mouthpieces" (Labica, "War, Conversation and Context," 80). As the war goes on, it is as though the visitors to Thames Lockdon compete more vigorously for the dubious honor of being the most ostensibly carefree and the least well behaved, as though committing outrages on the tedium of the extended wartime moment.

Miss Roach herself ascribes the behaviors she cannot otherwise account for in others to the fact that, in her words, "the war was on their nerves" (*Slaves of Solitude*, 232). The phrase raises the troubling idea that the war itself might rewire affective responses so that subjecting a person to social humiliation disguised as acceptable drawing room or public house behavior can proceed with impunity. And like the war itself, which, once started, provides its own momentum, Miss Roach's tormentors do not need a reason to torment her. All they need is to have started it—a distraction from their own anxieties perhaps—for it to seem worth continuing. Furthermore, if the war "infects" these characters and drives them to perform actions and make statements that are largely without meaning—something that is more obvious, because less explicable, when it occurs outside the war's chief theaters of action—one wonders what the consequences would be, should this effect turn out to have occurred in the world beyond the novel, for posterity.

Some consequences can be readily imagined. Lieutenant Pike, for instance, who is driven by his wartime lack of stability to offer marriage to several women who happen to be available to him in different nearby places, will likely escape the consequences of these impulsive offers by departing for the Second Front. The consequences will instead be encountered by the women. For a person like Miss Roach, however—conscientious, law-abiding, and well-meaning—the question is more difficult. Her personal situation is resolved when, bullied too far, she pushes Mr. Thwaites, as a result of which he falls down the boarding-house stairs and, soon after, dies of peritonitis with which the fall may or may not have been connected. Having fortunately come into some money at this point, she escapes to Claridge's Hotel in London.

Yet there are other, subtler instances in the novel of a war-wrought absence of meaning, or instability of context, gaining a charged, unsettling quality on the level of feeling, and affecting our protagonist in particular. Lieutenant Pike, with his invitations to drinks and blithely offered promise of marriage, is thought of by Miss Roach as "inconsequent" (*Slaves of Solitude*, 46), a word designating a disruption to intention, or a lack of rational connection to accompanying circumstances.[17] As the pair sit in the local pub, Miss Roach realizes that the Lieutenant is "not only inconsequent, as most human beings are, in drink": he is "chronically and inveterately inconsequent." All of his actions seem to be undertaken without thought of any "social consequences" at all (46).

"Inconsequence" might simply be an accurate descriptor of an American serviceman killing time in a nondescript town before participating in combat. The prospect of dying or being injured in battle perhaps inevitably charges the present moment with a corresponding increase in importance. It may also charge that moment with a corresponding emptiness of specific purpose: it is arguably more difficult to perform the acts one might wish to perform before one dies if one is in an urban backwater in a country one has not chosen. But while the Lieutenant's tendency to make offers of marriage without due thought to their consequences can be explained with reference to his situation, Miss Roach finds herself increasingly hampered by the opposite problem. Inhibitions, or precautionary withholdings of energy and freedom, are a tendency to which she is already prone. Yet her inhibitions seem to multiply in would-be compensation for the increasingly uninhibited behavior of others. These reductions in Miss Roach's freedom, or at least her freedom of thought and equanimity, cause her to operate rather like an invisible, well-meaning antidote to the maleficent Mr. Thwaites and

Vicki. Where they enact plans to terrorize fellow diners or disturb long-suffering publicans and other, quieter customers, Miss Roach is involved in laborious acts of thinking ahead about proprieties, or others' likely readings of certain actions (*Slaves of Solitude*, 48, 249, 252–53).

For Miss Roach, it is as though each thoughtless act, physical or verbal, performed by others has to be doubly processed by her, as though indeed the populace at large is bound to take up and engage the overflow of others' war-generated behaviors. Miss Roach more than once feels "shame," for instance, at Vicki's arch expressions, such as when Vicki represents herself as a seductress with the phrase "Slow but sure," or describes her ability to make cocktails as "Wizard!" a shame Vicki obviously does not feel (*Slaves of Solitude*, 73, 154). Yet the absence of purpose and artificiality that seem to fuel Vicki's speech do not disappear when Miss Roach takes them up. Rather, the enigma attaching to certain phrases and a larger, war-charged purposelessness seem to replicate themselves. Courting sleep—ordinarily, the absence of consciousness—Miss Roach is frustrated in the attempt, experiencing a troubling absence of unconsciousness (and thus a doubling of an absence) in which she "invent[s] conversations with Vicki, invent[s] Vicki's answers, and then get[s] white with anger at Vicki's answers." In asking herself what Vicki thinks (*Slaves of Solitude*, 180–81), Miss Roach invents the depth of meaning that, in Vicki's conversation and actions, is clearly lacking. But since the question of what Vicki thinks cannot be answered, Miss Roach in turn wonders what she thinks herself. "Perhaps she, Miss Roach," she opines late in the novel, and not Vicki, was the person who "had the wicked, distorted mind" (294, also 127–28, 178).

It is as though the boarding house residents, removed from the imminent dangers of bombing while owing their raison d'être to the war, have had their "personal, private ethics and desires . . . transformed" by wartime but not "elevated and merged" into the general pattern of a "whole community." Rather, these characters' personal desires seem to have been placed at a remove from themselves by the war, without the war's providing anything sufficiently distracting, involving, or uniting to occupy their hearts and minds instead. This means, paradoxically, that the feelings that have been placed at a remove from the characters by the intervention of wartime, rebound upon those same characters in ways that can be difficult to recognize and mobilize. The characters' "violent hatreds" are not quite externalized, since they are mostly indirectly leveled at fellow residents, becoming a source not of motivating clarity but, certainly for the protagonist, one of acute emotional unease.

Quite early in the novel Miss Roach observes that "it was the same everywhere: everyone, in the same way, was different: this was the war, the war" (*Slaves of Solitude*, 136). Throughout England, people's behavior changes so that everyone becomes different from how they were before, many of them, apparently, without noticing the alteration. If "everyone, in the same way, was different" because of the war, then daily life might also be regarded, in wartime, as a performance, and this seems to be the ultimate message of Hamilton's novel. Everyone is living with a heightening of the impact of their thoughts, words, and actions, even when they seem not to be doing so or when they are not being directly invited to scrutinize their words and actions for how they might impact on the progress of the war ("Is your journey really necessary?" and "Careless talk costs lives!").[18] Everyone is living a life they would not ordinarily live, interacting, to some extent, with people with whom they would not normally interact. For those who are not in immediate danger, this overplaying of everyday life can be toxic. The affective fallout of the behavior of Vicki, Mr. Thwaites, and the inconsequent Lieutenant Pike towards Miss Roach means that this sensible, thoughtful woman cannot escape a heightened self-consciousness—being the same, but different—as she strives to make sense of actions for which the only justification seems to be "the war."

This point gives rise to another question. If ordinary wartime civilians did not always know how they were feeling, the pressures of war work and domestic life being such that this question was not, understandably, always prioritized, and if their neighbors might have felt a similar internal estrangement, how would these people know how they were behaving with, and to, others? Does the rerouting of passive into active feelings, of inward hatreds into outer ones also necessarily come between people and their own knowledge, or reflective awareness, of themselves as social agents? And if the pressures of wartime mean that one's social alienation, as well as self-alienation, passes, so to speak, "under the radar" while more important events are going on, what happens to this sense of social dislocation *afterwards*? Hamilton's novel raises the question of what relation the things people say in wartime bear to their actual feelings about those to whom they direct them, and the extent to which it is possible to discern these feelings. In this way, it raises the question of whether personal dissociation of more negative, because more ubiquitous, kinds is an inevitable byproduct of the war, especially in the lives of those who, like Miss Roach, are destined to remain unremembered.

War marks "the end of privacy," and of secrecy, as the narrator of *The Slaves of Solitude* implies, with each day's waking to the "uncanny" sounds of one's immediate neighbors (83, 82). But on the other hand, war creates greater secrets and opacities than exist in peacetime. In peacetime we all functionally depend upon not knowing our neighbors' true desires—this is, after all, the working principle of democracy, of secret voting—largely without noticing that we do so, but in wartime we may not even know our own. The Second World War ended with the use of a weapon, the atom bomb, that helped usher in another conflict: the Cold War. And in that war, democratic governments necessarily increased, rather than decreased, their mandate for not sharing information with the public, lest it fall into the hands of the enemy.[19] The populace, worn down by the years of privation and conflict, was inevitably challenged by the impossibility of thinking anything useful about the quotidian prospect of unsurvivable nuclear death.[20] They inhabited, in some ways, a world at least as unreal and estranging as the one they had imagined they would, with the close of active hostilities, be leaving behind.

At the close of Hamilton's novel, Miss Roach's perspective on her Thames Lockdon life is described, from the bar at Claridge's, as a "clarification of mind," but also, more problematically, as "something else [that] was added" to it (*Slaves of Solitude*, 322). If wartime London were really offering this stoical, quietly heroic protagonist a reliable perspective on her time in boarding-house land, that perspective would presumably be described as the result of an erroneous framing falling away to reveal a truer insight, a more disinterested view. Instead, London "add[s]" clarification, and as the final page of the novel shows, that clarification, too, is based on a significant measure of unknowing. Miss Roach goes to sleep "knowing nothing of the future . . . of the February blitz shortly to descend on London . . . of flying bombs . . . of rockets . . . of Berlin, of the Atom Bomb" (*Slaves of Solitude*, 326), and so too did most citizens know little of the challenges that awaited them after the war. "Was this really her line of country?" our heroine wonders, comparing Claridge's with the Rosamund Tea Rooms, recalling her days and nights of suffering (*Slaves of Solitude*, 325). Perhaps not. But a war is a strange line of country, and stranger still may be the people it calls into being. All of them, in some way it seems, do things differently there.

Notes

1. C. Madge and T. H. Harrisson, *War Begins at Home* (London: Chatto and Windus, 1940), 424.

2. Sigmund Freud, *Inhibitions, Symptoms, and Anxiety*, in *The Standard Edition of the Complete Psychological Works of Sigmund Freud*, ed. James Strachey (London: Hogarth Press and the Institute of Psycho-Analysis, 1926), 87–156, at 138; Lyndsey Stonebridge, *The Writing of Anxiety: Imagining Wartime in Mid-Century British Culture* (Basingstoke, Eng.: Palgrave Macmillan, 2007), 20.

3. Patrick Hamilton, *The Slaves of Solitude* (London: Constable, [1947] 2006), 10.

4. Sandra Koa Wing, ed., *Our Longest Days: A People's History of the Second World War*, by the Writers of Mass-Observation, ed. Sandra Koa Wing (London: Profile, 2008), 32, 35, 214; John Welshman, *Churchill's Children: The Evacuee Experience in Wartime Britain* (Oxford: Oxford University Press, 2010), 130, 156, 206–7.

5. Mass Observation online archive, http://www.massobservation.amdigital.co.uk.ezproxy.auckland.ac.nz/contents/publication.aspx?documentid=282972. Diarist 5349, November 11, 1939; Directive respondent 2450, June 5 and 25, 1940; Directive respondent 2248, August 16, 1940; Diarist 5426, August 22, 1940; Directive respondent 1072, September 4, 1940; Directive respondent 2368, September 19, 1940; Olivia Cockett, June 20, 1940, Cockett 2009, 102. Olivia Cockett, *Love and War in London: The Mass-Observation Wartime Diary of Olivia Cockett*, ed. Robert Malcolmson (Stroud, Eng.: History, 2009).

6. Directive respondent 2265, October 10, 1939; Directive respondent 1668, January 7–8, 1942.

7. Mass Observation online archive, Directive respondent 2248, August 16, 1940; also Directive respondent 2886, September 18, 1941. Directive respondent 1668, January 7–8, 1942.

8. Mass Observation online archive, Directive respondent 1668, January 7–8, 1942.

9. Mass Observation online archive, Diarist 5349, November 11, 1939.

10. See Françoise Davoine, and Jean-Max Gaudillière, *History Beyond Trauma: Whereof One Cannot Speak, Thereof One Cannot Stay Silent*, trans. Susan Fairfield (New York: Other, 2004); Cathy Caruth, "Introduction," in *Trauma: Explorations in Memory*, ed. Cathy Caruth (Baltimore: Johns Hopkins University Press, 1995), 3–12; Cathy Caruth, *Unclaimed Experience: Trauma, Narrative, and History* (Baltimore: Johns Hopkins University Press, 1996).

11. See Tom Harrisson, *Living Through the Blitz* (London: Collins, 1976), 76–84.

12. See Thierry Labica, "War, Conversation and Context in Patrick Hamilton's *The Slaves of Solitude*," *Connotations* 12, no. 1 (2002–2003): 72–82, http://www.connotations.uni-tuebingen.de/labica01201.htm; Gerard Barrett, "Hamilton and the Nets of Language," *Critical Engagements* 1, no. 1 (2005): 212–34; John Mepham, "Varieties of

Incomprehension: Patrick Hamilton and Elizabeth Bowen," in *British Fiction after Modernism: The Novel at Mid-Century*, ed. Marina MacKay and Lyndsey Stonebridge (Basingstoke, Eng.: Palgrave Macmillan, 2007), 59–76.

13. Philip Ziegler, "Foreword," in *Our Longest Days*, by the Writers of Mass-Observation, vi; Harrisson, *Living Through the Blitz*, 326–27.

14. Angus Calder, *The People's War: Britain, 1939–1945* (London: Jonathan Cape, 1969).

15. Sigmund Freud, "Screen Memories," in *The Freud Reader*, ed. Peter Gay (London: Vintage, 1995), 117–26, at 123; Serge Leclaire, "Unconscious Transcription: Another Memory," in *Psychoanalysis, Creativity, and Literature: A French-American Inquiry*, ed. Alan Roland (New York: Columbia University Press, 1978), 75–84, at 75; Cormac Gallagher, "Lacan's Summary of Seminar XI," *The Letter: Lacanian Perspectives on Psychoanalysis* 5 (1995): 1–17, at 11.

16. Malcolm Smith, *Britain and 1940: History, Myth and Popular Memory* (London: Routledge, 2000); Mark Connelly, *We Can Take It! Britain and the Memory of the Second World War* (Harlow, Eng.: Pearson Longman, 2004); Kristine A. Miller, *British Literature of the Blitz: Fighting the People's War* (Basingstoke, Eng.: Palgrave Macmillan, 2009).

17. *Oxford English Dictionary*, online version 2014: www.oed.com.

18. John D. Cantwell, *Images of War: British Posters, 1939–45* (London: Her Majesty's Stationery Office, 1989), 24.

19. Peter Hennessy, *The Secret State: Whitehall and the Cold War* (London: Allen Lane, 2002), 77–120; Eluned Summers-Bremner, "'Another World than This': Muriel Spark's Postwar Investigations," *Yearbook of English Studies* 42: "Literature of the 1950s and 1960s" (2012): 151–67, at 153, 158–59.

20. Peter Hennessy, *Having It So Good: Britain in the Fifties* (London: Allen Lane, 2006), 320.

ALLAN HEPBURN

Facing the Future
Children in Postwar Britain

In postwar British culture, children represented broken continuity and grim futurity. Although plans for rebuilding Europe after the war resulted in discussion about the welfare of children, children themselves had little to say about their own destinies. In fact, they are relatively scarce in British fiction and film of the period.[1] When they do appear, they are treated either as precociously wise or as incidental to the tasks of social reconstruction. In many ways, children who lived through the war never had a childhood. Their wartime experiences of evacuation, deportation, and endangerment loosened family bonds. After the war, legislation mediated the uncertain role of children in Britain, both as members of families and as wards of the state. Young people bore the burden of the past and the promise of the future at the same time. In Elizabeth Bowen's *The Heat of the Day* (1949), Louie Lewis wheels her illegitimate son, Thomas Victor, to the place where her parents' house stood before it was razed by a bomb. His inheritance is a void in space and time; his future, consequently, remains uncertain. Postwar children win pity or charity, but their emotional lives remain obscure, especially to their parents. Their future, whatever it might be at a personal level, is inseparable from the destiny of the nation.

At the beginning of the war, British children were evacuated to the countryside or to destinations overseas, usually in the Dominions. Billeting children on farmers or landowners did not always prove successful. As Angus Calder observes, city children were not necessarily accustomed to indoor plumbing or outdoor play.[2] In *Put Out More Flags* (1942), Evelyn Waugh satirizes the program of sending lower-class children from the city to the country; the sly Connolly siblings terrorize the families upon whom they are foisted. Similarly, in Henry Green's *Loving* (1945), an English boy named Albert arrives at an Irish castle for the duration; although he appears at first to be a "refugee," one maid refers to him as a "little storm trooper" after he wrings the neck of a peacock on the grounds.[3] During the Phoney War, when aerial bombardment did not materialize as expected, some children returned to their parents in the city (Calder, *The People's War*, 45).

Honor Croome's novel, *O Western Wind* (1943), opens with a boatload of mothers and their children zigzagging across the Atlantic towards the United States. In reality, evacuation of British children abroad ended after U-boats torpedoed two ships filled with young passengers. On August 29, 1940, a U-boat attacked the *Volendam*, with 1,152 people on board, including 320 children and their escorts. All the children survived: ships in convoy with the *Volendam* picked up adults and children from lifeboats off the northern coast of Ireland and took them to Glasgow. Such good luck was not repeated two weeks later. On September 17, 1940, a Nazi submarine sank the *City of Benares*, which was en route to Canada with dozens of children aboard. Among the dead were 77 children, 5 adults, and 121 crew members. Because of this disaster, the Children's Overseas Reception Board abruptly ceased its evacuation program (*The People's War*, 129). The British protested that the Nazis had murdered innocent children on the *City of Benares*; the Nazis replied that they did not know there were children on the ship. In short, the dead children became pawns in a propaganda campaign.

From the Spanish Civil War through the Second World War, visual representations emphasized children's vulnerability for propagandistic purposes. In the appendix to Arthur Koestler's *L'Espagne ensanglantée* (1937), photographs of dead children lying on their backs with numbers draped around their necks, some of them with bullet wounds in the head or spatters of blood on their faces, create a graphic intervention in the propaganda campaign of the Spanish Civil War. (See figure 1.) The war destroys children even though they are peripheral to the conflict. A poster published by the Spanish Ministry of Propaganda with the French caption, "QUE FAIS-TU POUR EMPÊCHER CELA?

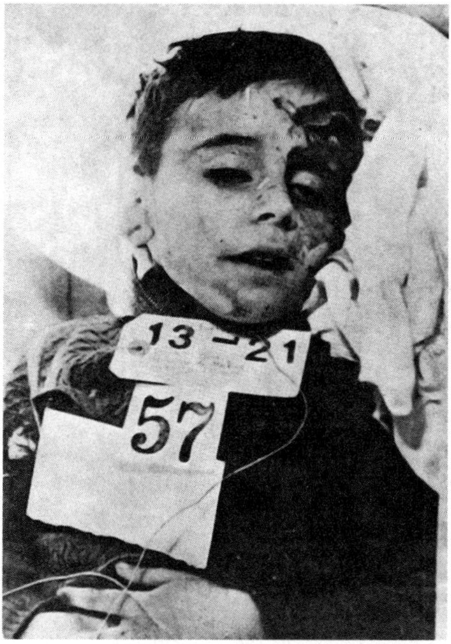

Figure 1. Dead child, L'Espagne ensanglantée.

MADRID," conveys the drama of vulnerability. (See figure 2.) Planes soar above a woman who clings to a child. A grey cloud, or what could just as easily be a roiling mass of dust, rises up behind the two figures. A bomb-blasted building juts ominously above the immobile figures. Fear, as the predominant affect produced by the image, is achieved through skewed frames. The rectangular geometry of the image—roughly boxed by the right angles of the caption, the building, and the planes—does not align with the square borders of the poster itself. The viewer implicitly crouches beneath the woman and child to create a steep vector that takes in people, building, and, in deep aerial space, planes. The woman looks down, not up, for salvation: danger comes from the sky. The child, gazing directly at the viewer, seems to be responsible for uttering the caption, "What are you going to do about this?" Squeezing the boy at the edge of the text-box visually cuts off his means of escape. He has survived the war so far, but he and the woman, assumed to be his mother, have no place to go and no place to hide.

Children are equally terrorized in Second World War images. In a

Figure 2. Poster, "Que Fais-Tu?"

poster designed by Abram Games in 1942 for a series called "Your Britain, Fight for It Now," a rickety boy pauses inside the ruins of a building. (See figure 3.) The Finsbury Health Centre, which offered free health care from 1935 onwards in the working-class borough of Finsbury, provides a front for the ruins.[4] As in the Madrid poster, an apocalyptic cloud looms over the war-ravaged landscape. The words "disease" and "neglect" appear on the walls. A tombstone in the background bodes ill, and nothing but ill. Like many surrealist paintings, the image floats in indeterminate space. The futuristic façade of the modern hospital contrasts with the blasted domain of disease and neglect; darkness lies ahead in the right side of the poster. Following a path from left to right, the natural direction of reading in English, the poster implies a regression from a bright future to a disastrous one. As in the Spanish Civil War poster, this image dwells on the boy's exposure: he is the only figure in the picture. The roofless building offers no shelter. Although the poster promotes early medical intervention to detect disease, the caption, "YOUR BRITAIN FIGHT FOR IT NOW," unambiguously links personal health to the future of the nation under attack.

Figure 3. Abram Games, "Your Britain, Fight for It Now." Courtesy the Imperial War Museum.

International crises complicated British national identity, with pronounced consequences for displaced and refugee children. Just prior to the outbreak of war, the Central British Fund for German Jewry, with the help of the Save the Children Fund and other agencies, appealed to the British government to allow unaccompanied German Jewish children under the age of seventeen into the country. After Kristallnacht in November 1938, the need to help Jewish refugees leave Germany intensified. On December 1, a group of 320 children left Berlin—via German railroads, Dutch relief stations, and British ferries—for England.[5] Ultimately, nearly 10,000 children, some of them orphans, others internees in concentration camps, were relocated to Britain and settled in foster homes, hostels, and schools. The Guardianship (Refugee Children) Act, passed in 1944, recognized the need to appoint guardians for "infants who have come to the United Kingdom in consequence of war or persecution."[6] Having designated guardians, however, did not alleviate the refugees' sense of alienation. As Phyllis Lassner argues, the children of the *Kindertransport* often experienced "discontinuity and disorientation," rather than acceptance in Britain.[7] Refugees did not necessarily assimilate: "For those Jewish refugees who stayed on after the war, becoming British would not mean assimilating to British culture but submerging their own history and culture under the weightier if tremulous traditions of Anglo-Jewry" (Lassner, *Anglo-Jewish Women*, 15). There was an abiding expectation that refugees would, to some degree, remain perpetual migrants. Indeed, from the 1930s through the 1940s, photographs, posters, and films depict children in motion. They have no permanent shelter.

By the end of the Second World War, shelter of any kind was scarce in Europe. On the Continent in 1945, 10 million dislocated people began to journey home, among them countless children. Many lived in displaced persons camps, under the jurisdiction of the United Nations Relief and Rehabilitation Administration (UNRRA). In 1947 Joseph A. Berger reported that

> the DPs comprise men, women, and children of all ages. Very few families are complete; one or more members of nearly all of them were killed, lost, or separated in some way during the war years. Although no statistics are available, it is known that large numbers of DP children are roaming round the country, lost and abandoned, while others are being brought up in German homes, unknown to their families. Many reclaimed children were sent to special UNRRA children's homes, pending the tracing of their relatives, while small numbers of other children have been allowed to enter countries overseas for permanent care and adoption.[8]

The Red Cross claimed that 13 million children had lost their "natural protectors" during the war.[9] UNESCO, founded in 1945, estimated that 8 million children in Germany, 6.5 million in the Soviet Union, and 1.3 million in France were homeless in 1946.[10] In the same year, the Polish minister of labour and social welfare announced that, of 7 million Polish children under the age of 14, one million had lost one parent; 650,000 had lost both parents; and a further 300,000 had parents who had been arrested and deported by the Nazis.[11] Visiting Germany in October and November 1946, Victor Gollancz photographed malnourished and diseased children; whether rooting in a garbage bin or dying in a hospital bed, these children are, implicitly if not actually, outcasts. UNRRA did not help the vanquished. Indeed, Gollancz notes that, "in the matter of food, Unrra was doing at least something for other countries, but nothing at all for Germany."[12] Having established a tracing service to reunite families, UNRRA helped settle 12,843 unaccompanied children by 1947. Yet the organization did not have a mandate to provide assistance to the 1.5 million German children expelled from Eastern Europe, because they were "enemy nationals" (Zahra, *The Lost Children*, 8). Nor did UNRRA have any jurisdiction over youths who lied about their age or who lived outside refugee camps. When UNRRA disbanded in 1947, it was replaced by the International Refugee Organization (IRO).

The IRO continued the tracing service that had been set up by UNRRA. Efforts were made to reunite families by consulting Nazi documents, along with other information. In Germany, one father located his two sons by having their photos flashed on the screen of German cinemas with commentary about their age and names. The boys were found in a Berlin orphanage. Tracing missing family members by bulletins in movie houses was restricted to the Russian zone in Germany; the Americans and British did not condone this method of putting families back together again.[13] In November 1949, more than four years after VE Day, the London *Times* tabulated the numbers of children still missing: "Poland lost the greatest number of children; altogether more than 100,000 children are still unaccounted for. Czechoslovakia and Yugoslavia also lost many. Five inquiries for British children were received, of whom one was found, and 33 British children have been located, the relatives being found in nine cases."[14] Finding children did not, of course, resolve the traumas that they endured during the Second World War.

The first European conference after the war, held in Zurich in September 1945, was devoted to "Children Victims of War" (Wyman, *DP: Europe's Displaced Persons*, 88).[15] Victimization took many forms. The Nazis kidnapped some youths for "Germanization": young girls and boys of Czech, Polish, Swedish, and other national origins were placed with German families and raised as members of the Third Reich. Nazis selected children with Aryan features from orphanages and foster homes. They also seized children in the street (Zahra, *The Lost Children*, 125). Assimilation of youth to the German language and culture was a means of securing the future of the Reich. "Wer die Jugend hat, hat die Zukunft," was a Nazi conviction: "Whoever possesses the youth, possesses the future" (quoted in Wyman, *DP: Europe's Displaced Persons*, 88). After the war, Germanized children were hard to locate and repatriate: "All means, administrative and psychological, had been used by the Nazis to obscure their origin."[16]

In an eyewitness report about the state of Europe, Katherine Lenroot cites statistics about the homeless and the orphaned that she had heard at the International Labour Congress held in Paris in 1945. At that meeting, participants from forty-eight nations discussed "the sufferings of the peoples of Europe and the effects of war and occupation upon children and young persons" (Lenroot, "Europe's Children Need Help Now," 40). Lenroot, representing the United Children's Bureau from the United States, subsequently visited a children's center in the American zone in Germany. She observed that "orphans and homeless children were receiving excellent care. Many, however, were stunted in growth, under-developed in muscular coordination, and greatly retarded in school" (41). She appealed to American readers to help rebuild liberated countries, with particular attention to "the needs of children and youth for food, health services and medical care, and educational facilities" (43). Disease, as Victor Gollancz observed, was rampant. "Hunger was the most common pain children experienced during and after the war," Nicholas Stargardt remarks, "and they soon learned that their parents could not take it away."[17]

The situation of children on the Continent right after the war was quite different from the situation in Britain. British children may have been underfed and badly clothed, or they may have been orphaned during the war, but they were not, usually, refugees in displaced persons camps. At the same time, news about European orphans, refugees, and homeless people filled British newspapers and magazines. Numerous photo essays and articles documented the plight of European children. On October 13, 1945, for example, the *Illustrated London News* ran a photomontage under the title "Europe's Homeless Refugees." In these pictures, women and children scavenge in a dump; a German boy holds aloft a loaf of moldy bread; people wait for trains among heaps of suitcases. Calling upon the spirit of New Year benevolence, the Oxford Famine Relief Society ran an ad in the December 29, 1948 edition of *The Times*: "AMONG THE REFUGEES, DISPLACED PERSONS, AND FATHERLESS CHILDREN / Millions, uprooted from their homes, face the new year with little to eat or to wear."[18] Requests for donations were ubiquitous, and they continued throughout the 1950s. The Ockenden Venture, founded in 1951, initially aimed to provide education, sustenance, and clothes to Eastern Europeans in displaced persons camps.[19] The Ockenden Venture funded its activities with charitable donations. The beneficiaries, children from Estonia, Czechoslovakia, Poland, and elsewhere, were welcomed for holidays in Surrey. The organizers behind this charity understood humanitarian action as international, not national, in its aims and ultimate effects. Like other agencies devoted to children's welfare, including UNESCO, the Ockenden Venture concentrated on education as a means of helping boys and girls towards a better future. From the perspective of the immediate postwar period, it was very difficult to imagine, let alone represent, the future without summoning up the figure of the child.

The proliferation of social services for children attests to postwar thinking about human rights, culminating in the Universal Declaration of Human Rights in 1948.[20] At the same time, increased legislation expresses ambivalence about who is ultimately responsible for children's welfare: the family or the state. In Britain, the Family Allowance Bill of 1945 granted payments to parents or others with children in their custody. The National Assistance Act of 1948 put an end to the Poor Laws, which had direct implications for the charitable assistance of children. Legislation covering the care and rights of children was further expanded in the Children Bill of 1947–48. As an extension of prior laws concerning the welfare of young people, particularly the Child Bill of 1908, the postwar law was intended to cover children who had no parents or unfit parents, or lived apart from their parents, or had been abandoned. The Children Bill specifically makes provisions, financial and vocational, for young people up to the age of eighteen and sometimes beyond. Issues dealing with juvenile delinquency, remand homes, employment, and financial responsibilities for children had been covered in the Children and Young Persons Act of 1931–32. The Children Bill of 1947–48 made modifications to that legislation, but dwelt at length on the social duties and expense of maintaining children. According to the estimates made in the House of Commons, the cost of expanded services to improve the lives of children would rise from £3.3 million to £4.5 million, to be paid by British taxpayers. In other words, postwar children became an obligation of the Welfare State.[21]

Missing Children

Yet children are, by and large, missing in postwar British culture. Their absence thwarts the compassionate ends of Welfare State legislation. Young people should be cared for, but they are not even present to receive aid. In various representations, missing children embody anxieties about the coming generations, particularly how young people differ from their parents and elders. More specifically, missing children point towards the vexed, potentially catastrophic future. In Marghanita Laski's novel, *Little Boy Lost* (1949), a writer returns to France after the war to trace a boy who went missing five years before. In Storm Jameson's *Cloudless May* (1944), set in the Loire Valley during the Fall of France, children express dynastic ambitions for a deputy with fascistic leanings, and unfulfilled futures for a prefect who resists the occupying Nazis; "I have ideas for the future," says a Frenchman who favors capitulation to the Nazis, "I have a son. You're not going to tell me he isn't the future?"[22] In *Children of Vienna* (1946), Robert Neumann documents the lives of children scrounging among urban ruins—a familiar trope in such films as *Rome, Open City* (1945) and *The Search* (1948). Reviewing Neumann's book, Elizabeth Bowen comments, "The children are now, apparently, no one's business. They ask, and receive, nothing from the outside world."[23] As no one's business, children fend for themselves and devise their future apart from the exigencies of governments and previous regimes.

On August 24, 1946, the *Daily Graphic and Daily Sketch* ran a poem entitled "The City Children," which demonstrates the ambiguous status of postwar children. The poem, by no means exceptional in its meter, rhyme, or asymmetrical stanzas, relates missing children to the Blitz:

> A host of little children run down the city street,
> They tell the time by flower clocks
> Through Cripplegate to Fleet;
> From dandelion and willow-herb
> The down lights softly on the kerb
> Beneath their soundless feet.
>
> The bombed and broken houses lie open, as they lay
> When with the dawn the red fires died

And morning paled to grey.
While in and out among the weeds
Run, silent as the floating seeds,
Still merrily at play
The little unseen children who tell the time of day.[24]

In its evocation of unchaperoned children in London, the poem recalls William Blake's "Holy Thursday" and "The Chimney Sweeper." Whereas the children are integrated into nature in the first stanza—they tread on down and tell time by flower clocks—they are as unattached as "floating seeds" in the second stanza.

The first stanza of "The City Children," while not immediately specified as postwar in its milieu, becomes distinctly so in comparison with the second stanza. The temporal ambiguity of the first stanza—it could be any year or any century—resolves into sometime after the Blitz. The children play in the streets because they have been routed from "bombed and broken houses." Weeds sprout up among those ruined buildings. As Leo Mellor observes, one species, "more than any other, recurs in the scientific and creative catalogs of bombsite plants: the pink flowers and jagged, down-coated leaves of *Epilobium angustifolium*—more commonly known as rosebay willow-herb."[25] Sometimes called "fireweed," the plant flourished in soil hardened by fire. The vivid red of willow-herb recalls the fires that raged during the Blitz in central London. The plant thus "offers a seeming after-image of destruction in the actuality of rebirth" (Mellor, *Reading the Ruins*, 180). In "The City Children," the willow-herb seeds float among bombed buildings. Even though the poem does not acknowledge this fact outright, Cripplegate was badly bombed during the Blitz. The city streets of London vaporize between the first and second stanzas; buildings and neighborhoods burn. The "host of little children" who run through the city streets also disappear. They are victims of the Blitz, not its survivors. Yet these children continue to "tell the time of day." Intimately connected to history, they are not released from the obligation to age and mature. They may be unseen, but they remain creatures of time. They haunt the city as a generation that never grows up because it has not survived the war. Soundless and invisible, they become part of the future of the city.

Even when missing, children shape political convictions. They embody principles of democracy, futurity, and human rights. John le Carré's bestseller, *The Spy Who Came in from the Cold* (1963), exemplifies the precariousness of children in terms of Cold War politics. Alec Leamas, a secret agent who has run a ring of spies in East Germany, has children, but he has no direct connection with them. They are mentioned in the most circumspect fashion: "somewhere there were children, now in their teens."[26] He sends money to them via a discreet bank in the City. Notwithstanding Leamas's remoteness from his children, le Carré's novel offers glimpses of children as emblematic of the future. A vignette involving an anonymous family embeds itself in Leamas's memory. One day on the autobahn, a father at the wheel of a Fiat suddenly swerves into the fast lane and nearly causes a collision: "Leamas stamped on the brake, turning his headlights full on and sounding his horn, and by the grace of God he missed it; missed it by a fraction of a second. As he passed the car he saw out of the corner of his eye four children in the back, waving and laughing, and the stupid, frightened face of their father at the wheel" (le Carré, *The Spy*, 97). The incident engraves itself on his memory. Just before he dies at the Berlin Wall, he thinks about the children in the car: "As he fell, Leamas saw a small car smashed between great lorries, and the children waving cheerfully through the window" (214). If Leamas fights for anything, he fights for the safety of children within Western democracies, even if those children sometimes become obstacles in his path. Despite having no particular attachment to his own children, Leamas believes, somewhat sentimentally, in the abstract concept of children as the promise of the future.

For Leamas, the image of children being crushed on the autobahn provides a screen memory of a specific incident during the war: Luftwaffe bombardiers strafing refugees as they fled along a road in Holland. The narrative provides background information on Leamas's wartime activities: he enlisted in 1939 with the Engineers, then transferred to specialist services because of his mastery of languages. He was in Holland from 1941 to 1943—during part of the Nazi Occupation. At key moments in *The Spy Who Came in from the Cold*, Leamas sees, in his mind's eye, "the long road outside Rotterdam, the long straight road beside the dunes, and the stream of refugees moving along it; saw the little aeroplane miles away, the procession stop and look towards it; and the plane coming in, nearly over the dunes; saw the chaos, the meaningless hell, as the bombs hit the road" (*The Spy*, 14). He remembers these bombed refugees when he nearly collides with the Fiat on the autobahn. Shaking and breathing heavily after the near-accident, Leamas pulls over and stares at the "hurtling stream of giant lorries. He had a vision of the little car caught among them, pounded and smashed, until there was nothing left, nothing but the frenetic whine of klaxons and the blue lights flashing; and the bodies of the children, torn, like the murdered refugees on the road across the dunes" (98). The definite articles—*the* refugees, *the* road, *the* dunes—indicate that he is thinking about a specific event: the wartime bombing in Holland. In Leamas's mind, violence inflicted on innocent people links the refugees in Holland during the Nazi invasion to the children in postwar Germany. The Cold War, as an extension of Second World War barbarity, demonstrates that civilian populations, especially children, remain at risk. Neither British legislation nor United Nations declarations can protect children from the dangers of war, no matter how honorable the intention of official proclamations.

Despite the historical emphasis on refugees and vulnerable children after the war, postwar literary representations downplay the presence of children, who are rarely seen and scarcely heard. In itself, such a strategy of underrepresentation might be taken as a means of sheltering children, but it generally has the effect of dismissing children instead. In Anthony Powell's twelve-volume series, *The Dance to the Music of Time* (1951–75), children have a negligible place amidst the love affairs and social ambitions of adults. Nick Jenkins, who narrates the series in the first person, fathers a couple of children, yet he leaves childbirth and child-rearing to his wife, Isobel. In *The Valley of Bones*, set during the early days of the Second World War, Nick tells an old acquaintance that Isobel is "having a baby soon."[27] When the baby comes, in a scene of "the utmost confusion and disquiet," Nick rushes off to his army bivouac in Northern Ireland, where he ponders "how it felt to be a father" (*Valley of Bones*, 167, 169). Pondering how to be a father does not mean interacting with the child. In *Books Do Furnish a Room*, Nick reports the birth of a second child with utter detachment: "Isobel gave birth to a son."[28] The child does not enter the novel except through this minor detail. The birth happens as if at a great emotional distance from Nick, as indeed it is. Implicitly, he worries that children could thwart his military obligations, or more importantly, his literary aspirations. As Cyril Connolly puts the case against children in *Enemies of Promise*, "there is no more sombre enemy of good art than the pram in the hall."[29] Nick cannot yield his advantage of age and position to younger generations. His preoccupation with social echelons and recurring figures in his own life prevents him from thinking much about children at all.

The representation of children as secondary and insignificant figures follows changes to social structures after the war: "In traditional families and communities, children remained children until they left school and went to work, at which point they were young adults."[30] The war changed the status quo by forcing new concepts of children into being. According to emerging definitions in the postwar, "children" were human beings below the age of fourteen, or sixteen, or eighteen, depending on who set the limit and for what reasons. In 1959 the United Nations adopted the Declaration of the Rights of the Child, which states that a child is a person under the age of eighteen. At the same time, "teenagers," a term that came into widespread usage in the 1940s, complicated the definition of "child" by taking over the middle ground between children and adults, the zone once called "adolescence."[31] Unease about categorical distinctions bespeaks uncertainty about the status of postwar children, specifically who cares for them and to what ends.

Children are to be protected, but not all children are pitiable or even pleasant. Some are downright villainous. During the war, children learned to fend for themselves by whatever means necessary. Drawing upon psychologists' findings, including Anna Freud's work with orphans and refugees in London, Dorothy Macardle thinks that war-traumatized children detached themselves from their families because of emotional distress: arrest, transport, incarceration, enforced labor, illness, sudden death. The "instinctive will to safeguard his health and balance partially insulated the child. Such a child was often very brave, and showed quickness of wit and courageous helpfulness" (Macardle, *Children of Europe*, 256).[32] Not just courageous and helpful, children who survived imprisonment in concentration camps or who lived by scavenging and begging had, of necessity, developed strategies for survival. In some cases, war hardened them into thieves and beggars: "survivors had often learned the value of lying, of cheating, and the penalties for not doing so" (Wyman, *DP: Europe's Displaced Persons*, 87). According to Macardle, the lawless underworld of postwar Europe "was inhabited by children—hordes of children whose moral natures seemed to have disintegrated under the impact of the conditions in which they lived" (Macardle, 260). Macardle nonetheless insists that they are delinquents in need of reform, not irredeemable criminals.

In Rose Macaulay's novel *The World My Wilderness* (1950), Barbary and her half-brother, Raoul, fight with the maquis during the Occupation in France. They are, respectively, seventeen and fifteen. Living by their wits during the war, beyond the help of their parents—their mother, Helen, is indifferent to what they do and where they go—they refuse to adapt to civilized life and indoor niceties in London. Self-reliant and tough, they haunt the ruins of bombed churches, especially St. Giles Cripplegate. Barbary and Raoul belong to the emergent generation of disaffected teenagers who bond with other young people as if in a club. As Helen claims, they "steal when they can; trespass on private property; sabotage motor cars; molest their fellow citizens. The same activities, in fact, that they pursued from patriotism during the war, they still pursue now from inclination and force of habit."[33] Those youngsters who lived through the war seem like a new species whose behavior has no precedent. Having survived disaster and war, postwar children face the future as a version of the past. They hold out little hope for improvement, let alone justice.

Facing the Future

In the 1945 elections, the Labour Party imagined how the future might take shape. The Labour Party slogan for the electoral campaign, "Let Us Face the Future," captured some of the cultural unease that had begun to accumulate around imaginings of postwar life in Britain. A pamphlet, as well as a longer statement about the Labour Party platform, was released under that title. The slogan does not identify who is included in the collective pronoun, "us." On the one hand, "us" refers to British soldiers and civilians who endured the war. On the other hand, the Labour Party, as against the Conservatives and Liberals, faced the future with ideas about how to implement the Welfare State. In this case, "us" signifies those who agreed with the 1942 Beveridge Report, which advocated planning for the future. The future should not just be an extension of the past; it had to be thought about and actively created. Despite being addressed to the nation, "Let Us Face the Future" implies that the nation is an ideal, not actual, concept. The nation needs improvement, and that can only happen as the future unfolds.

On the home front during the war, the national "us" was something of a political fiction. British citizens were given no alternative but to surrender their civil rights under the Emergency Powers (Defence) Act (1939). "Let Us Face the Future" recalls the wartime suspension of rights: "The Labour Party will see to it that we keep and enlarge these freedoms [of worship, speech, and opinion], and that we enjoy again the personal civil liberties we have, of our own free will, sacrificed to win the war."[34] "Us" signifies those who gave up their civil and political rights during the conflict as a temporary necessity. In exchange for that sacrifice, they want safety nets—workers compensation, family allowances, national health, education—for a wider spectrum of the British population as a way to close the gap between the "us" of 1945 and the "us" of the future. The slogan "Let Us Face the Future" therefore has an ambiguous rhetorical relation to the British population: the population is united as an entity, but that unity is a goal not yet achieved. "Us" includes Britons as they are and Britons as they might become.

As a slogan, "Let Us Face the Future" evokes several temporalities. Permission is being sought to face the future as if some obstacle inhibited "us" from doing so. Although unspecified, that obstacle is the immediate past: let us face the future and break with the privations and traumas brought about by the Second World War. In April 1945, when the Labour Party pamphlet was published, it was time to put the past to rest and to turn with renewed vigor to planning the future. The text in the pamphlet makes this meaning explicit: "The gallant men and women in the Fighting Services, in the Merchant Navy, Home Guard and Civil Defence, in the factories and in the bombed areas—they deserve and must be assured a happier future than faced so many of them after the last war. Labour regards their welfare as a sacred trust" ("Let Us Face the Future," 1). At stake is the enfranchisement of all those who fought in the war, either as combatants or volunteers.

The Labour Party keeps the specter of war, both past and future, in the minds of its readers. Wartime spirit on the home front should merge with the courage of the fighting forces abroad: "We need the spirit of Dunkirk and of the Blitz sustained over a period of years" ("Let Us Face the Future," 3). The shadow of the war overlaps with the possibility of further war. "We must prevent another war," declare the authors of "Let Us Face the Future" (3). Prevention occurs through international peace-keeping alliances and a strong national base: "No domestic policy, how-ever wisely framed and courageously applied, can succeed in a world still threatened by war" (11). From the Labour Party perspective in April 1945, war clouded the national future just as war determined the national past. The generation of tomorrow, it seemed, faced the possibility of a third global conflict.

Notwithstanding that eventuality, "Let Us Face the Future" implies that generations to come will benefit from social interventions. Facing the future means creating social mechanisms for the children born during or just after the war. They are to benefit from farsightedness and state protections. Yet children are virtually absent from the pamphlet and Labour thinking. In a passing comment, the Labour Party advocates an education system "that will give every boy and girl a chance to develop the best that is in them" ("Let Us Face the Future," 3). Under the provisions of the Education Act (1944), schooling was free for all pupils, and the school leaving age was raised to sixteen. The point of education, after all, is to create "individual citizens capable of thinking for themselves," as the authors of "Let Us Face the Future" phrase the issue (9). In such a formulation, children do not enter into the equation; they matter only insofar as they will develop into reasonable citizens later on. Education enhances citizenship in the long term, not the welfare of children in the short term. The health of children underlies the health of the nation: "Labour will work specially for the care of Britain's mothers and their children—children's allowances and school medical and feeding services, better maternity and child welfare services. A healthy family life must be fully ensured and parenthood must not be penalized if the population of Britain is to be prevented from dwindling" (10).

Healthy family life was not the order of the day in postwar British fiction. The children of postwar fiction tend to be unhappy, if not existentially tormented. An example of extreme familial neglect is Ivy Compton-Burnett's novel *Manservant and Maidservant* (1947). Horace Lamb deprives his five children of coal for the fire in their nursery. At Christmas, he refuses to give them gifts on the grounds that they are too old to receive them. (They range from seven to thirteen years old.) Although they often speak with oracular wisdom in perfectly grammatical sentences, they are far from grown up. Dressed in secondhand clothes, they attend church, where they draw comment from the other parishioners. Their appearance recalls the ubiquitous images of famished, ragged children that circulated in the postwar years. In many ways, *Manservant and Maidservant* offers a meditation on the changes wrought by the Welfare State, specifically the obligations of elders to children. Everyone in this novel thinks about the future, while resolutely denying that the future will alleviate the suffering of the children. Bullivant, the butler, says, "we have to think of the future, when our own day will be done."[35] With a view to the intransigence of his own children, Horace declares, "It is not easy to mould the future" (*Manservant and Maidservant*, 55). In the meantime, Horace's five children languish. They wait for time to pass without any hope that the future will be an improvement upon the present.

Many children in postwar fiction die before they can thrive. In Evelyn Waugh's *Brideshead Revisited* (1945), Julia Flyte's daughter, "born dead," is taken away before she is even seen.[36] So, too, in Nancy Mitford's *Love in a Cold Climate* (1949), Polly Hampton's baby does not survive. In Graham Greene's *The Third Man* (1949), Harry Lime sells adulterated penicillin on the black market. When children with meningitis receive penicillin mixed with sand, they "simply died, and a number went off their heads. You can see them now in the mental ward."[37] A father euthanizes his daughter in Neville Shute's *On the Beach* (1957) to prevent her from dying of radioactivity. In *Saturday Night and Sunday Morning* (1958), Brenda aborts a baby by drinking gin and lying in a tub filled with boiling water; she has two children already and does not want another. Arthur Seaton, her sometime lover and father of the unborn child, shows no compunction whatsoever about the abortion. He is as indifferent to Brenda's dilemma as he is to his own responsibility. Although children represent futurity, in the sense that they promise the continuation of families across generations, they have a diminished probability of survival in postwar British fiction.

Children who do survive often behave like grown-ups. In Elizabeth Taylor's first novel, *At Mrs. Lippincote's* (1945), seven-year-old Oliver, aspiring to omniscience, forecasts the time when he will look back on his childhood escapades "like Father talking about when he was a boy."[38] An only child, Oliver bears the weight of the world on his shoulders—the burden of survival, as well as the burden of British traditions. Despite his tender age, he reads *Jane Eyre* and *Tess of the D'Urbervilles*. The responsibility of carrying British traditions into the future rests with him, as a citizen and as a reader.

Looking Forward

Postwar children are never just children: they are historical in magnitude. In 1944–45 Humphrey Jennings made a 37-minute film called *A Diary for Timothy* for the Crown Film Unit. Michael Redgrave, reading the script by E. M. Forster, provides an eerie voice-over summary of wartime events. Although the film pretends to be a diary that accounts for the first six months of Timothy James Jenkins's life, the diary is written *for* him, not *by* him. The diary never assumes Timothy's point of view. A swaddled babe in his cradle, he is silent yet alert in the opening shots. "You are one of the lucky ones," threatens the narrator: "You are alive. You are healthy. You have parents who will take care of you."[39] His luck depends on his not being born on the Continent, where the war, in its fifth year, drags on.

The narrator, speaking in the second person, lectures Timothy about history. He addresses the newborn from some unspecified time in the future with glances back to the late phases of the war: "And it was on the third of September, 1944, that you were born" (*A Diary for Timothy*, 1:21). The narrator ranges over temporalities with ease. While the image on the screen offers a present tense—Tim in his crib—the voice-over speaks in the past tense. With omniscient powers at his disposal, he puts Tim's birth into a grand perspective. Throughout *A Diary for Timothy*, news on the radio cuts in and out with messages about the Battle of Arnhem, the bombing of Berlin, the Yalta Conference, and other crucial events in the war. Meanwhile, Tim's father fights overseas; a photograph on the wall metonymically substitutes for his being at home with his wife and son (5:41). In the father's absence, the narrator assumes a paternalistic role with regard to Tim. Like the BBC announcers who share the soundtrack, the narrator is irrefutable, matter-of-fact, male, and authoritative. Four other men—Goronwy the miner, Allan the farmer, Bill the engine driver, and Peter Roper the wounded pilot—all stand in for Tim's father. Women are unnamed and relatively incidental to Timothy's diary. Tim's mother seems pensive about having given birth, and she says virtually nothing throughout the film. By implication, Timothy is a son of Britain, not just an average child born into a British family.

Using his historical authority, the narrator lectures Tim about his British inheritance and responsibilities. Using the imperative voice, he guides Tim's eyes and ears to specific information: a stand-down parade, the drone of fighter planes, and—"listen to this" (*A Diary for Timothy*, 8:24)—an American reporter giving details of the Allies' advance into Germany. Although just born, Tim is already deeply implicated in European conflicts: "And now, Tim, we will show you a little of the history of your first days on earth, the start of your life, the end of our war in Europe. By the time you were born, we were invading the enemy's country, and sure that we were going to beat him" (4:26). The group called "we"—British countrymen, it should be assumed, and by extension the Allies—have been fighting on his behalf: "We were fighting for you, you and all the other babies. You were part of the war even before you were born. You see, this was total war" (2:27). In a sense, the diary lays out Tim's obligations to his protectors, those who fought on his behalf long before he entered the world. Not only is Roper the pilot wounded, but so is Goronwy; wounds to the national, male body, in contrast to Tim's undefiled infant's body, have to be healed before the nation can rebuild. In tandem, bombed houses are repaired while Roper and Goronwy recover from their injuries. The narrator obliges Tim to take up the weight of historical duty by reminding him what sacrifices have been made to preserve his future as a continuance of the past.

But the future cannot repeat the past, as the montage of *A Diary for Timothy* proves. Radical dislocations in time and place occur in sound and image. Blasts punctuate the film, as reminders of war and danger (*A Diary for Timothy*, 6:43, 7:13, 17:05, 23:00, 35:36). The visual content jumps from global events to Timothy gurgling in his cradle. The events exceed the personal witnessing implicit in the diary form. At the same time, as if it were the only way to counteract the disruptions of war, months are announced in terms of occasions: birth in September, baptism in October, danger on the beaches in November. Time flows on in a linear fashion. Nonetheless, Tim's innocence is no protection against harm to come. "What's going to happen in 1945 and in the years to follow," asks the narrator with a hint of malice, "when we are not here

Figure 4. A Diary for Timothy. *Timothy receives a letter from his father.*

and you are?" (28:11). Interjected into the future, Tim is imagined going to London or running down to the beach where barbed wire barriers have been dismantled and the danger of being blown to bits has passed. Like Oliver in *At Mrs. Lippincote's*, Tim appears to be precociously literate; he receives a letter from his father, as if he were capable of reading. (See figure 4.) The narrative implies that Tim should be old before his time, wise before he is out of the cradle. He guarantees the meaning of history: his survival redeems the senseless destruction of the Second World War. If his obligation to uphold the traditions of history were not clear enough, shots of Christmas celebrations are accompanied with the carol, "O Come, All Ye Faithful." The refrain, "Oh, come let us adore him, Christ the Lord," provides the soundtrack for a close-up of Tim, British baby, inheritor of democracy, the messiah of postwar Europe. He is called upon to make the world a different place: "You and the other babies" (36:48). As the film ends, Tim in his crib is six months old. His future remains up in the air, even as the narrator lectures him about his civic obligations and the dangers that await him in the future.

The parallels between *A Diary for Timothy* and Elizabeth Bowen's *The Heat of the Day* are striking. Both narratives feature women whose husbands are fighting abroad. In Jennings's film, Tim sleeps as the war happens around him; in *The Heat of the Day*, Louie Lewis wheels her baby to Seale-on-Sea to look at the site where her parents' house once stood. In both narratives, the baby boys have their symbolic roles heightened by muteness. Saying nothing because they are too young to speak, they face the future because their elders require them to do so. Tom, like Tim in his pram, remains unaware of history happening around him. Their unresponsiveness reproaches their elders; they resist the expectations imposed upon them. Louie Lewis's child, like Timothy in Jennings's film, promises a connection between present and future: "The baby's intention to survive put itself across her and taught her sense: the clearance, across at the other side, of the last of the enemy out of the Channel ports made it possible for her to return to Seale-on-Sea, an orderly mother."[40] The baby teaches his mother sense, rather than the other way round. At the same time, the clearing of the enemy from coastal waters gives a further impetus to make Louie "orderly." She adjusts her behavior to postwar mores.

Although no aspersions are cast on the mother's virtue in *A Diary for Timothy*, in *The Heat of the Day*, Louie Lewis steps out with various servicemen. She accosts Harrison in Regent's Park after she has spent the afternoon lying under an ilex bush with an "Air Force friend" (*Heat of the Day*, 15). Nonetheless, Louie sees herself in virtuous roles sanctioned by the press: "Was she not a worker, a soldier's lonely wife, a war orphan, a pedestrian, a Londoner, a home and animal-lover, a thinking democrat, a movie-goer, a woman of Britain, a letter-writer, a fuel-saver and a housewife" (168). In moments of misgiving, she suspects that she also belongs in the categories of "flighty wives or good-time girls" who dishonor their absent husbands (169).

Like Timothy's birth in *A Diary for Timothy*, Thomas Victor Lewis's birth is historical in its implications. He is not the son of Louie's husband. His claim on the future of Britain and the future of Europe is a form of symbolic illegitimacy. The child represents a mixed heritage: a foolish mother and an unknown father. Both Tim and Tom are offspring of contingencies. "It's a chancy world" (15:23), muses the narrator of *A Diary for Timothy* with regard to Goronwy's accident in the mine. The homespun observation applies to Tim as well; he is said to have been born lucky. "Let's hope the luck lasts" (*A Diary for Timothy*, 14:28), says the narrator with an air of doubt. Tim's security cannot be guaranteed by any external power, certainly not the narrator's. The war creates randomness that affects all the living. Bombs drop on one house but not another. One person is injured while his neighbor is spared. "It's only chance that you're safe and sound" (36:13), castigates the narrator, with reference to Timothy's luck at being born British.

At the end of the war, Bowen wondered about the future of children. As a writer, she was particularly attuned to the disconcerting effects of displacement on people. She concludes the essay, "Folkestone: July, 1945," with an observation about the fate of British children: "For the child of 1945 Folkestone bristles with barbed wire."[41] Like all children, fictional or real, the child in Folkestone faces a difficult passage to the future. Historical forces mount up around them. While they inherit the future, they also bear the burden of history that comes with that inheritance. Whether they want to or not, they shoulder the obligation to remember and perpetuate British traditions. Postwar disillusionment makes that obligation difficult to fulfill. For the child of 1945, passage to the future meant facing the barbed wire that lined the beaches. (See figure 5.) As the narrator promises in *A Diary for Timothy*, once the wire is cleared,

Figure 5. A Diary for Timothy. *Removing scaffolding and barbed wire from beaches.*

"there'll be nothing between you and the sea" (5:02). Taking down wartime barricades opened up possibilities for a different Britain. There was, however, no assurance that an unexploded land mine was not hidden in the sand, or that the war would not continue to haunt the children playing in the surf long after 1945.

Notes

1. Many films in the late 1940s featured Victorian orphans, such as *Great Expectations* (1946) and *Oliver Twist* (1948), as surrogates for postwar orphans. Other cinematic children are treated as exceptional, such as the intuitive boy in *The Rocking Horse Winner* (1949) or the deaf-mute girl in *Mandy* (1952).

2. Angus Calder, *The People's War: Britain 1939–45* (London: Jonathan Cape, 1969), 41–45.

3. Henry Green, *Loving* (London: Harvill, 1996), 45, 44.

4. Museum of Modern Art. Century of the Child 1900: Growing by Design 1900–2000, http://www.moma.org/centuryofthechild.

5. Lynn H. Nicholas, *Cruel World: The Children of Europe in the Nazi Web* (New York: Knopf, 2005), 162–63.

6. Guardianship (Refugee Children) Act, Chapter 8, March 1, 1944.

7. Phyllis Lassner, *Anglo-Jewish Women Writing the Holocaust: Displaced Witnesses* (New York: Palgrave Macmillan, 2008), 19.

8. Joseph A. Berger, "Displaced Persons: A Human Tragedy of World War II," *Social Research* 14, no. 1 (March 1947): 48.

9. Mark Wyman, *DP: Europe's Displaced Persons, 1945–1951* (London: Balch Institute, 1989), 87.

10. Tara Zahra, *The Lost Children: Reconstructing Europe's Families after World War II* (Cambridge, Mass.: Harvard University Press, 2011), 4.

11. Katharine F. Lenroot, "Europe's Children Need Help Now," *World Affairs* 109, no. 1 (March 1946): 40.

12. Victor Gollancz, *In Darkest Germany* (London: Gollancz, 1947), 18.

13. "The Screen Finds Germany's Lost Children," *Picture Post* (June 7, 1947): 21–23.

14. "Lost Children of Europe," *The Times*, November 5, 1949, 5.

15. At the Zurich conference, "a range of professionals such as medical doctors, lawyers, psychologists, psychiatrists, educators and social workers visited Swiss model reform and educational institutions for children and adolescents and discussed the future of the children." Delegates agreed that children should be helped regardless of the country in which they were located. They further agreed that children should preserve their nationality and should be helped "materially, spiritually and psychologically." Eva Simonsen, "Children in Danger: Dangerous Children," in *Children of World War II: The Hidden Enemy Legacy*, ed. Kjersti Ericsson and Eva Simonsen (Oxford: Berg, 2005), 276.

16. Dorothy Macardle, *Children of Europe* (Boston: Beacon, 1951), 234.

17. Nicholas Stargardt, *Witnesses of War: Children's Lives Under the Nazis* (New York: Vintage, 2007), 364.

18. "New Year in Europe," *The Times*, December 29, 1948, 7. Appeals continued throughout the 1950s and into the 1960s. "Amid the pageantry of this great and joyous occasion [the coronation of Queen Elizabeth in 1953], it is easy to forget the millions of men, women and children suffering as refugees and displaced persons throughout the world," read an ad from the British Churches Refugee Appeal in *The Listener* (May 28, 1953), 900. "There is still time to help a refugee!" exclaimed an ad in *The Times* (July 16, 1960), 4.

19. Ockenden Prizes History, www.ockendenprizes.org/about-ockenden/history.

20. The Universal Declaration of Human Rights has little to say about children per se. By the same token, its articles cover the rights of all human beings, including children. Article 26 declares that "motherhood and childhood are entitled to special care and assistance. All children, whether born in or out of wedlock, shall enjoy the same social protection." www.un.org/documents/en/udhr.

21. The Children Bill 1947–48, Financial Memorandum, ¶ 5.

22. Storm Jameson, *Cloudless May* (London: Macmillan, 1943), 194.

23. Elizabeth Bowen, "Elizabeth Bowen Reviews," *Tatler* (November 6, 1946): 184.

24. Diana Darling, "The City Children," *Daily Graphic and Daily Sketch*, August 24, 1946, 2.

25. Leo Mellor, *Reading the Ruins: Modernism, Bombsites and British Culture* (Cambridge: Cambridge University Press, 2011), 179.

26. John le Carré, *The Spy Who Came in from the Cold* (Toronto: Penguin, 2009), 10.

27. Anthony Powell, *The Valley of Bones* (London: Mandarin, 1964), 111.

28. Anthony Powell, *Books Do Furnish a Room* (London: Flamingo, 1983), 194.

29. Cyril Connolly, *Enemies of Promise* (New York: Persea, 1983), 116.

30. Tony Judt, *Postwar: A History of Europe Since 1945* (New York: Penguin, 2005), 347.

31. The *Oxford English Dictionary* gives the first usage of "teen-ager" in 1941. Cognates such as the adjective "teen-age" date from the 1920s and 1930s, but acquired currency in the 1940s and after.

32. Macardle does not mention John Bowlby or W. D. Winnicott, but their theories of attachment and separation anxiety derive from their studies of evacuated British children.

33. Rose Macaulay, *The World My Wilderness* (London: Collins, 1950), 12.

34. "Let Us Face the Future" ([n.p.]: Labour Party, 1945), 3.

35. Ivy Compton-Burnett, *Manservant and Maidservant* (New York: New York Review of Books, 2001), 5.

36. Evelyn Waugh, *Brideshead Revisited* (London: Penguin, 1962), 245.

37. Graham Greene, *The Third Man* (New York: Penguin, 1950), 107.

38. Elizabeth Taylor, *At Mrs Lippincote's* (London: Virago [1945], 2006), 118.

39. "A Diary for Timothy," dir. by Humphrey Jennings, written by E. M. Forster (Crown Film Unit, 1945), 1:49. Subsequent references to this film give minute and second.

40. Elizabeth Bowen, *The Heat of the Day* (New York: Anchor, 2002), 371–72.

41. Elizabeth Bowen, *Collected Impressions* (London: Longmans, Green, 1950), 230.

PAULA DERDIGER

"We Shall Never Make a Home of This"
Elizabeth Taylor's Postwar Reconstruction Fiction

Second World War billeting narratives depend dramatically on the problem of shared space. In this essay, I investigate how novels from the immediate postwar period such as Elizabeth Taylor's *At Mrs. Lippincote's* (1945)[1] take up this scenario as part of a mid-century trend that I term "reconstruction fiction." As architects, planners, and government officials set to work on reconstructing the physical and socioeconomic landscape of a bombed and war-weary nation, novelists contributed imaginative reconstructions of daily British life that responded to wartime conditions. Through the conceptual framework of rebuilding as it emerges through both literary and architectural and planning discourses, postwar novels set in wartime billets can be read as contributing to British reconstruction culture with their central interest in the shifting relationship between individual and community brought on by the exigencies of wartime life and continuing into the postwar period. The Emergency Powers (Defence) Act of 1939 demanded that individual citizens subordinate their desires to the state in the name of the war effort; housing, food, and clothing, among other basic provisions, became subject to rationing regulations and military necessity. The socialist policies of the Welfare State and the physical rebuilding resulting from its reconstruction initiatives continued to emphasize the needs of the collective, directing individual desire away from the promise of individual vertical advancement toward horizontal visions of socioeconomic equality for all. Cities like London and Coventry were reconstructed, and New Towns like Stevenage and Milton

Keynes were created with the aim of creating harmony between the individual and the community through long-range planning techniques.[2]

Novels such as *At Mrs. Lippincote's* register this shift in spatial and ideological orientation toward horizontality by setting novelistic action in the shared living space of the wartime billet. Despite the utopian rhetoric of the 1942 Beveridge Report, building and planning documents, and the 1945 Labour campaign and election victory, reconstruction was not a swift process that only focused on the future. Rather, it was a lengthy and laborious undertaking that necessitated first and foremost a realistic assessment of the effects of wartime destruction and instability—what Elizabeth Bowen described as "taking stock."[3] Indeed, reconstruction efforts had to account not only for destroyed housing but for general residential disruption: over the course of the war 60 million changes of address were registered for a civilian population of 48 million.[4] As one woman who housed numerous evacuees over the course of the war described the transition to peacetime in 1945, it was a time when "the old landmarks had disappeared and the new ones were not yet clearly defined."[5] *At Mrs. Lippincote's* is representative of immediate postwar novels that thus contribute to reconstruction culture not by forecasting an as yet unrealized future but by fleshing out the experience of shared household space that defined wartime life for many and would continue to shape it going forward. The war insisted on the normalcy of makeshift communities and shared housing instead of "proper" nuclear families and private space, which effectively made every house a potential billet and every individual a potential "guest." No one was permanently at home.

In addition to Taylor, writers such as Elizabeth Bowen, Graham Greene, Patrick Hamilton, and Evelyn Waugh took stock of the connection between citizen and the state through meditations on the transformed relationship between individuals and their once-private homes. Domestic interiors were disrupted by billeting, evacuation, and bombs, which laid bare to strangers the most intimate corners of people's living spaces. In her 1945 essay "Opening Up the House," Bowen identifies the dramatic potential inherent in this disruption of interiors; she reflects on "those unnumbered human beings who came and went [. . . , who] have left something behind them, something that will not evaporate so quickly as the smell of unfamiliar cigarettes."[6] Shared wartime housing, for

Bowen, was a new source for the gothic and ghostly depictions of domestic space that consistently characterized her fiction. For Evelyn Waugh, the responsibility of billeting evacuated children of a decidedly lower class was a subject for satire in *Put Out More Flags* (1942). While evacuees generally "were tolerated now as one of the troubles of the time," the Connolly children in Waugh's novel are an extreme, troublemaking exception: they are housed in one place for no longer than ten days and for as little as an hour and a quarter. "Everyone agreed that the only place for the Connollys was 'an institution.'"[7] The class implications of Waugh's depiction of the Connollys and billeting are poignant as a result of the allegedly socially leveling "people's war" and also as a result of prewar socially conscious texts such as George Orwell's *The Road to Wigan Pier* (1937). In his analysis of working-class communities, Orwell had emphasized the belief held by many 1930s intellectuals that shared living space, as in the slum-like lodging house described at the beginning of the text, would not promote upward mobility and an improved, middle-class lifestyle for the impoverished working classes.[8] Given the historical value placed on domestic privacy and permanence in middle- and upper-class British life, the forcible opening up of the house was a significant cultural turning point that encouraged writers of these classes to contemplate the consequences of losing individual privacy and property.

In what follows, I read Taylor's *At Mrs. Lippincote's* alongside the history of wartime and postwar debates about the value and nature of planning in architectural reconstruction. My approach dovetails with recent critical attention to mid-century British literature.[9] I follow Marina MacKay and Lyndsey Stonebridge, who argue in the introduction to *British Fiction after Modernism: The Novel at Mid-Century* that the period between the late 1930s and the 1960s has been neglected and "too often characterized as a conservative literature of retreat."[10] Against such views, they observe that "for those writing at mid-century, after two wars and in the middle of an undeclared chilly third, the historical resonances of what had come before loomed as large as (and as part of) the task of imagining the present and the future" (MacKay and Stonebridge, *British Fiction after Modernism*, 2). My attention to reconstruction as a broad cultural phenomenon born out of the war and the immediate postwar decade allows for a new way of considering how mid-century fiction takes up "the task of imagining the present and future."

In mid-century fiction, a realist mode dominates. Yet the effects of wartime life and the literary legacy of modernist experimentation challenge conventional realist expectations of linear plot progression and individual character development, let alone the promise of romance. In billeting texts written in the reconstruction period in particular, individual characters such as Taylor's Julia or Eleanor are depicted as struggling to find meaningful social and literary positions; private personal space has been made scarce by the war, and the goal of upward mobility for the individual no longer has historical or narrative relevance. In his study of the nineteenth-century novel, Alex Woloch argues that "the minor character is always drowned out within the totality of the narrative."[11] In the mid-twentieth-century context, as writers like Taylor and Patrick Hamilton rework nineteenth-century realist conventions, all characters, arguably, are made minor by the Second World War. Like food and clothing, character and plot become rationed goods. Accordingly, Taylor's narrative is characterized by the presence of multiple minor characters rather than a strongly developed individual protagonist, and plot lines do not advance in conventional realist or romantic directions. The billet as a setting thus allows writers like Taylor to assess the horizontal ethos of reconstruction plans in which individual desire is being recalibrated according to collective needs—an incorporation of necessary wartime practices into voluntary postwar initiatives. Against romantic notions of character development and plot progression, the narrator has a leveling effect. Functioning like a centralizing planner, the narrator continuously limits the growth and progress of any single character by emphasizing, through comic description, how individualistic fantasies have become untenable. *At Mrs. Lippincote's* is, in this sense, a demonstrative example of the immediate postwar moment in which realist fiction and the individual are in ruins and on the brink of reconstruction.

Reconstruction Culture

Reconstruction was not solely a postwar phenomenon. It began as early as 1940, when the first German bombs fell on England, and it was in full swing by 1942, when 2.5 million people were living in houses that had only received temporary repairs after bombing damage (Calder, 885). Literature and other forms of artistic expression joined the countless articles, speeches, treatises, broadcasts, and planning documents of the period in talking about housing and thereby communicating visions for a particular kind of postwar society. Louis MacNeice's 1941 observation that "the new division, the vital division, in this country will be between Planners and Non-Planners (or Anti-Planners)" indicates the significance that many invested in debates about housing and town planning.[12] After the destructive and disruptive conditions of wartime life, writers often thought about the craft of literature, the goals of representation, British literary history, and culture in general in terms of an architectural discourse. In a 1944 essay, for example, Elizabeth Bowen expressed a desire for renewed, clarified vision in metaphors of plans and glass: "The old plan for living has been erased, and you do not miss it. . . . No doubt . . . , everyone else, like you, is standing still, taking stock, looking round. . . . When the war is over, there will be no more of this nonsense; we shall look out through glass" ("Calico Windows," 184, 186). George Orwell also contemplated representation in terms of glass when he claimed in his 1947 essay, "Why I Write," that "good prose is like a window pane."[13] V. S. Pritchett wrote in his introduction to a new edition of *Wuthering Heights* in 1956 that the logic of Emily Brontë's "construction is masterly," and he went on to say of the novel that "there is nothing careless or amateur about its architecture."[14] Although Orwell and Pritchett were not directly writing about postwar reconstruction in these instances, their reliance on an architectural vocabulary to discuss literature points to the rich overlap between the two discourses in the immediate postwar years.

Housing is a major theme in fiction rewritten in the era of reconstruction. Postwar writers returned to the wartime home as a setting to explore the consequences of life among ruins, physical impermanence, the social tensions of billeting, and demobilization challenges for veterans and their families. Bowen offered an assessment of the attraction of wartime homes in a 1945 BBC Home Service broadcast: "Poor houses, how fragile they have become! Bombs plucked out the hearts of their mysteries! But do they, perhaps, for this very reason, appeal, today, more strongly to our imaginations?"[15] The domestic spaces of wartime literature are in clear need of reconstruction. In Rose Macaulay's novel *The World My Wilderness* (1950), for instance, "shells of flats" in the heavily bombed City of London "soared skyward on twisting stairs, staring empty-eyed at desolation."[16] In Patrick Hamilton's *The Slaves of Solitude* (1947), Miss

Roach is bombed out of her London home and relocates to a boarding house where she lives in a room that has been decorated and furnished by a strict landlady. Hamilton depicts Miss Roach's struggle to "reconstruct" this communal living space to accommodate her individual belongings: "in one corner were piled her 'books,' treasures of which she had saved from the bombing in London, but for which she had not yet obtained a shelf."[17] Representing a time when the notion of a permanent home was under siege, postwar fiction explores makeshift dwellings in which personal possessions and private space are scarce, if available at all.

The imaginative worlds and structural components of fiction that was engaged with reconstruction discourse intersected with those of architectural plans and building projects as both tried to account for individual and collective needs. Physical reconstruction initiatives supported by both Labour and Conservative parties in the early 1940s aimed to harness wartime technologies and large-scale organization techniques for peacetime projects. The goal was to preserve a humanizing architecture that valued individual privacy and identity within scientifically grounded plans to rebuild and rehouse the nation efficiently. The planning ethos that emerged during the war and that prioritized mass production was balanced by a consistent strain of skepticism in the name of individual freedom. In his 1944 book, *Building and Planning*, economist G. D. H. Cole summed up the anxiety about the implications of large-scale planning initiatives:

> Are we to plan? If so, what are we to plan, and what are the essential instruments for making our plans and for carrying them into effect? And, first and foremost, what is planning, and how much substance is there in the allegation that it is inconsistent with liberty? . . . Would it mean less real and tangible freedom for ordinary people, or would it mean an enlargement of the kinds of freedom that most people want and value?[18]

Cole's questions echo the cautionary attitude toward planning expressed by Mass Observation in a 1943 article for *Town and Country Planning*. Mass Observation resists the possibility of a totalitarian bureaucracy in which individual lives lose value within the planned, technologically modern environment:

> Mass-Observation's job is to provide the link between expert and amateur, planner and planned-for, the democratic leader and the democrat. In the increasing complexity of modern civilisation the specialist's job tends to become more specialized and he to become more remote from the people in whose interests he is working. In this article we have tried to suggest some of the lines along which experts in housing might stiffen their knowledge a little, in order to ensure that the houses they plan are not only beautiful, hygienic and convenient, but also lived-in, lived-for and demanded.[19]

Planners are reminded, in an official capacity, that houses must be built for individual human beings in a democratic, community-oriented society, not for sweeping principles of technological efficiency or aesthetic vision. Modernist intellectuals like Lewis Mumford and Louis MacNeice saw no conflict between efficient planning and a political system that valued the individual citizen. In *The Culture of Cities*, Mumford advocated large-scale "biotechnic planning" that employed the most up-to-date building materials (glass and steel, as opposed to stone) to provide a version of the traditional single-family home that was both technologically advanced and decidedly humanistic.[20] MacNeice also favored new techniques and technologies in the rebuilding of London; he argued in 1941 that "it is possible to become more efficient at the same time as, *and by reason of*, becoming more democratic" (MacNeice, *Selected Prose of Louis MacNeice*, 112).

As specific town plans began to emerge during the war, modern building, design, and planning techniques were put to work with clearly humanistic goals. Utopian visions of a community in harmony with the individual dominated, from the New Town to the suburban-style council estate to the tower block. The *County of London Plan* (1943) and New Towns Act (1946)—major examples of official planning documents and legislation—lobbied for reconstruction that would happen at a community level. A combination of single-family homes and blocks of flats were arranged within neighborhood units with the explicit aim of socializing inhabitants to an entire lifestyle centered on pubs, churches, and pedestrian shopping areas. The *County of London Plan*, devised by Patrick Abercrombie and J. H. Forshaw for the London County Council, made a strong case for carefully planned reconstruction—as opposed to quick, cheap, haphazard building to solve the immediate shortage crisis.[21] Long-range, community-oriented planning became the preferred methodology for reconstruction, as it was for all aspects of the emerging Welfare State, including education, health, insurance, and employment.

The *Plan* sought to balance the single-family home ideal, with the individual as its centerpiece, with the realistic demands of the housing shortage that made it impossible to turn this ideal into a reality for every citizen. "A good house," the *Plan* argues, "with all the amenities necessary for a full and healthy life, is a primary social need for everyone and must be the constant objective" (Abercrombie and Forshaw, *County of London Plan*, 74). Although the *Plan* contends that houses are preferable to flats because they have private gardens and "fit the English temperament. . . . houses would provide for only a quarter or a third of the present population" (77). For the Welfare State to meet its sociopolitical mandate of providing housing for all, non-single-family homes had to be built or created through conversion and incorporated into planned communities. For a density of 100 people, the *Plan* put 55 in houses and 45 in apartments (83). With its neighborhood maps and building elevations, the *County of London Plan* calls a particular postwar city into being: one in which individuals live in harmony with their local and national communities, where citizens are "ready and alive" to "the opportunity that [is] before London, as before the world, to create an environment that is worthy of our sacrifices" (19).

The 1951 Festival of Britain, conceived by Gerald Barry as a "tonic to the nation" that was still subject to strict austerity measures, further contributed to the vision of harmonious individual-community relations put forth by documents such as the *County of London Plan*.[22] Innovations in home and community design were a key component of the festival. Lansbury Estate, a "live architecture" exhibition, was created in the heavily bombed neighborhood of Poplar in the East End as an example of urban and New Town reconstruction initiatives. The Festival of Britain, like the *County of London Plan*, promoted projects that at once sympathized with the needs of the individual and demanded continued sacrifice of personal needs to national socioeconomic recovery. Alongside public, nation-building exhibitions like the festival, pamphlets, articles, and books related to housing and intended for consumption by the general public were generated in vast quantities. Publications such as *Homes for the People* (1946), put together by the Association for Building Technicians, promoted community-oriented reconstruction while also clearly laying out the desire for private individual living space as one of the most important goals of postwar building initiatives: "No part of the housing problem is so obvious as this: that there are not enough houses. *Very large numbers of the British people have no dwelling to themselves*."[23] With the experience of wartime living conditions and postwar austerity measures in the forefront of the public mind, community-based living would have signaled continued deprivation just as much as, if not more than, utopian promise. As journalist and novelist Mollie Panter-Downes wrote in 1945, Britain was by that point an "island of tired people" (Hartley, 264).

Building initiatives after the war attempted to recast the idea of the collective through neighborhoods that emphasized groupings of nuclear families as well as individuals: both the individual and the community were to be hallmarks of postwar modernity. *Homes for the People* emphasized to the general public that a balanced view of the debate about housing in single-family buildings versus housing in apartments "requires not only a consideration of how the advantages and disadvantages of houses and flats affect (a) the individual at home, but also how they affect (b) the town as a whole with its citizens" (*Homes for the People*, 21). Given the plans for continued austerity conditions after the war, citizens were encouraged to recalibrate their sense of individual identity to accommodate the needs and desires of others. The town, city, and nation were to be aligned with, not pitted against, the individual. The Association of Building Technicians assured the public that its ultimate goal was not to neglect the individual and the value of spatial privacy: "We cannot be content, our standards will not be really civilized, until every unmarried person other than a young child can have a separate bedroom" (27). Postwar architecture imagined a society in which the possibility of consequence for individual lives would be reinstated in the community-centered living space, and postwar fiction set in wartime billets created a critical space for assessing this postwar vision.

At Mrs. Lippincote's and the Limits of Postwar Space

In *At Mrs. Lippincote's*, Elizabeth Taylor contributes to reconstruction culture by exploring the particular task of rebuilding life and literature for the British middle classes at the end of a war that privileged the needs of the collective and fundamentally disrupted the relationship between individuals and their private possessions and households. In the latter part of the nineteenth century, property and possessions had become important avenues for developing and advancing middle-class social identities. As Deborah Cohen puts it,

> The question, as late nineteenth-century observers noted, was no longer merely who you were, but what you had. . . . Among the middle classes, whose numbers more than tripled in the second half of the nineteenth century, possessions became a way of defining oneself in a society where it was increasingly difficult to tell people apart. Homes . . . became flexible indicators of status, which could be exchanged for better accommodation as fortunes allowed.[24]

In literary terms, things, objects, and households took on a new level of narrative significance in the nineteenth century, especially for representations of middle-class and lower-middle-class characters.[25] Jane Austen's Fanny Price and Charlotte Brontë's Jane Eyre are two notable examples of nineteenth-century protagonists whose social and literary development rely on advancement in property occupation and ownership. In both of these cases, impoverished characters are relocated multiple times and live on the periphery of nuclear families. Their narratives arcs conclude only when poverty and domestic instability are reversed through marriage, as in the case of Fanny Price, or marriage and inheritance, as in the case of Jane Eyre. Modernist literature exploded the accepted realist connection between subjectivity and the exterior world, but wartime conditions—bombings, blackouts, evacuations—necessitated a realism that would reclaim and recalibrate the relationship between character and material circumstances that had been significantly transformed.

Taylor's novel participates in this revamping of realist conventions by constructing two female characters, Julia and Eleanor, who are limited, and indeed overcrowded, in the narrative by the shared household spaces they inhabit. The novel dramatizes the unromantic circumstances of evacuation and billeting for the middle-class Davenant family—Roddy and Julia, their son Oliver, and Roddy's cousin, Eleanor. This nuclear family plus one is evacuated out of London and billeted in the country, close to Roddy's RAF base. They move into Mrs. Lippincote's house, a Victorian structure complete with a locked tower attic—a clear allusion to *Jane Eyre*. To accommodate the military family, Mrs. Lippincote has been relocated to a nearby hotel; her move is another in a series of evacuations that destabilizes the relationship between individual and household. Surrounded by Mrs. Lippincote's things, furniture, and décor, the Davenants are depicted as struggling to find clear roles within the household and within the narrative itself. Indeed, Taylor's novel is one of a number of wartime or immediate postwar novels that depict home-front life for middle-class women who have to confront the realities of life in a billet (such as Betty Miller's *On the Side of the Angels*)[26] or life without servants (such as Mollie Panter-Downes's *One Fine Day*). Middle-class property, in the case of the wartime billet, is stripped of its historic power to confer social standing and to signify character development. Without their properly ordered and personally owned possessions, Taylor's novel suggests, the British middle classes are without physical as well as fictional space. This reading extends N. H. Reeve's interpretation, which considers the novel in terms of the problem of ownership for the Davenant family, as "an intricate study of dispossession, of losing what one owns, or finding one may never really have owned it, and of the mixture of damage and opportunity such losses can afford."[27] As reconstruction plans for the Welfare State promise to tether the individual to the community in an unprecedented way, the exigencies of the wartime billet and the dispossession that Reeve identifies loom as a new reality.

The wartime billet, as opposed to the permanent home, has to accommodate material possessions that belong to multiple occupants, and rooms once designated as servants' spaces become storage compartments for miscellaneous items that do not logically belong together. The Davenants cannot make a proper home in the billet partly because Mrs. Lippincote's things simply take up much of the available storage space. Julia "went to the bureau and opened the drawers one after another. All full: knitting-needles, playing-cards, paper-patterns, photographs . . . , some black-edged visiting cards and letters. . . . She felt burdened by Mrs. Lippincote's possessions. 'We shall never make a home of this,' she cried."[28] When Julia asks Roddy, "Where did you put all the rubbish?" he responds, "In the maid's room along with the dressmaker's dummy and the fishing rods" (*At Mrs. Lippincote's*, 73). As Taylor depicts the Davenants' frustrated attempts to make themselves at home in the midst of cluttered rooms and full drawers, she exposes a central task of middle-class fiction in the reconstruction period: to reassess the relationship between middle-class individuals and their living spaces.

Taylor develops a critical assessment of this relationship by highlighting a conflict between past cultural traditions—nineteenth-century realism, romance, modernism—and present-day demands. In doing so, she recalls E. M. Forster's critique in his 1939 essay on Jan Struther's "Mrs. Miniver" columns. For Forster, romantic attachment to past aristocratic traditions prevents the middle class from "build[ing] itself an appropriate home":

> That . . . is the trouble with Mrs. Miniver and with the class to which she and most of us belong, the class which strangled the aristocracy in the nineteenth century, and has been haunted ever since by the ghost of its victim. [. . . It] has never been able to build itself an appropriate home, and when it asserts that an Englishman's home is his castle, it reveals the precise nature of its failure. We who belong to it still copy the past. The castles and the great mansions are gone, we have to live in semi-detached villas instead, they are all we can afford, but let us at all events retain a Tradesman's Entrance. The Servants' Hall has gone; let the area-basement take its place. The servants themselves are going; Mrs. Miniver had four, to be sure, but many a suburban mistress batters the registry office in vain. The servants are unobtainable, yet we still say, "How like a servant!" when we want to feel superior and safe. Our minds still hanker after the feudal stronghold which we condemned as uninhabitable.[29]

Taylor depicts Julia as battling with this "ghost" of past traditions that are no longer appropriate for postwar society. For example, Julia is initially nostalgic for the Edwardian world of Mrs. Lippincote, in which social positions and material life were more stable:

> She looked at Mrs. Lippincote on her wedding day as she was often to look at her in the future. Nothing of her security, in these

> days. What would she have said to this? No home of one's own, no servant, no soup tureen, no solid phalanx of sisters, or sisters-in-law, to uphold her; merely—she glanced at Eleanor—merely an envious and critical cousin-in-law. (*At Mrs. Lippincote's*, 12).

Julia's wistful daydream romanticizes the prewar possibility of a middle-class "home of one's own" while alluding more symbolically to Virginia Woolf's "A Room of One's Own." The Woolfian tradition of modern female liberation through having one's own private space in which to think and work cannot be realized easily in the wartime billet for women or men. This unavoidable reality becomes clear as Julia continues to imagine Mrs. Lippincote's wedding day: "But it was only something which perished very quickly, the children scattered, the tureen draped with cobwebs, and now the widow, the bride, perhaps at this moment unfolding her napkin alone at a table in a small private hotel down the road" (*At Mrs. Lippincote's*, 10). For Taylor, modernist prescriptions for women's liberation have become romantic middle-class fantasies that must be revealed as such in the context of a war that has altered the relationship between the individual and the space she inhabits.

Julia's approach to domestic life—marriage, sex, parenting, cooking—reveals the wartime middle-class housewife as caught between a romantic, privileged past and a practical present. As a counterbalance to her nostalgic daydreams about Mrs. Lippincote's wedding and marriage, Julia looks to popular books for guidance such as *Happy Marriages, How to Make, Maintain, and Endure Them* (*At Mrs. Lippincote's*, 10). When Oliver asks where babies come from, she awkwardly attempts to explain through drawings, according to advice "she had read once in a pamphlet on sex-instruction" (68). After Oliver tells her, "I was dreaming I was killing you," Julia says to Eleanor, "I don't believe in all that nonsense about Freud. . . . Dreams just happen—any old nonsense comes out of the tangle. It doesn't *mean* anything" (78). Despite the fact that she claims to understand Freud only to reject his theories, and that she gets her cooking inspiration from *Villette* and *To the Lighthouse*, Julia's day-to-day life is "not quite so much like Emily Brontë learning German grammar while she kneaded bread as Julia liked to suppose" (99). Julia looks to past literary and intellectual models—Freud, Woolf, the Brontës—to bolster her sense of identity as wife, mother, and protagonist, but Taylor's narrator consistently undercuts any suggestion of high-brow sophistication or romantic fantasy through comic description.

In the spaces of the billet, Julia is forced to eschew prewar practices for new responsibilities. She cannot assume the role that Mrs. Lippincote once played in her home with the help of servants, and at the same time, she is not fully prepared to take on the duties associated with servants' rooms: sculleries, maids' quarters, tower attics. As Julia hesitantly moves from kitchen to scullery to dining room, Taylor depicts the challenge faced by many middle-class women as they found themselves unexpectedly in someone else's domestic world without help:

> Through an archway hung with plush, she came into the kitchen. It was like the baser side of someone's nature. Beyond the plush curtains, the house put aside all show of decency. Here, there was no doubt about the suggestion of damp. . . . This room, she supposed, represented what was fitting for the working class. On this side of the arch, varnished deal was preferred, wallpaper of brown and pink flowers, a brown tablecloth reaching to the floor and a plant with thick grey velvety leaves. Then down a hollowed stone step into a brick scullery where a refrigerator whirred and water dropped bleakly and with regularity into a bowl. She opened a cupboard and was frightened by a soup tureen the size of a baby's bath. In another cupboard a dozen meat dishes of very slightly varying sizes, white with a wreath of inky flowers, the glaze traced with faint sepia cracks. "That is how Mrs. Lippincote set up house," she told herself. (*At Mrs. Lippincote's*, 8–9)

Julia's ambivalence and discomfort in someone else's kitchen, without the help of servants, is typical of postwar novelistic depictions of middle-class domestic life.[30] As Phyllis Lassner, Gill Plain, and Karen Schneider have pointed out, women's lives were dramatically transformed during the war as they served in military organizations or worked in factories supporting the war effort.[31] The relative freedom and independence that women experienced on the home front was abruptly challenged in the immediate postwar decade. Alison Light explains that the dispersal of the servant class (all but complete by the late 1930s) put the average middle-class housewife in a newly limited position: "The well-off woman of the 1930s could indeed be far freer than her Victorian grandmother, wrestling with the Angel in the House, or her daughter in the 1950s suburb, servantless."[32] After the war, many middle-class women like Julia went into the kitchen, as it were, for the first time. Phyllis Lassner has interpreted Julia's ambivalent female position as a "first step toward the possibilities for change in British domestic society" (Lassner, *British Women Writers*, 186). With the context of the wartime billet and reconstruction plans in mind, however, this ambivalence can also be interpreted as Taylor's critique of middle-class attachment to outdated values. Julia is nostalgic for a prewar relation to household space and objects, and she is resistant to domestic responsibilities that put others' needs before her own. When the narrator describes Julia comically as being "frightened by a soup tureen," Taylor creates a critical gap between the life that Julia fantasizes for herself and the real conditions that demand her participation.

Julia is not the only object of the narrator's critical gaze. Eleanor is also depicted as having a frustrated relationship to conventional household space and literary development. She flails between plot lines that never quite get beyond the fantasy stage: a minor character, in Alex Woloch's sense of the concept, that is repeatedly prevented by the narrator from becoming anything more "major." Her doomed romantic attachments—to her married cousin and to a soldier whom she has never met—will never become marriage plots. She has a romantic view of marriage, which is made even more unrealistic by her particular wish to marry Roddy, whose infidelity behind Julia's back makes him a less-than-worthy object of desire: "'If I had Roddy,' thought Eleanor, 'my greatest happiness would be to go out with him to meet the other wives.' . . . She could not forgive Julia for wanting more than her own dearest dream" (*At Mrs. Lippincote's*, 11). Taylor emphasizes Eleanor's misguided romanticism when she describes the grim reality of Julia's marriage and identity as a wife: "having no life of her own, all she could hope for would be a bit of Roddy's" (20). Although Eleanor tries "not to behave like a spinster in a book," Taylor limits her to precisely this minor literary position by "what Roddy called her 'little ways,' by which he meant the trivial comforts, consolations, cups of tea and patent medicines, small precautions against draughts and a gentle fussing" (20).

Taylor depicts Eleanor as being limited romantically as well as politically. She is curious about communism but conducts her explorations in secret and ultimately remains politically ambivalent. She attempts to find a sense of empowerment and belonging outside the billet, in which she has no clear role beyond that of a spinster, but her one-night move into a house shared by a group of unmarried communists does not provide the narrative mobilization she needs to emerge as a strong political character. Upon entering the communist house, Eleanor immediately scans and feels alienated by the shabby décor: "two sash windows there were, not clean, a fawn, characterless wall paper, a deal table covered with a typewriter, a duplicator; then, the worn moquette sofa and an empty grate littered with cigarette ends and toffee papers. A breakfast cup full of faded dog-roses stood on the mantelpiece and a large clock with a brass plate" (*At Mrs. Lippincote's*, 64). The unkempt and unfamiliar décor prompts Eleanor to confront her lack of secure individual identity as she lies awake on the sofa where she has been invited to sleep: "'Everything so strange,' she thought. 'Who am I? Lying here, under this coat, which is heavy but certainly not warm. It is not I. Or is it, at last, I, myself? The adventurer, the liar, the hypocrite?'" (127). Like the neighborhood units and blocks of flats that make up the *County of London Plan*, this house explicitly depends on property relations that privilege the community over the individual. Eleanor, however, cannot give up her middle-class approach to defining herself through the things that surround her. Not quite part of the Davenant family, Eleanor is also not part of the communist community. As an unmarried middle-class woman at the end of the war, she can be peripherally accommodated in the shared spaces of fiction, billets, and communes only as a minor spinster.

In *At Mrs. Lippincote's*, the literary consequences of shared living space and limited individual ownership that characterize wartime life and reconstruction initiatives are made clear by the identity crises experienced by both Julia and Eleanor. These characters cannot find solace in outdated literary or social identities that require secure middle-class property ownership and the possibility of upward mobility, and as a result, they can both be considered as minor protagonists. Although Julia tries to determine whether she will be "a Madame Bovary" or "a good mother, a fairly good wife," she ultimately does not have the privilege to make such a choice. Despite the presence of the narrative components of romance, she does not have an affair with the Wing Commander and take up the romantic role of the bourgeois adulteress (*At Mrs. Lippincote's*, 204). Without the physical or literary space to return to prewar conventions, characters like Julia demonstrate a moment at which the middle-class novel is forced to reconsider the significance of the individual within literary and domestic structures in the postwar period. Julia's qualities—jealousy, vanity, nostalgia, cruelty—are not those of a romantic heroine or a modern feminist, but those of a middle-class housewife coming to accept that she will be neither Jane Eyre nor Madame Bovary nor Lilly Briscoe, as she fantasizes; those models no longer work. As the narrative unfolds, nostalgia for prewar traditions is ultimately discarded in exchange for a willingness to reconstruct middle-class identities without the assurance of private property as Britain transitions to the Welfare State.

By taking up the scenario of makeshift families and domestic impermanence, *At Mrs. Lippincote's* lays the foundation for a novelistic theme that occupied Taylor throughout the 1940s and 1950s: what defines the idea of "home," and what is the role of this idea in fiction? In *At Mrs. Lippincote's*, Oliver associates home with the idea of return after walking back to the billet: "It has made it seem more like my home, because I am coming back to it" (149). Taylor's subsequent fiction tests and ultimately undercuts the possibility of a peaceful, postwar return. Her late 1940s novels, *A View of the Harbor*, *Palladian*, and *A Wreath of Roses*, are tragedies—not comedies—of domestic reorganization. Love affairs break up marriages only to lead to further disillusion within the household. Children die. Men commit suicide or suffer from mental illness. Following the pattern established in *At Mrs. Lippincote's*, characters in these novels cannot find solace in private domestic space or prewar domestic conventions. In *Palladian* (1946), for instance, Taylor depicts the decline of a Victorian household once upheld by servants and governesses. The death of prewar social traditions plays itself out in the decay of the estate house at the center of the novel:

> The fewer people were in the house, the less it seemed able to support its existence. The sound of voices, of doors slamming, seemed to have prolonged its life beyond what was natural and to be expected. But as the life was gradually withdrawn, the house became a shell only, seeming to foreshadow its own strange future when leaves would come into the hall, great antlered bee-

> tles run across the hearths, the spiders let themselves down from the ceilings to loop great pockets of web across corners; plaster would fall, softly, furtively, like snow, birds nest in the chimneys, and fungus branch out in thick layers in the rotting wardrobes. Then the stone floor of the hall would heave up and erupt with dandelion and briar, the bats wing up the stairs, and the dusty windows show dark stars of broken glass. As soon as grass grows in the rooms and moles run waveringly down passages, the house is not a house any more, but a monument, to show that in the end man is less durable than the mole and cannot sustain his grandeur.[33]

Taylor's depiction of the decaying, servantless house resembles that of a house that has been bombed: plaster falling, the floor erupting open, glass breaking. Man-made "civilization" has destroyed itself by ruining the very concept of "home" over the course of the war. In the wake of this destruction, according to Taylor's novelistic vision, the wilderness, rather than the architect or town planner, reasserts itself. In literary terms, the romantic and gothic traditions of the past can be conceived of within mid-century fiction only as monuments that are no longer capable of producing and sustaining human life. Indeed, *Palladian* concludes when the young boy who would inherit the house is killed by a statue on the estate grounds. For Taylor, the war has made past definitions of "home" nostalgic, unavailable, or at worst, fatal.

After the bombing of Virginia Woolf's Bloomsbury home in 1940, Elizabeth Bowen wrote to Woolf, "All my life I have said, 'Whatever happens there will always be tables and chairs'—and what a mistake."[34] Narrative negotiations of material destruction and reconstruction unfolded out of Bowen's simple but profound realization. As British citizens learned to get on without the security of permanent furniture, British writers constructed fictional worlds that depicted both what had been lost and what might be gained in a reorganized society that no longer privileged the house-holding individual. Where town plans, building legislation, and project blueprints outline *what* can be built, reconstruction fiction more fully dwells on *how* and to what end that building should happen. In her discussion of postwar British architecture, Karen Shonfield contends that "utopian aspirations . . . lie behind the very act of building. At the smallest scale building involves transformation, and some investment in the future."[35] William Beveridge, Clement Attlee, and the architects and planners who created the Welfare State keenly demonstrated their faith in the utopian dimension of building. Writers like Taylor, Bowen, and Patrick Hamilton also invested in the future with their constructions that took stock, even if they critiqued rather than condoned the realities they depicted. Indeed, postwar fiction, with its realist attention to the war and its aftermath, helps to clarify and add nuance to our hindsight vision of the reconstruction period that, I argue, lasted until the late 1950s. On the one hand, it was a time of concerted efforts to transform social, political, and economic inequalities. On the other, it was a time of unfulfilled promises and neglect—a trajectory realized most starkly in the 1960s when homelessness became an acute problem in Britain despite the fact that it was the high point of the construction of tower blocks, a form of housing that progressive architects proposed would solve spatial and social problems but that came to symbolize, instead, the failure of Welfare State architectural modernism. The next generation of postwar writers, including J. G. Ballard, Anthony Burgess, Colin MacInnes, and Muriel Spark, would take up this trajectory critically in their fiction. The story of reconstruction, told through fiction, plans, and buildings, continually emphasizes that no structures or worldviews are permanent, and that the imagination can play an invaluable role in determining what is preserved and what is pulled down.

Notes

1. Elizabeth Taylor, *At Mrs. Lippincote's* (London: Virago, [1945] 2006).

2. For an extended discussion of the history of wartime and postwar planning, which has its roots in the nineteenth-century Garden City as well as 1930s innovations in surveying and construction techniques, see Iain Boyd Whyte's edited volume, *Man-Made Future: Planning, Education and Design in Mid-Twentieth Century Britain* (London: Routledge, 2007).

3. Elizabeth Bowen, "Calico Windows," in *People, Places, Things*, ed. Allan Hepburn (Edinburgh: Edinburgh University Press, 2008), 182–86, at 184.

4. Angus Calder, "UK: Domestic Life, War Effort, and Economy," in *The Oxford Companion to World War II*, ed. I. C. B. Dear and M. R. D. Foot (Oxford: Oxford University Press, 2005), 885.

5. Jenny Hartley, *Hearts Undefeated: Women's Writing of the Second World War* (London: Virago, 1994), 280.

6. Elizabeth Bowen, "Opening Up the House," in *People, Places, Things*, ed. Allan Hepburn (Edinburgh: Edinburgh University Press, 2008), 131–33, at 132–33.

7. Evelyn Waugh, *Put Out More Flags* (London: Penguin, 2000), 82.

8. Orwell describes the interior layout and furnishings of the working-class lodging house in detail, emphasizing the overcrowding: "There were generally four of us in the bedroom, and a beastly place it was, with that defiled impermanent look of rooms that are not serving their rightful purpose. Years earlier the house had been an ordinary dwelling-house, and when the Brookers had taken it and fitted it out as a tripe-shop and lodging-house, they had inherited some of the more useless pieces of furniture and had never had the energy to remove them. We were therefore sleeping in what was still recognizably a drawing-room. Hanging from the ceiling there was a heavy glass chandelier on which the dust was so thick that it was like fur. And covering most of one wall there was a huge hideous piece of junk, something between a sideboard and a hall-stand, with lots of carving and little drawers and strips of looking-glass, and there was a once-gaudy carpet ringed by the slop-pails of years, and two gilt chairs with burst seats, and one of those old-fashioned horsehair armchairs which you slide off when you try to sit on them. The room had been turned into a bedroom by thrusting four squalid beds in among this other wreckage." George Orwell, *The Road to Wigan Pier* (London: Penguin, [1937] 2001), 3.

9. See, for example, Jed Esty's work on "late modernism" in *A Shrinking Island: Modernism and National Culture in England* (Princeton, N.J.: Princeton University Press, 2004); and Kristin Bluemel's edited volume *Intermodernism: Literary Culture in Mid-Twentieth-Century Britain* (Edinburgh: Edinburgh University Press, 2009). Both works address, in different ways, material that has been neglected in studies that operate within more conventional definitions of modernism.

10. Marina MacKay and Lyndsey Stonebridge, eds., *British Fiction after Modernism: The Novel at Mid-Century* (Houndmills, Eng.: Palgrave, 2007), 2.

11. Alex Woloch, *The One vs. the Many: Minor Characters and the Space of the Protagonist in the Novel* (Princeton, N.J.: Princeton University Press, 2003), 38.

12. Louis MacNeice, *Selected Prose of Louis MacNeice* (Oxford: Clarendon, 1990), 114.

13. George Orwell, "Why I Write," in *A Collection of Essays* (New York: Doubleday, 1954), 313–20, at 320.

14. V. S. Pritchett, "Introduction," in Emily Brontë, *Wuthering Heights* (Boston: Houghton Mifflin, [1847] 1956), x.

15. Elizabeth Bowen, "Book Talk" (1945), in *Listening In*, ed. Allan Hepburn (Edinburgh: Edinburgh University Press, 2010), 79–84, at 81.

16. Rose Macaulay, *The World My Wilderness* (London: Book Club, 1950), 110.

17. Patrick Hamilton, *The Slaves of Solitude* (New York: New York Review of Books, [1947] 2007), 5–6.

18. G. D. H. Cole, *Building and Planning* (London: Cassell, 1945), 38.

19. Mass-Observation, "File Report 1622: Some Psychological Factors in Home Building," 1943, *Mass-Observation Online*, University of Sussex, http://www.massobs.org.uk/index.htm, 7.

20. Lewis Mumford, *The Culture of Cities* (London: Secker and Warburg, 1938).

21. Patrick Abercrombie and J. H. Forshaw, *County of London Plan* (London: Macmillan, 1943), 18.

22. Gillian Whitely, "Festival of Britain," in *Designing Britain: 1945–1975*, SITE Design Archive, University of Brighton, http://www.vads.ac.uk/learning/designingbritain/html/festival.html.

23. Association of Building Technicians, *Homes for the People* (London: Paul Elek, 1946), 18; emphasis in original.

24. Deborah Cohen, *Household Gods: The British and Their Possessions* (New Haven, Conn.: Yale University Press, 2006), xi–xii.

25. Bill Brown's essay "Thing Theory" and Susan Stewart's book *On Longing: Narratives of the Miniature, the Gigantic, the Souvenir, the Collection* have been especially influential in shaping critical discussions of the relationship between narrative and things or possessions. Bill Brown, "Thing Theory," *Critical Inquiry* 28, no. 1 (2001): 1–22; Susan Stewart, *On Longing: Narratives of the Miniature, the Gigantic, the Souvenir, the Collection* (Durham, N.C.: Duke University Press, 1993, 2007). Elaine Freedgood's *The Ideas in Things: Fugitive Meaning in the Victorian Novel* (Chicago: University of Chicago Press, 2006) is also notable for assessing this relationship for the middle classes in the nineteenth century, as in her discussion of mahogany furniture in *Jane Eyre*.

26. Betty Miller, *On the Side of the Angels* (New York: Penguin-Virago, [1945] 1985).

27. N. H. Reeve, *Elizabeth Taylor* (Tavistock, Eng.: Northcote House / British Council, 2008), 21.

28. Taylor, *At Mrs. Lippincote's*, 13.

29. E. M. Forster, "Mrs. Miniver" (1939), *Two Cheers for Democracy* (London: Edward Arnold, 1972), 307.

30. In *One Fine Day* (1946), for example, Mollie Panter-Downes tells the story of a woman much like Taylor's Julia who sits in her empty, postwar house thinking nostalgically of her servants from the prewar period: "What had happened? Where had they gone? The pretty, hospitable house seemed to have disappeared like a dream back into the genie's bottle, leaving only the cold hillside . . . They would never come back into the tame house again. Everyone said so." Mollie Panter-Downes, *One Fine Day* (New York: Penguin-Virago, [1946], 1985), 19.

31. See Phyllis Lassner's *British Women Writers of World War II: Battlegrounds of Their Own* (Houndmills, Eng.: Palgrave, 1998); Gill Plain's *Women's Fiction of the Second World War: Gender, Power and Resistance* (Edinburgh: Edinburgh University Press, 1996); and Karen Schneider's *Loving Arms: British Women Writing the Second World War* (Lexington: University Press of Kentucky, 1997).

32. Alison Light, *Forever England: Femininity, Literature, and Conservatism between the Wars* (London: Routledge, 1991), 121.

33. Elizabeth Taylor, *Palladian* (New York: Viking, 1947), 234.

34. Victoria Glendinning, *Elizabeth Bowen: Portrait of a Writer* (London: Weidenfeld and Nicolson, 1977), 131.

35. Katherine Shonfield, *Walls Have Feelings: Architecture, Film, and the City* (New York: Routledge, 2000), 29.

ELIZABETH MASLEN

"Someone Should Put It on Record"

Storm Jameson and "Witness Literature"

In the wake of World War I, at a time when the form and function of the novel were hotly debated, Storm Jameson was one of a small number of novelists who addressed not only issues at home, but also issues in Europe as events in the interwar years became increasingly perilous; for she was never insular, always aware of how closely England's fate was bound up with that of Europe. Moreover, a literature of commitment was what, from the mid-1930s on, Jameson saw as the novel's main function, and in this she was, and would remain, more aligned with writers in Europe than with those at home; in France, for instance, "*littérature engagée* (committed literature) was the watchword on both left and right."[1] So Jameson was one of those who set out to construct what Nadine Gordimer would later call "witness literature." But this does not mean that her work can be dismissed as journalistic; as Gordimer would say in the wake of the felling of the twin towers, there is a key difference between a reporter's job and that of a creative writer: "Witness literature is fiction, not non-fiction, an interplay of sometimes real events or a context that is real, with fictional events and characters, combined with the aesthetic qualities of fiction." And Gordimer goes on to spell out how fiction can enrich the reader's perception of events: "Meaning is what cannot be reached by the immediacy of the image, the description of the sequence of events, the methodologies of expert analysis . . . it is seeing what is really taking place."[2] Of course, to see what is really taking place requires a strong sense of context, and Jameson was always acutely conscious of this, both for herself as a writer addressing contemporary readers, and as the creator of situations and characters in her novels. Interpretation of one's own age will always be a daunting task, as Jameson conceded in 1947: "Every age asks its artists, its thinkers, a question. In the end it is always the same question: What is man? Why was I born? What does my life mean? But every age asks it in a different form, and it is quite easy for an artist to spend his whole life struggling to find out exactly what the question is that he is being asked."[3] In this Jameson has much in common with the social historian for, as Raphael Samuel has acknowledged, echoing R. H. Tawney, a historian friend and mentor of Jameson herself:

> [Historians] are in fact constantly reinterpreting the past in the light of the present, and indeed, like conservationists and restorationists in other spheres, reinventing it. The angle of vision is inescapably contemporary, however remote the object in view. Even when we produce words and phrases verbatim, the resonances are those of our time. However faithfully we document a period and steep ourselves in the sources, we cannot rid ourselves of afterthought. However jealously we protect the integrity of our subject matter, we cannot insulate it from ourselves. History is an argument about the past, as well as a record of it, and its terms are forever changing.[4]

And that remains true, even of the very recent past that Jameson regularly explores in her novels.

Jameson had experienced the effect of World War I on the years that followed, seeing that war "as a boundary mark in the history of values and attitudes."[5] So she was one of those who, both during and after World War II, feared that the mistakes made as a result of the earlier war would be repeated after the next. Indeed, as Marina MacKay and Lyndsey Stonebridge argue, "for those writing at mid-century, after two wars and in the middle of an undeclared chilly third, the historical resonances of what had come before loomed as large as (and as part of) the task of imagining the present and the future."[6] It is not for nothing that Jameson's two novels written in the immediate aftermath of World War II, *Before the Crossing* (1947) and *The Black Laurel* (1947), have as central characters men who started life in her interwar works, and who were shaped by their experiences of World War I. The character Renn (like Jameson's own husband) was not only gassed but emotionally drained by his time in the trenches; something in him has been perilously dehumanized despite his integrity and commitment to justice. Gary, once his friend and now his opponent, suffered a wound in the war that castrated him, his innate, frustrated virility eventually leading him on an obsessive, dehumanizing quest for material power, his sense of values warped by his legacy from World War I. For, as Mark Mazower argues, it is ultimately "the question of values which lies at the heart of [twentieth-century] history—the values which drove people to act, which shaped and transformed institutions, guided state policy and underpinned communities, families, individuals."[7] And after World War I, the old vocabulary of widely shared humanitarian values, under threat for decades, had been finally shattered: words like "justice," "peace," and "freedom" meant different things to different people, depending on their political and cultural allegiances.

So writers like Jameson, like George Orwell, brought to their concerns about the next war and its aftereffects what they had experienced as the legacies of World War I: at home, there had been what would now be called post-traumatic stress disorder, unemployment, a sense that the social hierarchy was unchanged by the terrible sacrifices made by so many families in that war, a sense that the establishment was simply carrying on as before, no lessons being learned. In Europe as a whole, they watched how the interwar years charted the conflict between the three dominant ideologies, liberalism, fascism, and communism. Inevitably, their fears that the mistakes of the past would be repeated haunted their hopes for the future, while the rise of dictators during the interwar years (Mussolini, Hitler, Franco, Stalin) preoccupied them. It is not surprising, therefore, that writers like Jameson and Orwell, from the outbreak of World War II, and increasingly as the war dragged on, speculated on what kind of world would emerge from the devastations of this conflict. While popular opinion about Russia was largely favorable after news of the heroic defense of Leningrad and Stalin's new role as an ally against Hitler and Nazism, more than one writer worried that the removal of one dictator and his followers might simply leave a vacuum for another dictator to fill. Orwell had completed his novel *Animal Farm* by 1943, in which, after the bullying farmer is removed by the pigs as the animals' champions, those champions become even worse tyrants than the one they replaced; but although in England censorship of fiction was by no means as repressive as censorship of nonfiction, thanks to the efforts of the Society of Authors, this novel was not published until the end of the war, since its interpretation as an anti-Soviet satire might offend the Soviet ally. In the meantime, Orwell went on with his journalism, where the subject of dictators continued to concern him: in one of his weekly articles for the *Tribune*, he lists among contemporary führers, "actual and would-be," de Gaulle and Churchill.[8] The Tehran Conference held in that same year, bringing Stalin, Churchill, and Roosevelt together to discuss current strategy and plans for "zones of influence" in the postwar world, generated (Orwell would later maintain) ideas that resulted in *Nineteen Eighty-Four*.[9] Meanwhile, Orwell's close friend, Arthur Koestler, invited a number of writers to contribute to an anthology in which he asked them to speculate on the kind of world that might emerge from the war, setting the scene in 1975. Jameson was one of those he approached, but she, like Orwell, was pessimistic about the legacies this war might leave. Her own visions of the future were nightmares, she said; she felt the human race was heading for another Dark Age.[10] Two years before she had, as she put it, balanced two conversations in her mind: the first was with a wealthy woman who told her that if Britain lost the war she would turn her house into a hospital for German officers and run it for them, while the second was with a young man in the RAF who was offered a job as an instructor, but preferred to remain a bomber pilot because, he told her, it was such rotten work he would prefer to do it himself rather than teach others. He was killed shortly afterwards, Jameson told a friend, while the woman was still alive, so she had not as yet worked out "the sum."[11] Her story for Koestler, "The Young Prisoner," infuses the implications of these conversations with nightmare, echoing the world of Zamyatin's *We* (1924), and anticipating Orwell's *Nineteen Eighty-Four*.[12] The action is set in a future totalitarian England, in a penal colony, where the young protagonist has been imprisoned for publishing his idealistic vision of freedom to live and love; inevitably he is sent to his "accidental" death by one of the all too dutiful guards.[13] Koestler thought this tale "outstandingly brilliant"; but the projected anthology never materialized.[14] Later that year, voicing a concern shared by a number of his contemporaries, Koestler would himself write:

> In this war we are fighting against a total lie in the name of a half-truth . . . We fight against Racialism and yet racial discrimination is far from abolished in the Anglo-Saxon countries; we fight for Democracy and yet our mightiest ally is a dictatorship.[15]

He went on to say that short-term pessimism was inevitable, but that it was the duty of what he termed "an active fraternity of pessimists (I mean short-term pessimists)" to warn, and to work to counter the ills that concerned them (Koestler, "The Fraternity of Pessimists," 111). And Jameson shared this view of the pessimist's task.

As World War II drew to an end, Jameson, committed as she was to "witness literature," faced "the problematic nature of representing an age of ambiguous victories . . . ; it has participated in the defeat of one version of totalitarianism only to feel the apocalyptic threat of another" (MacKay and Stonebridge, "Introduction: British Fiction After Modernism," 7). Moreover, there was not only the fear of a repetition of the mistakes of the interwar years; there was also the fear that the authoritarianism that World War II had bred on both sides of the conflict would continue; historians have pointed to "the alarming approximation between totalitarian regimes and democratic cultures under wartime conditions."[16] Elizabeth Bowen commented on these tendencies: "outwardly we accepted that at this time individual destiny had to count for nothing: inwardly, individual destiny became an obsession in every heart."[17] And Jameson and Vera Brittain had shared, in their correspondence of the late 1930s and early 1940s, this sense that the counter to fascism was perilously close to fascism itself; they were, like Bowen, acutely aware of the importance of maintaining the integrity of the individual.[18] Mark Rawlinson, looking at the situation they deplored, sees it as having "the effect of dissolving rather than clarifying the differences between the warring ideologies," and he quotes pacifist Brittain's bitter, postwar comment that: "'Taking It,' now universally extolled as a major virtue . . . meant submitting our standards, our consciences, and our thoughts to progressive brutalization."[19] Sartre had warned in 1943 that "to render myself passive to the world is still to choose the person I am," while Camus argued in one of his *Letters to a German Friend*, in July 1944: "You never believed in the meaning of this world and therefore deduced the idea that everything was equivalent and that good and evil could be defined according to one's wishes . . . I continue to believe that this world has no ultimate meaning. But I know that something in it has meaning and that is man."[20] In her two novels written as the war ended, Jameson would have Renn and Gary represent both sides of this existential crisis. There was also the need to confront the revelation of the Holocaust and Hiroshima, the extent of the betrayal of humanism. As Jameson's friend, George Steiner, says:

> We come after. We know now that a man can read Goethe or Rilke in the evening, that he can play Bach and Schubert, and go to his day's work in Auschwitz in the morning. To say that he has read them without understanding or that his ear is gross, is cant . . . It is not only the case that the established media of civilization—the universities, the arts, the book world—failed to offer resistance to political bestiality, they often rose to welcome it and to give it ceremony and apologia.[21]

And he concludes, echoing Sartre, "Men are accomplices to that which leaves them indifferent" (Steiner, *Language and Silence*, 129). In *The Black Laurel*, Jameson would show the Jew Kalb as a victim of just such indifference.

Jameson's commitment to "witness literature" also meant that she must confront that other taxing problem for the postwar writer: the recognition of what had happened to language over the past thirty years or more. Wars and the burgeoning of different ideologies had intensified the fragmentation of what had once been perceived as shared meanings throughout "civilized" society, and writers were faced with the effects of wartime propaganda, which had increased the complexity of transmitting any shared code of values. For as Foulkes has argued:

> Most people claim the ability both to recognize and to resist propaganda, but when pressed for examples of its methods and manifestations, they usually point to the "distortions" of the politicians they do not vote for, the "slanted" editorials of the newspapers they tend not to read, or the "lies" put out by the foreign power which they happen to regard as the greatest threat of the day . . . What they fail to see is that the interests they perceive as being attacked by inimical propaganda may themselves be

the product of propagandistic processes far more subtle than the ones employed by the "other side."[22]

It was the duty of the writer, as Jameson saw it, to recognize all such usage, whether blatant or subtextual. For she was all too aware of one of the legacies of World War I and its echoes in World War II; as Sherry puts it:

> The distortions that total war enforced on the discourses of culture . . . the exaggerations that stimulated the required popular involvement, the hate campaigns, the cartoon enmities, all in all, the mechanism of oppositional thinking and the bogus extremities it effected. Gigantism is a feature equally of the political and military dimensions of mass warfare, and it scales much of the subsequent experience of the century to its intimidations, at once intimate and immense (Sherry, "Introduction," 2).

In *Before the Crossing* and *The Black Laurel*, young Arnold, one of the younger generation that Jameson presents as a fragile hope for the future, is shown as gradually penetrating the propagandist language of such characters as Gary. At first Arnold is impressed by Gary's clear view of the lure of Hitler when he tells the young man:

> It's the mass who suffer, the millions, poor or well-off, who daren't ask themselves why they were born—because the only truthful answer terrifies them. They'll clap anybody—a politician, a successful general, Hitler—who palms off on them a comfortable answer.[23]

Gary sees the young man as his heir, employing him as his pilot and trying to indoctrinate him with his ideas. For a time, Gary and Renn act as young Arnold's good and bad angels, and during that time Gary's apparently selfless arguments have the more seductive appeal. But then the boy comes to see that Gary's descriptions of the New Order he wants to impose after the war has as its subtext Gary's own need for power, a need all too akin to the driving force of the totalitarian regimes it is supposed to counter: as Arnold tells Gary, "you don't care what happens to people you can't use" (*The Black Laurel*, 338). He has come to see the truth of

Renn's comment, stemming from his awareness of his own mistakes, that "in any society where some men are of no importance, the only justice these get is the cheap legal sort. You can't separate justice and freedom" (329). Here, Jameson gives Renn the chance to rescue key concepts in the novel from the slippage within the language and actions of Gary and his confederates, both German and English.

Distortions of language used against an enemy, or one who could be presented as such, had also been used, Jameson was well aware, to bolster a sense of unity at home. As Gill Plain argues, during World War II

> the national identity was a composite picture. It drew extensively upon the imagery of an anachronistic rural myth, which was combined with a reaffirmation of long-established opinions about the nature of the British character—the paradoxes of which can be juxtaposed to create a truly conservative Everyman. Insular yet tolerant, anti-intellectual but full of common sense, the British were a nation of home-loving imperialists crowned above all by their irrepressible sense of humour.[24]

It was these comfortable myths of Englishness that Jameson set out to challenge in such postwar novels as *The Green Man* (1952) and *A Cup of Tea for Mr. Thorgill* (1957);[25] she was intent on combating the propagandist use of language that insisted on the difference between "us" and "them," whether at home or abroad. In these works, as in *Before the Crossing* and *The Black Laurel,* it is the shared human follies, the fragility of the hopes for the future that Jameson threads through the narrative. She had always in mind the failure to establish a lasting peace after World War I.

There was another decision she had made during the 1930s, as the rising tide of fascism grew ever more threatening: she had to devise the kind of novel that would best serve as "witness literature." In several of her works during the 1930s and 1940s, she experimented with a realism that was far from naive. She was in fact choosing the kind of approach that a range of postcolonial writers, such as Lamming, Naipaul, and Lessing, would also adopt. All of them were seeking

> in distinctive ways to retain realism's strengths, particularly its attention to the social and intersubjective nature of human life,

> while at the same time confronting the problem of representation . . . They all extend realism by disclosing the constitutive function of language and narrative in human beings' production of meaning. This emphasis on the construction of meaning is predominantly the counterpart of a textuality rooted in a particularized and historicized social domain.[26]

Jameson's powerful empathy with the refugees she had encountered in her work for the P.E.N. Club and her concerns for issues beyond the bounds of her own country inevitably resulted in her sharing many of the priorities of postcolonial and other overseas writers.[27] But of course there are problems in addressing sensitive issues in realist mode; for "the novels that emphasize how deeply cognition is embedded in language also insist that it is confronted by a recalcitrant, external world with which it must perforce engage" (Gasiorek, *Post-War British Fiction*, 183). Jameson's postwar novels often fell foul of this "recalcitrant, external world" in the form of reviewers and some readers who refused to accept the version of the world that she presents, for she was, repeatedly, revisionist in her view of contemporary or near-contemporary events and issues. And this, as John Orr has argued, creates problems for the novelist who espouses realism, for his or her novels are "used to promote an illusion of the Real," and "the Real depends upon a fragile consensus about reality, about what it is and will become. Yet the major novelists of realism are always shattering the consensus by uncovering new forms of the Real which are disputed and disavowed. The Real is never a fixed object with a fixed definition. It changes historically over time with the development of the novel itself."[28] Orr builds on Auerbach's discussion of tragic realism; he sees it as the particular province of such postcolonial writers as Gasiorek names, but what he says is equally applicable to a writer like Jameson:

> The disclosures of tragic realism are both contemporary and prophetic, examinations of past and present. . . . We are thus speaking of worlds *where fiction gets there first*, where it uncovers a world buried or repressed, but where it also imagines events and gives them fictive meanings before they are nailed to the masthead of fact . . . a close reading of tragic realism over the space of the last century offers little scope for liberal complacency. It

> reveals racism and fascism as the monsters of liberal civilization, just as it reveals Stalinism as the monster of a derailed revolution. (Orr, *Tragic Realism and Modern Society*, 8–9).[29]

This was very much Jameson's aim in all her postwar novels: she was so often "getting there first," in novels set at home and abroad, which makes it important to see her reviewers as not always responding to the quality of her writing, but rather to the challenges her themes posed and which they were not ready to face.[30]

Clearly, Jameson's commitment to "witness literature" was no simple task. But, despite postwar weariness, she shared with the youthful Kafka a passion for writing that engages with difficult issues. As Kafka wrote in a letter:

> If the book we are reading does not wake us, as with a fist hammering at our skull, why then do we read it? So that it shall make us happy? Good God, we would also be happy if we had no books, and such books as make us happy we could, if need be, write ourselves. But what we must have are those books which come upon us like ill-fortune, and distress us deeply, like the death of one we love better than ourselves, like suicide. A book must be an ice-axe to break the sea frozen inside us.[31]

Youthfully melodramatic this certainly is, but Jameson in her fifties and sixties had not shed her passion for liberal values. During World War II she was determined to make the readers of her novels confront what it felt like to be in Europe as Nazism and its allies gained the upper hand. In 1943, for instance, her novel *Cloudless May* was set in a small French town, but her characters mirror the many factions and private agendas inherent in government and the wider society. Jameson was adept by now at mirroring actual happenings and personalities in her contemporary world and bringing them to life in an intimate setting that houses recognizable people rather than faceless names in a newspaper report. So her small-town mayor mirrors the French prime minister, Reynaud, as the German tanks rolled into France; we see how fatally his mistress, Marie, confuses his judgment (an echo of the real life minister's liaison), yet Jameson rounds the woman's character out, the insecurities of childhood poverty driving her greed, as she lives a life of "hunger and stratagems."[32] We see her lover, the mayor Emil, at first fighting off would-be Nazi collaborators, and then finally succumbing to her pleas; Jameson shows his ugliest moment (again a mirror of a real life situation) as he refuses to free an interned German Jew because, Marie insists, such people could be seen as revolutionaries by definition, they are simply "enemies in an enemy country invaded by their enemies" (*Cloudless May*, 67). Jameson analyzes with shrewd insight the many reasons for France's internal divisions and capitulation. She shows those driven by self interest—"Hitler understands how to govern," says one such character (67)—as well as those who believe passionately in peace, or are simply sickened by their experiences of the last war. Jameson shows the insidious workings of prejudice and propaganda, as when the word "realist" is bandied about to describe each person's differing view of a situation. The confusions of intentions, good, bad, and wavering, are interwoven into a very human tapestry, while issues like the widespread horror in France at destruction inflicted by the British on the French fleet at Oran (to prevent its seizure by the Germans, but resulting in great loss of life), or the fact that the retreat from Dunkirk was seen by many French as betrayal, reminded the British reader of how differently "reality" could appear when seen from another point of view.

Jameson took on another sensitive issue in *The Other Side* (1946);[33] the novel centers on Marie, the young French widow of a German officer, living with his family, and having to face the initial contempt of the officer Aubrac, a member of the French army of occupation billeted in the German family's *Schloss* after the war. Marie's loyalties are severely tested as she realizes the head of the German family is involved in a plot against the Allies. When she reveals the plot, she is of course seen as a traitor by the family, but finally, after coping with many insults from both French and Germans, not to mention her own lack of self-esteem, she allows herself to be saved by Aubrac who eventually shows a grain of grim compassion for her lot; and the young son of the German family, despite his Hitler Youth background, insists on keeping the copy of Ronsard's poems she had left behind. In this novel, realism takes on a fabular guise, not so much witnessing as offering hope for at least a measure of reconciliation.

For the end of World War II brought Jameson two experiences that would strengthen her urge to continue to write "witness literature." She was the first civilian woman to be invited to Poland by the Polish government in the autumn of 1945, a few weeks later traveling to Czechoslovakia, this time as a guest of the Czech Ministry of Foreign Affairs.[34] Jameson's accounts of her visits are starkly graphic. In Poland, she was appalled by the extent of the destruction of Warsaw, where "people are killed every day by bits of wall collapsing on them," as they struggle to survive amidst "ruins and rubble." She was told of the brutalities both suffered and witnessed by so many, meeting women recently released from death camps as well as those who had been involved in the Warsaw Uprising. But she was also dismayed by the brutalization that war inevitably left behind, commenting that "to kill, lie, rob, loot is heroism one day and evil the next"; she was warned not to go out at night as "thugs and things keep shooting in the streets."[35] However, her role in P.E.N. had honed her skills in listening without judging, and she tried, where she could, to see for herself. Later, in Prague, she met friends from before the war, broken by what they had suffered; she was taken to the room where a young man she had known had been tortured beyond recognition before he was killed. But she also insisted, against considerable local opposition, on visiting the detention centers where German prisoners and those accused of collaboration or fraternization were interned; she was particularly dismayed by the bleak, underfed conditions in which girls who had formed relationships with German soldiers were kept, their babies dying as the mothers' milk dried up. Gazing at one dying baby, Jameson had a horrifying insight:

> The tiny face dissolved and for less than a breath I saw through its soft skull the guillotine in Pankrác . . . , the terror of a boy in the instant before he is killed, the decent bodies of women heaped, naked as maggots, in Terézin and Auschwitz—the spume of agony flowing back and forth across Europe.[36]

What the Czechoslovak people had suffered, and the complex repercussions after the war, when the boundaries between justice and vengeance were all too often crossed, would color her writings for years to come. For what would haunt her, along with the suffering, was the propensity for cruelty within humankind as a whole.[37] Before World War II she had visited Czechoslovakia with a P.E.N. delegation, and been deeply moved by the evidence of democracy she had seen, evidence of what appeared to be the living manifestation of the preamble to the 1920 constitution that asserted its aim "to form a more perfect union of the nation." Yet there remained, behind the scenes, the question as to whether "the country's Slovaks, Jews, Hungarians and Germans regarded themselves as included in such a phrase" (Mazower, *Dark Continent*, 24). Certainly, what Jameson witnessed after the war confirmed that all was far from well, and her own experiences did nothing to allay her pessimism.

Indeed, like a number of her fellow writers, Jameson was confronting something of an existential crisis. Her pessimism, her warnings against the repetition of the mistakes emanating from World War I, had been warnings against more of the same; what she now confronted was a world altered by the sheer scale of the atrocities being uncovered, by the dropping of the atom bombs, by the threats posed by Soviet influence and ambitions. The bleak world of Sartre's *La Nausée*, published in 1938—its philosophy very much a legacy of World War I—expressed for many the existential angst following World War II: his powerful portrayal of a defamiliarized world, his protagonist living only in the present without reference to past or future, haunted many creative minds at this time. This is the world that Jameson's protagonist, Renn, experiences in *Before the Crossing*;[38] he is, like so many postwar protagonists, an antihero, one who demonstrates the contention that

> the adventure of the Real cannot be extricated from [its] historical passage, . . . a passage of material descent which cannot overlook its aspiration to the ideal. Yet sooner or later the noble and the ideal expire. The question then becomes: What is left? And what can take its place? (Orr, *Tragic Realism and Modern Society*, 10)

Jameson's antihero, damaged physically and emotionally by his experiences in World War I, embodies the vulnerability of humanist values during the interwar years and the risk of a descent into barbarism, even as he sees himself as a champion of justice. Jameson is also challenging her post–World War II readers with a revisionist account of the national character that had become "more indebted to official wartime propaganda than to an accurate and differentiated understanding of wartime history" (Rau, *Our Nazis*, 6).[39] By setting Renn in the midst of a number of characters representing industry, the press, and politics, most of whom have lost sight of a shared standard of values in the interwar years, she shows an England that has disturbing signs of the corruption that she had charted in the French society of *Cloudless May*. In a lecture given in 1938, on "The Novel in Contemporary Life," she had developed ideas put forward in her "Documents" article for the journal *Fact*.[40] In this lecture she had urged writers to strive to recognize what was essential in the life of their age, and what was "dead and done for" (24); but if the whole was too much to encompass, the novelist must "take soundings" (24). She had developed this method in several novels since, and now she was taking "soundings" in the dark side of the national character that had been largely ignored in the wartime image made so much of during the war. She was not depicting an England that is overall "a country of cruelty, selfishness, greed, and subservience to power."[41] What she was out to show was how easily fascist traits in a range of English characters could have changed the course of history: she was resisting what Rau calls "the insistence on the alterity of fascism, on its exotic nature" (Rau, *Our Nazis*, 10), and she was fully aware of what Virginia Woolf had called "the subconscious Hitlerism in the hearts of men."[42] For in *Before the Crossing*, Renn illustrates what Bowen's Mephistophelean character, Harrison, observes in *The Heat of the Day*: "War, if you come to think of it, hasn't started anything that wasn't there before."[43] In Jameson's novel, the narrative explores traits in her characters that might well be the breeding grounds for the treacheries and cruelties of the interwar years and World War II; her central theme gives voice to her anxieties about fascist tendencies developing in any of the warring states, both enemy and ally, and her conviction that such tendencies exist even in the most principled individual. For while Renn sees clearly such tendencies in the murderer he pursues, and in associates who gradually shed democratic values they once held dear, his own single-minded quest for justice becomes so obsessive that it takes on the character of the very cruelty he is out to destroy; his humanity is all but obliterated. This, Jameson would pinpoint in 1947 as the flaw in Sartre's philosophy: "How to reconcile, except in the practice of a Resistance or Revolution, the belief that conflict is the only relation of one human being to another, with the belief that respect for the freedom of others is a basic virtue?"[44] She felt Sartre could not, "within the human situation as he conceives it, erect brotherly respect as a universally valid human value" (*The Writer's Situation*, 25).

The opening paragraph of Jameson's novel *Before the Crossing* sets the scene in the late 1930s, depicting Renn as observer, very much as Esk was in her novel *Europe to Let* (1940), or as the French officer Rienne was in *Cloudless May*.[45] Renn is in Paris, outside a café, observing

> the street, the girl hanging on the arm of her pallid furtive young man, the sharp corner of the rue Soufflot, railings of the Luxembourg, the light. This light ran against him from all sides: he saw himself as a dark knot at its centre, which it did not penetrate. (*Before the Crossing*, 1)

Here Renn's view of himself as "a dark knot" is the key for the reader: such bleak detachment will have its dangers, but as yet Renn has not recognized the full implications for himself. The same is true for his erstwhile friend, the once life-loving Gary, who has, without realizing it, "lost his nature," becoming eventually nothing more than an "international usurer" (*Before the Crossing*, 145). Images of light and dark weave their way through the novel, as do mirrors and eyes: what characters see or think they see in others or themselves is central. It is telling that the murdered man, whom Renn is out to avenge and whose eyes the murderer has gouged out, was a man of integrity. Most of the characters in the novel do not share the murdered man's clear sight: the state of the world seeps into them, each in their own way corrupted. Renn himself, standing apart and observing, is also vulnerable; Jameson, through her experience of the war and what came after had come to see that reason, detachment, could both be corrupted in a world where people were adrift, without any stable code of values. It is only in his final confrontation with the murderer he has been pursuing that Renn realizes that his commitment to justice has deteriorated into revenge: the murderer, Hunt, demands to know what Renn has done to Hunt's girlfriend, the young woman Renn bullied into flight in his determination to track down Hunt himself. Jameson deliberately skews the reader's sense of right and wrong by having the "villain" accuse the "good guy," and be justified in so doing. Yet she allows Renn the ability to observe how far he had fallen: "He had pressed roughly on the human being least able to bear it," he realizes (279), so his one claim to be the "good guy" is that he can recognize and admit to himself his lost integrity. And Jameson, at the end of the novel, picks up the image of her first paragraph, allowing a hint of hope: "The light, when he stepped from the dark sunken lane into the road, pressed against his eyes, so warm, massive, living, that it was purely a joy" (279). Renn's "dark knot" has gone, as he starts a new quest, the quest to find the young girl he bullied into flight, and so to redeem himself. This ending shows Jameson striving to keep alive the idea of progress, of peace bringing a better world, even as her pragmatism is all too aware of what human nature is capable of, and she is determined that her readers must accept this. Throughout, her aim has been to get under the reader's skin, "prodding at inconsistencies in nationalist narratives and calling them to account for their blind spots" (Carlston, *Double Agents*, 10).

Jameson was no romantic, as she had accused Sartre of being (*Writer's Situation*, 26); the dilemma at the heart of her next novel, *The Black Laurel*, set initially in Scotland and then in the ruins of Berlin, infects a range of characters of different nationalities, generations, and ideologies: the loss of a common moral perspective explored in *Before the Crossing* now intensifies in the problems that war and opposing ideologies bring in their wake. The immediate aftermath of World War II in this novel catches the spirit of a time that Stevie Smith memorably labeled not "peace" but the "postwar."[46] In the postwar world of Jameson's novel, all too often an individual's private agenda justifies their choice of action, and what was once familiar territory is defamiliarized repeatedly, both for the characters and for the reader. For the landscape of the bulk of the work—a Berlin that graphically mirrors the devastation Jameson saw in Warsaw—reflects what Jameson says of Sartre's philosophy as conveyed in *La Nausée*:

> Life has no purpose, except the meaning and purpose we give it when we act. In action we create ourselves, and provide ourselves with a reason for living . . . Man is alone, in a situation he did not choose, and within this situation totally responsible for his own acts. In this lies the tragic ambiguity of the human

> situation—given, obstinately fact-circumscribed—yet in which we choose, freely to act; can, indeed, only choose to act . . . , condemned to be free. And responsible before nothing. (Jameson, *Writer's Situation*, 21)

Jameson's Renn, in *Before the Crossing*, is very much a Sartrean figure: his world view has been shattered by the experiences of one world war and its inexorable march to a second. Rejecting a past idealism that he sees now as unrealistic, together with a future of "progress" that he cannot envisage, he is the product of an uprooted present, which, as we have seen, leaves him open to a loss of moral perspective. In *The Black Laurel*, where Renn struggles to redeem himself, Jameson throws light on the inadequacies of military rule in occupied Berlin and the ambivalences of big business interests that often undermine any clear view of right or left in politics, of what can be justified and what is beyond the pale. Her depictions of treachery are very close to those of Rebecca West;[47] like West, she never allows her "villains" to be black all through—all are capable of kindness, all are recognizable human beings who do not allow us to distance ourselves from their uglier moments. Jameson, like West, is very aware of what is in danger of being lost in this defamiliarized world. But theirs is no tired nostalgia for the flawed world of the prewar days, a world both Jameson and West excoriated in their interwar writings, and which Jameson shows as dangerously flawed in *Before the Crossing*; what they deplore is the increasing tendency, as they see it, of individuals to pursue their own ends without concern for the community their actions undermine. As a character in *The Black Laurel* says despairingly:

> Any bloody thing can be justified, gas chambers, cutting a schoolroomful of Bolshie children's poor little throats, injecting poison into the veins of old girls of sixty or seventy—anything. Once you decide to call a private murder justice you're done for—you and your country are going straight to hell (16).

In both *Before the Crossing* and *The Black Laurel*, Jameson's central characters face the dilemma that Sartre posed for himself, as Iris Murdoch argued in 1953:

> Sartre has in himself both the intense egocentric conception of personal life and the pragmatic utilitarian view of politics which most western people keep as two separate notions in their head, only since he is a metaphysician Sartre wishes to join them by a theory of action.[48]

Moreover, in *The Black Laurel* Jameson draws attention to the extreme instability of Europe in the immediate postwar years. As Tony Judt has argued:

> It is widely believed by scholars today that for all the contemporary gloom the initial post-war recovery and the reforms and plans of the years 1945–47 laid the groundwork for Europe's future well being. And to be sure, for western Europeans at least 1947 would indeed prove the turning point in the continent's recovery. But at the time none of this was obvious. . . . With the precedent of the post-World War I mistakes uppermost in their thoughts, many European and American observers indeed feared the worst. At best, they calculated, the continent was in for decades of poverty and struggle. German residents of the American Zone [of occupation] expected it to be at least twenty years before their country recovered . . . But long before that, in the pessimists' view, continental Europe would collapse back into civil war, fascism, and Communism.[49]

Committed as she was to "witness literature," Jameson always researched the background to her novels meticulously, and she was particularly careful over the background to *The Black Laurel*, consulting members of the occupying forces in the British zone, as well as refugees who had returned and brought back details of the conditions they had found. There was good reason for this, as she had not actually visited the postwar Berlin she was portraying, although she had known the city well before the war. She had, however, the vivid experience of her visit to Warsaw and it was there, as she told her Macmillan publisher, that she learned how people lived in ruins.[50] She was clearly anxious that her use of the Warsaw experience to reveal the situation in Berlin would not undermine the essential "witness" of her work; and we can still raise the question as to whether she was justified. A recent article in *The Guardian* addresses this very problem, the Sierra Leonian writer, Aminatta Forna, telling how she was inspired by Nadine Gordimer's essay, "Witness: The Inward Testimony." This essay, Forna says, showed her how writing fiction could give a meaning to real-life events:

> Witness literature is . . . not autobiographical fiction. . . . In Sri Lanka, Colombia, Nigeria, India and even Spain, readers recognise a description of their lives and experiences even though the stories are set on another continent. . . . Writing is a process of synthesis, the taking of strands from one place and another, using form and language to fashion something new. It does not constrain the artistic liberty of the writer, as some might argue . . . Sometimes the outsider bearing "witness" can bring a new dimension to familiar events. (Forna, "A Book That Changed Me," 30)

This is very much the way Jameson views her own "witness literature" over half a century earlier. And she was very careful about how she presented the ingredients of her tale. Aware as she was of wartime propaganda, she establishes the horrors of life in the wastelands of Berlin, where physical ruins not only exist in their own enormity but also stand for the ruins of shared cultural and moral values—the old humanist Gerlach is killed by his own nephew, a young man brutalized by his experiences under Nazism during the war. Only after establishing the situation in Berlin does Jameson show the mirror image of that suffering in the Warsaw the Nazis destroyed, showing it chillingly through the indifferent eyes of a German art expert sent to oversee the "final stripping of the city's galleries and museums" (*Black Laurel*, 81). Her decision was a daring one, given Europe's raw wounds, but her priority is to show the common ground of suffering, brutalization, and tragedy. So she has Renn go to Prague on his quest to find the young woman he bullied into flight, and to see, as Jameson saw herself, the fate of the young mothers in prison, where he is dismayed, as she was, to see the dying babies. She gives him the same words of horrified insight that she would use herself, many years later, in the passage in *Journey from the North* quoted above. It is not without interest that it was this chapter on Prague that her publisher wanted her to remove as too harrowing, but Jameson refused, insisting that someone should put it on record.[51]

At the core of the novel is the little Jew Kalb, the ultimate victim of prejudice and expendability, as German and British collude for material gain. He had escaped to England in 1934, and now returns to Germany on his self-appointed mission to identify paintings stolen from occupied countries. But this "mission" gets in the way of those who are out to make gains for themselves. In this novel, as Phyllis Lassner says, "it is less important what the Jew is than how others react to and then represent him . . . As the novel is shaped, when no one can find reason enough to save the Jew, the fate of Europe is sealed in its past and the future of democratic justice is cloudy at best."[52] The other victim of this haunting example of tragic realism is the old German Lucius, recently released from Buchenwald, and intent on resurrecting the humanist standards that he stood for in his youth; here is Jameson's "sounding" of a type of German already savaged by his own people, but who keeps his integrity, refusing to be corrupted by prewar friends like Gary. Yet he cannot speak the same language as his young fellow countrymen who have been brutalized. His killing by his own kind is not only a family tragedy but an image of the death of humanist values as a result of the war. For communication throughout this work is shown as never more than partial; Jameson gives the reader glimpses of the motivation underlying and often contradicting words apparently shared, and the images of ruin and desolation make their own comment on the dialogues of corruption. As Renn comments bitterly: "There are some very respectable families living in cellars, over the sewage, and in a few other cellars you can have quite a decent young woman for a bar or two of chocolate" (*Black Laurel*, 39) . But Jameson allows the novel to end with some hope. There is the hope that young Arnold's insights bring; but also, early on, Jameson comments on the incongruous sight of a pot of geraniums on the windowsill of a building in ruins (126). This is no mere sentimentality—it was to be a common sight in many ruined cities of Europe—but rather an assertion of continuities in ordinary human life. For in the end, Renn agrees to take the child of the girl he damaged under his care, as she aims for a new life in America: and Jameson has him echo the hope proclaimed by that pot of geraniums, and unknowingly echo what Lucius had hoped to offer his nephew's generation. Because Renn recognizes he must himself learn, with the child,

> existence, from the beginning—in the humbler existences: of the child's toys, or of herbs, pots, jugs, rooms; and, so small and weak as yet, of the child . . . Renn bent over him, and touched his cheek with one finger. The child opened his eyes and smiled at him. (*Black Laurel*, 349)

Some forms of simplicity, of the ordinary details of daily life must be learned if there is to be any hope for the future. Jameson had little faith in the bigger issues.

Indeed, the situation in Europe, for those who looked that way, continued to disturb: there was no clean break between "the hot and cold war," and by 1950, communists and anticommunists "each saw the other as the successor to Hitler, themselves as his true opponents" (Mazower, *Dark Continent*, 217, 222). There was a sense that just as World War I had been the prelude to World War II, yet another world war might emerge from the wreckage of World War II. This fear did not seem so remote when the Korean War got under way in June 1950, as was clear from the fate of Jameson's little novel, *The Moment of Truth* (1949). Written against a background of the growing aggression of Soviet policy in Eastern Europe, and still haunted by the ideas embodied in *The Black Laurel*, Jameson had produced a novel of deceptive simplicity, set in a future England undergoing a Soviet invasion, just as her novel *In the Second Year* (1936) had envisaged an England under Hitler a decade before. The Drama Department of the BBC adapted it as a radio play to be broadcast in September, 1950. But on August 3, Jameson was told that the play had been withdrawn as the BBC would be thought irresponsible if it broadcast a play whose setting was the defeat and occupation of England by the Soviet Union, and in which the response of the Allies was portrayed as inadequate.[53] The notion of England as a land never to be invaded was being stoutly defended; myths and the propaganda inherent in them die hard. And Jameson's novel *The Hidden River* (1955) also ran into trouble.[54] Postwar France, like Czechoslovakia, had seen many reprisals taken against those who had collaborated or fraternized, or were thought to have done so. Jameson's novel originally provided a tale of a French family echoing the Greek tale of Orestes and Electra;[55] but both her London publisher and her American agent insisted that she water down the grimness of the plot, making much of the originally slight love interest, and (in the serialized version for *The Saturday Evening Post*), even turning her haunted Orestes figure into a responsibly bourgeois farmer. The complex historical reality she had subtly probed in the original version was all but overlaid with such obfuscating elements; ironically, the altered version was one of her most successful novels financially.

The fate of *The Hidden River* did not turn Jameson away from writing "witness literature," but she endured increasingly hostile reviews as the official versions of World War II took hold. Yet she was one of the few who demonstrates what Eric Hobsbawm argues, that "history needs mobility and the ability to survey and explore a large territory, that is to say the ability to move beyond one's roots . . . Anachronism and provincialism are two deadly sins of history, both equally due to sheer ignorance of what things are like elsewhere" (Hobsbawm, 415). Her work cannot be judged by its reception at the time of writing; as I have argued, her challenges to what many perceived as received wisdom made many of her reviewers refuse to accept precepts in her novels that have been proved all too well founded in later years. But equally her work demanded at the time and demands now that we reject, or at least modify

> the notion that the essence of literature should be seen as a sort of aesthetic timelessness which has the power to speak to us across the ages. The very concept of timelessness, if it is to represent more than a personal and unprovable value judgement, can derive only from a succession of accumulated acts of reception, each one of which is subject to its own historicity. (Foulkes, *Literature and Propaganda*, 105)

"Witness literature," as for Nadine Gordimer and Aminatta Forna, is of its time. Its strength is that when, as in Jameson's case, it speaks so eloquently from its own time, daring to challenge propagandist notions and insisting on the commonness of human nature, it gives us a way into a complex human heritage that points the way to where we are now.

Notes

1. Catharine Savage Brosman, "French Writing of the Great War," in *The Cambridge Companion to the Literature of the First World War*, ed. Vincent Sherry (Cambridge: Cambridge University Press, 2005), 166–90, at 184. See also Elizabeth Maslen, "The Case for Storm Jameson," in *British Fiction after Modernism: The Novel at Mid-*

Century, ed. Marina MacKay and Lyndsey Stonebridge (Basingstoke, Eng.: Macmillan Palgrave, 2007), 33–41.

2. Nadine Gordimer, "Witness: The Inward Testimony," quoted by Aminatta Forna, "A Book that Changed Me," *The Guardian*, August 21, 2013, 30.

3. Storm Jameson, "The Writer's Situation," in *The Writer's Situation and Other Essays* (London: Macmillan, 1950), 1–36, at 1. Originally given as a lecture for the Lyceum Club in May 1947.

4. Raphael Samuel, *Theatres of Memory*, vol. 1: *Past and Present Contemporary Culture* (London: Verso, 1994), 430. See also R. H. Tawney, *Social History and Literature* (London: for the National Book League, 7th annual lecture by Cambridge University Press, 1950); and Eric Hobsbawm, *Interesting Times: A Twentieth-Century Life* (London: Allen Lane, Penguin Press, 2002), 100.

5. Vincent Sherry, "Introduction," in *The Cambridge Companion to the Literature of the First World War*, ed. Vincent Sherry (Cambridge: Cambridge University Press, 2005), 1–14, at 4.

6. Marina MacKay and Lyndsey Stonebridge, "Introduction: British Fiction after Modernism," in *British Fiction after Modernism: The Novel at Mid-Century*, ed. Marina MacKay and Lyndsey Stonebridge (Basingstoke, Eng.: Palgrave Macmillan, 2007), 1–16, at 2. See also Jane Dowson, *Women's Writing, 1945–1960: After the Deluge* (Basingstoke, Eng.: Palgrave Macmillan, 2003), 1–14; and Adam Piette, *The Literary Cold War, 1945 to Vietnam* (Edinburgh: Edinburgh University Press, 2009).

7. Mark Mazower, *Dark Continent: Europe's Twentieth Century* (London: Penguin, 1999), xv.

8. See George Orwell, "As I Please" (1944), in *Collected Essays*, vol. 3, no. 13 (Harmondsworth, Eng.: Penguin, 1970), 91. See also Elizabeth Maslen, "A Cassandra with Clout: Storm Jameson, Little Englander and Good European," in *Intermodernism: Literary Culture in Mid-Twentieth-Century Britain*, ed. Kristin Bluemel (Edinburgh: Edinburgh University Press, 2009), 21–37.

9. George Orwell, letter to Roger Senhouse, December 26, 1948, in *Collected Essays*, vol. 4, no. 132, 519.

10. See Storm Jameson, letter to Arthur Koestler, March 1, 1943, University of Edinburgh Library, Koestler Archive, 2399/11.

11. Jameson letter to Basil L. Hart, May 30, 1941, King's College London: Liddell Hart Centre for Military Archives: 1/408, 1937–1973, 1986.

12. Yevgeny Zamyatin, *We*, trans. anon. (New York: E.P. Dutton, 1924).

13. See Siegfried Lenz, *The German Lesson* (1968), trans. Ernest Kaiser and Eithne Wilkins (New York: New Directions Books, 1986), for comparison, a novel which shows where the duty of an ordinary German man might lead in World War II.

14. See Hermon Ould, letter to Jameson, June 7, 1943, University of Texas at Austin, Harry Ransom Center, PEN archive); Jameson, "The Young Prisoner," in *Modern Reading* no. 9 (1944): 111–26; see Jameson, letter to Arthur Koestler, May 20, 1943.

15. Arthur Koestler, "The Fraternity of Pessimists" (1943), in *The Yogi and the Commissar* (London: Jonathan Cape, 1945), 106–12, at 106.

16. Petra Rau, *Our Nazis: Representations of Fascism in Contemporary Literature and Film* (Edinburgh: Edinburgh University Press, 2013), 8.

17. Elizabeth Bowen, *The Demon Lover and Other Stories* (London: uniform edition, Jonathan Cape, 1952), 220.

18. See the Vera Brittain Archive, McMaster University, Hamilton, Ontario.

19. Mark Rawlinson, *British Writing of the Second World War* (Oxford: Clarendon, 2000), 31; Vera Brittain, *Testament of Experience: An Autobiographical Study of the Years 1925–50* (London: Gollancz, 1957), 274–75; see also Vera Brittain, *Seeds of Chaos: What Mass Bombing Really Means* (London: New Vision, for the Bombing Restriction Committee, 1944).

20. Quoted in Mazower, *Dark Continent*, 195.

21. George Steiner, *Language and Silence: Essays 1958–1966* (Harmondsworth, Eng.: Penguin, 1969), 15.

22. A. P. Foulkes, *Literature and Propaganda* (London: Methuen, 1983), 2.

23. Storm Jameson, *Black Laurel* (London: Macmillan, 1947), 21. See Hannah Arendt, *The Origins of Totalitarianism* (New York: Schocken Books, [1951] 2004). Jameson shows how legitimate argument can be used for Gary's own ends and so be twisted.

24. Gill Plain, *Women's Fiction of the Second World War: Gender, Power and Resistance* (Edinburgh: Edinburgh University Press, 1996), 5.

25. Storm Jameson, *The Green Man* (London: Macmillan, 1952); Storm Jameson, *A Cup of Tea for Mr. Thorgill* (London: Macmillan, 1957).

26. Andrzej Gasiorek, *Post-War British Fiction: Realism and After* (London: Edward Arnold, 1995), 181.

27. P.E.N. stood for Poets, Playwrights, Editors, and Novelists, but the acronym became standard when referring to the Club.

28. John Orr, *Tragic Realism and Modern Society: The Passionate Political in the Modern Novel* (Basingstoke, Eng.: Macmillan, [1977] 1989), 4.

29. See Erich Auerbach, *Mimesis: The Representation of Reality in Western Literature*, trans. Willard B. Trask (New York: Princeton University Press, 1974), 464–66.

30. See, for example, J. D. Scott, reviewing *The Moment of Truth* in *The New Statesman and Nation*, July 23, 1949. After a synopsis, he comments: "there is a clash between the potential resistance leader and the potential collaborator, and it illustrates the danger of trying to annex a piece of the public drama for literary use. The young communist's apologia, for instance, is intolerably vapid, dated even as a parody. . . . Since the great argument has not been emotionally or mentally digested, it tends to issue in incoherent intensity. . . . Danger—hunger—the defeat; they are clearly tempting subjects, but the results of succumbing to temptation are superficiality and pretentiousness." It is telling to set this beside one of the few good reviews such as Bowen's in *The Tatler*, June 1949: "This tense story is a masterpiece. So much carried along was I by the excitement, the rapid twists and turns of events that I took for granted the excellence of the writing. But re-reading *The Moment of Truth*, how I relished it!" Jameson's novels never reveal their full subtlety and complexity to a reader who skims the surface.

31. Quoted in Steiner, *Language and Silence*, 90.

32. Storm Jameson, *Cloudless May* (London: Macmillan, 1943), 65.

33. Storm Jameson, *The Other Side* (London: Macmillan, 1946).

34. See Storm Jameson, diary of Polish visit, Churchill College Library, Cambridge: Churchill Archive, JMON2; notes on Czechoslovakian visit, King's College London Library: Liddell Hart Centre for Military Archives, LH1/408. See also "Poland," *Fortnightly Review* 165 (January–June 1946, January 1946): 28–34; reprinted as "Poland 1945," in *The Windmill*, ed. Reginald Moore and Edward Lane, vol. 1, 1944–1946

(London: William Heinemann 1946), 127–32; "The New Czechoslovakia," *Fortnightly Review* 165 (January–June 1941, February 1946): 73–80.

35. Quotations from Storm Jameson's diary in Churchill College, Special Collections: Guy Chapman archive JMON2.

36. Storm Jameson, *Journey from the North*, vol. 2 (London: Virago, [1970] 1984), 194.

37. See Rebecca West's similar dismay at the Nuremberg trials concerning the ordinariness of those who had overseen such monstrosities: *A Train of Powder* (London: Macmillan, 1955). See also Erin G. Carlston, *Double Agents: Espionage, Literature, and Liminal Citizens* (New York: Columbia University Press, 2013); also Christopher R. Browning, *Ordinary Men: Reserve Police Battalion 101 and the Final Solution in Poland* (New York: Harper Perennial, 1998).

38. Storm Jameson, *Before the Crossing* (London: Macmillan, 1947).

39. See Juliet Gardiner, *Wartime Britain 1939–45* (London: Review, Headline Publishing, 2004), for examples of the darker side of wartime Britain.

40. Storm Jameson, *The Novel in Contemporary Life* (Boston: The Writer, 1938), reprinted with some additions in *Civil Journey* (London: Cassell, 1939), 277–309; see also "Documents," in *Fact*, no. 4 (July 15, 1937): 9–18.

41. Jennifer Birkett, "'Waiting for the Death Wind': Storm Jameson's Fiction After the Second World War," in *Margaret Storm Jameson: Writing in Dialogue*, ed. Jennifer Birkett and Chiara Briganti (Newcastle, Eng.: Cambridge Scholars, 2007), 127–46, at 129.

42. Quoted in MacKay and Stonebridge, *British Fiction after Modernism*, 8.

43. Elizabeth Bowen, *The Heat of the Day* (London: Penguin Books, [1948] 1962), 33.

44. Storm Jameson, "The Writer's Situation," in *The Writer's Situation* (London: Macmillan, 1950), 1–36, at 23–24.

45. Storm Jameson, *Europe to Let: The Memoirs of an Obscure Man* (London: Macmillan, 1940).

46. Stevie Smith, *The Holiday* (London: Virago, [1949] 1979), 13.

47. See, for instance, West, *A Train of Powder*. See also Carlston, *Double Agents*; and Lyndsey Stonebridge, *The Judicial Imagination: Writing after Nuremberg* (Edinburgh: Edinburgh University Press, 2011).

48. Iris Murdoch, *Sartre* (London: Bowes and Bowes, 1953); reprinted as *Sartre: Romantic Realist* (London: Vintage, 1999), 68.

49. Tony Judt, *Postwar: A History of Europe Since 1945* (London: Pimlico, 2007), 89–90.

50. Storm Jameson, A4 typescript entitled "Background to Black Laurel," British Library: Macmillan archive, AD73144, unbound.

51. See letter of Jameson to Lovat Dickson, May 28, 1947, British Library: Macmillan archive, AD73144, unbound.

52. Phyllis Lassner, *British Women Writers of World War II: Battlegrounds of their Own* (Basingstoke, Eng.: Macmillan, 1998; New York: St Martin's, 1998), 248.

53. See letter of Donald Stephenson to Jameson, August 3, 1950, BBC Written Archives, Caversham.

54. Storm Jameson, *The Hidden River* (London: Macmillan, 1955).

55. See letters of Jameson to Lovat Dickson, Macmillan archive, May 27, 1953, May 29, 1953.

ADAM PIETTE

Postwar Espionage Fiction
Memory and Fascism in Emergency-State Thinking

As the traitor Haydon argues in John le Carré's *Tinker, Tailor, Soldier, Spy*, the secret services are "the only real measure of a nation's political health, the only real expression of its subconscious."[1] One of the premises of postwar espionage fiction is that the secret state is not only the source of all secret political story, but that, as covertly as its subject, the spy thriller aims to reveal the tradecraft and dirty information which characterize that open secret, the national security state, at the level of the political "subconscious." The national security state became a global force once the United States consolidated its secret service institutions with the National Security Act of 1947. But it is arguable that it was the United Kingdom which had the world's first fully operational national security state, when MI5 and MI6 were set up during the First World War, as Nicholas Hiley has shown.[2] As a wartime institution, the national security state will always tend to characterize the political situations with which it has to deal as national crises, sanctioning covert actions only conscionable in states of emergency, as Giorgio Agamben has argued.[3] The Cold War was fought at the level of the secret state with the ruthlessness and totalizing logic characteristic of national security states of emergency, using powers developed during the Second World War. The espionage thriller thrives on acts of textual betrayal of this open secret: that the national security state in its Cold War form operates artificially to prolong and maintain Second World War states of emergency. Cold War NATO may have had different ideological objectives to the Allies during the war, may have functioned as an unprecedented super-bureaucratic information machine, may have had other means to penetrate defenses and counter-penetration, and of course faced very different spectral enemies. Yet its secret service procedures and ideology were driven by the dark energy which is national security state-of-emergency thinking, creature of the two world wars. The Cold War spy thrillers I will be reading take the discovery of this dark energy as their principal duty, and raise questions about the aftermath of the Second World War as a fascist survival deep within the West's secret services.

Fascist Infiltration and Secret Power

The figure of the fifth columnist insider infecting home country government has as long a history as the spy thriller itself, originating most clearly with the Professor and Verloc in Joseph Conrad's *The Secret Agent* and John Buchan's Black Stone in *The Thirty-Nine Steps*. For both Conrad and Buchan, invasion fears are at their most paranoid when considering the possibility of the enemy within. Conrad merges Verloc's political treachery with intimations of sexual and psychological secrets, thematized in the seedy pornography sold as cover from Brett Street. Hannay's Scottish/colonial identity and the fact he is being hunted down for murder by the British police forces bring him uncomfortably into mimetic relation with the German spy network, who secrete themselves within England with very English cover stories. The genre thrives on theatricalized subject positions, and raises questions concerning the covert resemblances between "us" and "them" at the level of the political unconscious.[4] Those questions turn on inner treachery as emanating from a dark Id-force, a black stone, or secret porn shop of the heart within the nation state. Something about the toxicity of the dark information at the core of power means that the counterespionage agent in pre–Second World War espionage fiction, whether it be the historian Latimer in Eric Ambler's *The Mask of Dimitrios*, or the mentally disturbed Pompey in Stevie Smith's *Over the Frontier*, is drawn to the fascist enemy as to a dark twin counterpart. Latimer becomes the double to Dimitrios as he tracks him across archives and covert history, becoming semi-criminalized in the quest for the fascist antagonist. Pompey, in the move to the sanatorium in Germany, enters an intelligence fantasy world where patriotic drives meld into proto-fascist power play: in the spy drama of her madness, she stars herself as "pitted against a most inhuman enemy, with an answering swift increasing power in my veins" (Smith, *Over the Frontier*, 244). As the world was drawn towards the antifascist Second World War, spy fiction registered the gravitational pull of Nazi violence on the citizen imagination. Ambler had succeeded in translating the conservative genre into a left-wing mode of cultural history, an antifascist analytic tool. Smith revealed the psychoanalytic fantasy formations which the spy thriller could be used to explore. 1930s espionage fiction, in setting its sights on the fascist enemy within, the Dimitrios thug concealed within capitalist history, or the "swift increasing power" of Nazi drives in the unconscious, prepared the terrain for the Cold War thriller.

It is with this thick tradition behind it that one must read Cold War espionage fiction; as really about the survival of 1930s and wartime fears both of fascist infiltration of the imagination and of the undue influence of secret establishment power in the United Kingdom.[5] Those fears are melodramatized to a certain extent by the massive solidity and nuclear power of the Soviet enemy; and also by the rivalries and resentments fostered by the post-imperial special relationship with the new American superpower. But it is the aftermath of the Second World War which characterizes most if not all of the Cold War thrillers: as if the memories and emergencies of wartime were the secret state's cryptic origin and sanctioning matrix. Many espionage thriller writers had wartime experience of intelligence, and what characterizes the reminiscences of this work in their postwar writing is what one might call "emergency memories" in their espionage fictions, by which I mean memories which act as secret endorsements for the emergency actions of the postwar period. The effect of this is not a deliberately deceptive set of fictions, however. The reminiscences read as genuine accounts of the political imagination as generated by the Second World War because they uncover the emergency state logic secretly underpinning postwar power structures.

Graham Greene served as an intelligence officer in London and abroad during the war, and counted Kim Philby as an acquaintance. His postwar "entertainments," as he styled his genre writing, dwelled often on the war as nurturing treacherous bonds as well as secret state paranoia. *The Third Man* (1949) is set in the zoned city of Vienna, and thematizes the amorality of surviving wartime ideology in the underworld of a still ostensibly fascist Austria. This takes concrete form with Harry Lime, creature both of the sewers secretly connecting the zones and of the Prater Wheel, construct of a lofty totalitarian subject position ("Would you really feel any pity if one of those dots stopped moving?" asks Lime, gazing down on the Viennese below).[6] The sewers and wheel figure a dual form of political unconscious as both dirty underworld, where secret intelligence work takes place as racketeering, and Machiavellian vantage point, with a bomber's point of view. Tracking Lime to his lair from Prater wheel to the sewer zone, Holly Martins discovers his oldest friend has been soiled and polluted by fascist history. The penicillin racket that kills and maims so many children conjures the worst experiments of the Nazi regime, but here as a perverted form of American capitalism. Lime's dark machinations are a postwar translation of Nazi ruthlessness into carpetbagging backstreet trading: "If I said you could have twenty thousand pounds for every dot that stops, would you really, old man, tell me to keep my money without hesitation? Or would you calculate how many dots you could afford to spare? Free of income tax, old man. Free of income tax. . . . It's the only way to save nowadays."[7] Given the careful ways Greene sets up comparisons between Lime and the cynicism of the British policeman, Calloway, and the unacknowledged drives motivating good guy Martins with his lust for his dead friend's girl, the unsettling nightmare of Cold War Vienna is revealed as a war-scripted zone of dreams: the war memories are everywhere in the form of ruins. In a scene in the film, Martins visits the sinister Dr. Winkel's house: it is packed with creepy Catholic curios, as though a crypt had been rifled. Winkel is sinister because he resembles the doctor of nightmare, recalling the Nazi medics at the Nuremberg Doctors' Trial (which took place two years before Greene and Reed began work on the project).[8] His house, where Winkel diluted and distributed the stolen drugs, is a zone of stagy history, at once summoning the rooms of Nazi Germany full of goods stolen from the dead, and a museum preserving the cryptic icons of a looted past.

For Greene, the Second World War is a sewer crypt of secrets beneath Cold War streets, a bomber memory-formation generating destructive Machiavellian wishes in the gaze down on cities, and a museum of horrors and looted icons in the history rooms of the political imagination. And it is the intelligence operations of the secret state, whether in the form of Martins's quest for his brother enemy, Lime's own racketeering, or the police actions of Cold War powers at the border zones, which preserve the sewer system, turn History's wheel, and curate the museum in the name of national security. The fear of totalitarianism which was such a powerful force in the construction of Cold War ideology in the West, was a fear that Nazi and Stalinist ruthlessness and bureaucracy might transmigrate into the secret states within Western democracies. That fear plays itself out in an intelligence satire such as *The Third Man*: the movie makes manifest the sewer and Ferris wheel perspectives of post-fascist Machiavellianism, troping the "Id" and "superego" temptations of totalitarian politics within the Cold War citizen.

War Records and Postwar Espionage Fiction

The war records of many of the pulp fiction spy thriller writers are coded in to many of the works. Ian Fleming's work for Naval Intelligence, specifically running the Commando 30 Assault Unit during the war, lies behind the character of James Bond. A Royal Navy commander, and secret agent with a license to kill, Bond is "a compound of all the secret agents and commando types I met during the war," Fleming admitted[9] and at key moments in the novels Bond becomes pure Commando. For instance, Dr. No's experimental mode of death for Bond is an assault course which forces Bond to squeeze along pipe shafts with a knife between his teeth. Nicholas Rankin's book *Ian Fleming's Commandos* gives the story of 30 Assault Unit, set up by Fleming to "pinch" enemy technology. The miniature submarines and frogmen of *Thunderball* recall the unit's underwater operations in Italy. The Spektor coding machine in *From Russia with Love* is based on the Enigma ciphers stolen for Bletchley. *Moonraker*'s rocket scientists remember the Peenemünde V1 and V2 scientists tracked down by 30 Assault Unit at the end of the war.[10] It makes a difference to register how far the Cold War gadgets Bond is equipped with, and the evil genius technologies the Secret Service has to defeat, are in fact thinly disguised substitutions for the war effort against Nazi technology. Bond's evil twins are fascist power-hungry maniacs. Dr. No spouts *Mein Kampf*-like Machiavellian nonsense, obsessed with the totalitarian godlike powers that war economies gave Hitler and Stalin: "Who in the world had the power of life or death over his people? Now that Stalin is dead, can you name any man except myself?"[11] His science is overtly compared to Nazi concentration camp experiments, as he reminds Honey: "The German experiments on live humans during the war were of great service to science. It is a year since I put a girl to death in the fashion I have chosen for you, woman" (*Dr. No*, 665). What comes through, uneasily, however, are the resemblances between Bond's license to kill and Dr. No's Nazi-fueled power of life and death. That power is structured as a compound of rampant criminal capitalism (Dr. No's guano and arms brokering), lust for totalitarian power, and sadistic fantasies of lethal science. Bond has an erotic attachment to deadly technology too; the novel begins with him having to give up his beloved Beretta .25:

> The thought of his fifteen years' marriage to the ugly bit of metal. He remembered the times its single word had saved his life—and the times when its threat alone had been enough. He thought of the days when he had literally dressed to kill—when he had dismantled the gun and oiled it and packed the bullets carefully into the singleloaded magazine. (*Dr. No*, 551)

Fifteen years takes Bond in 1958 back to the war: he is dressed to kill in the Cold War because of this internalized bond to war technology, prompting dreams of the license to kill given to combatants in the Second World War.

Fantasies of Permissible Murder

Francis Clifford, the pseudonym of Arthur Bell Thompson, and author of the best-selling 1966 espionage thriller *The Naked Runner*, had fought behind enemy lines in Burma with Karen tribesmen, only escaping with his life after a 1,000-mile trek, a tale he tells in his war memoir, *Desperate Journey*. The hero of *The Naked Runner*, Sam Laker, is recruited as a Cold War spy by a Special Operations friend, Slattery, who is still in the game: and much of the novel turns on the ways "the permissible murder of war" continues into the postwar in the form of the violence sanctioned by secret state intelligence.[12] Laker travels to Leipzig as both a businessman going to the trade fair, and a "postman" for secret intelligence:[13] the trip is a rerun of his wartime Special Operations Executive operations in Germany during the war. Flying in a Czech plane with his son (soon to be kidnapped to blackmail him into becoming a sniper for the enemy), Laker can't stop remembering:

> It was impossible to block out the past. His first time to the Fair, yes; but he'd flown this way before, in cloudy moonlight, with a diversionary raid on Magdeburg to distract attention, and he suddenly remembered the dispatcher, a New Zealander, leaning back from the intercom and bawling: "Skipper says we've passed the Weser. Hanover to starboard. Two-fifteen and not a mouse stirring." (Clifford, *The Naked Runner*, 398)

Other situations trigger allusions to the Second World War: the text is full of recall trip wires. His cover blown, his son Patrick abducted, Laker is subjected to a mock-execution by the Stasi Hartmann in a pine forest eight miles outside the city designed to recall wartime killings. Laker in East Germany is perpetually on "the border-line of nightmare" (*The Naked Runner*, 420), and that nightmare is the sense of the easy killings of the Second World War recurring twenty years later: "Death and violence were commonplace when he had found it possible to kill. The whole world was at it then. But he had grown, learned to pity, acquired sentiment, was softened. Jesus, how could he go about it now—even for Patrick's sake?" (438). The choice between sacrifice of his son or becoming a Cold War assassin is itself a fantasy that reveals the secret ruthlessness inherited from wartime and buried as instinct within both ex-combatant and secret state. It turns out that Laker has been manipulated into killing his enemy Hartmann by the false news his son has been killed; but Hartmann is a double agent and the man he actually shoots is a defector. Hartmann's fascist antics in the pine forest are part of a complex *British* deception designed by Slattery to trigger the killer instinct learned in the war, as he tells Laker:

> "I haven't forgotten what you were like in Green Park that night during the war or the way you were when you got back from Gardelegen. No one who knew you in those days could ever forget. And we don't change, Sam—not underneath, not where it matters." (*The Naked Runner*, 530)

The night Slattery remembers is a couple of nights after Laker has learned his parents and sister have been killed by a flying bomb, when "sodden with whisky and hatred, he swore what he would do when they let him loose in Germany" (*The Naked Runner*, 375). The deception, tricking him into believing his son has been killed, is the trigger for the war frenzy that makes a sniper of him twenty years after the war. The stage management of the trigger mechanism, the borderline of nightmare, the replay of wartime killings through the distancing technology of the telescopic sights, the double identity of Hartmann, the close proximity of the deaths, son repeating parents and sister: the elaborate fiction is only partly about the ruthlessness of secret intelligence. More clearly, it is about the survival of war trauma into the postwar period in the form of fantasies of permissible murder, reprise of wartime hatreds and violent instincts let "loose in Germany," borderline states of hysterical repetition of war stories as dirty government lies, secrets, and deceptions. It concerns the ways in which the technology of the Second World War, like Bond's Beretta, and Laker's sniper rifle, become fetish objects that attract to themselves the complex of memory and instinct that constitutes the war's aftermath. The darkest drives of the mind as historically determined, the war hatred leveled at the enemies who have killed your family, survive the war in terms of spectral resemblances which dreamwork can revive if only in the form of the monstrous hoax of extreme prejudice. The Cold War was the Second World War fought at the level of the national security state's dark conspiracies, occupying the mind as a violent family romance:

> seeing a resemblance between that wartime gamble and this, that prolonged bout of murderous rage and this, gazing out on the country once openly trampled and fought over which was now the hunting-ground of backroom entrepreneurs who'd devised their stealthy games of blackmail and death, catch-as-catch-can, their own dirty laws, their own ethics. (*The Naked Runner*, 496)

Francis Clifford wrote his thrillers to try and compensate for the dark years of the war.[14] Those dark years are transposed and projected onto the secret state as stealthy games of family resemblances; in so doing, Clifford discovers some of the impetus driving, and contradictions shaping, the Cold War national security state as a construct of the Second World War.

Deception Intelligence Fiction

Muriel Spark worked for a deception intelligence outfit during the war, and its fabrications colored the way she thought about fiction-making in the postwar. She was drafted to work for Sefton Delmer's black propaganda radio broadcast project. Delmer had been German correspondent for the *Daily Express* and had been asked by the Political Warfare Executive to set up the black propaganda unit at Milton Bryan in order to mimic German radio broadcasts, and then weaken morale and sow confusion by speaking with the voice of disaffected and cynical patriots. For instance, the first station, Gustav Siegfried Eins (GS1), featured "Der Chef," a ruly, traditionalist Prussian whose complaints about the Nazis were designed to hit the right chords. Two further stations were set up when GS1 was disbanded (with Gestapo machine-gunning Der Chef "live" on radio): Soldier's Radio Calais and Atlantic Radio, with "Vicky," the sailor's sweetheart as false radiophonic friend and mock confidante. The broadcasts were beamed as though from Germany into occupied Europe using a powerful half-a-million-watt transmitter shipped over from America, nicknamed the "Biggest Aspidistra in the World!"[15] The black propaganda stories disseminated by the stations filtered down into both British and German ordinary people's beliefs, as Spark revealed in her autobiography, *Curriculum Vitae*. She quotes Delmer's own account of the unit, *Black Boomerang*, especially his strange defensive pride in having convinced the conspirators against Hitler that the Nazi hierarchy was in disarray: "I am sorry the generals ended their lives on Hitler's meat hooks. But I cannot say I have any compunction about having raised false hopes in them."[16] As Victoria Stewart has shown,[17] Muriel Spark explores the ethical problems involved in the war work, specifically the deception and inhabiting of Nazi subject positions, in the strange dramatization of the Milton Bryan story in *The Hothouse of the East River*.

In the novel, the characters are lost in a hyperreal fantasy of 1970s New York, are ghosts reliving and endlessly exploring their wartime up to their destruction by a V-2 bomb. The ghosts spookily act out their past as spooks at "the Compound," elaborated into a spy thriller story once one of the anti-Nazi Germans who worked for the unit is spotted mysteriously walking the New York streets. Elsa and her entourage play out a 1940s novelette of adultery and espionage as though locked into a parody of spy fiction. The Helmut–Elsa–Paul triangle repeats itself as if in traumatic dream recall, an acting out which bears the traces of always having happened before, with some eerie suspicion of treacherous (and postmodern) faked-up performance. The end of the war was a watershed, but it left the postwar survivors and new generations with an obscure triple relation to the victims of the war, the novel could be said to be arguing: partly the traumatic compulsion to remember them, just as Elsa and Paul learn to wind their New York stories back to the events of 1944; partly an envy of the radical life lived by men and women during the war ("In the summer of 1944, [Paul] is telling his son, life was more vivid than it is now");[18] and partly a difficult acknowledgment of how the postwar period is haunted, still, by the measures taken during the war.

For what Elsa, Paul, and Helmut are engaged in at the Compound is "black propaganda and psychological warfare" which involves a mimicking of fascist beliefs to the point of infection: "the propagation of the Allied point of view under the guise of the German point of view [entailing] a tangled mixture of damaging lies, flattering and plausible truths" (*Hothouse*, 52). This is the state of mind Elsa and Paul are stuck in after the war, in a dead afterlife of damaging lies and flattering, plausible truths, based on points of view tangled up with the enemy's. Their deaths in 1944 have not put paid to the habits learned by Anglo-American culture during the war. The lies and half-truths of the war survive, Spark's ethical allegory implies, in the damaging pop psychology of psychoanalysis, in the advertising dreams of commodity culture, in the vulgar, self-seeking and godless hatreds between members of the nuclear family. The covert anti-Americanism of the book senses relations between the empty postmodernism of the postwar metropolis and the lying propaganda invented by fascism to subdue and seduce a dream-rapt populace. As Victoria Stewart has argued, the novel stages the doubts and subterfuges of postmodern fiction as a creature of wartime black propaganda: "Gaps between what is thought and what is said, uncertainty about the consequences of one's actions, and the need for the reader to interpret on scant evidence: all these characteristics seem suited to a novel dealing with wartime propaganda" (Stewart, *Second World War in Contemporary British Fiction*, 47). The roots of Spark's own fictionalizing skills point back to the black propaganda work of the Second World War, and their "infection" by the Nazi ideology they were forced to mimic so well to get their subversive job done. The dubiety of espionage and black propaganda has infiltrated fiction-making itself. The invention of character, the construction of cover story, the mimicking of the "enemy," the subterfuge of plot trails, fake evidence, red herrings, the fictionalization of "true" stories, the fabrication of beliefs, and the raising of false hopes: all these staple elements of espionage fiction, and indeed of Sparkian fiction more generally, recall Delmer's ingenuities, his black arts of persuasion, the grim lack of compunction about the suffering caused. Cold War postmodernism is in many ways an exploration of the relations between the networks of simulacra late modernity creates and the systems of persuasion fabricated in the wartime information wars. The black hole at the heart of postwar culture is a shadow cast by those intelligence operations.

Two further considerations can be understood from Spark's foray into the espionage thriller genre: one to do with the "special relationship" (Churchill's term for the bond between the United Kingdom and the United States) as a product of the war; and the other with communications technology as an uncanny channel for anxieties about the national security state. The iconic image that dominates the book of Elsa looking down on New York from her skyscraper apartment, with her little cloud of unknowing at her feet, is a fine remake of the Harry Lime Prater Wheel point of view. Elsa gazes down on the city from Olympian heights, queen of all she surveys. The image can serve as icon for the new surveillance powers generated by wartime secret intelligence and military technologies, and bearing fruit in the National Security Act of 1947. The allegorical hinted drama of Spark's novel links black propaganda operations in the United Kingdom to the Olympian power of surveillance of the new superpower. That link is thematized by the novel's scripting of the special relationship as the exchange of British intelligence savvy (Milton Bryan and its psywar box of tricks) for American wealth and goods. Paul and Elsa's wealth and elegance as high society specters in 1970s New York is a wry parodic survival of the glamorized envy of America in wartime Britain, a vision of commodity riches like the presents Paul brought back from his secret trip to the United States in 1944, "all unobtainable in England": "One by one they were looked at and smiled over and gasped about" (*Hothouse*, 123). How that pans out is through a mystification of the technology of communications and surveillance:

Elsa and her fellow spooks remain as ghosts in the machine generated by the black ops radio war, voices, and fabricated characters emanating from scripts written in the Second World War and still reverberating into the Cold War. America may be NATO ally and brother in arms; spectrally, however, to the political imagination of the postwar United Kingdom, the new national security state which is governing all citizens in the West, with an Olympian power of surveillance and propaganda, is haunted by the wartime stories speaking of those powers as *British* dark arts. For the Office of Strategic Services (OSS) and the body it became in 1947, the CIA, were created by William J. Donovan specifically according to British models he had learned to respect during the war when stationed in London.[19] The first headquarters of the Coordinator of Information, then OSS, was in New York, Room 3603 of Rockefeller Center, the former offices of MI6. It was there that the British Security Coordination under Sir William Stephenson taught the Americans everything the British knew about secret intelligence, counterespionage, and special operations. Elsa's apartment looks out onto Welfare Island, now Roosevelt Island, which housed the asylums of New York: very close to the United Nations building, it is also only blocks away from Rockefeller Center, with its famous "top of the rock" panoramic and panoptical view over Manhattan. The skyscraper perspective of the national security state is a Prater Wheel deranged dream of the world, still ghosted by the security coordinations of British wartime. At the heart of the crazy plot of *Hothouse* is the adultery triangle circling round Keil, the double agent and secret Nazi: as though the whole security of the world, from the United Kingdom to the United States to the United Nations, was always already infected by the Nazi propaganda and surveillance systems that wartime "black" intelligence operations were designed to outwit. British dark arts in the postwar period, as registered by Spark's uncanny fictionalizing of the political unconscious, are hardly distinguishable from the Nazi propaganda machine and secret state.

The Thriller and the Children of the War

The next generation of espionage fiction writers were children during the war, and in many ways their writing exemplifies a special form of postwar memory wherein war stories are channeled to the child writers' experiences so deeply as to seem to constitute memory systems they have access to as writers of fiction. Len Deighton and John le Carré were born in the early 1930s and so took in the war as boys. Deighton witnessed the arrest of the German spy, Anna Wolkoff, who had lived next door to his family's house in Marylebone.[20] As a seventeen-year old, he worked for the RAF's Special Investigation Branch as a photographer. The war looms large in everything Deighton wrote, from straight war history with *Blitzkrieg*, through *Bomber* and the alternative history *SS-GB*.[21] Le Carré spent the war at a public school paid for by his con-man of a father before doing his national service in Vienna with the Army Intelligence Corps. He spent his time there, as he has said in interview, "strolling through the displaced-persons camps, looking for people who were fake refugees, or for people whose circumstances were so attractive to us from an intelligence point of view that we might consider returning them, with their consent, to the countries they came from. For a person of, as I was then, barely twenty-one, it was an immense responsibility at an extraordinary moment in history, which, horrible as it was, I was very pleased to have shared."[22] He later worked for MI5 and MI6 in the early 1960s, spending some years in Germany, and in many ways his early thrillers blend the sinister refugee camp stories with Cold War intelligence tales to create a historical critique of the weakened security state of the postwar United Kingdom. For both Deighton and le Carré, the spy thriller is a space to confront the fascist core within the national security state, dark remnant of the Second World War.

Le Carré's 1963 *The Spy Who Came in from the Cold*, published while he was still working for MI6 in Germany, has a clear subtext: its plot concerns the secret and unholy Cold War alliance of the British secret service with ex-fascists in the struggle against German communism. Double agent and head of the East German intelligence service Mundt wants Liz Gold killed along with Fiedler—both Jewish. If for Haydon in *Tinker, Tailor, Soldier, Spy* the secret services are "the only real measure of a nation's political health, the only real expression of its subconscious," then the secret of secrets is the "subconscious" fascism at the core of the British establishment (*Tinker, Tailor*, 407). Leamas is spirited into East Germany as a fake defector, and the view of the airport reminds him of the war, all the "machines, half hidden in the fog" and "everywhere the air of conspiracy."[23] As with Clifford's *The Naked Runner*, two plots are running simultaneously: one where Leamas is in control of the plot with a view to incriminating Mundt; the other, where he is a pawn in a game to incriminate Fiedler and rehabilitate Mundt. He is asked by Control to act the traitor to fulfill the requirements of the first fiction. Once in Germany, he discovers that the secrets he has to betray under interrogation and trial take on ghastly reality once the tables are turned: Liz and Fiedler are sacrificed and he is destroyed by the revelation. The recall of the war in the machines and atmosphere of conspiracy at the airport become actualized in the interrogations, trial, and death. The two colossi of the story are the Circus and the Centre, two security states threatening the Cold War citizen on either side of the Iron Curtain. Liz and Leamas die on the Berlin Wall, at the exact demarcation line between the two enemies, acting out a nightmare of citizenship in the newly emergent national security state. The panoptical gaze of the state is figured in "the beam of the searchlight" in the last chapter—"the watchtower's searchlight began feeling along the wall towards them" (*The Spy*, 217). The whole journey to the Wall is one taken through systems of interrogation and fake justice, but also through intelligence archives: the photostat minutes analyzed by Leamas, the Praesidium minutes, the COMECON draft, and so on. Leamas as fantasy Cold War citizen is subjected to the nightmare of a post-Nazi bureaucracy and information state, locked into the systems and archives that preserve a fascist potential at its control center in the form of the monstrous Mundt. Le Carré's experience of the displaced-persons camps in postwar Austria is staged in this allegory of complicity through pseudo-denazification in Germany.[24] Mundt's anti-semitism figures the victimizing forces at the heart of the security state.

The double interpretation necessitated by the plot enacts the turn back to the Second World War and postwar memory of Nazi Germany: readers must first dismiss Fiedler's view of the links between Mundt and Karl as we believe him to have been taken in by British deception intelligence—but later when we realize Mundt *is* a British agent, then Fiedler's case becomes *retrospectively valid*. That retrospective validity is a historicizing move that uncovers a direct line back from the Berlin of the Wall to the Nazi city. This becomes most clear not in Fiedler's arguments, though, but in the Kafkaesque trial, where the witness stand nightmare suffered by Liz Gold plays out a totalitarian theater of political anxiety. The "they" that sit and watch in judgment are creatures of citizen paranoia as an internalized form of security state terror: "All the time they were listening, watching, waiting for a word, a gesture, perhaps, that could do terrible harm to Alec" (*The Spy*, 184). Memories of wartime persecution haunt the courtroom as the paranoia draws inwards toward Orwellian dread at the silent totalitarian prosecutor of the political unconscious:

> There was a terrible silence in the courtroom, more terrible to Liz because like a blind child among the seeing she was cut off from all those around her; they could measure her answers against some secret standard, and she could not know from the dreadful silence what they had found. (*The Spy*, 187)

Zeroing in on East Germany, the Cold War espionage thriller writers could reflect on the aftermath of the war as Nazi postwar memory coded into security state systems, the archives and covert law-enforcement and intelligence-gathering structures and institutions that originated in wartime.

Cold War Thriller and the War Dead

A similar geopolitical logic runs through Len Deighton's 1964 *Funeral in Berlin*. It also looks to the Wall as a seemingly solid and monolithic structure dividing West from East, yet as with *The Spy Who Came in from the Cold* (and with the sewers in *The Third Man*), the fixed border becomes a fluid zone of crossings and secret communications, as well as a historical zone of contact with Second World War tropes and memories. The anonymous hero is as suspicious of Gehlen and Hallam as he is of Stok and the KGB, and it soon becomes clear that it is the identity of Vulkan which is key to the political enigma. Vulkan begins as a Harry Lime figure, contemptuous of the British, but is revealed as a faked-up Nazi war criminal. The Cold War may be frozen into the Wall, but the real war is a mess of crowded and conflicting bodies, Soviet, British, French, West and East German, Israeli, and Egyptian intelligence operatives, all turning round the fascist continuities issuing from the Second World War.

The plot turns on an elaborate scheme to smuggle the "dead" body of a Soviet defector through the Berlin Wall. The Wall is countered and rendered fluid by the elaborate coffin scam and dead body, as though figuring the circumvention of Cold War structures by deeper levels of dead history and deception. And as the "Harry Palmer" hero investigates, he discovers that the two Cold War cities of London and Berlin lead to another: Prague, and a war story that will reveal the true identity of Broum. Prague is Kafka's city of the Jewish ghetto, in the communist zone, but also a space of wartime history, dominated by the list of death camps (given in chapter 35). The backstory of the Broum alias takes both Stok and "Harry" back into Nazi history, the dark secret underpinning Cold War Europe. The real enemy is the secret fascism within every state. The CIA operative in Prague, Harvey, is spokesman for this recognition:

> Harvey said "Fascists," quietly. He looked around. "There is a deal of semantic confusion around that word. A sort of implied, inbuilt suggestion that there is a special counter-productive network of every bully, crook, swindler, rapist and short-order artist in the world confronting the gentle, honest, helpful, long-suffering, scholarly underpaid remainder." Harvey swayed slightly and tapped his chest violently. "Fascism is something in here. Right here in everyone in the world." Stok and the Czech officer were looking at Harvey in surprise.[25]

Vulkan turns out to have been a concentration camp guard whose identity had been assumed after his assassination by a wealthy prisoner, Broum, collaborating with a Nazi camp doctor. Fascist history is "right here" in the dark heart of all citizens, operating at the heart of European security systems. Like the secret Nazi room which is a cover for the Egyptian surveillance of the Israeli agent Steel, the covert environment is where fascism is both disguise, remnant, and secret motive. In many ways, the anonymous British agent is waging a fantasy war through the double perspective of Cold War and Second World War politics; the Cold War is a chess game of ethical crimes and their punishment for the hero (chess advice figures at the head of each chapter): he gets the fascist Gehlen operatives killed; he destroys the fascist Vulkan/Broum; he punishes Steel; and he judges the Stalinist communists whilst admiring the antifascist communists. The Cold War, in other words, is for "Harry

Palmer" at least, a continuation of the antifascist struggle of the Second World War. This is made clear in an odd plot diversion which sees the counterintelligence operative track Vulkan and Samantha Steel to Bordeaux: he tips off French intelligence and both are arrested after Vulkan makes a mysterious trip to meet a man across the Spanish border. He turns out to be Ernst Mohr, the doctor in the concentration camp who'd helped him assume the concentration camp guard identity. Deighton presents Mohr's background in the form of a case file:

> Captured Hamburg 1945. Witness at British Army War Crimes Inquiry Hamburg 1946 (ref. 275/Crime/nn). Released to work British military hospital 1946. Released to work in German civilian hospital 1946. Under contract to Bonn Government (Intelligence, not Gehlen) 1948. Began work as representative radium therapy machine 1948. Assigned to Northern Spain as radium therapy machinery 1949. (*Funeral in Berlin*, 140)

Deighton cryptically fashions a small-scale political history here which establishes the coded relations, at the "subconscious" level of secret case file information, between war crimes in Nazi-occupied territory during the war, denazification deals in the immediate postwar period, and the continued presence of fascism in Europe with Mohr's Cold War-inflected business (the radium therapy machine) in Franco's Spain. Mohr and Vulkan meet at the border between fascist and non-fascist states and are themselves enmeshed in machinations crisscrossing major intelligence information systems—Vulkan/Broum is being tracked by the British, the French, the Israeli, the Stasi, and Soviet intelligence services, as victim/killer/fascist/capitalist/collaborator amalgam coded into the shadowy systems of emergency Europe.

Deighton's style achieves a merger of techniques that help gear the narrative into memory mode. The noir and hard-boiled register and delivery gives a 1940s texture.[26] The case file structure of the chapters makes the reading experience archival. The point-of-view switches cede narrative control every so often away from the British perspective: so we have chapters delivered by Vulkan (chapter 10); Jan-im-Glück (chapter 32); Stok (chapter 34); and Hannah Stahl (chapter 43). These act as secret storytelling intrusions into the memories of the more ambiguous geopolitical figures of the text, and these merge with the chapters which are set out as files: the Broum request (chapter 9), the Mohr file (chapter 29), as well as the appendixes. All this textual play serves as a nest for the key wartime stories at the heart of the secrets—Jan's and Josef's and Vulkan's stories. The book, like the security state, is a set of files, stories, investigations which harbor as emergency memory wartime stories that are at once originatory (source for all shape-shifting deceptions and identity shifts of the postwar period) and non-assimilable. For their force and horror twist and distort the Cold War plot and present time into empty duplication of the lethal stories of the war. The Cold War is figured by Deighton as a field of memories of past wartime deaths, and generating deaths in the postwar aftermath as ritual and covert repetitions of those deaths. Death and the war dead haunt the novel's climatic scenes: with the Berlin funeral of the man who died in the war; the Guy Fawkes bonfire scene where the English traitor, collaborator with fascism and dark capital, attempts to murder the anonymous hero; and the final scene at the Cenotaph.

The novel does not leave it at that, however. The Second World War is not simply an imaginary field of violent drives within the security state. It is also the source of a very material relationship between wartime atrocities and Cold War weapon systems. The appendix on the covert use of poisonous insecticides as bioweapons states: "The films and the research came into Allied hands during the war and the research continued by UK, USSR and USA and still continues to be important as a military weapon."[27] The very material way the insecticide is weaponized—"two tiny harmless amounts get together and make a lethal combination" (Deighton, *Funeral in Berlin*, 299)—not only stands as a trope for the relationship of postwar to war memory, as well as between Cold War security states, but as a real and material fact about the transmission of lethal technologies. The Second World War bequeathed to the postwar world killing technologies that equipped the secret state and military-industrial complex with the tools, both material-technological and discursive, to discipline dissentient populations, and to occupy each security state citizen with a death-entranced imagination, hallucinating Second World War destruction as a postwar memory of cenotaphs, bonfires, and concentration camp nightmares.

Notes

1. John le Carré, *Tinker, Tailor, Soldier, Spy* (London: Sceptre, [1974] 2009), 407.

2. Nicholas Hiley, "Counter-Espionage and Security in Great Britain During the First World War," *The English Historical Review* 101, no. 400 (1986): 635–70. See also Nicholas Hiley, "Decoding German Spies: British Spy Fiction 1908–18," *Intelligence and National Security* 5, no. 4 (1990): 55–79.

3. Giorgio Agamben, *State of Exception*, trans. Kevin Attell (Chicago: University of Chicago Press, 2005).

4. Graham Greene's thug villains in *Brighton Rock* and *A Gun for Sale* are clearly in this tradition of internal fascists.

5. For work on espionage fiction in the Cold War period, see John Atkins, *The British Spy Novel: Styles in Treachery* (London: OneWorld, 1984); Michael Denning, *Cover Stories: Narrative and Ideology in the British Spy Thriller* (London: Taylor and Francis, 1987); Alex Goody, *Technology, Literature and Culture* (London: Polity, 2012); Christoph Lindner, *The James Bond Phenomenon: A Critical Reader* (Manchester: Manchester University Press, 2003); Lars Ole Sauerberg, *Secret Agents in Fiction: Ian Fleming, John le Carré and Len Deighton* (London: Macmillan, 1984); and Allan Hepburn, *Intrigue: Espionage and Culture* (New Haven, Conn.: Yale University Press, 2005).

6. *The Third Man* (London Film, 1949), dir. Carol Reed. The novella was written as a treatment for the movie.

7. Graham Greene, *The Third Man and the Fallen Idol* (London: Vintage Classics, 2005), 81. The film script can be accessed here: http://www.aellea.com/script/the_third_man.txt.

8. Robert Jay Lifton connects Nazi doctors in the Holocaust to "the nuclear technology of genocide which now haunts us all." Robert Jay Lifton, *The Nazi Doctors: Medical Killing and the Psychology of Genocide* (New York: Basic Books, [1986] 2000), 503.

9. Quoted in Ben Macintyre, *For Your Eyes Only: Ian Fleming and James Bond* (London: Bloomsbury, 2008), 50.

10. See Nicholas Rankin, *Ian Fleming's Commandos: The Story of 30 Assault Unit in WWII* (London: Faber and Faber, 2011).

11. Ian Fleming, *Dr. No* (1958), in *Great Spy Stories* (London: Sundial Publications, 1978), 651.

12. Francis Clifford, *The Naked Runner* (1966), in *Great Spy Stories*, 374.

13. The compromised contact is a woman called Karen Gisevius, her name a compound both of the Burmese people Clifford fought with during the war and of the only anti-Nazi conspirator in the plot to kill Hitler to survive the war.

14. He became a Catholic on reading Graham Greene; his obituary in the *Catholic Herald* stated: "He said a sort of melancholy lay at the base of his urge to write. 'I am driven by an inward despair at myself and at the world,' he said. He began writing after the Second World War because he felt unsettled after his experiences and wanted 'to find out what I thought.'" http://archive.catholicherald.co.uk/article/5th-september-1975/3/novelist-francis-clifford-dies-at-58.

15. See Robert Rowen, "Grey and Black Propaganda Against Nazi Germany," New York Military Affairs Symposium, http://bobrowen.com/nymas/radioproppaper.htm.

16. Muriel Spark, *Curriculum Vitae: A Volume of Autobiography* (New York: New Directions [1992] 2011), 146.

17. Victoria Stewart, *The Second World War in Contemporary British Fiction: Secret Histories* (Edinburgh: Edinburgh University Press, 2011).

18. Muriel Spark, *The Hothouse of the East River* (Harmondsworth, Eng.: Penguin, 1973), 29.

19. Donovan's plan for the CIA and the national security state it would be housed within was prepared in 1944, the year of the V2 blast that kills the Compound characters.

20. "One night, I leaned from the window to see our next door neighbour Mrs. Wolkoff being arrested. My mother worked for her as a cook and saw the VIPs she had as dinner guests. Dear old Anna was an important spy working for the Germans. After a trial at the Old Bailey she went to prison." Deighton interview with Mike Ripley, 2008, http://deightondossier.blogspot.co.uk/2009/06/origins-of-fascination-with-espionage.html.

21. As Deighton remarks in his preface to *SS-GB*: "I remembered London in wartime: the dimly lit streets, gas lights that hissed and spluttered, tin baths in front of the fire, rationing that made food a constant subject of thought and conversation, and bombed homes that spewed their intimate household contents into the streets." Len Deighton, *SS-GB* (London: HarperCollins, [1978] 2009), vi–vii.

22. John le Carré, interview with George Plimpton, *The Art of Fiction* 149 (Summer 1997): 14, http://www.theparisreview.org/interviews/1250/the-art-of-fiction-no-149-john-le-carr.

23. John le Carré, *The Spy Who Came in from the Cold* (London: Coronet Books, [1963] 1990), 65.

24. East and West Germany of course dealt very differently with the Nazi past: denazification procedures and failures are specific to the ideologies of the occupation forces/regimes in place at the time. See Perry Biddiscombe, *The Denazification of Germany: A History, 1945–1950* (Stroud: Tempus, 2007); and Frederick Taylor, *Exorcising Hitler: The Occupation and Denazification of Germany* (London: Bloomsbury, 2011).

25. Len Deighton, *Funeral in Berlin* (London: Grafton [1964] 1978), 171–72. It was made, as the first of a series, into a 1966 film starring Michael Caine as Harry Palmer.

26. For studies linking noir to the war and immediate postwar aftermath, see James Naremore, *More Than Night: Film Noir in Its Contexts* (Berkeley: University of California Press, 2008); and Sheri Chinen Biesen, *Blackout: World War II and the Origins of Film Noir* (Baltimore: Johns Hopkins University Press, 2005).

27. This story of bioweapons research parallels the ways nuclear technology was secured by the United States in Operation Paperclip. To state this so clearly, in 1964, years before historical novels like Joseph Kanon's *The Good German* or Philip Kerr's Bernie Gunther series turned critical attention to the ways Nazi science was incorporated into postwar military systems, is a tribute to Deighton's clarity of political analysis and research.

PETRA RAU

"Knowledge of the Working of Bombs"
The Strategic Air Offensive in Rhetoric and Fiction

> Never believe the statement that a nation's character is purified by trial. It is simply not true.
> —BRYHER, *The Days of Mars*

Much of the popular memory in Britain is taken up with narratives and images of *being bombed*, notably of the Blitz of 1940–41 and the little Blitz of 1944, with London taking center stage over the provincial towns and coastal cities. The German bombing raids affected very particular areas within a clearly defined interval, but being bombed is commonly regarded as the most important experience of total war on the British home front; it holds a synecdochal place in the collective memory, not least because it celebrates national virtues (resilience, stoicism, humor) while also acknowledging civilian suffering. By contrast, even recent academic studies of the representation of bombardment such as Leo Mellor's *Reading the Ruins* (2012) pay little attention to bombing by the British.[1] In other words, it is the metropolitan ruin that is being critically read rather than the Continental one. To be fair, cinematic and literary representation of Britain's share in the bombing was not ample, and much falls under the heading of propaganda. Wartime films such as Ealing's *The Big Blockade* (1942) and the documentary *Target for Tonight* (1941) sustained the fallacy of precision bombing at a time when less than a quarter of planes even got within five miles of a target.[2] Alexander Korda's short propaganda film *The Biter Bit* (1943) included footage of bombed German cities, but has never been shown on British TV, nor is it released on DVD.[3] *The Way to the Stars* (1945), based on Terence Rattigan's play *Flare Path*, focused on bombing as an Anglo-American effort and a dangerous mission, but it is set on an air base and neighboring village, much like the bestselling fiction written about bomber crews at the time, notably Nevil Shute's *Pastoral* (1944) and H. E. Bates's stories in *The Greatest People in the World* (1942) and *How Sleep the Brave* (1943). The actual bombing happens offstage, as it were. In much wartime fiction and film, British bombs literally have no direct impact, that is, they are hardly ever seen to land and explode. This representational gap, as we shall see, would help shape the lack of cultural engagement with the Allied bombing campaign in the postwar period.

In this essay I am concerned with the reasons why the memory of the Blitz has overwritten any wider cultural awareness of the bombing of Germany; why bombing does not easily fit into the hegemonic narrative of Britain at war. Only two British novels, Len Deighton's *Bomber* (1970) and A. L. Kennedy's *Day* (2007), have engaged with the moral complexity of the Strategic Air Offensive over Germany. Both manage the tightrope walk between empathy with aircrew and a more skeptical point of view about state-sanctioned violence and popular memory. Kennedy in particular delivers a caustic verdict on that archive of popular memory, the 1950s war film, by turning her protagonist, the former rear gunner Alfred Day, into an extra on a film set where he can witness how badly his real wartime experiences translate into cinematic storytelling. These books suggest a trans-generational shift away from an almost hegemonic narrative strongly informed by wartime propaganda and wartime rhetoric, away from heroism and national unity towards trauma, moral doubt, and social tension. *Bomber* and *Day* indicate a change in sensibility about war in general and bombing in particular: for Deighton, a more comprehensive perspective—one that includes the enemy's experience—is crucial to understand this war. Almost four decades later, Kennedy is also concerned with the traumatic impact of war on veterans whose experiences have no place in the popular narrative of that war. For both writers, fictionalizing the bombing of Germany is also a way of thinking about the controversial conflicts of their own time—Vietnam and Iraq. These novels, then, offer a critical commentary on the importance of popular memory (and its gaps) for shaping political attitudes towards subsequent conflicts.

The Uneasy Path to Bombing: Unruly Colonials, Bouncing Bombs, Heroic Airmen

The bomber has no long and honorable national tradition such as the navy, which also has a peacetime and merchant component and can be used defensively. Bombing stands outside the tropes of chivalric combat that were extended, during the Battle of Britain, to the lone fighter pilot fending off attacks on the homeland. On the contrary, bombing was initially seen as an unequivocally aggressive act and as the next step in the escalation of modern warfare; fear of it caused great anxiety in the interwar years.[4] However, this anxiety only applied to its use by a perceived proximate enemy. As David E. Omissi has argued, when the British themselves resorted to bombing, notably in colonial territory in Africa and the Middle East, this was rhetorically presented as a defensive strategy: "police bombing" or "morale bombing" quelled unrest and tamed unruly natives; qualms about the indiscriminate destruction of bombs that could hardly distinguish between hostile forces and noncombatant civilians were brushed aside by redefining civilians as combatants or by impugning "collective guilt."[5] Resistance to bombing via tactical adaptations, ground artillery—biplanes proved highly susceptible to rifle fire—as well as resorting to natural and underground shelters already caused some doubt about the efficacy of bombing when it was practiced in the colonies. Yet the most potent argument for such pacifying measures was their cost-effectiveness over the deployment of huge land armies in lengthy campaigns and expensive occupations. Bombing as strategic "air policing," particularly in Iraq, ostensibly ensured the survival of the Royal Air Force (RAF) after the First World War (Omissi, *Air Power and Colonial Control*, 211). As we shall see, the justifications given for bombing then—the morally inferior state of the enemy, the collective guilt of the population and their wholesale involvement in colonial resistance (or the war effort), the economic aspects of bombing—prefigure the arguments that would be marshaled from 1942 onwards to legitimize the "morale bombing" of German cities. This has little to do, I would argue, with any similarity between unruly colonials and citizens of the Third Reich; rather, it tells us something about the way in which the British Empire rationalized the use of air power.

Not everyone took care to couch air power in ideologically palatable terms. Stanley Baldwin's statement on bombing in an address to the House of Commons in 1932 was unashamedly blunt but encapsulated the logic that justified this strategy: "The bomber will always get through. . . . The only defence is in offence. You have to kill more women and children more quickly than the enemy if you want to save yourselves."[6] Baldwin's lack of distinction between incidental and deliberate casualties would be deeply distressing to most civilized people; he certainly offended the RAF at the time. It was also a harbinger of the kind of highly technological modern warfare of the future in which blunt talk of "women and children" would have to be replaced with the obfuscations of "collateral damage."

Bombing required considerable moral and rhetorical agility before it became acceptable as a strategy. The nightly raids over Germany caused tremendous losses for the RAF—47,268 crew killed in action or as POWs and 8,195 in accidents[7]—and subjected flyers to intense flak fire and attacks from Luftwaffe fighter planes. Both the physical and psychological strain on these very young men was severe. Focusing on the crew of technicians who manned the bombers and turning them into the homosocial nation in miniature was the only available strategy to lend this military practice a human and heroic face. It shifted attention away from the lethal cargo and from the victims on the ground onto the peril of the mission and the crew's technical skills. It is the bombs that do the killing; the crew merely fly the plane.

In the postwar films about bombing, *The Dam Busters* (1955) and *663 Squadron* (1964), the strain of these risky missions is consistently emphasized while "women and children," and civilians in general, are curiously absent. *The Dam Busters* presents the destruction of the Ruhr dams with a bouncing bomb as a feat of precision engineering and ingenuity; with its rousing anthem, it remains an afternoon staple on British TV screens (a slot reserved for senior citizens). Yet it is the exceptionality of this mission—the accuracy with which the bomb was dropped on an industrial installation—that makes bombing palatable in this instance.

The film can enter popular memory because it offers a sanitized version of war: it is essential that no "women and children" die on screen. They don't die in museum displays either. In the summer of 1998, the cultural historian Sven Lindqvist traveled around England to see how museums represented Bomber Command. In all the places he visited, from the Imperial War Museum and the RAF Museum in Hendon to small private institutions, he found that not a single exhibit acknowledged what bombing had done to people on the ground. If the displays showed damage, this concerned industrial installations, thus giving the impression of effective precision bombing.[8] The lack of attention to the civilian victims of bombing is also evident in the official four-volume history of the bombing campaign published in 1961. Among over a hundred pages of tables, lists, and statistics documenting cities bombed, tonnage of bombs dropped, percentage of "built-up area (target)" destroyed, there is not a single German corpse to disrupt all these orderly numbers, although the Federal Statistical Office in Wiesbaden could have provided a conservative figure untainted by Dr. Goebbels's propaganda (figures range from 350,000 to 600,000 dead).

It is hard not to think of these silences and gaps as symptoms of an *ongoing* moral discomfort with the bombing campaign (a discomfort that certainly informed the mixed responses to the memorial to the dead of Bomber Command, erected in London's Green Park in 2012).[9] The campaign's efficacy was disputed among politicians and military commanders, and has remained contentious, not least because of the fabulous claims made by Bomber Command's commander-in-chief, Sir Arthur Harris, who wished to prove the value of his service against rival claims from the army and navy.[10] At the time, the moral opposition to bombing among the British public was given voice by a tiny articulate minority, notably Bishop Bell of Chichester, the military theorist B. H. Liddell Hart, pacifists such as Vera Brittain, author of *Seeds of Chaos* (1944),[11] and the MP for Ipswich, Major Sir Richard Stokes, who asked probing questions in the House of Commons. Mass Observation, too, noted increased discomfort about bombing over the period of the war, particularly among women, but no overt objections.[12] The bombing campaign enjoyed at least the tacit consent of the British public but as we shall see, the *feelings* underlying this consent could not be meaningfully integrated into the national narrative of the British at war.

The Language of Bombing: Prangs, Whirlwinds, and Mere Acts of Terror

Deighton's unprecedented achievement in *Bomber* lies in representing the bombing campaign from both sides: the men flying these nightly missions and the German civilians on the ground. It took twenty-five years for a British novelist to describe the comprehensive impact of bombing German cities: the horrific manner in which airmen died; the equally horrific inferno on the ground; the shortcomings of technology to identify targets and the consequences of navigational errors; the trauma of the survivors. His style is consistently realist, not least to counter wartime rhetoric, and he does not lose much time leading up to the controversy. The first chapter includes a conversation between the crew and an émigré civilian about the missions; this introduces some of the key characters via their attitude towards bombing. Lambert, the skipper, does not need post-operational photographs to realize that city centers hardly accommodate heavy industry or workers' housing, but he knows that that evidence is available to anyone who cares to look at it. Flight Lieutenant Sweet, an arrogant and mendacious careerist and Lambert's rival, has not only failed to grasp the relationship between target and casualty numbers but simply does not care about it. His euphemism for the mission is to "put a little salt on Hitler's tail."[13] The public school–educated, upper-middle-class Sweet and the cricket-obsessed Group Commander are Deighton's indictment of the British class system. Sweet and the Group Commander on the air base are part of a social stratum for whom "killing Huns" (*Bomber*, 311) and playing cricket are on the same level of importance, but it is refusal to serve the team in the latter skill that incurs blackmail and demotion. *Bomber* moves away from the focus on middle-class officers that characterized 1950s films such as *The Dam Busters*, *Angels One Five*, or even *The Way to the Stars*. They stay closer to John Boulting's *Journey Together* (1945) in their emphasis on the social diversity of Bomber Command crews and their technical competence.[14] In Deighton's novel, Sweet becomes the mouthpiece of wartime propaganda, not because he is stupid but because spouting such phrases produces a safe "official" position with his men and his superiors alike, a position he hopes will secure his future.

It is worth dwelling for a moment on the language of bombing, not least because one of its functions is to cloak the tremendous violence it unleashes. Alfred Day, Kennedy's rear gunner, adopts the phrase of a putative French commando he encounters pranking with an explosive:

> "You have knowledge of the working of bombs? I am trained in bombs." . . .
> *But you don't talk about death.*
> *You only ever say you have a knowledge of the working of bombs.*
> (*Day*, 201; 203)

The foreigner's unidiomatic phrase, both too vague and too formal, focuses on the means of war, its science, its technology, rather than its result or its use. The later repetition in italics, the focalization of Day's memory, knowingly appropriates this wording because it screens off reality: someone who has a knowledge of bombs is not necessarily a bomber. Military personnel, of course, develop their own slang for violence inflicted ("a good prang!") and suffered ("Gone for a Burton") and weapons of destruction (a 4,000-pound bomb becomes a "cookie"), not least to cope with the tremendous strain of dangerous missions and the fear of death. The ostensibly nonchalant attitude to violence and destruction is less an expression of gallantry or callousness, but an intra-service linguistic code of belonging as well as a carefully cultivated attitude to keep thought and emotion at bay. In many ways, this circumlocutory and periphrastic rhetoric enables the crew to do their work, but the clichés used as Deighton suggested in his novel could also make it hard for debriefing staff to extract precisely what happened on raids.

The wartime Briton was confronted with a curious paradox in the public rhetoric surrounding the bombing campaign.[15] Government officials and the War Cabinet often used euphemistic language for bombing. Vera Brittain in *Seeds of Chaos* lists a number of examples of "soporific words" that she felt had begun to characterize the language of this war: "softening up" an area; "neutralizing a target"; "area bombing"; "blanketing an industrial district"; "saturating an area" (95). Steven Poole calls this rhetorical obfuscation "unspeak" and sees it as an important linguistic strategy for governments to shroud the reality of state-ordained violence in anodyne terms in order to manufacture consent or indeed escape criticism or opposition.[16] For Richard Overy, such vocabulary creates a deliberate abstraction in place of the real bodies that bombing damages (*The Bombing War*, 48). Precisely because this language hides the truth of violence it is part of the barbarization of modern warfare.[17] On the side of the British government, public statements about the bombing campaign had to cloak the certain knowledge that "area bombing" would necessarily cause large-scale civilian deaths because precision bombing was simply not technically possible at night, under prevailing weather conditions and when confronted with heavy anti-aircraft defenses. The bombing of workers' residential areas was called "dehousing" and generally featured in reports as "built-up (target) area" or "percentage of buildings destroyed." "Strategic bombing" implied a legitimate focus on those targets clearly identified as supporting the German war industry: transport routes, railway lines, canals and bridges, oil and heavy industry particularly in the Ruhr valley, aircraft manufacturers, armaments factories, and workers' housing. As early as September 1941, Charles Portal, wartime chief of the Air Staff, justified to Churchill the attack on "the general activity of the community" in Germany with an analogy to successful morale bombing and air policing in the colonies: "it is an adaptation, though on a greatly magnified scale, of the policy of air control which has proved so outstandingly successful in recent years in the small wars in which the Air Force has been continuously engaged" (cited in Overy, *The Bombing War*, 49). The pragmatic switch in policy from "strategic bombing" to "area bombing" in October 1942 was not officially communicated to the public. It *lifted* the rules governing bombardment policy in German, Japanese, and Italian territory, that is, the prohibition to intentionally bomb civilians, the necessity to clearly identify the target and to take reasonable care to avoid undue loss of civilian life in the target vicinity.[18] In fact, this dismissed the morally relevant distinction between incidental and deliberate casualties. What *was* communicated, both in ministerial and media rhetoric, was that "enemy morale" now constituted a target and that this aggravation was justified by Germany having started both the conflict and the practice of "unrestricted air warfare" (Hastings, *Bomber Command*, 211). The Casablanca directive of January 1943 stated that the "primary object will be the progressive destruction and dislocation of the German military, industrial, and economic system and the undermining of the morale of the German people to a point when their capacity for armed resistance is fatally weakened" (cited in Webster and Frankland, *Strategic Air Offensive*, 2:12). As Tami Davis Biddle has argued, such general language gave plenty of latitude for interpretation to field commanders.[19] It was not clear what precisely morale was and why the enemy's should be susceptible to deterioration under bombardment when the British experience suggested the opposite.[20] (Rather tellingly, civilians far away from bombed areas were most strongly in favor of bombing Germany while those who had lived through the Blitz often showed greater reluctance to inflict a known calamity.)[21] In fact, the term "morale bombing" is so semantically flexible as to include the widening of physical targets while also implying that its chief benefit might be to raise morale on the home front.

Communication between ministry officials in the vast machinery of wartime bureaucracy was also remarkably careful to adhere to official bombing rhetoric. Minutes and cables that did not correspond to it had to be withdrawn and rephrased. The most notorious example of outrageous candor was Churchill's original minute to the Chief of Air Staff after Operation Thunderclap, which included the bombing of Dresden.[22] In it, Churchill famously distanced himself from the campaign: "The destruction of Dresden remains a serious query against the conduct of Allied bombing."

> It seems to me that the moment has come when the question of bombing of German cities simply for the sake of increasing the terror, though under other pretexts, should be reviewed. . . . I feel the need for more precise concentration upon military objectives, such as oil and communications behind the immediate battle-zone, rather than on mere acts of terror and wanton destruction, however impressive. (Cited in Webster and Frankland, *Strategic Air Offensive*, 3:112; Taylor, *Dresden*, 375–76)

Impressive acts of "wanton destruction" had only troubled pacifists. This minute admitted that area bombing was so imprecise that it caused indiscriminate destruction, and that the purpose of the campaign was to inflict "terror" while government directives and official rhetoric merely provided "other pretexts." In other words, both military commanders and the government knew exactly that bombing killed large numbers of civilians and had condoned this. Yet it also implied that somehow Bomber

Command was acting independently of the government, and needed to be reined in. Churchill's revised minute exchanged terror bombing with the euphemistic "so-called 'area bombing'" and emphasized that bombing should not impede occupation (Webster and Frankland, *Strategic Air Offensive*, 3:117). It now suggested that Harris was a poor military strategist since he did not bear British postwar plans in mind. In his habitually frank reply, Harris simply dismissed any qualms over wartime destruction as sentimental nonsense over "German bands and Dresden shepherdesses" (cited in Hastings, *Bomber Command*, 476).

The timing of Churchill's original minute gives us a clue about his change in rhetoric. It dates from March 28—six weeks after the Dresden bombing—when victory was within grasp. He queried the Dresden raid after the *public* in Britain and America showed signs of moral doubt. They, in turn, had responded to reports by an Associated Press war correspondent that the "Allied Air Chiefs" had made the "long awaited decision to adopt deliberate terror bombing of German population centers as a ruthless expedient to hastening Hitler's doom" and that this would include attacks on "residential sections" of Berlin, Dresden, Chemnitz, and Cottbus (cited in Webster and Frankland, *Strategic Air Offensive*, 3:113). "Terror bombing" had been Goebbels's choice phrase; now it entered war reportage and made its way into British ministry correspondence until it would find its way into the *Official History* as a "perhaps not inaccurate description" (3:116).[23] American citizens were perturbed by such news because they had been told that, in Europe, the USAAF was capable of selective and precise bombing. For educated Britons, Dresden was a center of German culture, the Florence of the Elbe, with well-known galleries, finishing schools, baroque architecture, and a world-famous opera house. It was part of the European landscape of art. In *Seeds of Chaos*, Vera Brittain had argued that the bombing was destroying German patrimony on a disproportionate scale.[24] A few months after her essay was published, Dresden drove that point home to a British public that was by then utterly exhausted by the war and *with* wartime rhetoric but also certain of victory. Crucially Dresden assumed a symbolic significance even beyond any later debates about its military importance. It became a sign of violent excess and deliberate punitive escalation that seemed somehow un-British and therefore incommensurate with the wartime rhetoric of British moral exceptionalism. It challenged the British sense of self as a civilized and reasonable nation; it produced anger and shame, and in the long run, helped marginalize the bomber offensive in the popular memory of the war.

These retrospective feelings perhaps also indicate the power of wartime rhetoric to suppress moral ambivalence and discredit opposition. Paul Fussell has noted that on all sides the Second World War had become a war of publicity in which presentation replaced actuality.[25] The cleft between rhetoric and reality was most pronounced in the fabulous claims about what bombing could achieve and its actual technical capability, particularly in the early stages of the war.[26] If the British government had been rather restrained about informing the public about what was actually being bombed, Harris's public statements as well as the directness of newspaper reportage or newsreel commentary and imagery made up for this lack of candor. Vera Brittain's analysis relied largely on statements in the public domain, which indicates that information about the scale of destruction was not hard to come by. And yet, for Richard Overy "the duplicity of the British position"—to deliberately target civilians while rhetorically redefining them as military targets—became so embedded in RAF propaganda and service language that it could actively shield officers from the truth (*The Bombing War*, 629).[27] As Mark Connelly has demonstrated in his analysis of media reportage about the bombing, the press resorted to Old Testament phrases, the best-known among them perhaps that having sown the wind, Germany would now reap the whirlwind—a phrase that dismissed proportionality as irrelevant.[28] In the language of the *Daily Express*, that translated into "The Vengeance begins!" (after the 1,000-bomber raid on Cologne in May 1942; Connelly, *Reaching*, 73). Propaganda films such as Alexander Korda's *The Biter Bit* (1943) presented the aerial footage of bombed German cities as a result of the German bombardment of Britain. Edward Blishen, a conscientious objector, blamed journalists for stoking a vindictive spirit with language that soon infected the mood of the land girls he was working with. One of the worst neologisms he cited was "Hamburg has been Hamburgered."[29] Air staff's notion of just retribution comes across in operational names, such as "Chastise" for the bombing of the Ruhr valley dams or "Gomorrah" for Hamburg.[30] Blishen noted a coarsening, "a bleak narrowing of ordinary human sympathies" in 1943 when the tide was beginning to turn, while the novelist Rose Macaulay, just listening to people in shops, wrote to her sister about the "lamentable lapse in moral outlook of the British people."[31] This barrage of morale-stoking reportage about German ruins and British air power sits rather oddly with the shock of Dresden towards the end of the war. It suggests the public's rather high tolerance for both state-sanctioned violence and violent rhetoric, and therein lies what Paul Fussell has called the "perceptual and rhetorical scandal from which total recovery is unlikely" (*Wartime*, 115). This unwelcome realization runs counter to the high-minded propaganda myths of moral exceptionalism with its epithets of the "good" or "just war" (which, incidentally, never held much truck in the literary representation of wartime). Scapegoating Harris and ignoring him in the postwar honors list was one immediate official "recovery" strategy; for the public, it would mean overwriting bombing with being bombed in the hegemonic commemoration of the Blitz.

Postwar Revisions of Forgetfulness

Neither Kennedy nor Deighton needs a "target" of the symbolic significance of Dresden. Their big raids happen during 1943, when the tide has turned in favor of the Allies but when the end is not yet in sight. Deighton invented a raid on the small, fictitious town of Altgarten, an erroneous target, to make his point about the fallacy of precision bombing: on radar screens acres of glasshouses are mistaken for factories (*Bomber*, 331), but even maps in this "new kind of war" are so abstracted and "faceless" (346) that they match radar screens rather than reality. Pathfinder planes mistake the target, bombers drop bombs too early, too late, or simply where fires are already raging, and it is impossible to gauge *what* is being bombed. *Bomber* was widely and favorably reviewed as an indictment of war at a time when the campaign had long fallen into disrepute. The *Official History* of the bombing campaign, published in 1961, was highly critical of its effectiveness on German civilian morale and wartime economy, and dismissed the claims made by Air Staff. In a return to prewar policies, British bombs were dropped to quench colonial unrest in Kenya and Malaya. Those conflicts happened far away and were barely noticed at home; in contrast, the American bombing in Vietnam became proximate and could be witnessed daily on TV screens. One of the epigraphs in *Bomber* is a simple statistic about the tonnage of bombs and rockets dropped on Vietnam from February 1965 to July 1968, which invites a parallel reading of the novel as both historical and contemporaneous: this is what happens to the young men who fly these missions; this is what happens to people on the ground. By 1974, Laurence Olivier would deliver ironic commentary on the ineffective technology of bombing in episode 12, "Whirlwind: Bombing Germany," of the highly acclaimed TV series *The World at War*. Historians such as Max Hastings and Angus Calder imploded some of the myths of popular memory, while on the American side Paul Fussell and Studs Terkel raised eyebrows at "good war" thinking in the 1980s. Early on, Deighton's *Bomber*, then, captured the mood of the time and the skepticism of a postwar generation that had grown up in its shadow but rejected its rhetoric. *Bomber* does not let Nazism as a genocidal regime off the hook, but it is the first British novel to offer a change in perspective on the bombing offensive by including the perspective of bombed German civilians on the ground. It dismisses chivalric visions of air war ("as though it was a manly duel instead of blowing people and their homes to pieces"; *Bomber*, 315) and asks awkward questions about the proportionality of the violence unleashed.

In an interview with Melvyn Bragg, Deighton described his fascination with the bombing campaign as a war of machines and technology in which the quality of a man is judged by the skill with which he operates machinery. He commented on the unreal quality of technological warfare in an otherwise remote encounter: men in planes came so close to cities hundreds of miles away from home but never set foot in them; instead, the only connection between plane and the ground was the radar beam and the bomb. Deighton rejected the glorification of violence or its harnessing in the service of a self-righteous cause:

> There is a school of writing that exists, particularly in Hollywood, that has a moral belief that if you show the bullies being violent you can end your story by having the people who were bullied show more violence than they ever believed was possible and we're all supposed to applaud and that's alright. And that's absolutely not alright with me. I don't want to write any books in which violence triumphs. I believe that there's a responsibility as a writer to try to show that intellect triumphs over violence.[32]

Deighton's moral purpose stands in marked contrast to the biblical rhetoric of the whirlwind and the just retribution. In its dispassionate descriptions of destruction it emphasizes an excess of violence concomitant with the manner of warfare (the remoteness of the bomber who never faces the results of his "work") and the ethical failures of those in charge of policy and campaigns. Kennedy's rear gunner, on being repatriated to England after his internment in a POW camp, can see Germany—for the first time by daylight from above: he finds himself "above the bombed thing that was Germany, above their work. As if the cities had been eaten, as if something unnatural had fed on them until they were gashes and shells and staring spaces, as if it was still down there like a plague in the dust" (*Day*, 271).

We should do well, here, to remember that the number of resources that were channeled towards the campaign—material and person hours to build factories, bombs, and planes; recruiting and training ground staff and crews; building airfields; coordination and cooperation with the USAAF—was simply stupendous. What the campaign unleashed in the later war years points to a frightful dynamic between economics, publicity, and military thinking: in the peak *month* of the Allied bomber offensive (March 1945) significantly more bombs were dropped than in the entire *year* 1942 (Biddle, *Rhetoric and Reality in Air Warfare*, 287). Quantity also ensured "precision": judging from the pitted landscape of craters in published post-operational aerial photographs, the likelihood of hitting a target of course increased with the number of bombs dropped; "precision" became a matter of weight dropped. Once the means for such destruction were ready for deployment, it would have required the will to restraint and proportionality as part of military decision-making and practice to *not* fully avail oneself of this arsenal. W. G. Sebald perhaps put it most acerbically: letting this machinery stand idle "ran counter to any healthy economic instinct" (Sebald, "Air War and Literature," 18). The will to restraint was never present in Harris, who firmly believed that bombing was a shortcut to victory, nor was it present in Churchill who needed to demonstrate a genuine British war effort to the Allies while deferring the Normandy landings to 1944, and who saw the propaganda value of daily reports of hitting back at the enemy. Restraint was hardly discernible in the press.

For A. L. Kennedy this dynamic is played out in the 1943 firestorm on

Hamburg—hardly reported, never the point of controversy, and therefore less known than Dresden. For Alfred Day, Operation Gomorrah is simply trip twenty-six and twenty-seven on his tour. The ferocity of this incendiary raid stirs thoughts of ambivalence in his crewmate Dickie Molloy: "When we did what we did this week—that was the end of heaven. . . . I'll have to go to hell now."[33] What the Catholic Molloy thinks of as a sin, becomes retrospective "ruination" (*Day*, 237) for Day. Trip twenty-eight, a few days later, again to Hamburg, is their last mission because they are shot down by flak: "*we burned up the sky and now it's come for us*" (245). The vague third-person pronoun "it" runs through the passages on the Hamburg raid. "It" can be traced back to the agents of death, among them phosphorus: "its true self is a harmful thing and so you keep it closed away" (232). The true self of the chemical becomes an objective correlative for the essence of war—its uncontrollable destruction—as well as Day's true self, a composite of his experiences the memory of which he needs to keep "closed away." The impact of his flashbacks, however, sears like the touch of phosphorus on human flesh:

> *And then it bares your teeth and licks them, holds them, holds you so you smell how glad it is you've let it out. The harmful thing. And it makes you forget Molloy and everything else but the way it was, the way it still is, repeating itself against your bones.*
>
> *Such a good job you did, such a perfect, perfect job—back over Hamburg and the target indicators had gone down so tight, backed up so tight, and then every stick of bombs—it didn't seem that anyone could miss, did miss.*
>
> *Its hand in your throat and pushing up, filling your mouth and the fist pressing on, cracking you, having your skull, fingers in your skull, digging this out of your brain to show you.* (*Day*, 236)

Day will never communicate "it" to anyone; the italicized focalization of the flashback never translates into direct speech. According to Victoria Stewart, this is part of the novel's engagement with different types of secrecy as part of the war's ambivalent legacy.[34] Yet Day's reticence is even more complex: part individual trauma, part personal guilt, part political realization that men like him have no voice in postwar British society, but perhaps most tellingly an ongoing acknowledgment of the level of violence he is capable of in his role as an agent of "just retribution"—killing his wife-beating father; bombing cities. There's a sense that his military training has leaked into domestic life, giving him the courage and the means to avenge his mother. Part of Day's struggle is not just to restrain himself from resorting to violence ("that harmful thing") but to unlearn wartime attitudes that legitimized its unrestrained use.

Kennedy's *Day*: Nothing Unpleasant for the Audience

Kennedy's novel allows the reader to trace Day's realization of the cleft between wartime rhetoric and reality. Early on in the novel he remembers how the individual men assembled into crews. As a group they transitioned from airmen to Bomber Boys: trained for the lonely position of the rear gunner in his turret, Day has to yield his shooting skills to the larger aim of getting through and bombing:

> "Course. We have to bomb. . . . he'll get his wish: the bombing will always be the thing, what you're for, what Chopper Harris says you're for, the big Boss. He says you're to be the boys who bring the whirlwind. And you don't only obey the skipper, you want to obey him and that makes a wonderful difference. Even if in the end it amounts to precisely the same thing. Saying more than you'd expected, 'We'll bomb. We'll bomb the bastards.'" (*Day*, 13)

Once Day has flown several missions, the enthusiasm for "the thing" has been replaced by the "knowledge of the working of bombs" and hearing jokes about bacon: "We're all just pork," comment a couple of drunken airmen (*Day*, 57). The transition from a knowledge of killing to an awareness of dying produces its own sensations: "You'd see a man take his seat in the briefing room, or pet his dog, or pass by a doorway, perhaps, and this kind of heaviness would spread inside you, unmistakable, and even the very first time you'd understand—they were dead. They were already dead" (78). The sense that war turns living men—even survivors—into the "already dead" never leaves Day. Like Henry Green's Charley Summers in *Back* (1945), also returning from a POW camp, he is stuck in time. Summers is usually "some sentences behind" in everyday civilian life,[35] while Day is suspended in his own sense of ghostliness, unable to articulate his experiences.

Kennedy also debunks the popular memory of the war as a very selective construct, particularly in the war films of the 1950s. Day is the only member of his crew to survive the bail-out after a mission; he spends the rest of the war as a "Kriegie" in a German prisoner of war camp. In 1949, the present tense of the novel, he returns to Germany as an extra in a film about POWs that invariably reminds the reader of *The Captive Heart* or, more famously in the United Kingdom, *The Colditz Story* and *The Great Escape*. Day soon finds that his own experience gets in the way of the story that is being put on screen: the truth is neither photogenic nor palatable. When Day faints in a delayed response to a dangerous situation the day before and due to the strain of flashbacks from his own camp experience, this incident is integrated into the film script for dramatic effect, and he has to concede that he finds this re-presentation "more convincing": The actor "is undoubtedly better than you are at being you" (*Day*, 33). "You," of course, is no longer an individual but a generic Kriegie. The film set utilizes a real camp, now used to hold Displaced Persons, and the film crew soon keep themselves apart from their extras and the DPs because they begin to realize that those with real war experiences do not fully appreciate the efforts to bend these into a script full of humor and bravery, "nothing that might be unpleasant, or disturb an audience" (41). Among all the phoniness of and on the film set, Day asks himself why he is there, realizing that his actual experience is not only not representable, not uplifting, not undisturbing, but simply not what sells movies: suffering has to be redemptive or meaningful and it needs to be integrated into a story of moral and military victory. Even if he found the words to tell his story, no one would listen.[36]

After the war, Alfred Day works in a bookshop owned by Ivor Sands, a heavily scarred former conscientious objector who lost one eye and an arm. Ivor is traumatized himself and haunted by his experiences of clearing up after bombing raids. Far-fetched as it may be to stage such an encounter in fiction, it offers Kennedy the possibility of an argument that pitches being bombed against bombing. By the time the reader confronts the ethical problems of the bombing offensive, Kennedy has already directed a great deal of empathy towards her protagonist: the reader sees him as a very young man, aged way beyond his years as a result of fear, strain, hunger, and violence, who volunteered to fight a war on behalf of a country that is now ashamed of its own capacity for violence: "Try telling [the girls] that you flew in bombers. You won't be so popular then, either" (*Day*, 146). Neither type of masculinity holds much currency in the postwar era: the bomber's is too violent, the conchie's too meek, when the real issue is of course how any of these men would find their way back into civilian life. Rather, the argument between Ivor and Alfred represents an impasse, a caustic comment on the rhetorical scandal that propagated collocations such as "good war" or "just war."

> "Oh, yes. What did you do in the war? Because I was on the ground, clearing up after bastards like you, putting out the fires, lifting out the bodies and the bits of bodies." His hands shaking, which you recognise, but ignore. "You ever carry someone melting?—they'll drip like a candle sometimes, runs all over you."
>
> "You were cleaning up after Germans, not bastards like me."
>
> "And your bombs were different, were they? When they landed? Opened up and rained down chocolate for the kiddies, did they? Nylons?" (*Day*, 145)

Both men, the reader understands, have more in common than they realize: trauma, disillusionment, a longing for the comfort of female company, a mother who did not survive the war, inexplicable outbursts of anger, hands that move over injuries in uncontrollable reflexes, and a "knowledge of the working of bombs" in the form of disintegrating corpses. Deighton, too, lets bodies explode and melt but the experience on the ground and in the air is never brought into conversation in this way. Years after the war, Ivor and Alfred see the world the same way, as vulnerable targets:

> *Walk anywhere and you'll catch yourself calculating out from where the first cookie would fall and blast the buildings open, let the incendiaries in to lodge and play. Difficult to pick where you should live— . . .*
>
> *And so you see targets beside targets: nothing but targets and ghost craters looping up from the earth, shock waves of dust and*

> *smoke ringing, crossing. You feel the aerial photograph staring down at you where you stand, waiting to wipe you away. You always are a target under naked air.* (*Day*, 202–3)

There is a sense that although the war is over, the world is not safer. Rather, in the weary consciousness of these men, individuals have become infinitely vulnerable to destruction. The passage above, focalized through Day, is in fact a collapsing of perspectives—the bomb aimer's and the fire fighter's. This is the only moment in the book when Day imagines himself as a target of bombs, and it is the moment when Ivor—"He's a fucker sometimes, Ivor. Sometimes he's a shit"—detects "a tiny bit of guilt" (*Day*, 204). It requires a change of perspective, the willingness to put yourself in someone else's shoes.

Later, in a second exchange, Ivor lifts the argument onto a more political and explicitly pacifist platform:

> Whoever crawls to the top of the heap will always think the rest of us are scum. That's the only law. So people like you go off and die and people like me go off and get burned, and all of us get bombed, because they think bombing will scare us and make us give up. But it doesn't. They bomb us and we don't give up. They have us bomb other people and the other people don't give up. Because people aren't scum. And we've nowhere to go. We can't give up. All the fuckers in charge, they don't understand. (*Day*, 275)

For Ivor, the pursuit of power necessitates disregard for ordinary people, negates the knowledge of common humanity. The elevation of being "in charge" turns you into a "fucker" without empathy, for whom people are then reduced to disposable "scum." Such fuckers are then also utterly blind to the poor logic of such policies as "morale bombing" because they exist in a system of hierarchies in which the enemy's qualities are by definition lower and lesser than one's own. "Morale bombing" can only be taken seriously if one truly believes that the much-lauded moral stoicism of bombed Londoners, for instance, is less a consequence of having "nowhere to go" than evidence of superior national character. Kennedy's conscientious objector explodes the narrative of British exceptionalism because he demonstrates this narrative to be a propaganda myth that does not so much elevate the ordinary Briton but rather reveals how suspicious the wartime government is of its own citizens' morale:

> And your type—they shoot you in the trenches—*pour encourager les autres*—they threaten you with Lack of Moral Fibre because they expect you to be scum. But we did so well—so many people did so well . . . and all it means is they learn that the next time they'll have to kill more and then more again, because maybe we're stupid scum and we don't know when we're beaten. (*Day*, 275)

The official censure in the RAF for cowardice or psychological breakdown, "Lack of Moral Fibre," features prominently in the films about bomber crews. The nervy protagonists in *Appointment in London* fear their superiors' and crew members' loss of respect more than the prospect of dying. And unsurprisingly, they do so well because, *particularly postwar*, the acknowledgment of their fear acts as a reassuring sign of humanity; they are not killing machines or people callously pressing buttons. In fact, in those films we are not encouraged to think at all of what these men do night after night on their missions, only of how perilous these missions are. It would be far too disturbing, to return to an undesirable audience emotion, to be reminded that being trained to kill people might be so traumatizing that these men might never fully recover from it. And they, too, have "nowhere to go" in a postwar world in which being bombed has made bombing unmentionable.

The second-person pronoun in the quotation above gradually becomes semantically wider and encompasses Day as well as general humanity, ordinary soldiers, just as the first-person "we" finally includes ordinary people at war irrespective of nationality. For Ivor, the Second World War is merely another episode in a series of escalating violence perpetrated by "the fuckers in charge." Deighton articulated the skepticism of the Vietnam generation about scandalous rhetoric through a plot that offered the reader both the perspective of the bomber and that of the bombed. Kennedy, writing during the wars in Iraq and Afghanistan, indicts the impact of questionable political decision-making on both soldiers and civilians. Both novels, I would argue, are deeply conscious of how popular memory has contributed to one of the modern fallacies of war: that state-sanctioned violence can be harnessed to good reasons or restrained by codes of conduct, and cleansed of its potential for excess, brutalization, and escalation. Once these forces are unleashed, the damage is not just done to the enemy but lodges deep in the minds and souls of those who are asked to wage war on our behalf.

Notes

The epigraph is from Bryher, *The Days of Mars: A Memoir, 1940–46* (London: Calder and Boyars, 1972), 178. I am grateful to Lucy Noakes, Gill Plain, and Christine Berberich for comments on an earlier version of this essay.

1. See for instance Mark Rawlinson's *British Writing of the Second World War* (Oxford: Oxford University Press, 2000); and Martin Francis's *The Flyer: British Culture and the Royal Airforce, 1939–1945* (Oxford: Oxford University Press, 2008). Anthony Aldgate and Jeffrey Richards discuss *The Way to the Stars* with a focus on Allied cooperation in *Britain Can Take It: The British Cinema in the Second World War* (Edinburgh: Edinburgh University Press, 1994). Robert Murphy's *British Cinema and the Second World War* (London: Reaktion, 2000) devotes a mere five pages to "the war in the air," while Philip M. Taylor's edited collection *Britain and the Cinema in the Second World War* (Basingstoke, Eng.: Macmillan, 1988) contains one paragraph on films broaching the strategic bombing offensive.

2. Based on the Butt Report, which analyzed photographic data from June and July 1941, that is, data from two thirds of sorties, since on average one third returned without attacking their primary target. Of the remaining two thirds, only one third came within five miles of their aim; in the Ruhr, where flak defenses and weather conditions were more difficult to overcome, it was only one tenth. At the time, only 22 percent of planes (or 6 percent in the Ruhr valley) came within five miles of their target, if a radius of five miles can justifiably be called accurate. See Charles Webster and Noble Frankland, *The Strategic Air Offensive Against Germany, 1939–1945*, 4 vols. (London: Her Majesty's Stationery Office, 1961), 1:178. See also Max Hastings, *Bomber Command* (London: Pan 1999), 127–28.

3. See BFI Film & TV Database at http://www.ftvdb.bfi.org.uk.

4. For prewar literary responses, see Leo Mellor, *Reading the Ruins* (Cambridge: Cambridge University Press, 2012), 11–22.

5. David E. Omissi, *Air Power and Colonial Control: The Royal Air Force, 1919–1939* (Manchester: Manchester University Press, 1990), 164–70. The tolerance of the British population of bombing colonials was considerable since the insurgents were habitually represented as unruly troublemakers, tax-avoiding tribal rulers, or religious maniacs. The impact of bombing on the bombed was also sufficiently remote to be far from the attention and the consciousness of the mainland citizen. Objection came largely from policy makers and from air personnel. However, air enthusiasts were treated to a taste of "police bombing" in the empire at the air shows in Hendon, notably in 1922 when an "Eastern Drama" against "Wottnotts" was staged where a tribal village and its inhabitants were subjected to incendiary bombs (ibid., 172).

6. Baldwin quoted in A.C. Grayling, *Among the Dead Cities* (London: Bloomsbury,

2006), 148. The same rhetoric was still being used by J. M. Spaight in 1944 in *Bombing Vindicated* (see Hastings, *Bomber Command*, 148).

7. See Webster and Frankland, *Strategic Air Offensive*, 4:440; and Richard Overy, *The Bombing War: Europe 1939–1945* (London: Allan Lane, 2013), 168.

8. Sven Lindqvist, A *History of Bombing*, trans. Linda Haverty Rugg (London: Granta, 2001), sections 391 and 200.

9. Recent discussions of the campaign and its controversy include Yuki Tanaka and Marilyn B. Young, eds., *Bombing Civilians* (New York: New, 2010); Igor Primoratz, ed., *Terror From the Sky: The Bombing of German Cities in World War II* (New York: Berghahn, 2010); and Wilfried Wilms and William Rasch, eds., *Bombs Away! Representing the Air War over Europe and Japan* (Amsterdam: Rodopi, 2006). Lindqvist's narrative is organized in an innovative and historically wide-ranging manner that allows some astonishing cross-referencing about the history of bombing. See also Eric Markusen and David Knopf, *The Holocaust and Strategic Bombing: Genocide and Total War* (Boulder, Colo.: Westview, 1995). Hastings's critical *Bomber Command* was followed by Mark Connelly's *Reaching for the Stars: A New History of Bomber Command in World War II* (London: I.B. Tauris, 2001). In the United Kingdom, Grayling has recently argued the case against the bombing as a moral crime. For influential German contributions to this debate, see Jörg Friedrich's *The Fire: the Bombing of Germany, 1940–45* (New York: Columbia University Press, 2008); and W.G. Sebald's "Air War and Literature: Zürich Lectures," in *On the Natural History of Destruction*, trans. Anthea Bell (London: Penguin, 2004), 1–107.

10. For the debate about efficacy, see summaries in Connelly, *Reaching for the Stars* (159–61) and Hastings, *Bomber Command* (452–57). The Ministry of Economic Warfare was ill-supplied with actual economists. Even for the period January 1943 to March 1944 "the area bombing was very far from inflicting any crippling or decisive loss on the enemy and had not prevented the great increase in armaments carried out in this period" (Webster and Frankland, *Strategic Air Offensive*, 2:268; see also 3:247 about "three fundamental errors" in assessing German industry). For a more optimistic economic assessment of the bombing campaign, see Adam Tooze, *The Wages of Destruction* (London: Penguin, 2007).

11. Brittain's pacifism remained unwavering throughout the war in contrast to other writers' attitudes such as Storm Jameson's, who came to believe that Nazism had to be defeated.

12. Cited in Grayling, *Among the Dead Cities*, 186–87; 194, who refers to an opinion poll conducted in April 1941 about RAF retaliation bombing, published in the *News Chronicle* and a Mass Observation report published in *The New Statesman* in February 1944. See also Vera Brittain, *Seeds of Chaos* (1944), in *One Voice: Pacifist Writings from the Second World War* (London: Continuum, 2005), 164–65.

13. Len Deighton, *Bomber* (London: Triad/Granada, 1980), 19.

14. See Martin Francis, *The Flyer: British Culture and the Royal Air Force, 1939–1945* (Oxford: Oxford University Press, 2011), 48–49.

15. For a fascinating analysis of Churchill's changing rhetoric about bombing, see Grayling, *Among the Dead Cities*, 187–90.

16. See Steven Poole, *Unspeak* (London: Abacus, 2007).

17. See George Kassimeris, ed., *The Barbarisation of Warfare* (London: Hurst, 2006).

18. The memorandum circulated to the Command and Group Air Officer Commanding of the RAF is reprinted in Hastings, *Bomber Command*, 211.

19. Tami Davis Biddle, *Rhetoric and Reality in Air Warfare: The Evolution of British and American Ideas about Strategic Bombing, 1914–1945* (Princeton, N.J.: Princeton University Press, 2004), 215.

20. As the official historians of the campaign concede, "Germany was a nation of far stronger morale and greater industrial strength and ingenuity than had been anticipated" (Webster and Frankland, *Strategic Air Offensive,* 3:309). Churchill had come to the same conclusion about so-called morale bombing: "all that we have learnt since the war began shows that its effects, both physical and moral, are greatly exaggerated" (ibid., 1:182).

21. Mass Observation report cited in Grayling, *Among the Dead Cities*, 186–87; see also Overy, *The Bombing War*, 623.

22. The bombing of Dresden has, perhaps, created its own mythology in the bombing controversy, not least because it was ideologically deployed in Goebbels's last-ditch propaganda efforts and by historiographers in East Germany. For the most recent assessment of Dresden see Frederick Taylor, *Dresden: Tuesday 13 February 1945* (London: Bloomsbury, 2004).

23. In contrast, the Dresden controversy is conspicuously absent from Churchill's history of World War II (Overy, *The Bombing War*, 396).

24. Brittain, *Seeds of Chaos*, 103; 119–51. For a fascinating study of modern warfare as "cultural cleansing," see Robert Bevan's *The Destruction of Memory: Architecture at War* (London: Reaktion, 2006).

25. Paul Fussell, *Wartime: Understanding and Behaviour in the Second World War* (New York: Oxford University Press, 1989), chap. 11 (143–64).

26. See Biddle, *Rhetoric and Reality in Air Warfare*, 176–214.

27. However, the flying officer in Roald Dahl's "Someone Like You" (1946), like his fictional successor Lambert in *Bomber*, has clearly realized that the casualties of his raids are civilians: "Same sort of people. Men and women and waiters. All drinking in a pub." Dahl, *Over to You* (London: Penguin, 1973), 158. Similar sentiments of moral doubt emerge among the veteran crew interviewed for Patrick Bishop's popular history *Bomber Boys: Fighting Back, 1940–1945* (London: Harper, 2007), 137–41.

28. Mark Connelly, "The British Debate," in Primoratz, *Terror from the Sky*, 181–203. See also Connelly, *Reaching for the Stars*, 73 and Hastings, *Bomber Command*, 216.

29. Edmund Blishen, A *Cackhanded War* (London: Thames and Hudson, 1972), 122–23.

30. Interestingly, German civilians also often thought of the bombardment as a form of payback. The term is ironized in Gert Ledig's 1956 novel about the Hamburg firestorm, *Vergeltung*. See also Sebald, "Air War and Literature," 14.

31. Cited in Paul Berry and Mark Bostridge, *Vera Brittain: A Life* (London: Chatto and Windus: 1995), 438.

32. Len Deighton in an interview with Melvyn Bragg, BBC 2, broadcast December 18, 1977. Available in the BBC radio web archive as "The Lively Arts: Len Deighton," http://www.bbc.co.uk/archive/writers/12212.shtml.

33. A. L. Kennedy, *Day* (London: Jonathan Cape, 2007), 236. All subsequent references to this edition are cited parenthetically in the text.

34. Victoria Stewart, *The Second World War in Contemporary British Fiction: Secret Histories* (Edinburgh: Edinburgh University Press, 2011), 87.

35. Henry Green, *Back* (London: Harvill, 1998), 73.

36. Indeed, in her acceptance speech for the international Eifel Literary Prize awarded for *Day*, A. L. Kennedy made precisely this point in relation to the returning veterans from the Iraq war: "In my own country men are coming home from war—and my country doesn't listen to their stories, even if they want to tell them yet. People don't want to hear about killing children when you fire into a crowd, people don't want to see the face of war—and so wars are easier and seem cleaner and more bearable. And we are Good Britons and we can say if someone asks us—'Oh, but we didn't know'" (original text unpublished; correspondence with author). The slightly shortened German translation of the speech was published in the *Frankfurter Allgemeine Zeitung* (August 16, 2008), no. 138, 33.

VICTORIA STEWART

"A Bomb Made of Words"
Letter-Writing in Fictions of the Second World War

In Elizabeth Taylor's 1945 novel *At Mrs. Lippincote's*, Eleanor's correspondence with Reggy, a prisoner of war, is described in this way:

> "My very dear Reggy," she wrote, without feeling any surprise whatsoever. She had not known Reggy well nor cared to know him better when he had gone overseas four years before, and had begun to write to him—"Dear Reggy"—simply because it was in her anyhow to be a prodigious letter writer. Then he was killed and she found that, barring Roddy [her cousin], he was all she had to offer up for her country, and wept. But after a month or two, he was not killed, but a prisoner-of-war. In her relief, he became "My dear Reggy." It was obvious that she was still only a short way up the scale that culminates, one supposes, in "Darling," "My Love," "My Own."
>
> She wrote her letter, signed it "Your E," wrote on the envelope that monstrous word *Kriegsgefangenenpost*, and put it proudly on the mantelpiece. Then she sat down by the fire with a rather bogus book about China, and fell asleep.[1]

That Eleanor puts the envelope "proudly" on the mantelpiece, in view of her cousin Roddy and his wife Julia, with whom she is living, and that Reggy is described as all she has to "offer up for her country," implies that this correspondence is not only, perhaps barely at all, about establishing a meaningful relationship with Reggy himself. It is, rather, a way for Eleanor to establish a meaningful relationship with the war. Later, though, the extent of what is concealed by the phrase "she wept," which here indicates her reaction to the news of Reggy's apparent death, is described more fully. Eleanor, who is teaching at a school, admits to her colleague Aldridge that she "had a breakdown . . . It sounds vague, but it isn't pleasant nor vague. One thing after another—voice went, and then, when I recovered that, alopecia . . . Then neuralgia, insomnia, loss of memory" (*At Mrs. Lippincote's*, 45). When Aldridge comments that these symptoms must have been caused by a "shock," she admits: "My—a dear friend was reported missing, then killed, then, after a long time, a prisoner of war" (45). She implies that she feels her reaction was excessive in the circumstances: "Other women go through all that and worse and never turn a hair" (45), but her unwillingness to discuss this with Aldridge is also, in part at least, a consequence of her feeling an attraction towards him. Eleanor's switch from "Dear" to "My very dear" in the salutation of her letters to Reggy is thus contextualized as expressing relief at hearing he is alive after believing him dead; his progress from missing, to killed, then eventually to prisoner of war, seems to deepen her feelings towards him, as much as the correspondence itself might. But the switch also seems to be a way for her to justify, retrospectively, the breakdown she suffers at the (false) news of him being killed: to produce that reaction, her feelings must, surely, have been intense.

As Eleanor becomes more closely drawn into Aldridge's circle, writing to Reggy ceases to be so important to her: "'I hope this . . . I hope that,' Eleanor wrote, with indifference" (*At Mrs. Lippincote's*, 129). The glimpse we get of Reggy's letters to her implies that for him too, the fact of having a correspondent is as important as any role the letters might play in the development of a relationship: "On the mantelpiece was propped a card with '*Kriegsgefangenenlager*' printed on it, and a few lines of writing in indelible pencil—'Keeping quite fit. Few games of Footer. Not heard lately. Mail irregular. See you soon. All the best'" (174). Here, half the brief message is taken up with complaints about not having had a letter back, emphasizing the fact that, from Reggy's perspective, simply receiving a letter at all is an event, and casting in a different light Eleanor's sense that putting pen to paper has become an effort. Most of the other half of his card seems to be almost meaningless filler: "See you soon. All the best";

these are the clichés resorted to by one who, perhaps, unlike Eleanor, is not by disposition a prolific letter writer.

The scenario depicted here of a woman at home keeping in touch by letter with a prisoner of war in Germany is one which recurs in representations of the Second World War and often, as is the case in *At Mrs. Lippincote's*, such a correspondence is used to express not only the difficulties of maintaining a relationship in wartime but also the wider shifts in gender roles that the war is bringing about. Jenny Hartley has suggested, with reference to Janet Altman's conceptualization of letter-writing, that the letter "acts as a bridge between two distant points, and . . . the writer can emphasise either the distance or the bridge."[2] In Hartley's view, Second World War letters from women to men abroad, particularly letters from mothers to sons, strive to emphasize the bridging function. As is evidenced by *At Mrs. Lippincote's*, in fiction at least, the ostensible nature of this bridging function is often revealed. In wartime fictional representations, incarceration can be constructed as emasculatory, with the prisoner deprived of the opportunity to prove his prowess on the battlefield; but for a former soldier to return home after a period in a camp rather than directly from fighting can also help to defuse some of the anxieties about the reintegration of soldiers into civil society that were circulating towards the end, and in the immediate aftermath, of the war.[3] In this regard, the prison camp, like the hospital, acts as a buffer zone, creating a distance between the individual soldier and the military organization and therefore placing him in closer proximity to the domestic. In some representations, the ways in which the domestic sphere and women's lives more generally have been changed by wartime are strategically muted in order to imply a smooth transition between war and peace, martial and civilian, but this is not always the case. In Taylor's novel, the reader does not learn what becomes of Reggy, and, at the end of the narrative, the household at Mrs. Lippincote's breaks up and is set to move on in the wake of the discovery that Roddy has been having an affair. There is certainly little sense that Reggy will be able to return to any semblance of stability.

Before discussing further the particular exigencies of wartime correspondence and how these are reworked in Gerard Woodward's historical novel *Nourishment* (2010), consideration of critical approaches to the letter as a form of life-writing, and to the epistolary novel, reminds us that the supposed qualities of the private letter—spontaneity, intimacy, the communication of domestic and personal detail—have historically been associated with women.[4] As Amanda Gilroy and W. M. Verhoeven point out, however, this gender alignment reflects historical concerns "about the place of women in the literary marketplace" ("Introduction," 5) as much as any intrinsic qualities of women's letter-writing. In wartime even more than at other times, it might be deemed necessary for both men and women to keep check on outpourings of feeling. Margaretta Jolly notes that "letters spring from and codify ideal relationships, preserving the self through appeal to the other and practicing the conduct of civility."[5] As she also comments in a different context: "It is not necessary to say that letters are deliberate lies or conscious fictions, although we might want to be suspicious of the assumption that they are the spontaneous outpourings of the true self. Rather, I see in them a subtle interchange among fantasy, writing, and relationship. . . . There is something expressive, excessive about all writing."[6] These elements of idealization, fantasy, and excess become particularly pronounced in more recent examples of the letter in fictional representations of wartime, but, as I will show, the notion of the letter as performative, rather than "spontaneous," was not an alien one during the 1940s, not least because of the sensitivities raised by censorship. Hartley notes that "discretion and reticence" were "drilled into letter readers and writers by wartime advice columnists" and suggests that in Taylor's novel letters "signify deception and failed communication."[7] A combination of prolonged geographical and temporal separation and a knowledge that the correspondence cannot be a completely private one means that wartime letters are often constructed as a means of maintaining a holding position rather than as a medium that can help existing relationships to develop.

The policing of ostensibly private correspondence through censorship can be seen as a literal example of what Nancy Armstrong has observed, alluding to Lacan's and Derrida's reflections prompted by Poe's "The Purloined Letter" (1845): "letters are now and always have been . . . purloined letters. Always present in the mind's eye of the letter writer is a third party who leaves the mark of such awareness on the letter."[8] Armstrong suggests that the unarticulated knowledge that a letter might not reach its intended destination undermines the illusion that a correspondence is an exchange involving only the sender and the addressee, a sort of long-distance conversation. Eleanor's postcard from Reggy, placed on display on the mantelpiece, and in fact mocked by her cousin Roddy ("'Just the sort of letter one likes to get,' he thought sarcastically"; Taylor, *At Mrs. Lippincote's*,174), is a reminder that the postcard is itself a form of correspondence that militates against secrecy.[9] Incorporating letters into fictional representations of the war can be a means of complicating the depiction of subjectivity, especially when, as in Eleanor's case, a degree of self-concealment is involved. Letters also serve to attenuate the time scale of a narrative, to slow down interaction between protagonists, although on occasion, as I will show, the temporal and spatial gap between the sending of the letter, its receipt, and the sending and receiving of a reply is closed down for the purpose of creating the illusion that the correspondence, and by extension the situation which has necessitated it, does not in fact place a barrier between the correspondents.

Although fictional rather than actual letter-writing will be my focus here, some consideration of real-life correspondence can further help to contextualize representations from the 1940s. Taylor herself, as Nicola Beauman revealed in her biography of the author, continued to correspond with Ray Russell, with whom she had been having an intermittent affair since 1938, during the four years that he was in a prison camp. Beauman estimates that "during that time Elizabeth wrote Ray hundreds of letters, perhaps a quarter of a million words in total."[10] Like Eleanor's Reggy, Ray was reported missing, though not believed killed; he was captured in Greece at the end of June 1941. Taylor was sure he was still alive and carried on writing to him; if letter-writing is a means of continuing an actual relationship in textual form, Taylor evidently held onto her belief that the letters written while Ray was missing would eventually reach their destination, and, indeed, at the start of August, she received news that he was in captivity in Austria. A correspondence can continue one-sidedly, for a time, but there is perhaps also an element of wishful thinking evident here: so long as he could be written to, Ray could still be alive. According to Beauman, the letters Taylor wrote to Ray while he was in the camp detail her domestic life, describing films she saw and books she read. For Ray, whose fellow prisoners were mostly from New Zealand and Australia and who therefore did not share his cultural background, these letters provided vital sustenance, as well as fueling a hope that he and Taylor might eventually be together for good. In fact, Taylor bore a child to her husband during this period, and her relationship with Ray eventually petered out after the war.

Although the aftermath of the retreat from Dunkirk caused long delays in the establishment of contact between prisoners and their families at home, by the time that Ray Russell was captured, it took an average of about three weeks for British families to receive news of the whereabouts of prisoners in Europe. Prisoners were allowed to send four postcards and two letters home a month, with a delivery time of about six weeks once the system was established.[11] The situation in the Far East was of course very different; there were much longer delays for families in finding out where their loved ones were and little if any post could get through. Julie Summers records a number of instances of men in Far Eastern camps waiting up to eighteen months for their first letters from home, and also notes that, on at least one occasion, unopened mail from home was burnt in front of prisoners as a punishment.[12] Post was sometimes held back from British prisoners in German camps as a reprisal for delays in receiving post experienced by German prisoners being held in Canada and Australia.[13] As I have noted, and as the "monstrous word *Kriegsgefangenenpost*" written on Eleanor's envelope further reminds us, the systematization of the army postal service involved censorship. This severely compromises any sense that letters can be a private communication between two individuals. It was not only post to and from prisoner of war camps that was read; as Mark Donnelly explains, all material being sent out of the country was censored, principally to "prevent information of military value from reaching the enemy," but there was also a desire to "restrict the circulation of material which brought into disrepute the Allied war effort."[14] Within Britain, censorship was imposed on "mail to and from ports and other sensitive areas" (Hartley, *Millions*, 223). In relation to letters to servicemen abroad, not bringing the war effort into disrepute extended to maintaining the morale of those who were fighting, or, indeed, had been prevented from fighting by being captured.

Both fictional and actual correspondents show varying degrees of awareness of the surveillance and censorship of letters that took place in wartime. Censorship did not only occur once letters had been written and sent; a form of self-censorship was also practiced by the correspondents themselves, not only to reflect their knowledge that their letters would be read but also in the light of advice about the need to maintain morale. As Robert Mackay notes, "all the while a pretence of optimism and cheerfulness had to be maintained . . . the prime consideration was *military* morale and how civilians might help sustain it."[15] Midge Gillies cites advice about letter-writing from a Red Cross magazine that was distributed to the families of men in prisoner of war camps:

What to tell him	What not to tell him
Film you saw	Dinner you ate
Book you read	Cold you caught
Sermon you heard	Bomb you dodged
Flowers you grow	Fright you had
Skirt you made	Pound you lost
Money you've saved	Vase you broke
Words baby's learnt	Ration book loss.[16]

The intention here is to steer (female) correspondents away from complaining about the privations of life on the home front, but, evidently, for such women, life continued, and indeed changed, in ways that was simply not possible for men sequestered away from the war in prison camps. Part of the reason why the scenario of a "free" woman writing to an imprisoned man recurs in fiction is its tendency to throw into relief the gendered nature of participation in the war. Once they are incarcerated, soldiers' ability to take an active part in the war is severely reduced, if not removed altogether. Those on the home front, and women in particular, were never simply passive in the first place, but part of what the letter-writing guide encourages is a focus on how the home is remaining the same. Women are requested to edit out the ways in which the war is impinging on their lives, ostensibly in the interests of reassuring their husbands or sons that they are safe, but also, presumably, as a means of avoiding implying that they, the civilians, may be having the worse time, or conversely, that they are managing quite well on their own or enjoying the challenges of war work. (Regardless of the hopes of the Red Cross, some women did of course become involved with other men while their partners were imprisoned and felt that honesty was the best policy.)

Guidance of the sort cited by Gillies emphasizes the extent to which letter-writing always involves the adoption of a persona, one which, as the depiction of Eleanor reflects, may be more or less convincing to the recipient: "I hope this . . . I hope that." In wartime, the factors overdetermining this performance are multiple, relating as they do to wider issues of morale and the war effort. This element of performance is explicitly thematized in the film *The Captive Heart* (1946),[17] featuring Michael Redgrave as a Czech concentration camp escapee called Josef Hasek who takes on the identity of a dead British officer, Geoffrey Mitchell, and is taken to a prisoner of war camp under this officer's identity. (His deception is facilitated by the fact that, having spent his childhood in England, he speaks perfect English, and none of his fellow prisoners know the man whom he is impersonating.) Letters are shown to be crucial in maintaining morale in the camp, but the news carried is not always positive. At one point, Mitchell, as Redgrave's character is known in the camp, writes a letter on behalf of an injured soldier, breaking off the man's relationship with his girlfriend, but, in accordance with the injured soldier's wishes, the letter does not reveal that the real reason he wishes to end the relationship is that he has been blinded. Another prisoner receives news that his wife has died in childbirth. But a desire to emphasize wartime correspondence as having a bridging function is brought to the fore when Hasek receives a letter from Geoffrey Mitchell's wife, which reveals that the pair's relationship has been troubled since before the war. "Geoffrey" replies and effectively initiates a relationship with a woman who believes she is writing to her husband. He asks her to continue writing "as though I were a stranger," which, of course, he literally is. Her letters prove to be both emotive and morale-boosting for all the men in Mitchell's hut, as he shares with them her descriptions of life in the Mitchells' home village, which has been changed in some superficial respects by the war, but still, by her account, continues in its immemorial cycles. Mrs. Mitchell's letters are a model of uncomplaining and sustaining wartime correspondence; they serve not only to provide a bridge back to civilian life for the men who hear their contents but they also provide a fantasy of belonging for Hasek, the deracinated European subject. This companionable sharing of letters between prisoners is given a nasty twist in Gerard Woodward's 2010 novel, *Nourishment*, as I will show.

The scenario evoked in *The Captive Heart* might seem rather ridiculous but the often bleakly realist aesthetic of the film contributes to its force. It was filmed at a recently decommissioned prisoner of war camp in Germany, a scenario that is evoked in A. L. Kennedy's novel *Day*

(2007), in which, after the end of the war, Alfred Day returns to the camp where he was incarcerated to perform as an extra in a feature film being made there, in an attempt to understand his traumatic war experience. When the war ends in *The Captive Heart*, and Geoffrey's wife (played by Redgrave's own wife, Rachel Kempson) learns the truth, she overcomes her initial shock and realizes that the relationship that the false Geoffrey has fostered is now as crucial to her as her original marriage once was. The film ends with Mrs. Mitchell admitting that she loves her substitute husband, and with the implication that Hasek will replace Geoffrey Mitchell as the head of the household. As I argue elsewhere, this literal substitution of one man for another encodes contemporary fears about the ways in which war might change men (Stewart, *Narratives of Memory*, 139–40). Narratives in which an imposter comes home instead of the expected son or husband express the fact that many men had profound difficulties in readjusting to civilian life, but can also, as in *The Captive Heart*, be a means of foreclosing the process of mourning for a deceased loved one, with the substitute either taking his place, or providing assurance that the death was in a noble cause.

In Taylor's novel and *The Captive Heart*, then, we see two very different approaches to the letter-writing and its multiple functions in wartime, one less optimistic than the other. Contemporary authors have also shown an awareness of the different purposes that wartime letters could fulfill and the different pressures that could be experienced during their composition. Kennedy's *Day* echoes Henry Green's *Back* (1946)[18] in focusing on what letters mean to the incarcerated recipient, and in particular, how they might continue to signify after the war, when reread in very changed circumstances. Thinking about his relationship with the married Joyce, which has been foiled by her husband returning home from action injured, Day laments the fact that he has "lost every letter she sent me before the camp, don't have a word of her left from any time when I was free."[19] Even though he receives letters from her during his incarceration, for Day, as for Charley in Green's novel, it is the letters from before then, reflecting a love affair at its height, that he values most highly. These letters represent for Day the hope that continuity might be possible, despite the fact that he and Joyce are now apart. Kennedy's novel, like texts from the immediate postwar period, such as *The Captive Heart* and *Back*, is able to provide a perspective that was only partially accessible during wartime, that of the prisoner himself. The extent to which the letter succeeded as a way of bridging the distance between those who are imprisoned and those at home could only properly be gauged retrospectively, at the end of the war. In more recent fiction, a fuller assessment is possible of the wider ideological and social divisions and struggles, particularly as regards gender roles, of which wartime letter-writing is emblematic. Kennedy is relatively unusual among contemporary British authors of literary fiction in privileging the soldier's perspective. When contemporary authors have reconsidered the narrative trope of wartime protagonists communicating by letter, they have tended to focus on the woman's side of the correspondence. Notably, on a number of occasions, women never get as far as actually putting pen to paper; in novels including Peter Ho Davies's *The Welsh Girl* (2007), Liz Jensen's *War Crimes for the Home* (2002), and Sarah Waters's *The Night Watch* (2006)[20] the letter is rejected as a means for a woman on the home front to communicate news of pregnancy to a boyfriend in the services. Such instances of unwritten and unwriteable letters are one way of expressing the gulf between male and female experiences of war in these novels. They also express, like Eleanor's "I hope this . . . I hope that," the fallibility of the written word, gaps and failures in communication.

Perhaps the most startling counter to the largely restorative and reparative letters of *The Captive Heart* are the letters that are exchanged in Gerard Woodward's novel *Nourishment*. The events of this narrative extend from wartime into the immediate postwar period. Tory Pace and her mother, Mrs. Head, are sharing a house in a London suburb while Tory's husband, Donald, is in the army and her children evacuated. Mrs. Head has previously lived alone in a village in the East Anglian fens, and wartime has therefore reversed her relationship with her daughter from a postal to an actual one. Tory has taken a job in a gelatin factory and her boss, George Farraway, is undertaking secret work in an (unsuccessful) attempt to develop the food of the future, in pellet form. At the center of the novel is the correspondence which develops between Tory and Donald once Donald is known to be a prisoner of war, and the kind of sustenance he expects her letters to provide.

Tory has received an official letter informing her that Donald is missing and has almost persuaded herself that he is dead when another envelope finally arrives, and is examined first of all by Mrs. Head:

> *Kriegsgefangenenpost* was written across the top. She knew that this meant it was a letter from a prisoner of war. And there was Donald's handwriting, overshadowed and cowering, it seemed, beneath the rubber stamps of officials and censors. STALAG-VII-C. A red crown with the word "passed" underneath. A German eagle. Hands from both sides of the war had touched this envelope, had read its contents. Enemies had co-operated in its journey across Europe. It thrilled Mrs. Head a little, and she became breathless.[21]

Mrs. Head can glean a good deal of information from the envelope alone: the fact that this communication has been read at least twice by other people is emphasized here, although she chooses to read the double surveillance of Donald's communication as cooperation rather than intelligence gathering. Like Eleanor's letter to Reggy, Donald's letter is left on display on the mantelpiece, though unlike Taylor, Woodward glosses for his reader the word "*Kriegsgefangenenpost.*" Tory is emotionally shaken at the sudden resurrection of her husband that is signified by the letter's arrival, and asks her mother to read it to her. The opening is anodyne enough: "*At last the Germans have given us pen and paper and allowed us to write letters home . . . I'm doing pretty well considering . . . . Good crowd here, some Australian and Canadians*" (*Nourishment*, 36). But then Mrs. Head comes to a halt: "Your husband seems to have quite lost his mind" (36). Tory reads the final paragraph of the letter herself:

> *Nothing else troubles me apart from not being able to pull your knickers down and give you a good fuck. Instead, could you write me a dirty letter, by return of post? I mean really filthy, full of the dirtiest words and deeds you can think of.*
>
> *I require this most urgently.*
>
> *Love to your ma*
>
> *Donald*
>
> XXX (*Nourishment*, 37)

Woodward reveals what could never come to light so explicitly in wartime representations: that imprisoned men may well have spent time thinking about giving their wives or girlfriends "*a good fuck.*" Donald's request is troubling for Tory not only because it has been seen by her mother, a situation which reflects the extent to which letters home in wartime would often be shared, partially or wholly, with individuals other than the addressee. Any reply she does write will be read by others en route to Donald, but, besides, her memories of her sexual relationship with her husband are neither especially pleasant nor vivid, and she lacks the imagination and vocabulary to comply with this request. She replies reprovingly to Donald, only to receive, all at once after having been held up in the post, several letters renewing the request: "They had all been written at fortnightly intervals, yet were delivered in the space of a few days . . . To have the months of Donald's frustration crushed into the space of a few days, gave them such density and weight—it was as though she had been struck by a bomb made of words" (*Nourishment*, 46). The letters become increasingly obscene, and she burns some without reading them, finally replying in what she hopes is a suitably officious tone:

> *Dear Donald,*
>
> *Your letters were delayed in the post and have arrived all at once this past week. I have destroyed them. Please do not write me any more letters like those. If you do so I will destroy all further communication from you without opening it, and will not write to you again.*
>
> *You have offended me grievously.*
>
> *Yours sincerely*
> *Tory Pace*

Tory thinks this letter, "as pointed and as efficient as an arrow" (*Nourishment*, 48), will put a stop to her husband's importunate requests, but an arrow is no defense against a bomb in this war of words, and Donald resorts to framing his desire as a consequence of the horrors that he has witnessed, essentially blackmailing his wife. Implicitly, deprived of the ability to exercise his masculinity on the battlefield, Donald looks to Tory to shore up his feelings of manliness, although, as becomes clear later in the novel, the motives for his request are, by his own account, as much to do with his relations with other prisoners as with his wife. Woodward implicitly mocks the romanticized evasions of sex and sexuality that characterize a text such as *The Captive Heart*, while at the same time exposing the multiple roles that Tory is expected to perform in exigent circumstances: she is a daughter, a mother, an employee, a wife, and now, explicitly, a sex object.

Her role as a mother is emphasized by the fact that, as well as keeping in touch with Donald, Tory is simultaneously attempting to maintain a relationship by letter with her children, who have been evacuated to the Cotswolds. The strains that this situation places on their relationship are initially depicted in semi-poignant, semi-comic fashion, although later, when the children return home, it becomes clear that Tory's relationship with her son Tom has been irreparably damaged, not only by their separation but also by her own actions. Early on, Tom reproves her in a tone that echoes the officiousness of her response to her husband: "*I refer to your letter dated 16–1-41. Your most recent letter (dated 21–3-41) repeats a lot of this information. There is really little point in writing to us unless you have something new to tell*" (*Nourishment*, 25). Tom is unable to find the appropriate register in which to address his mother, imitating the form of the model business letter that he may have been taught to write at school and refusing to engage in the polite fiction that receiving a letter at all is a sign that she cares, regardless of the contents. More affecting for Tory is the "simple, contradictory honesty" of a letter she receives from her younger daughter:

> *Dra Mama,*
> *I cant think of anything to rite*
> *Yours truly*
> *Albertina* (*Nourishment*, 26)

This letter collapses the distinction Hartley identifies between letters which emphasize the bridge and those which emphasize the gap. Albertina is too young to realize that writing that she has nothing to say defeats the purpose of writing at all. In Tom's analysis, however, this is what his mother's inadvertently repetitive missives have been saying: that she, essentially, has nothing new to tell them. The more Tory tries to use letters to maintain the relationship, the clearer it becomes that she has lost touch with how her children might themselves be growing and changing, and that this type of sustenance is not enough. The correspondences conducted by Tory in the novel seem to signify not only that she is the one who, as best she can, is acting as the linchpin for the family, but that circumstances are calculated to make the task of bringing the family together again at the end of the conflict almost impossible. During the wartime portion of the novel, the reader is presented with events from Tory's and her mother's perspective, with letters providing elusive glimpses of what the other members of the family are experiencing. Once the family is reunited at the war's end, Woodward fleshes out the context for their missives to Tory, revealing to the reader, and to some extent to Tory herself, how partial the accounts contained in the wartime letters actually were.

Donald's renewal of contact is at least some good news to share with the children, though he appears to show little interest in them, even when Tom helpfully sends some ideas, via Tory, for how he might make his escape from the camp (*Nourishment*, 51). Donald continues to demand a sexually explicit communication from his wife, brushing aside her concerns about censorship. She eventually decides that she must at least attempt to comply, but can only draw on her own limited experience of sex with Donald, and her letter is returned with "*NOT GOOD ENOUGH!!!*" written across it (59). Part of Tory's problem is that she has qualms about blurring the divide between actuality and invention. At this point in the narrative, she reflects that "if she was capable of writing a dirty letter, it would have had to be a work of fiction" (41). What she seems unable to acknowledge is the extent to which all letters partake, as Jolly notes, of fantasy, and that the divide between fact and fiction is not an absolute one. But Tory has a further problem, in that she is restricted not only by the limitations of her own experience but also by her very vocabulary: "It was one of the curious side effects of Donald's letters that Tory's mind was permanently filled with sexual thoughts she was unable to express" (87). What she can imagine, she does not have the words to articulate.

Having failed to find any help from literary works, and after an embarrassing exchange on the subject with one of her workmates at the factory, Tory eventually embarks on an affair with Mr. Farraway, the factory owner, almost, it would seem, so that she will have something to write to Donald about. Having been unable to imagine what Donald wants described, she is led to actually do some of those things, so that her letters contain not imagined, but remembered actions. Later, however, after his return, Donald wants her to reenact with him what he initially believes to have been sexual fantasies on her part, producing precisely the blurring of fantasy and reality that Tory wishes to avoid. Tory and her letters ultimately seem to be merely the conduit for Mr. Farraway's preferred types of sexual behavior, and indeed his language, to be communicated to Donald (and, it eventually emerges, to the other prisoners as well). She fills her letters with "long descriptions that mostly used [Farraway's] rich sexual language but which, with a subtle and deft change of tense and viewpoint, became passionate erotic missives from a wife to her imprisoned husband" (*Nourishment,* 129). Having previously sent a letter with the weedy force of an "arrow," she now launches a "spring offensive of sexual narrative" (130). By enunciating sexual desires that are actually Mr. Farraway's, Tory unwittingly colludes in the logic of pornography, which typically attributes to women sexual fantasies that are in fact expressive of male desires. Donald is unaware of Mr. Farraway's role in Tory's life at this point, but Gayle Rubin's classic discussion of how women can function in relationships between men is pertinent here: when women are "transacted . . . it is the men who give and take them who are linked, the women being a conduit of a relationship rather than a partner to it."[22] Tory's own sexual desires are not central either to her relationship with Mr. Farraway or to her relationship with her husband; she pleases one in the attempt to please the other on the terms that he demands.

As though to acknowledge further the highly mediated nature of her letters to her husband, Woodward also has Tory adopt another writing persona, when she embarks on a novel about her wartime experiences, suitably sanitized, with a protagonist called "Charlotte Maugham" (*Nourishment*, 163). "Charlotte Maugham" might be closer to the voice Tory wishes to offer the world but she also represents a different form of constraint; if her letters to her husband are too frank, what she writes under Charlotte's name is not frank enough. Writing the novel becomes a means not only of reflecting, and reflecting on, her own experiences, but also a way of trying out alternatives: in one draft, in an echo of *The Captive Heart*'s substitute husband plot, Charlotte's husband returns after having been declared dead, to find that his wife has remarried (242). Tory's war novel is no closer to evoking her "authentic" voice than the letters to Donald are. To please Donald she has to put on paper a particular kind of sexual fantasy; to be Charlotte successfully, she has to distort her experience in other ways. Charlotte echoes a figure like Mrs. Mitchell in *The Captive Heart*, accepting the role offered to her by a wartime ideology of uncomplaining resilience in the face of the exigencies of life on the home front.

The consequence-less sex of Donald's fantasy collides with reality when Tory becomes pregnant by Mr. Farraway. When Donald returns, he is evidently unconvinced by her tale of having found her new son, Branson, in a bombed-out house during a visit to friends in Leicester. Returned from evacuation, her son Tom begins to believe that she is not actually his mother, but an actress brought in to replace her, thus explaining her extra child. Tom eventually acts out this fantasy of displacement when, forced to leave school by Donald, he hangs himself in a barn in the village to which he was earlier evacuated (*Nourishment*, 218). Branson, the product of a fantasy made reality, and the focus of a paranoiac fixation on Tom's part, manages actually to displace him in Donald's affections. The blow of Tom's loss is swiftly followed by Tory's discovery of what the reader has known for some time, that the letters she has written to Donald were nothing more than a form of "currency" (139) in the camp, passed around among the other soldiers in return for cigarettes, a way of keeping face and asserting sexual potency. In a switch to Donald's perspective at the start of the second part of the novel, his feelings during the period when, as the reader has seen, he was essentially harassing Tory, are revealed: he "derived little pleasure from the letters . . . his requests had been made purely for expedient reasons" (135). What might seem like a crude means of reestablishing and nurturing intimacy had little to do with Tory as an individual at all. Instead, it is about Donald being able to retain a particular status within the all-male environment of the camp. In this respect too, then, Tory, or at least her letter, is a "conduit" for relations between men. In a way, this is a twisted rewrite of *The Captive Heart*. The sharing of letters is framed as legitimate in the film because, in some respects, their actual recipient was already usurping the true addressee's role. Mrs. Mitchell's lyrical descriptions of village life strike a chord with all the men because of their assertion of apparently changeless values; even Hasek, a foreigner, is enchanted. Misunderstandings, betrayals, and "Dear John" letters are not absent from the film nor indeed from other wartime representations of men either on active service or in captivity, but such upsets are almost always reparable: the blinded soldier's girlfriend stands by him; the wife dies in childbirth, but the child lives. In Woodward's novel, the prisoners are bound together not by a longing for a vision of England of the sort depicted in Mrs. Mitchell's letters but by a desire for sexual release that can nevertheless ensure that the bonds between them remain of a safely homosocial kind. For the prisoners in each text, it is not the reality of Mrs. Mitchell or of Tory that is the point; it is the conviction with which she expresses the desired "morale boosting" sentiments that is most important.

At a historical distance, Woodward can be franker about issues of sexuality, but he also implies that the passing round of the letters from Tory is just one aspect of a particularly modern, indeed postwar, form of the commodification of female sexuality. Notably, Woodward does not include any of her "dirty" letters to Donald within the novel, avoiding indulging in or replicating what he is attempting to critique. The commercial exploitation of her sexuality is expressed most bluntly by the fact that Donald borrows the typewriter on which Tory has been secretly composing her middlebrow novel about a woman's war experiences, types her letters up, and submits them to the Olympia Press for publication as an under-the-counter pornographic novel (*Nourishment*, 289). It is only at this point, when he is already in discussions with the publisher, that Tory discovers his treachery. The private function of the letter is comprehensively subverted, but the joke is also on Donald, who only belatedly realizes that his request prompted Tory to turn to her boss Mr. Farraway, and Donald's retyping of the letters is a reminder for the reader that these fantasies were male-authored in the first instance. However, Woodward does not suggest that the novel featuring Charlotte Maugham will be much truer to Tory's experiences. Instead, the novel seems to imply that the kind of self-censorship that characterized wartime letter-writing extended itself into postwar literary fiction, particularly literature by women, but Woodward is in danger of equating reticence with repression, and offers no middle way between the uncensored, albeit illicit, version of the war contained in Donald's epistolary novel and Tory's literary evasions. Woodward asks us to question the honesty of a text such as *The Captive Heart* or Tory's novel, but it is evident that *Nourishment* itself is as much, if not more, interested in how the war and its consequences have been mediated as in attempting to evoke a realistic sense of wartime experience.

Tory pays Donald back for the humiliation of seeing the letters in print by ejecting him from the household, but a final example of letter-writing, which emerges towards the end of the novel, should also be considered. When Tory is going through Mrs. Head's belongings after her death, she discovers some letters that her mother exchanged with Major Brandish, a neighbor from the village where Mrs. Head was living prior to the war. It becomes clear that, while Tory was struggling with Donald's request for a dirty letter, Mrs. Head was sending letters of just this kind to the Major, and that, when reading the Major's replies out loud to Tory, was editing out paragraphs of a personal kind. Tory is horrified to think that "somewhere on the Kent marshes a retired major was hoarding a stash of her own mother's letters" (*Nourishment*, 315). For the reader, this revelation causes a reconsideration of Mrs. Head, who has been on the fringes of the narrative throughout, showing her to be a more complex individual than Tory has given her credit for. But this hidden correspondence also underlines the extent to which private life has been opened to public view by the war, and can never revert to its earlier shape afterwards. Any gains that Tory has made in terms of sexual knowledge are undercut by the humiliation of exposure and the pain of loss. Woodward points here to the paradox that freedoms or apparent freedoms offered especially to women in wartime were always compromised by the very conditions which enabled them.

Woodward's novel is at times overly schematic in its structuring and imagery, and its often fantastical incidents undercut its effort to engage with the impact of the war on the home front, but it does condense, in its use of correspondence in particular, many of the concerns about men, women, and wartime that authors have grappled with over the past sixty years or more. Recent novels show an increased awareness of the ways in which war invaded individuals' privacy, with the censorship of private correspondence emblematic of the surveillance of domestic life more generally. Writers in the 1940s were of course aware of the corralling of private life towards the war effort that was emblematized by the notion of the home front, but expressed this awareness in more covert, perhaps more subtle ways. To return to Taylor's novel, as I have noted, both the letters received by Eleanor and those she sends are placed, for a time, in view of the rest of the household, on the mantelpiece. This gesture acknowledges the importance not only of fulfilling the perceived duty of upholding morale and therefore contributing to the war effort, but also of being seen to do so.

Notes

1. Elizabeth Taylor, *At Mrs. Lippincote's* (London: Virago, [1945] 2008), 24. This chapter draws on a keynote paper delivered at "War and Gender," a War and Representation Network conference held at the University of Newcastle in March 2011. Thanks to Katherine Cooper for inviting me to speak at this event.

2. Jenny Hartley, "'Letters Are *Everything* These Days': Mothers and Letters in the Second World War," in *Epistolary Selves: Letters and Letter-Writers, 1600–1945*, ed. Rebecca Earle (Basingstoke, Eng.: Ashgate, 1999), 183–95, at 187.

3. See Victoria Stewart, *Narratives of Memory: British Writing of the 1940s* (Basingstoke, Eng.: Palgrave, 2006), 141.

4. Amanda Gilroy and W. M. Verhoeven, "Introduction," in *Epistolary Histories: Letters, Fiction, Culture*, ed. Amanda Gilroy and W. M. Verhoeven (Charlottesville: University Press of Virginia, 2000), 3.

5. Margaretta Jolly, "Myths of Unity: Remembering the Second World War Through Letters and Their Editing," in *Arms and the Self: War, the Military, and Autobiographical Writing*, ed. Alex Vernon (Ohio: Kent State University Press, 2005), 144–70, at 164.

6. Margaretta Jolly, *In Love and Struggle: Letters in Contemporary Feminism* (New York: Columbia University Press, 2008), 7.

7. Jenny Hartley, *Millions Like Us: British Women's Fiction of the Second World War* (London: Virago, 1997), 134.

8. Nancy Armstrong, "The Case of the King's Cabinet Opened," in *Epistolary Histories: Letters, Fiction, Culture*, ed. Amanda Gilroy and W. M. Verhoeven (Charlottesville: University Press of Virginia, 2000), 191–93, at 192.

9. There can, however, be room to hide even here. Pat Reid recalls postcards bearing news of successful escapes arriving at Colditz Castle: "sometimes a picture postcard slipped through the censor's net, written in a disguised hand from a fictitious character, but leaving no uncertainty in the mind of the recipient as to the meaning of the seemingly innocuous phrases in the text." A card received from Switzerland, signed by Hariette and Phyllis Murgatroyd, with the message: "We are having a holiday here and are very sorry you are not with us" is soon decoded as issuing from two successful escapers called Hank and Pat. Pat Reid, *The Latter Days at Colditz* (London: Pan, 1955), 178.

10. Nicola Beauman, *The Other Elizabeth Taylor* (London: Persephone Books, 2009), 82.

11. S. P. Mackenzie, *The Colditz Myth: British and Commonwealth Prisoners of War in Nazi Germany* (Oxford: Oxford University Press, 2006), 163.

12. Julie Summers, *Stranger in the House: Women's Stories of Men Returning from the Second World War* (London: Pocket Books, 2008), 36–37.

13. S. P. Mackenzie, *The Colditz Myth: British and Commonwealth Prisoners of War in Nazi Germany* (Oxford: Oxford University Press, 2006), 245.

14. Mark Donnelly, *Britain in the Second World War* (London: Routledge, 1999), 46. After May 1940, mail sent within Britain was also subject to spot checks.

15. Robert Mackay, *Half the Battle: Civilian Morale during the Second World War* (Manchester: Manchester University Press, 2002), 98.

16. Midge Gillies, *The Barbed-Wire University: The Real Lives of Allied Prisoners of War in the Second World War* (London: Aurum, 2011), 21.

17. *The Captive Heart*, directed by Basil Dearden (1946; Ealing).

18. Henry Green, *Back* (London: Harvill, [1946] 1998).

19. A. L. Kennedy, *Day* (London: Jonathan Cape, 2007), 198.

20. Peter Ho Davies, *The Welsh Girl* (London: Faber and Faber, 2007); Liz Jensen, *War Crimes for the Home* (London: Bloomsbury, 2002); Sarah Waters, *The Night Watch* (London: Virago, 2006).

21. Gerard Woodward, *Nourishment* (London: Picador, 2010), 33.

22. Gayle Rubin, "The Traffic in Women: Notes on the 'Political Economy' of Sex," in *Toward an Anthropology of Women*, ed. Rayna R. Reiter (New York: Monthly Review, 1975), 157–210, at 174.

MICHAEL PERFECT

"He Wished to Defend a Country That Wasn't His"

British Subjects/British Servicemen in Zadie Smith's White Teeth *and Andrea Levy's* Small Island

In a section of Zadie Smith's *White Teeth*[1] (2000) that takes place in 1984, three nonwhite, British-born children who are not yet ten years old—black British Irie Jones and British Asian twins Millat and Magid Iqbal—are, as part of their school's celebration of Harvest Festival, enlisted in a project of helping their local community. The three are "assigned" (161) to a Mr. J. P. Hamilton of Kensal Rise, an elderly man to whom they are to deliver charitable donations of various, largely canned foodstuffs. When they arrive at Hamilton's house, their arms full of their offerings, Hamilton appears and is alarmed to be "confronted on his doorstep by three dark-skinned children clutching a myriad of projectiles" (168). It is immediately made clear that Hamilton is a war veteran, and a proud one at that; he has "four argent medals perched just above his heart," and even his choice of cigarette brand seems to have been determined by his dedication to the British armed forces: he has the "silver rim of a Senior Service packet peeping over [his] breast pocket" (169).

Initially anxious that the children might attempt to rob him, Hamilton eventually invites them into the "town house gloom of his hall" with its "battered and chipped Victoriana" (170) and leads them to his living room, offering them tea. Disappointedly professing that he is unable to eat the vast majority of the items that the children have brought him because of his false teeth, Hamilton begins—in a passage to which the novel's title refers directly—to talk about teeth more generally and about his experiences serving in the army during the war:

> "Clean white teeth are not always wise, now are they? Par exemplum: when I was in the Congo, the only way I could identify the nigger was by the whiteness of his teeth, if you see what I mean. Horrid business. Dark as buggery, it was. And they died because of it, you see? Poor bastards. Or rather I survived, to look at it in another way, do you see?" . . . "Those are the split decisions you make in war. See a flash of white and bang! as it were . . . Dark as buggery. Terrible times. All these beautiful boys lying dead there, right in front of me, right at my feet. Stomachs open, you know, with their guts on my shoes. Like the end of the bloody world. Beautiful men, enlisted by the Krauts, black as the ace of spades; poor fools didn't even know why they were there, what people they were fighting for, who they were shooting at. The decision of the gun. So quick, children. So brutal. Biscuit?" (171–72)

While Hamilton's racism and his graphic description of the horrors of armed combat cause Irie to start crying quietly, Millat—who is rather more self-assured than his friend—is made "furious" (172) by what he has heard and yet senses an opportunity both to offer something of a corrective to Hamilton's racism and to find common ground with him; Millat tells Hamilton that he and Magid's father not only "played for England" during the war (172) but that he did so alongside Irie's father. Hamilton rejects this out of hand, stating authoritatively that there "were certainly no wogs"; "no . . . no Pakistanis . . . what would we have fed them? No, no, ... Quite out of the question. . . . No Pakistanis. The Pakistanis would have been in the Pakistani army, you see, whatever that was" (172). As Magid chimes in, telling Hamilton that their father "really was" in the war—and that, like Hamilton, he "has medals" that show he was "a hero"—Hamilton goes on to tell the children to stop telling "fibs" or their teeth will rot (173).

White Teeth is a novel that is as much about forgetting the past as it is about remembering it, and with this passage Smith addresses Britain's tendency to memorialize and mythologize the war as a defining moment in British history while forgetting the role that its colonial subjects played in the conflict. As Raphael Dalleo observes, Hamilton

> conveniently forgets . . . the presence of colonial subjects in British history. His memory produces a hermetic, albeit fictional, past world in which the English fought in the British army, and the Pakistanis in the Pakistani army, and never the twain did meet. One of the novel's purposes appears to be to combat this decontextualization with the historical realities of contact.[2]

Indeed, while the scene in Hamilton's house takes place some four decades after the war itself, in the novel it occurs only fifty or so pages after an account of the experiences of Bangladeshi Samad Iqbal—father of Magid and Millat—fighting alongside white Briton Archie Jones, the father of Irie. As such, the novel is careful to ensure that its reader is fully aware of just how erroneous Hamilton's comments are as soon as he makes them.

Irie, Millat, and Magid quickly elect to escape the house and, with it, Hamilton's ill-informed sermonizing; they find themselves "running to get to a green space, to get to one of the lungs of the city, some place where free breathing was possible" (174). The three children, we are told, not only know the city itself but are also aware that "the city breeds the Mad" (174), at which point the novel gives brief sketches of a series of bizarre, outlandish characters who seemingly occupy their time roaming North London unselfconsciously drawing attention to their own mental illness (one of whom, "Mad Mary," has a confrontational encounter with Magid and Millat's father, Samad). Interestingly, the figures referred to collectively as "the Mad" are immediately contrasted with Hamilton: "But these people *announced* their madness—they were better, less scary than Mr. J. P. Hamilton—they flaunted their insanity, they weren't half mad and half not, curled around a door frame. They were properly mad in the Shakespearean sense, talking sense when you least expected it" (174, italics in original). Here, the novel suggests that what is particularly frightening about Hamilton is that, as a veteran of the war who asserts that there were "certainly no wogs" fighting for the British, he represents—in marked contrast to "the Mad"—the talking of nonsense when one would most expect sense. The clear implication is that the events and the legacies of the greatest human conflict that the world has ever known can be grossly misremembered and misrepresented even by those who actively participated in it.

Critics have noted that Hamilton serves as one of many examples of the ways in which "the essentialist argument is challenged" in *White Teeth*.[3] However, perhaps even more troubling than his essentialism and the fact that he is grossly mistaken in terms of his historical facts is the probability that Hamilton was quite *disastrously* mistaken during the war itself. Given that, after Belgium came to be occupied by the Nazis, the Congo (then a Belgian colony) remained loyal to the Belgian government (which was in exile in London), and given that many thousands of Congolese troops fought for the Allies, it is highly likely that the "niggers" that Hamilton shot and killed in the "split decisions you make during war" were, in fact, his allies rather than his enemies. It is somewhat ironic that, four decades later, as he thinks of them pityingly, he remarks that they hadn't even known "what people they were fighting for, who they were shooting at." Indeed, Hamilton himself seems not to have known—nor, indeed, does he even know some four decades later—who the Congolese were fighting for, nor who he himself was shooting at. While it is clear that J. P. Hamilton functions in *White Teeth* as a means of commenting on Britain's tendency to forget about the role played in the war by its colonial subjects, here the novel also seems to suggest that Britain is often monumentally mistaken about the nature of its own actions during the war.

Smith's debut novel is one of two phenomenally successful British novels of the early twenty-first century which deal with the experiences of British colonial subjects who serve in the British armed forces during the war and which, in so doing, seek to explore the relationship between the legacy of the war and the nature of contemporary, multicultural Britain. Like Smith's novel, Andrea Levy's *Small Island* (2004)[4] has proved a literary sensation; it has, like *White Teeth*, proved incredibly popular both critically and commercially, has won multiple awards, has found its way onto book club reading lists and academic syllabi, and has been adapted by the BBC. While both novels have been applauded for exploring the experiences of immigrants from former British colonies traveling to the former imperial center following the end of the war, what has received rather less attention is the fact that both feature major characters from British colonies who fight for Britain during the war before deciding to migrate there following its conclusion. In *Small Island,* Jamaican airman Gilbert Joseph serves in the Royal Air Force before traveling to London on the *Empire Windrush* in 1948. In Smith's novel, Bangladeshi Samad Iqbal—the father of Millat and Magid, the British-born children who, as above, encounter Britain's tendency towards rewriting its own history in its own interest early on in their lives, in the form of Mr. J. P. Hamilton of Kensal Rise—serves in the army during the war and moves to London some time later in 1973. After returning to their home countries following the end of the war, both Gilbert and Samad come to feel that their countries of origin simply do not offer them, and will not offer their future children, the kinds of socioeconomic opportunities that they desperately crave. (While it takes Samad some three decades to reach this conclusion, Gilbert does so rather more quickly, in less than three years.) Both see the chance to move to the very heart of the former empire as a tremendous opportunity; understandably, having fought for Britain, each expects to be welcomed there and to be treated as an equal. Upon their arrival, however, both quickly discover that the reality is rather different.

While the precise numbers of British subjects who served in the war are impossible to determine, statistics suggest that "[a]t the end of the War over three million men [from Commonwealth nations] were under arms, 2 million of them in the Indian Army, over 200,000 from East Africa and 150,000 from West Africa."[5] It is thought that more than 12,000 West Indians saw active service in the Royal Air Force.[6] However, that the roles of such servicemen have far too often been overlooked cannot be doubted. In research into the content of history textbooks in 2005, for instance, Stuart Foster found that

> despite the global sweep of the war, analysis of textbooks commonly used in England suggests that schoolbooks devote almost exclusive attention to the "principal" Allied and Axis powers. Accordingly, the actions of Britain, USA, and the USSR, routinely are portrayed fighting the Axis powers of Germany, Japan, and to a lesser extent, Italy. . . . [T]he widespread absence from textbooks of other nations, cultures, and ethnic groups determines that history students will learn about the war from a disturbingly

> limited and narrow perspective. Absent from their understanding of the war will be any knowledge of the contributions of other nations and any sensitivity to the accomplishments, actions, and complex perspectives of peoples from other diverse cultural and national backgrounds.[7]

Efforts have been made by major institutions in Britain to address the problem which Foster's findings point towards; the Imperial War Museums, for instance, have made some progress in attempting to ensure that information about the roles of Commonwealth servicemen is present within national spaces of education and commemoration, and the BBC's online "WW2 People's War" archive has helped to call attention to the diverse range of people(s) who were involved in and affected by the war.[8] In addition, the publication in the last few years of a number of insightful new studies into the contributions of Commonwealth servicemen to the war effort may reflect growing public and academic interest in the field.[9] However, there is still some way to go before those contributions receive the full recognition that they deserve.

As the present volume demonstrates, the war has, for some seven decades, remained an incredibly popular—and unquestionably fertile—subject for novelists. However, it must be said that the enormous body of literary fiction which has engaged with the war has tended to suffer from the problem that Foster identifies in history textbooks. Given that so many British colonial subjects served in the war, it is perhaps somewhat surprising that there have not been many more literary works that have attempted to address their experiences; indeed, such works are, relatively speaking, rather few and far between. Michael Ondaatje's Booker Prize–winning novel *The English Patient* (1992), which features as one of its major characters a young Indian sapper who serves as a bomb disposal expert, is perhaps the most celebrated;[10] a more recent example is Biyi Bandele's 2007 novel *Burma Boy*, which takes as its title character a fourteen-year-old Nigerian boy who, after lying about his age, finds himself fighting for the British in Burma in 1944.[11] While such novels play an important role in reminding us that the war was not, as Foster points out, fought by the inhabitants of just six nations, it might also be said that they serve to reposition the war itself within the field of postcolonial studies. While analyses of the relationship between the war and postcolonial studies are, of course, far from uncommon, such analyses have tended to focus almost exclusively on the ways in which the war functioned as a catalyst for decolonization, with the end of the war often referred to as marking the beginning of a period that can be spoken of as "post-colonial." Accordingly, discussions of postcolonial *literature* in relation to the war have, most commonly, focused on anticolonial literatures written after 1945, when—despite the Allied victory—Britain's power and its hold over its colonies was seen to have been irrevocably weakened.[12] Rather than simply identify the war as a precursor to the postcolonial, Smith's and Levy's novels ask us to consider the war itself from a postcolonial perspective. Not only do they address the experiences of nonwhite men who are first British colonial subjects, then British servicemen, and finally migrants to Britain; they also draw attention to the fact that such men contributed to the war effort and to Britain's subsequent failure to recognize their contribution. Indeed, Gilbert and Samad both discover that their service has done nothing to alter British prejudices about their being interlopers; about their being "darkies," "wogs," "niggers," or "Pakis." The fact that they ever served at all seems to have been forgotten altogether. In this sense, *White Teeth* and *Small Island* both suggest that, long after violent conflict between the Allies and the Axis had ended, acts of violence continued (and continue) to be committed against history itself. This is something that both novels seek to address.

Samad and Gilbert both volunteer to fight for the British. Moreover, for both, the experience of having been colonized by the British plays a key role in their decision to do so, albeit in very different ways. In the former novel, in the final year of the war Samad and Archie Jones, just nineteen and seventeen years of age respectively, are "assigned to each other" (*White Teeth*, 83) by the British army and find themselves rolling through northern Greece and southern Bulgaria in a Churchill tank, together with three other white Britons. Reactions to Samad's presence are rather mixed. While Archie—whose job it is to drive the tank, and who seems never to have seen anyone of South Asian descent in the flesh before—spends much of his time simply staring at the tank's brown-skinned wireless operator, co-driver Roy Mackintosh absolutely despises Samad and Captain Will Dickinson-Smith secretly lusts after him. (The fifth man, gunner Will Johnson, is rather too simple-minded to have much of a reaction to anyone or anything.) Mackintosh takes it upon himself to frequently insult Samad, calling him an "Indian Sultan bastard" (85) and a "poof" (86); while Samad offers dispirited but eloquent retorts to these insults, seemingly trying to demonstrate his mastery of the English language so as to convince his white British counterparts that he is not so different from them after all, Mackintosh takes this very eloquence as further proof of his being a "poof." Dickinson-Smith, meanwhile, desperately tries to conceal his sexual desire for his exotic wireless operator by largely allowing Mackintosh to continue with his torrent of verbal abuse, while Archie simply continues to stare, secretly fascinated by Samad and yet outwardly frosty towards him because of a reluctance to incur the wrath of his compatriots.

This conflict and drama that take place within the tank stand in pronounced contrast to everything outside it; the five soldiers quickly discover their journey through southeastern Europe is to be "a long tiresome one, rarely punctuated by any action" (86). Indeed, their task is "not so much to fight the war as to make sure it ran smoothly" (86), and even the adolescent Archie realizes that, at this late stage of the war (it is April 1945), the "real war, the one where cities were brought to their knees, the war with the deathly calculations of size, detonation, population, went on many miles above [his] head" (86–87). Frustrated by the ignorance and intolerance of his British colleagues and by the dreariness of their labors together, Samad complains that this is not what he should be doing:

> [A]s Archie checked their route to Sofia, to no one in particular Samad said, "I should not be here."
>
> As usual he was ignored; most fiercely and resolutely by Archie, who wanted somehow to listen.
>
> "I mean, I am educated. I am trained. I should be soaring with the Royal Airborne Force, shelling from on high! I am an officer! Not some mullah, some sepoy, wearing out my chappals in hard service. My great-grandfather Mangal Pande"—he looked around for the recognition the name deserved but, being met only with blank pancake English faces, he continued—"was the great hero of the Indian Mutiny!"
>
> Silence.
>
> "Of 1857! It was he who shot the first hateful pigfat-smeared bullet and sent it spinning off into oblivion!"

> A longer, denser silence.
>
> "If it wasn't for this buggery hand"—Samad, inwardly cursing the English goldfish-memory for history, lifted five dead, tightly curled fingers from their usual resting place on his chest—"this shitty hand that the useless Indian army gave me for my troubles, I would have matched his achievements." (87)

This is the first of many speeches that Samad gives over the course of *White Teeth* on the subject of his great-grandfather and his supposedly glorious role in the Indian Mutiny. Based on the historical figure Mangal Pandey, Pande becomes a much-disputed figure whose actions and reputation are exalted by Samad at every opportunity, and variously challenged and mocked by other characters. Significantly, here Samad reveals his rather ironic motivations for wanting to take part in the Second World War; somewhat paradoxically, he claims to want to "match [Pande's] achievements" by fighting *for* the very power that his grandfather *opposed*. As Z. Esra Mirze notes, by "replicating the courageous actions of his ancestor against Britain, he now hopes, by fighting *for* Britain, to inscribe himself in British history books. Samad's desire to please the empire reflects the extent of his colonial subjectivity."[13] Indeed, the extent of Samad's "colonial subjectivity" becomes even clearer as he continues to lecture Archie in the tank. Before revealing that an Indian soldier accidentally shot him through the wrist, an unfortunate occurrence which resulted in the permanent impairment of his hand, Samad curses Indians in general (while reserving particular acrimony for Sikhs) and tells Archie that, while serving in the Bengali Army, he was tricked into thinking that he was being given a "great honour" by being allowed to fight in Europe:

> "And then they take me, hero of the 9th North Bengal Mounted Rifles, hero of the Bengal flying corps, and say, 'Samad Miah Iqbal, Samad, we are going to confer on you a great honour. You will fight in mainland Europe—not starve and drink your own piss in Egypt or Malaya, no—you will fight the Hun where you find him.' On his very doorstep, Sapper Jones, on his very doorstep. So! I went. Italy, I thought, well, this is where I will show the English army that the Muslim men of Bengal can fight

> like any Sikh. Better! Stronger! And are the best educated and are those with the good blood, we who are truly of Officer Material." (88)

For all his idolization of his British-defying, anticolonial grandfather, whose achievements he explicitly hopes to emulate, Samad's ultimate desire is to impress the British; to prove his worth to the empire. While the novel purposefully portrays this desire as confused and as rather infantile—as akin to a child attempting to curry favor with a parent by demonstrating superiority over siblings—it also suggests that the British were only too happy to turn Samad's "colonial subjectivity," and that of millions of others like him, to their own military ends.

As with Samad in *White Teeth,* in *Small Island* Gilbert only comes to question his motivations for signing up to serve in the British armed forces (in his case, the Royal Air Force) after he has actually done so. He recalls how, stationed at a military training camp in Virginia, he and his fellow West Indians immediately thought that "America [was] Paradise" (126) on account of the food that they were served there, but soon came to realize that America might not be quite the utopia that it had initially seemed. When an American officer informs them that they cannot leave the camp because they have to "minimise the risk of contracting disease" (128), the realities of racial segregation in the United States—concealed from them at first by the walls of the compound—are momentarily glimpsed. In time, these realities become increasingly clear; as the American hosts show their West Indian guests (now British servicemen) around the camp, they attempt to elaborate on the various problems with the "American nigger" (131) and on their country's "nigger problem" (132). Significantly, Gilbert and the other West Indian recruits are told by the American officer that, even though they cannot leave the compound, they are in fact extremely lucky:

> "I know, I know, you're all disappointed. But while you are at this military establishment," his voice was rising, "and guests of the Government of the United States of America you will have the run of this camp. Everyone here has been ordered to see that your stay with us is the best welcome Uncle Sam could give to the negroes of an ally." He was shouting now. "You will mix with

> white service personnel. Have you boys any idea how lucky you are? You will not be treated as negroes!" (128–29)

Much like Samad, then, Gilbert begins his career as a British serviceman by being told that he is uncommonly fortunate, and that he should be extremely grateful for the magnanimous treatment that he is receiving. In each case, what the British subject is told upon becoming a British serviceman has distinct echoes of the rhetoric of colonialism itself; apparently, colonial subjects should be thankful for the opportunity to fight for the colonial power, just as they should be grateful for its "civilizing" them in the first place.

Gilbert's experiences in the United States push him to reconsider his reasons for wanting to join the RAF. When he decided to enlist he was, as he recalls here, berated by his cousin Elwood:

> "Man, this is a white man's war. Why you wanna lose your life for a white man? For Jamaica, yes. To have your own country, yes. That is worth a fight. . . . But you think winning this war going to change anything for me and you?"
>
> Anthropoid—I [Gilbert] looked to the dictionary to find the meaning of this word used by Hitler and his friends to describe Jews and coloured men. I got a punch in the head when the implication jumped from the page and struck me: "resembling a human but primitive, like an ape." Two whacks I got. For I am a black man whose father was born a Jew. (129)

While he does not completely disregard Elwood's warning, Gilbert remains resolute in his decision because, he says, he has experienced for himself the ugliness of racism. Gilbert recalls how, led by his father—who converted from Judaism to Christianity on a battlefield during the First World War—his family would go to an Anglican church each Sunday and would be stared at by the "haughty and aloof" (130) white people there. Significantly, it is this specific experience that Gilbert is reminded of when he comes across news coverage of what is happening in Europe: "The picture in the newspaper was of a German Jew. He wore a cloth star on a dirty coat. He walked along a street, hunched and humbled, while non-Jews eyed him with an expression of disgust Lester and I knew only too well from those Sunday services" (130). It is this identification with a persecuted German Jew that ultimately persuades Gilbert that he must participate in the struggle against what he refers to as "this master race theory" (131). While Gilbert's motives for deciding to join the British forces and fight against the Nazis are both understandable and extremely admirable, there is also a sense in which they are highly ironic. The very experiences of racism of which Gilbert is reminded by the plight of the German Jews are those of a British colonial subject; somewhat paradoxically, then, Gilbert's decision to fight *for* the colonial power is brought about by the very racism inflicted upon him *by* that colonial power. While Gilbert does not choose to fight for Britain for the same reasons as *White Teeth*'s Samad (namely, on account of a desire to impress the colonial power), like Samad his experiences as a British colonial subject are central to his decision to become a British serviceman.[14]

While *Small Island* certainly never questions the validity—or, indeed, the absolute necessity—of the Allies' violent struggle against the Nazis and against an ideology based on biological racism, one of the novel's greatest strengths is that it challenges the assumption that the powers who led that fight were not themselves racist. In Virginia, upon being informed by his American hosts of their "nigger problem," Gilbert explicitly links the situation in the United States to the very ideology that he resolved to fight: "They had a name for it—no, not master-race theory: Jim Crow!" (132). Here Gilbert uses exactly the same terminology to describe segregation in the United States as he previously used to refer to the fascism of the Nazis (while wryly noting that the Americans themselves choose to employ somewhat different terminology). Moreover, while 1940s Britain certainly did not have the kind of racial segregation that the United States did, Gilbert is made aware even before he enlists in the RAF that racism is deeply ingrained in the British armed forces. It transpires that Gilbert's brother Lester had in fact attempted to enlist in the RAF some time before Gilbert, but despite his fervent desire to fight the Nazis—he is as moved by the newspaper photograph of the German Jew as his brother is—Lester was rejected on account of his not being "of pure English descent" (131) and returned home "burdened with the knowledge that the Mother Country only required members of the white races for this fight" (131). It is, of course, deeply ironic that Lester was prevented from participating in the fight against a racist, absolutist ideology by military recruitment policies that were themselves absolutist and deeply racist.

When Gilbert himself decides that he wants to enlist, he is only able to do so because the "colour bar" in the British forces has, by this point, been lifted; however, he soon discovers that many other "colour bars" are still in existence, and not just in the United States. After leaving the training camp in Virginia, Gilbert (together with many other West Indians) is sent to a camp in Yorkshire, and when he encounters England for the first time he is shocked by the disparity between what he had been led to believe about the country—and, moreover, his own connection to it—and the reality. In a particularly poignant passage, he personifies Britain as a distant but cherished matriarch and reveals that, as well as wanting to fight against the racism of the Nazis, he had also wanted to come to the aid of the "mother country" in its hour of need:

> Let me ask you to imagine this. Living far from you is a beloved relation whom you have never met. Yet this relation is so dear a kin she is known as Mother. Your own mummy talks of Mother all the time. "Oh, Mother is a beautiful woman—refined, mannerly and cultured." Your daddy tells you, "Mother thinks of you as her children; like the Lord above she takes care of you from afar." There are many valorous stories told of her, which enthral grown men as well as children. Her photographs are cherished, pinned in your own family album to be admired over and over. Your finest, your best, everything you have that is worthy is sent to Mother as gifts. And on her birthday you sing-song and party.
>
> Then one day you hear Mother calling—she is troubled, she need your help. Your mummy, your daddy say go. Leave home, leave familiar, leave love. Travel seas with waves that swell about you as substantial as concrete buildings. Shiver, tire, hunger—for no sacrifice is too much to see you at Mother's needy side. This surely is adventure. After all you have heard, can you imagine, can you believe, soon, soon you will meet Mother? (139)

While Gilbert is certainly shocked to discover that Britain[15] is, in fact, dilapidated and ugly—that "Mother" is, in fact, a "filthy tramp" who has "a blackened eye, bad breath and one lone tooth that waves in her head when she speaks"—what shocks him even more is that it fails to recognize him: "she looks at you through lordly eyes and says, 'Who the bloody hell are you?'" (139). Indeed, on his first day in the country, Gilbert discovers that nobody in Britain even seems to know where Jamaica is; on account of his skin color, they assume that it is probably somewhere in Africa (142). This is a problem that is also reported by another Jamaican airman, Michael Roberts, later in the novel (298).

Britain itself is not the only thing that is to prove a great disappointment to Gilbert during his time as a British serviceman. Just as he has been misled about the "Mother" country, he has also, it transpires, been greatly misled about the nature of the role that he will actually have during his time in the Royal Air Force. When enlisting, he was assured that his role would be an important, highly respected one:

> A wireless operator/air-gunner or flight engineer. With my excellent . . . education and my exemplary grades in all exams, those pompous men sitting in the recruitment office in Kingston had told me that, when reaching England, I would be trained as a wireless operator/air-gunner or flight engineer. I would be a valuable member of a squadron, second only to a pilot in respect and responsibility. (145)

Despite these assurances (and despite both his protests and his pretending not to know how to drive), Gilbert is assigned to "motor transport"; that is, for the duration of his service, he is to work as a driver. He wryly notes that, in stark contrast to what he was led to believe about the kind of training that he would receive and the valuable role that he would fulfill, he is in fact going to be trained to do something that he has been doing since he was ten years old (147).

Much like *White Teeth*'s Samad, then, when he enlists as a British serviceman Gilbert is actively misled about the kinds of responsibilities and opportunities that he will have; like Samad, he comes to feel (quite understandably) that the role that he is assigned is a mundane and tedious one that is not befitting someone of his education. Indeed, for both, the war turns out to be—if not entirely uneventful—fairly uninteresting. When enlisting, both see the chance to serve in the war as a British serviceman as an opportunity to do something heroic and, moreover, as a means of finally demonstrating that they are the equals of their British colonizers. That is, both see gaining the status of "British serviceman" as a means of transcending the status of "British subject." However, both are to be severely disappointed, both by the lack of "action" and by the way in which they are treated. Significantly, neither of them actually encounter very much conflict with members of the Axis powers, their official enemies; they do, though, come into conflict with their own (white) allies as a result of being nonwhite colonial subjects. (While Samad is, as above, verbally abused by his immediate colleagues, Gilbert is abused by white American soldiers who are stationed in Britain at the same time as him; their racist objections to him sitting with a white woman in a cinema lead to a riot as well as to a death.) As such, while it is certainly the case that *White Teeth* and *Small Island* both seek to remind us that British subjects played a significant role during the war, neither novel is particularly concerned with portraying that role as a glorious, heroic one. While Ondaatje's *The English Patient* explicitly draws attention to the kinds of courageous, selfless, heroic roles that millions of British colonial subjects played in the war (as above, in Ondaatje's novel young Indian Kirpal Singh works as a bomb disposal expert), this is not a central concern in either *Small Island* or *White Teeth*. Rather, in addressing the experiences of British subjects who become British servicemen, both novels explore ways in which the war served to cement rather than to eradicate the boundaries between colonizer and colonized.

While Samad and Gilbert both come to question their motivations for enlisting in the British services, it is notable that both have a stronger sense of what they are fighting for than do their white British counterparts. In *White Teeth*, Archie is puzzled over why Samad has decided to "defend a country that wasn't his" (95) but also expresses confusion over his own motivations for fighting. When pushed by Samad about what exactly it is that he thinks he is defending, he responds rather weakly: ". . . 'For England. You know,' said Archie, scratching his brain, 'democracy and Sunday dinners, and . . . and . . . promenades and piers, and bangers and mash—and the things that are *ours*. Not *yours*'" (120, italics in original). In *Small Island*, while Gilbert decides to enlist because he wants to fight against racism, Queenie's husband Bernard—who serves in India—gives a totally different account of what he has fought for: "The war was fought so people might live amongst their own kind.

Quite simple. Everyone had a place. England for the English and the West Indies for these coloured people" (469). Accordingly, while Samad and Gilbert are both portrayed as feeling cheated and deceived by the British—as having been lied to about their opportunities both during and after the war, and as coming to question whether they should ever have volunteered to fight—both novels present us with white Britons who serve in the war but whose motives for doing so are questionable. While, in *White Teeth*, Archie's uncertainty about what it is that he is defending is highly comic, in *Small Island* Bernard's racist certainties are deeply alarming.

Perhaps the most significant experience that both Gilbert and Samad have during the war is their meeting and befriending a white Briton who will play a key role in their lives. For Samad, this person is Archie. While the two are initially unsure of what to make of each other, they forge a strong friendship after an unexpected occurrence leaves them as the only surviving members of their crew. On May 6, 1945, the day before the signing of the German Instrument of Surrender, their Churchill tank breaks down near a small Bulgarian village, abruptly halting the progress of their journey. Archie and Samad walk into the village, where they spend three hours drinking Sambuca, and then return to find Mackintosh, Johnson, and Dickinson-Smith dead; while the first two have been murdered by two Nazis that Samad and Archie have heard are traveling through the area, the latter, it seems, chose to take his own life. Suddenly alone, stranded and without means of making contact with their superiors—their radio has, as Samad puts it, been "stripped to buggery" (92)—they remain in the village together for another two weeks, not even realizing that Germany has surrendered until Russian troops arrive in the area and inform them. Samad complains that their chance to play any kind of significant role has vanished: "Like a bus, Jones. We have missed the bloody war" (105). He later tells Archie that, in order to render their service meaningful, they—or, more specifically, Archie—must kill "Dr. Sick," a French scientist who lives nearby and who, they have heard, worked for the Nazis on their sterilization program. Lying about their ranks, they take command of their Russian allies and lead a team of twelve men to the house where "Dr. Sick" lives; Archie confronts him and, after a gunshot is heard, emerges, seemingly having killed him.

As Phyllis Lassner notes, in *White Teeth* "we witness the end of Empire as a cross-cultural friendship is formed between two subalterns in the British army."[16] Indeed, while 1945 marks the end of the war and the beginning of the end of the British Empire, in Smith's novel it is immediately clear that it also marks the *beginning* of something. The friendship that Samad and Archie forge comes to be the very cornerstone of *White Teeth*'s plot, a kind of foundational moment in the novel. As John Clement Ball argues, "Samad's belief that Archie did kill the scientist cements their friendship and leads to their later reunion in London and the mutual involvement of their wives and children."[17] Indeed, after Samad moves to London with his wife in 1973 and seeks out his old comrade, the Iqbals and the Joneses are to be not only connected to but also crucial to each other; the two families eventually converge when, in the final stages of the novel, Irie Jones bears a child to which either Magid or Millat Iqbal is the biological father. Another occurrence in the final stages of the novel is the reappearance of "Dr. Sick"; to Samad's shock and dismay, it transpires that Archie did not, in fact, kill the scientist. Again, then, *White Teeth* suggests that the events of the war are often totally misunderstood by those who actually took part in them; while, quite unbeknown to himself, Mr. J. P. Hamilton seems to have killed people that he shouldn't have, Archie, quite unbeknown to Samad, did not in fact kill the person that he was supposed to have.

Much as Samad meets Archie during the war, *Small Island*'s Gilbert meets Queenie Bligh while he is in the RAF serving in Britain. As in the case of Archie and Samad, Queenie is a white Briton who will have a pivotal role in Gilbert's life and in his family's future; as in the former novel, the friendship that Gilbert and Queenie forge proves to be the cornerstone of *Small Island*'s plot, the thing which brings the novel's major characters into contact with each other. With her husband Bernard fighting overseas (he is also in the RAF), Queenie encounters Gilbert after her father-in-law, a shell-shocked veteran of the First World War, confuses him with Michael Roberts, a Jamaican airman with whom Queenie has an affair and who is the cousin of Hortense, the woman that Gilbert will later marry. Upon meeting for the first time, Queenie and Gilbert quickly become friends; although, to his disappointment, she might not have any idea where Jamaica is, Gilbert is relieved to have encountered someone in Britain who does not seem to judge him based on his ethnic origin. Indeed, Queenie sees Gilbert as being the equal of her husband; she refers to Gilbert as a "boy in blue fighting for this country just like Bernard" (116). After the war, when he has decided to make a life for himself in London, it is in Queenie's house that Gilbert finds somewhere that he can lodge. So, much like the relationship between Archie and Samad in *White Teeth*, for Gilbert Queenie not only represents a friendly, familiar face in a society that is largely hostile to immigrants, but is also—having encountered him as a British serviceman during the war—someone who sees him as an equal who has every right to make a life for himself as a British citizen.

It is only after investigating a great many advertisements for rooms to let, and being refused all of them, that Gilbert eventually thinks of Queenie, remembers her address, and then goes there in "desperation" (215). Trying to secure accommodation that is suitable for both him and Hortense, his new wife who is currently still in Jamaica but is soon to join him in London, he discovers that British landlords are unwilling to rent rooms to black people:

> So how many gates I swing open? How many houses I knock on? Let me count the doors that opened slow and shut quick without even me breath managing to get inside. Man, these English landlords and ladies could come up with excuses. If I had been in uniform—still a Brylcreem boy in blue—would they have seen me different? Would they have thanked me for the sweet victory, shaken my hand and invited me in for tea? Or would I still see that look of quiet horror pass across their smiling face like a cloud before the sun, while polite as nobility they inform me the room has gone? (215)

Significantly, Gilbert wonders whether his old RAF uniform would have any effect on the racist attitude of the British landlords. Only three years have passed since the end of the war and yet the very idea that he, a black immigrant, could have served in the British forces seems to be totally unthinkable to the British themselves. Moreover, Gilbert finds that accommodation is far from the only thing to which his not being white is a barrier; he has as little "luck" with investigating advertisements for jobs as with those for rooms, and is often subjected to openly racist abuse. While Gilbert was certainly disappointed with Britain when he went there during the war (as above, he personifies wartime Britain as a "filthy tramp"), after the war has ended he finds that very little seems to have changed. In fact, if anything, Britain is even more hostile to him now than it was before. Having been a British serviceman, he quite reasonably expects to command at least some respect and to be seen as an equal and yet, ironically, now that his service is complete and he is no longer in uniform, he is perhaps even *more* looked down upon and despised.

Upon moving to Britain some twenty-five years later than Gilbert does, *White Teeth*'s Samad similarly finds that far fewer opportunities are open to him there than he had hoped and that, far from securing him the respect or esteem of most Britons, his wartime service to the country might as well never have happened. Living, initially, in East London, he is forced to work as a waiter in an Indian restaurant (despite having a degree in science) and attempts to engage his customers in conversation and to show them that he is not "really" a waiter. However, as Shiva, one of his younger colleagues, makes extremely clear to him, nobody cares in the slightest about his opinions, his education, or his service in the war (57). While Samad wishes that he could wear a plaque that explains to his customers that he has been "A STUDENT, A SCIENTIST, A SOLDIER" (58, capitalization in original), it is patently clear to him that, as Shiva mockingly points out, his customers are not at all interested, and simply want him to serve them.

After a year of working in the Indian restaurant and living in East London—which, "with its NF gangs" (59), proves to be particularly hostile to immigrants—Samad and his wife relocate to Willesden in North West London, an area which is hesitatingly described as being "more . . . more . . . liberal" (59) and where, crucially, they are only "four blocks down" (54) from Archie and his wife. Samad's proximity to his old wartime comrade is crucial—while he often agonizes over his own lack of opportunities and respect in Britain, the secularism and immorality of British society, and his sons' failure to live up to his expectations for them, the one thing which Samad finds he can rely on is his friendship with Archie, who clearly sees him as an equal. Moreover, as above, the Joneses and Iqbals finally become one family when Archie's daughter gives birth to a child fathered by one of Samad's two sons. Born at the dawn of the twenty-first century, the baby has white British, black Caribbean (Archie's wife Clara is black), and South Asian ancestry, and as such seems to represent a happy, familial convergence of Britain with its postwar, postcolonial immigrants.[18] While Samad often grumbles that his life has been without meaning, as the novel excitedly endorses the new generation of millennial, multicultural Britishness that the child represents, the implication is that this new generation could not have come about had Samad not made the decision to fight for Britain and, subsequently, to migrate there. As such, in *White Teeth* the primary importance of the war is that it is identified as a (perhaps even "the") foundational moment in the history of contemporary, multicultural British society. As Phyllis Lassner suggests, the novel "imagines the grand finale of Empire as the construction of a multicultural, multiclass British bazaar" (Lassner, *Colonial Strangers*, 193).

Like *White Teeth*, *Small Island* ends with the birth of a baby. In the extremely moving final moments of the novel, Queenie gives birth to a child fathered by Michael Roberts and begs Hortense and Gilbert to adopt it, reasoning—as John McLeod has phrased it—that in the Britain of 1948 "the best place for a child who looks black is with a black family."[19] While they are initially shocked by Queenie's request, Gilbert and Hortense eventually agree to adopt the child; Hortense, it seems, is never to realize that she has adopted a child that is in fact the son of her cousin and first love, Michael. While it seems that the two couples are unlikely to ever encounter each other again, like *White Teeth*, *Small Island* ends with the arrival of a child whose birth connects the two families and who, as such, seems to represent a new, multicultural generation of Britishness. In Levy's novel—which, it might be said, is rather more cautionary than celebratory in its portrayal of Britain as a multicultural nation—the baby born in 1948 seems to represent a new, postwar generation of multicultural Britishness that will never fully understand the complexities of its own ancestry.[20]

In both *White Teeth* and *Small Island*, then, the most significant experience that the British colonial subject has while serving in the British forces during the war is that of meeting and befriending a white Briton who will play a key role in their life after they relocate to London, the former center of empire, following the end of the war. Moreover, in both novels this friendship proves to be foundational in terms of the beginning of a new generation of multicultural Britishness (a postwar generation in Levy's novel and a millennial generation in Smith's). Accordingly, while it is certainly true that both novels seek to remind us that British subjects played important roles in the Second World War and that these roles are often overlooked, this is not the major concern of either novel. Rather, given that both identify the war as foundational in bringing about an ethnically and culturally diverse Britain and that both novels are obsessed with portraying the war as something that is constantly misremembered and misrepresented (indeed, even by those who fought in it), ultimately *White Teeth* and *Small Island* both suggest that failing to understand the war means failing to understand the nature of contemporary, multicultural British society. In *White Teeth*, seventeen-year-old Archie Jones expresses bafflement over why nineteen-year-old Samad wanted to "defend a country that wasn't his" (95), and in *Small Island* Gilbert's cousin Elwood expresses a similar sense of puzzlement. However, both novels identify the war as a key moment in Britain coming to "belong" to men like Gilbert Jones and Samad Iqbal as much as to anyone else. As such, both novels suggest that, since the war, fighting for Britain has, necessarily, meant fighting for multiculturalism.

Notes

1. Zadie Smith, *White Teeth* (London: Penguin, 2000).

2. Raphael Dalleo, "Colonization in Reverse: *White Teeth* as a Caribbean Novel," in *Zadie Smith: Critical Essays*, ed. Tracey Walters (New York: Peter Lang, 2008), 91–104, at 96.

3. Molly Thompson, "'Happy Multicultural Land?' The Implications of an 'Excess of Belonging' in Zadie Smith's *White Teeth*," in *Write Black, Write British: From Post Colonial to Black British Literature*, ed. Kadija Sesay (Hertford, Eng.: Hansib, 2005), 122–44, at 125.

4. Andrea Levy, *Small Island* (London: Review, 2004).

5. Ian Thomas, "Black History Month 365: For Whom the Bells Toll," http://www.blackhistorymonth.org.uk/article/section/bhm-heroes/for-whom-the-bells-toll/.

6. Richard Smith in *The Oxford Companion to Black British History*, ed. David Dabydeen, John Gilmore, and Cecily Jones (Oxford: Oxford University Press, 2007), 436.

7. Stuart Foster, "The British Empire and Commonwealth in World War II: Selection and Omission in English History Textbooks," *International Journal of Historical Learning, Teaching and Research* 5, no. 2 (July 2005): 1–19, at 1–2.

8. See "WW2 People's War" at the BBC website, http://www.bbc.co.uk/history/ww2peopleswar/.

9. See for example, David Killingray, *Fighting For Britain: African Soldiers in the Second World War* (Oxford: James Curry, 2010); Alan Jeffreys and Patrick Rose, eds., *The Indian Army, 1939–1947: Experience and Development* (Farnham, Eng.: Ashgate, 2012); Stephen Bourne, *The Motherland Calls: Britain's Black Servicemen & Women, 1939–45* (Stroud, Eng.: History, 2012).

10. Michael Ondaatje, *The English Patient* (London: Bloomsbury, 1992).

11. Biyi Bandele, *Burma Boy* (London: Jonathan Cape, 2007).

12. See, for example, Elleke Boehmer's seminal study *Colonial and Postcolonial Literature: Migrant Metaphors* (Oxford: Oxford University Press, 1995).

13. Z. Esra Mirze, "Fundamental Differences in Zadie Smith's *White Teeth*," in *Zadie Smith: Critical Essays*, ed. Tracey Walters (New York: Peter Lang, 2008), 187–200, at 189, italics in original.

14. For a discussion of colonial subjects' ambivalence about fighting for the British, see Ritchie Ovendale, "The Empire-Commonwealth and the Two World Wars," in *The Oxford History of the British Empire*, vol. 5: *Historiography*, ed. Robin W. Winks (Oxford: Oxford University Press, 1999), 354–65.

15. Like other characters at various moments in the novel, Gilbert actually refers to "England" rather than to "Britain" in this passage. It should be noted that there is a great deal of slippage between "England" and "Britain" throughout the novel, which never particularly seeks to address the question of the difference between the two nor the problems of conflating them.

16. Phyllis Lassner, *Colonial Strangers: Women Writing the End of Empire* (New Brunswick, N.J.: Rutgers University Press, 2004), 198.

17. John Clement Ball, *Imagining London: Postcolonial Fiction and the Transnational Metropolis* (Toronto: University of Toronto Press, 2004), 241.

18. See Michael Perfect, *Contemporary Fictions of Multiculturalism: Diversity and the Millennial London Novel* (Basingstoke: Palgrave Macmillan, 2014), 76–101.

19. John McLeod, "Postcolonial Fictions of Adoption," *Critical Survey* 18, no. 2 (Summer 2006): 45–55, at 50.

20. See Michael Perfect, *Contemporary Fictions of Multiculturalism: Diversity and the Millennial London Novel* (Basingstoke: Palgrave Macmillan, 2014), 52–75.

SUE VICE

The Nazis in Britain

Representations of the Wartime Occupation of the Channel Islands

THERESA: Where are the Channel Islands?
LYDIA: Near France.
THERESA: Near France. Is that safe?
LYDIA: Don't worry, they're safe. They're British. We'll all be safe there.
—JULIA PASCAL, *Theresa*

The Channel Islands were the only part of the British Isles to be invaded by the Nazis during the Second World War and were occupied between June 1940 and May 1945. Yet this remarkable fact is often either forgotten or subject to polarized stereotypes about the islanders' heroic endurance as much as their abject accommodation to the invaders. This is due in part to the complex and specific nature of the occupation, and because of the Channel Islands' relation to the rest of the British Isles. The Bailiwicks of Guernsey and Jersey's status as crown dependencies means that although their inhabitants are British citizens, the islands are not part of the United Kingdom nor, postwar, of the European Union. In 1940 the islands were invaded after they were demilitarized by Britain, since they were seen by Hitler as a staging point for the German invasion of the British mainland. While the islands' wartime experience has been compared to that of occupied western Europe, including Belgium, the

Netherlands, and France, it was not characterized by the organized resistance that took place in those countries,[1] although some independent initiatives did occur.[2]

The varieties of forgetting that have accompanied the occupation's history arise from the fact that these events do not fit comfortably with the British national myth of wartime heroism and a united front against evil, both at home and overseas. This is the case for several reasons: Churchill's paradigm of triumphant "victory at all costs"[3] is at odds with the islanders' grueling experience of a five-year-long occupation, while the pragmatic and moral accommodations made on the islands during that time do not always accord with British self-conceptions of wartime tolerance and righteousness. Yet it is precisely such "rivalry"[4] between incompatible national myths, and the occupation's "moral ambiguities,"[5] that make for the formally varied and ethically challenging representations that I discuss here. Mary Horlock's novel *The Book of Lies* (2012) is narrated by the Guernsey schoolgirl Catherine Rozier, whose fascination with the occupation that took place over forty years earlier leads to her conviction that the familial secrets and betrayals of the war are being repeated in her own life. Julia Pascal's play *Theresa* (premiered in 1990) extends the notion of betrayal and collaboration beyond the family to include the government of the Channel Islands, where the institution of the Nuremberg Laws on crown territory goes unopposed and results in the deportation of the play's eponymous protagonist, Theresa Steiner, to her death in Auschwitz. In Pascal's play, wartime "lies" about collusion are shared and maintained by a whole community, and the theatrical form of *Theresa* is enlisted to represent this.

Several events in the 1990s altered perceptions of wartime history on the Channel Islands, acting in the contradictory directions that appear in aesthetic form in the works under discussion here. The release of Public Record Office and local records in Jersey and Guernsey began in 1993, followed by that of information on forced laborers from Russian archives.[6] In 1995, the fiftieth anniversary of liberation saw the beginning of an explicit recognition of the difference between the islanders' wartime experience and that on the British mainland, as well as the commemoration of the occupation's victims (Carr, "Examining the Memorialscape," 176). This took the form of public memorials, while the posthumous award in 2010 of "British Hero of the Holocaust" to four Jersey people who had assisted their Jewish fellow islanders has contributed to a narrative of "righteous" resistance. This is set against the kinds of "horror"[7] represented in Pascal's *Theresa*, whose protagonist is murdered in Auschwitz.

The title of Madeleine Bunting's history of the islands' war, *The Model Occupation*,[8] which was written in the wake of the opening of the Jersey archives, uses the phrase, originally that of Ambrose Sherwill, Guernsey's wartime attorney general, to double-edged effect. "Model" refers at once to the Nazis' view of the invasion of the Channel Islands as a trouble-free version of its kind, overseen by German soldiers rather than the Gestapo, and to the potential significance for Britain of that history as an imagined or counterfactual template of what the invasion of the British mainland might have been like. The critic Gavriel Rosenfeld argues that such an "allohistorical subtext" to Bunting's study is a corrective one, designed to "debunk the myth of Britain's moral exceptionalism" during the war. This takes place through Bunting's demonstration of the historical reality of collaboration that occurred in the British Isles on Guernsey and Jersey. In the post–Cold War era, Rosenfeld argues that such an act of British self-reflection could establish commonalities in contrast to an insistence on a different history, and "a new sense of national identity, less aloof from . . . a united Europe."[9] However, as implied by the texts that I discuss in this essay, the more the details of the occupation are known, the more local and specific this history may seem, and the less applicable to the rest of Britain. For instance, Mary Luckhurst notes the "shocked" reaction of mainland audience members to the story of Theresa Steiner represented in Pascal's play, since they claimed to know little of the occupation and "did not associate the history of the Channel Islands with British history" (Luckhurst, "The Case of Theresa," 266).[10] Each of these texts makes a radical effort to reassess the Channel Islands' wartime history. That record is reexamined as part of British history, rather than a localized example of collaboration that has no relation to Britain's moral exceptionalism, and the islanders' accommodation of the occupiers is used as a way of speculatively foreshadowing what the invasion of the mainland might have looked like.[11]

Mary Horlock, *The Book of Lies*

Mary Horlock's novel *The Book of Lies* directly juxtaposes the Channel Islands' past and present by interleaving the diary, written in the 1980s, of disaffected Guernsey schoolgirl Cathy with her uncle Charles Rozier's wartime memories tape-recorded twenty years earlier. These two stories about secrecy and betrayal unfold in parallel. Cathy tells the reader on the first page of her diary that she has killed her schoolfriend Nicolette by pushing her off a cliff; while Rozier's taped memoir, transcribed by his brother, Catherine's father Emile, gradually reveals the ways in which Charles's boyhood rebellion against the occupiers resulted in his father's death and his own deportation to Europe under the Nazis' "Night and Fog" decree. The novel concludes with Cathy's discovery that her grandmother had an affair with a German officer, and she determines to leave the islands. Cathy blackmails her mother into keeping her own murderous secret quiet by threatening to reveal what she believes to be her mother's complicity in Emile's death.

The overdetermination of narrative conceits and generic tropes in *The Book of Lies*, which such a summary reveals, is motivated and necessitated by its wartime secrets. While the schoolgirl-gothic plot replicates wartime animosities, it is equally fitting to this story about the ghosts of the past that Cathy frightens her schoolmates with stories of "flesh-eating Nazi Zombies"[12] haunting the Guernsey cliffs. As well as resounding with the bathos of what is clearly Cathy's preferred genre of film, such invocation of the living dead is psychically apt, since the destructive past has not been laid to rest. The narrative device of interleaving past and present by juxtaposing Cathy's diary and Charles's memoir has several functions. In particular, it gives substance to Cathy's declaration of belief in historical determinism, since "some things are destined, as per Shakespeare and his tragedies," such that the secrets and unresolved conflicts of the past will be enacted in her own life. "It turns out I was a murderer before I was even born," as she puts it (*The Book of Lies*, 5).

Yet Cathy's and Charles's stories are not just interleaved, but interanimating. Although Horlock has observed in an interview that the past "interrupts and predicts the present" in her novel,[13] it is rather the reverse: in a version of Freud's notion of *Nachträglichkeit*, or belated awareness, the past as represented in her uncle's diary often appears after Cathy's writing about the present moment. This is made clear in linguistic terms. It is as if Charles overhears Cathy and repeats her words, although the reader is aware that it should be the other way round. In her opening diary entry, Cathy introduces the reader to the psychogeography of her world by questioning the Germans' description of Guernsey as "a small paradise" with a viewpoint of contemporary cynicism: "*Excusez-moi*, but since when did a few manky palm-trees make a paradise?" (*The Book of Lies*, 1–2), and likens the killing of Nicolette to an act of wartime resistance:

> My so-called best friend was a Liar and a Traitor who deserved everything she got . . . Bullies should be punished, right? They are like the Nazis, picking on poor, isolated people and pulling them to bits. What I did was not an Abomination (excellent word). (*The Book of Lies*, 3)

Cathy's comments reveal her self-exonerating interpretation of events, since Nic was the one who attacked first, and Cathy's action in pushing her over the cliff was taken in self-defense. While Nic's deadly feud with her former friend seems trivially motivated—Cathy's betraying the news of Nic's mother's affair prompted her parents to separate—here Cathy mingles incompatible registers of discourse about schoolyard bullies with that of Nazi persecution. However, it turns out, with the hindsight accorded by reading further, that these were originally Charles's words, now refracted through Cathy's distinctive satirical voice. He describes the Guernsey of his birth in 1928 in prelapsarian terms as "that small and perfect paradise," before he, like his niece, fell in with the wrong friends, including Ray Le Poidevoin, whom he describes as, "Murderer. Traitor." For Charles, it is the view from Clarence Batterie—site of Nicolette's death some forty years later—that is an "abomination," obscured as it is by the "German concrete" of massive fortifications (*The Book of Lies*, 6–7). Others of Cathy's unmarked analepses draw ironic attention to what has become of the events of the occupation in the present. These events seem to have devolved simply into kitsch signifiers of present-day anomie, as shown by her descriptions of the local bad boy Michael Priaulx, who wears a New Order T-shirt and spray-paints a swastika and the legend "The Nazis Won" on a watchtower built during the war (78–

82). Recalling the war in his memoir, Charles describes his first sight of a swastika on Guernsey, "whipped up" by Creasey's, the local draper's shop (85), and quotes the warning given to his family by *Unteroffizier* (Corporal) Anton Vern, to the effect that local people are to adhere to the rules of the occupation and that "the Bailiff and Attorney General have agreed to the new order" (86). Charles even echoes narratively, by prefiguring historically, Michael's slogan, in reporting a conversation between himself and his father: "'You cannot be serious,' I told [Hubert]. 'You cannot believe the Germans will win.' And of course he couldn't answer me because in truth they already had" (89). Yet this devolution of wartime events into the epithets and slogans of present-day pop culture is not represented straightforwardly. Despite their differences, Michael's graffiti and Charles's apparent defeatism concern the same notion of the islands' moral capitulations; and Charles's seemingly authentic oral record, transcribed by his brother, complete with exclamations and use of Guernsey patois, turns out to be unreliable. Ray Le Poidevoin did not betray Charles and his family to the Nazis, and Vern was not simply the "good German" that he seemed, but also his mother's lover.

Indeed, the containment of Charles's story within Cathy's increases its unreliable appearance, partly because of the reversed linguistic influence, and partly because Cathy's own first-person narrative is unreliable. This is the case despite the fact that it is possible to account for the temporal reversals of the two stories in terms of the novel's diegesis. The story is in Cathy's charge, and framed by her narration. Charles's memories do not appear unmotivatedly, despite at first seeming to be interpolated by an invisible implied narrator, but because Cathy is in the process of "carefully putting in order" and transcribing her dead father's papers (*The Book of Lies*, 29, 246). Like unreliable modernist narratives such as Ford Madox Ford's *The Good Soldier*,[14] where rumor, hearsay, and the voices of others are enlisted to apparently confused but actually self-exculpatory effect, it is as if Cathy is constructing a historically determinist alibi for herself and her killing of Nic by means of intertextuality. She laments to her history teacher Mr. McCracken that "it's like everything has been decided. My life is set on this crap course of crapness" (235).

As in the case with John Dowell's narrative in *The Good Soldier*, if expressed in a rather different idiolect from his orotund narration, it is only with hindsight or on rereading that the details of Cathy's diary are revealed as inconsistent and hard to account for. In a predictive utterance that gives away the fact that she has not only read Charles's account but might be modeling hers on it, Cathy observes that "Nic was like the sister I'd never had but always wanted. And remember: two sisters, like two brothers, can be completely different" (*The Book of Lies*, 19). It seems that she is not only drawing upon, but is profoundly influenced by, Charles's rhetorical question to Emile just a page later but forty years earlier: "How can two brothers be so different, eh? You got the good stuff, the brains, the looks, our mother's love, while I, biân sûr, was poisoned" (20). Hints at the ways in which Cathy too is "poisoned" are made in passing, for instance her preface to falsely accusing the schoolteacher Mr. McCracken of sexual abuse: "And now I get to the bit where I say kids tell stupid lies because they don't know any better, but actually I should know better, because I've read it all before" (105). Cathy's phrase "I've read it all before" is not a cliché about general life lessons, but a deceptively low-key admission of the extent of Charles's influence upon her story. She has read his memoir thoroughly, along with learning the content of all her father's occupation-related history books and files "off by heart and inside out" (152). Indeed, the next installment of Charles's memoir opens, "Pour continua, Emile," as if it is Cathy's and not his own story that he is seamlessly carrying on, as he adds: "You know the story of the boy who cried wolf? He told so many lies nobody would believe him when he finally told the truth" (106). Cathy's enlisting her uncle's wartime narrative for her own purely personal ends is symbolic of the islanders' ambivalent relationship to the past, and their mixture of self-pity and defensiveness. She is an embodiment of the contemporary revisioning of the past, and one who is aware of this very technique.

Eventually Cathy allows the distinction between her diary and her uncle's memoir to blur, and simply incorporates his narrative within her own to imply a parallel, this time between her being unjustly ignored by her schoolfellows, and Charles's inglorious return home at the war's end:

> But it was like I didn't exist. It was like I was dead.
>
> When my uncle was shipped back to Guernsey after the war, he wasn't given much of a welcome . . . people said he'd

> been very foolish for causing so much upset, and it was his word against theirs so he never stood a chance. (*The Book of Lies*, 210)

Cathy does not conceal her own unreliability as a witness to and interpreter of events. Such admission is couched in two contradictory ways. On the one hand, Cathy sees her misleading narration in terms of an inability to represent either the past or the present, since it is "weird how I can learn things off by heart but still not understand them" (*The Book of Lies*, 63), and claims that she does not "understand the first thing about living people—why they make the choices they make, why they keep secrets" (251). On the other hand, Cathy also admits to the deliberate shaping of events. She has "made things up" (17), places truth and fact in opposition (2), admits that she has a "brilliant imagination" (143), and quotes her mother saying she knows her daughter "exaggerates" (249). Indeed, the extent of Cathy's unreliability is never certain. We might simply take it that her view of events, including her feelings about Nicolette—whom she claims at different moments to have loved or hated—fluctuate. At the other extreme, it may appear that the whole narrative is invented, either intradiegetically, in the sense that nothing Cathy says can be trusted, or extradiegetically, since the story is the product of an implied narrator beyond Cathy, and is, after all, a novel entitled *The Book of Lies*. It does not require any radical skepticism to view this title as a reference to the novel's *énonciation* as much as its *énoncé*. As a consequence, despite its immersion in the topography of Guernsey and its wartime history, the novel's concerns are, rather, the literary ones of invention, memory, and distinctive but unreliable first-person utterance, located in this overdetermined setting.

Yet again like John Dowell in Ford Madox Ford's novel, who gives varying estimates of the eponymous "good soldier" Edward Ashburnham and his history, Cathy relates contradictory versions of what happened to her uncle during the war. Despite the partial renditions Cathy gives, she refers to Charles's tale as "The Whole Grim Truth." To Nicolette, she outlines the story of "Uncle Charlie, Dad's older brother, who got in trouble with the Germans and ended up being starved and tortured and driven mad" (*The Book of Lies*, 29). To Mr. McCracken, she "explains" that "Dad's elder brother was my age when he betrayed his entire family to the Nazis, shot his father in the head and was then sent to a concentration camp" (35). The strategic nature of Cathy's distortions is evident when she informs Nicolette that the reason for Charlie's "trouble" was his choice of the "wrong friends" (29), while Mr. McCracken is told that "children can do and say terrible things without realising the consequences" (35), as if anticipating not only her responsibility for Nic's death, but her false accusations against him. Even such obviously intentional variation seems small-scale in relation to the sensationalist version of patricide that Cathy relates to Mr. McCracken: "I was aware, as I was saying it, that I'd got the facts slightly muddled, but I didn't like to backtrack" (35). Yet "backtracking," in a version of Michael André Bernstein's notion of backshadowing in *Foregone Conclusions*, is exactly what Cathy does throughout her narrative, in order to establish both precedent and justification for her actions. On this occasion, her apparent honesty sounds like John Dowell's, to the extent of echoing his confession of "impressionist" narration: "I have, I am aware, told this story in a very rambling way so that it may be difficult for anyone to find his path through what may be a sort of maze" (Ford, *The Good Soldier*, 182). Like Cathy, Dowell has told his tale, which resembles a "maze" morally as much as in terms of its plot, in "rambling" fashion because, as he puts it, "this is a real story and . . . , after all, real stories are probably told best in the way a person telling a story would tell them. They will then seem most real" (*The Good Soldier*, 183). Dowell's use of "real" to mean, on first mention, something akin to "important" or "historical," and, on its second mention, "true," is akin to Cathy's divided concern in *The Book of Lies*. It similarly fails to make clear whether "seeming" real suggests authenticity or simulacrum.

It is only in an interpolated document from another source, a letter from Cathy's father Emile to the editor of the *Guernsey Evening Press*, that we read his version of what really befell the Rozier family during the war, one that is partial only in the sense of being concise:

> My father, Hubert Wilfred Rozier, was shot dead by the Germans whilst allegedly "trying to escape," my brother, Charles André Rozier, was arrested and tortured by the Nazis at the notorious prison of Paradis before being deported to a concentration camp in Germany, where he remained for the rest of the war. (*The Book of Lies*, 52)

Cathy's reportage of her uncle's fate gives way towards the end of her narrative in the face of her assertion that "the biggest secret so far" is the fact that "I wasn't ever very interested in the Bloody-Stupid German Occupation, but I thought I might find something in Dad's books and journals and letters to explain what Mum wouldn't. Shouldn't History explain everything?" (*The Book of Lies*, 271). This admission that Cathy is searching for information about her father's recent death appears to accomplish two feats: the subordination of public to a personal, oedipally inflected history, and of the past to the present. In terms of the former, Cathy wishes to love her father in his paternal and his historian's role, as she says at the beginning of her story in a conflation of public with personal history: "This is Guernsey, please remember, where there are plenty of secrets no one's ever meant to talk about . . . Usually we blame the Germans. Me? I blame Dad" (4). The historical record, at least in terms of Charles Rozier's diary, is valuable to Cathy only in its links to her own life. Indeed, she sees both life and history as open to what she calls "revisionism":

> What I like most about History is that you can change it. Yes, that's right . . . Just look at what happened with the Occupation. Once it was over, most islanders decided that it hadn't been that bad, and even called it character-building. (*The Book of Lies*, 222)

Cathy's remark knowingly makes her a figure for the islanders' transformation of their part in a history of equivocation and accommodation into the personal triumph of survival. Such a statement about historical relativity also relates to the ontological status of Cathy's story and her self-conscious fictionalizing. The father whom she idolizes has not been presented to us as he was, as she implies in a posthumous address to him: "I tell everyone you were a champion swimmer and a hero and a genius, even if you weren't" (223).

Cathy's wish is to understand the details of her father's death as well as what might be missing from her mother's "Official Version" of events (*The Book of Lies*, 279), but this question is only settled in terms of her father's own oedipally inflected discovery, which seems to make the public and private narratives of Guernsey life coalesce. A second documentary source, this time a letter from the German soldier Anton Vern, now living in Vienna, offers another perspective on the events of the war. Vern describes how he and Mrs. Rozier had a clandestine love affair and that it was he who instigated the search of the Roziers' house that resulted in Charles's arrest and Hubert's death. Yet Vern succeeds in adding only another interpretive layer to Cathy's text, rather than revealing an explanatory truth about the past. Not only is his perspective shown to be subjective—"I have now had more experience with women and as far as can I see they often act impetuously" (289), as he puts it—but the nature of the affair that he describes is not identified, and Mrs. Rozier's feelings and motives remain opaque. Such lack of overt judgment successfully defamiliarizes debates about the "horizontal collaboration" on the part of Channel Island women who had relationships with members of the occupying army.[15] Vern's affair with Mrs. Rozier is not represented either as a tragic romance or a "shameful and unpatriotic" betrayal (Knowles Smith, *Changing Face*, 176),[16] except by implication in terms of its negative effects. However, Vern's letter suggests an uncomfortable merging of the imperatives of war with those of romance. He quotes Hubert Rozier admitting to ownership of a notebook in which German military locations were recorded while shielding his wife from knowledge of it: "There shouldn't be any secrets between a man and wife, but the War's changed all that, hasn't it?" Yet this rhetorical question is also a challenge to the adulterous couple, and is followed by Hubert's statement to Vern, "You have got what you wanted" (*The Book of Lies*, 287). Both utterances have a double reference, to the spoils of love as well as those of war.

The two central themes of *The Book of Lies*, Cathy's fabrications and the occupation of Guernsey, are united by her efforts to understand the pressure of past events on the present. Although she declares that her interest all along was in her father rather than the war, the two are not separable, not least because the occupation was Emile Rozier's obsession and underlay his conviction that "you couldn't choose your fate because History had already dictated it" (*The Book of Lies*, 319). As we have seen, such a fatalistic abnegation of agency is one shared with his daughter, who equally insists that her fate has been determined by the past. Like many of the novel's details, Emile's remark is no truism, but implies that the specific events of Guernsey's wartime history accord with those of the present. Cathy's account uses the atrocities of the past, some of which she invents, for present-day purposes. Mentioning the forgotten mass graves at the bottom of the cliffs is a ruse to engage Nicolette's interest by means of a "little story of shameful lies and death" (18), as well as constituting a moment of dramatic irony since we know that Nic's body will end up in the same place. Historical detail appears in footnote form in Cathy's narrative, not so much as a way of acknowledging the past as affirming its consignment to a subsidiary status. The inventions, such as the bibliographical detail of Emile Rozier's extensive oeuvre (he is the author of such works as *The Bunker Baedeker*, Patois Press 1977), are sometimes a part of the text's fictional world, while at other times, as the novel's title suggests, they are intradiegetic lies—for instance, about the use of Guernsey's "Underground Hospital as a gas chamber" (29)—told by Cathy to the reader as much as to the characters. The effect of this is to cast her reliability into further doubt. While we might agree that *The Book of Lies* represents what Christian House calls "the domino-topple of such mistakes from one generation to another,"[17] this seems to be exactly the result Cathy has aimed for. Although the events of the past do hang over the novel's present, she exploits them as a way of explaining away her own actions.

Julia Pascal, *Theresa*

In *The Book of Lies*, one of Cathy's footnotes claims that "no one wants to talk about the Jews ever ever ever" (208), and the challenge of such a deliberate silence is taken up by Julia Pascal in her play *Theresa*, based on the fate of its real-life eponymous heroine, Theresa Steiner. In the play, we witness Theresa's journey from Nazi-occupied Austria to being a refugee in Britain, followed by her journey with her employer, Lydia Askew, to Guernsey as a governess. When Lydia and her children flee the island back to the mainland at the outbreak of war, Theresa is prevented from leaving by a Guernsey policeman, William Sculpher, although the Germans have yet to arrive. These fateful acts—the abandonment of Theresa by Lydia, and in particular Sculpher's preemptive initiative—are the central dramatic and moral focus of the play.

Like Horlock's novel, Pascal's play places in parallel different historical moments to ironic effect. Rather than such a juxtaposition taking the form of the interleaving of accounts written at different times, as it does in *The Book of Lies*, in *Theresa* the imagery of Nazi Germany and Anschluss-era Austria is used to foreshadow events in occupied Guernsey. Theresa's long opening monologue is spoken simultaneously in English and German, to both mimetic and alienating effect. Although it fulfills Pascal's wish to reproduce the multilingual world of prewar Jewish life,[18] it also acts to make the audience work hard to relate to the play's varied format, which features music, dance, stylization, and use of the different national languages of Polish, German, and French within the English dialogue. At the play's outset, Theresa describes scenes of cruelty and atrocity witnessed by a "well-dressed" and, it is implied,[19] Jewish man in a Viennese café in 1938: "He looks out of the highly polished crystal glass window" to a scene in which an old Jewish couple are being forced to scrub the street, and "a group of pretty prostitutes are screaming with laughter at the pair old enough to be their grandparents" (*Theresa*, 20). Although the unnamed man stares in "frozen fascination," the other customers "continue sitting in the café and ordering 'another cake!'" (21). In a review, Mark Jenkins describes the effect of Theresa's personal anecdote and reportage of this kind as a "melody line" or leitmotif, since its substance is echoed in altered form later in the play, in the manner of a musical composition.[20] Indeed, this is the play's consistent technique: words and events are repeated to modified and ominous effect in different settings. For instance, the action of characters "throw[ing]" a "case, hat and coat" at Theresa to convey her escape from Austria to Britain reappears in Guernsey at the moment of her forced deportation, when her fellow nurses "throw case, coat and hat" after her (25, 52). The sound of the train that seemed to convey successful evasion in the earlier scene of leaving Vienna becomes the way in which the audience apprehends Theresa's death: the play's last moments consist of the "*high sound*" of trains going to Auschwitz.

We see such an effect of melodic yet malign echoing in the play's opening scene at the level of both utterance and action. Theresa's repeated mention of the Viennese café's "crystal" window that separates its patrons from what is happening in the street prefigures historical violence even more clearly in its German version as a "Kristallfenster." Kristallnacht, the "Night of Broken Glass" pogrom of November 9, 1938, emerges syllabically in the next scene following this invocation of the window as an invisible barrier to acknowledging the pain of others. The prophet Cassandra appears as a character during Kristallnacht, and observes of this state-sponsored violence that "they'll say, 'It never happened. How could it happen? Who would do such a thing?'" (*Theresa*, 25). Cassandra is a figure for denial of what is known to have taken place as much as one of prophecy that goes unheeded. The effect of such bleak historical irony is compounded by the same actor assuming both this role and that of Auguste Spitz, the other Viennese refugee who was deported from Guernsey to Auschwitz. Auguste's experience provides implicit answers to Cassandra's rhetorical questions: like Theresa, she was sent to her death by a British policeman, whose character in the play embodies a challenge to any unquestioning assumption of moral superiority.

Like the "lies" of Horlock's novel, the doubling of characters in *Theresa* is a technique that operates both within and outside the fiction. In the play, its function is to deconstruct any notion of exceptionalism.[21] Although the small number of actors in the play—the script notes suggest four, for a cast of twenty-four—operates for the most part to represent a "fusion" (Lassner, *Anglo-Jewish Women Writing the Holocaust*, 159) of perpetrators and collaborators in different national settings, even Theresa herself acts as the conduit through whom discordant voices speak. The Polish of her childhood, used elsewhere to signify youthful innocence as she sings nursery rhymes (Pascal, "Introduction," 7), returns as a startlingly oppositional utterance about the Holocaust:

> THERESA: (*Momentarily breaking character to express a Polish antisemitic view*): *Wynalazek zydowski!*

Such a technique disrupts the customarily seamless identification of voice and individual; instead, Theresa embodies here the utterances of her cultural background. In the play, the Polish phrase—meaning, "It's a Jewish invention!"—is made clear only by means of its repetition in French and German. Elsewhere, such an effect is accomplished by means of a soundtrack. Noel Coward's wartime song "Don't Let's Be Beastly to the Germans" is heard when Theresa first arrives at Lydia Askew's home, sounding an ambivalent note of both satire and capitulation;[22] while an "echo" of the *Blue Danube* waltz that we heard at the play's opening in Vienna mingles with the sounds of the final train transporting Theresa to Auschwitz.

The play's opening scene does not just establish Theresa's plight, as a Jewish woman who has been dismissed from her university post as a professor of architecture and has no safe future in Vienna. This sequence also enlists the audience's horror at the spectacle of the old people's mistreatment, and their relief on Theresa's behalf when she is able to depart for Britain. Yet this offers a highly ironized sense of escape, since just the same elements appear in different form in Guernsey, as Cassandra's prediction suggests. Theresa's questions to Lydia perform the Cassandrian function of a warning that goes unheeded, as the quotation from my epigraph emphasizes:

> THERESA: Where are the Channel Islands?
> LYDIA: Near France.
> THERESA: Near France. Is that safe?
> LYDIA: Don't worry, they're safe. They're British. We'll all be safe there. (*Theresa*, 35)

Lydia's response confuses geography with politics in implying that the Channel Islands' Britishness will act as a protection, and she turns out to be mistaken in both senses. The islands' proximity to France eventually enables not only their invasion but also Theresa's deportation to Bordeaux and thence to Auschwitz; and no British virtues prevent the institution of anti-Jewish measures by "the Islands' highest officials, all British-trained lawyers."[23] Indeed, Britishness offers little comfort to Theresa when she first arrives in Britain and is treated ungenerously in the households where she is employed as a maid. Lydia appears more humane, and, as a single mother with a history of patriarchal victimization, has less investment in the status quo. However, even she has to keep apologizing for her gaffes and assumptions about Theresa's age, nationality, and Jewishness. Lydia's expressions of regret in this domestic context function as a premonition of her abandoning Theresa in Guernsey. The scene is played first conventionally, and then, as we see below, in the stylized form of Theresa's recurring nightmare:

> LYDIA: I need tickets.
> SCULPHER: This lady stays.
> LYDIA: My responsibility.

SCULPHER: Vienna. J. Jew.
THERESA: Yes. I am a Jew. I am a Jew. I am a Jew.
SCULPHER: Belongs to Germans.
LYDIA: Haven't invaded.
SCULPHER: Stays with me. (*Theresa*, 37)

The scene's importance is conveyed by its being "*replayed*," as the stage direction has it, six times, in a way that emphasizes the freezing of a historically and personally traumatic moment that Theresa cannot forget. In its combination of individual fearfulness on Lydia's part and overzealous bureaucracy on Sculpher's, this incident encapsulates the play's concern with ethical choice and action in revealing how Theresa's fate was determined. The only change in the rendition of this recurrent nightmare occurs in the sixth replay, in which Lydia repeats "Forgive" three times, and the fragmentary form of the word signals an uncertain meaning: Lydia appears to be asking for Theresa's forgiveness, but the omission of a first-person pronoun—she does not say, "Forgive *me*"—makes it seem both ineffectual and generalized. It is as if Lydia is asking history's forgiveness for Theresa's death. The nightmare's fragmentary utterances offer condensed meaning that escalates in significance with every repetition. Lydia's phrase, "My responsibility," seems in its truncated state to be an admission of culpability for Theresa's fate, but in its full form implies a more mundane employer's obligation: "She is my nanny . . . She's my responsibility." Sculpher's assertion, "Belongs to Germans," emphasizes the political and existential irony of any notion of "belonging" for Theresa as a stateless Austrian refugee, while his uncomfortably intimate "[she] stays with me" allies him with the approaching Germans: they will all be on Guernsey together. This motif of Sculpher's apparently personal possessiveness arises from what Christopher Browning has described as the "agentic state" in which ordinary people in extreme situations may come to experience themselves not as responsible agents but as "instruments of another's will," and do not question their orders but strive to fulfill them properly.[24] The motif is repeated at the moment of Theresa's deportation, when a Gestapo officer uses a phrase that echoes Sculpher's:

GESTAPO OFFICER: Theresa Steiner. You have three minutes to pack one suitcase before you leave with me. (*Theresa*, 51)

Sculpher's stubborn insistence that Theresa should "stay" is fatally matched by the Gestapo officer's that she must "leave."

Theresa's vision of prostitutes amused by the indignities undergone by an old Jewish couple in the street in Vienna has its contrapuntal echo in the Channel Islands. Although it may appear an uncomfortable use of a symbol, the image of the prostitute reappears in both a literal and more coded guise. A stark contrast is drawn between "Jewish French Resistance fighters" locked in a tunnel on Alderney, while, as one of the play's narrator-figures observes, "above the tunnel French prostitutes sunbathe. In Alderney." This dichotomy between suffering and oblivious self-concern is extended to the "jerrybags" who consort with Germans on Guernsey:

> 1ST NURSE: Who can blame [the women] for wanting a little bit extra? (*To* GESTAPO OFFICER.) Herr Kommandant. My brother is breaking the law. He's got a radio.
>
> 2ND NARRATOR: That woman eats well tonight. (*Theresa*, 40)

The Nurse's phrase, "wanting a little bit extra," combines the notion of wishing for romance with that of expecting payment, as if the Guernsey women were little different from the "French prostitutes." Indeed, the consistent implication of a likeness between the Channel Islands and Vichy France strikes a warning note (see Behlau-Dengler, *Zakhor!* 312). The change in role the Nurse undergoes in this dialogue, from apologist—"Who can blame them . . . ?"—to betrayer of her brother, conveys the play's understanding of the islanders' shared responsibility for collaboration. We are reminded that apparently distinct roles may become blurred.

Such interchangeability is enacted in the moments before Theresa's deportation. At Castel Hospital where she works, Theresa and the other nurses shake out sheets in time "to the Radetzky March," that rousing celebration of Austrian military victory. The scene represents a condensation of historical material into symbolic form, since not only is Sculpher "looking on," but Auguste Spitz is also present. Dialogue that is shared between the characters ominously blends Vienna with Guernsey:

> THERESA (*Beckons Spitz*): Vienna? (*Spitz nods*) I remember you. One day in the park. I was walking with my son. I saw

you on the bench. The bench where Jews were forbidden to sit.

SCULPHER: No Jews

GESTAPO OFFICER: . . . are allowed

THERESA: . . . to sit.

AUGUSTE: To sit. (*Theresa*, 50)

Once more, fragmentary utterance has a double-voiced effect. Theresa's opening question to Auguste—"Vienna?"—sounds initially like an invitation to identify Guernsey as Vienna, then turns into one about an earlier site of discrimination. The completion of Sculpher's sentence by the Gestapo officer is an enactment of the way in which his partially formulated actions not only fed into Nazi genocide but enabled it. The notion of "sitting" is turned by Auguste's repetition into another way of expressing the idea of not being allowed to rest in one place, a "belonging" catastrophically denied. Indeed, the varied form of the play signifies, by means of "collaging different styles together,"[25] what might be lost to the deadly and homogenizing threat of Nazism: as Teresa says to Lydia of the possible future, "There will be no room for our . . . quirky individual differences" (*Theresa*, 22).[26] Although the technique of doubled characters and shared utterance might appear to threaten a homogenizing of crucial differences, for instance, between Theresa and a Polish antisemite, and Herschel Grynszpan and a neo-Nazi, it serves rather to defamiliarize conventional distinctions, between victor and loser, collaborator and cooperator.

The technique of shared utterance is used to convey the appearance of the series of "Orders Relating to Measures Against Jews" in the *Guernsey Evening Express*, which Pascal describes as drawing upon "Living Theatre techniques" (Pascal, "Introduction," 8) in which extracts from historical documents are enacted, signaled in the text by quotation marks and onstage by the actors' delivery. A verbatim practice is used to ironic effect, since the orders appear in this local newspaper in abbreviated form in between news items about a bicycle accident and the events of the war:

1ST NARRATOR: *La Gazette Officielle*. (*Gives everyone a newspaper.*)

1ST NURSE: The *Evening Press*.

1ST NARRATOR: "Second Order relating to Measures Against Jews" . . .
GESTAPO OFFICER: Jews cannot take part in
SCULPHER: "Wholesale and retail trade."
GESTAPO OFFICER: "Hotel and catering industry." (*Theresa*, 43)

Among these speakers, the Nurse is an unnamed colleague of Theresa's who later leads the Germans to her, and Sculpher himself assumes a central role. Although the Gestapo were not present on Guernsey, this officer's voice stands for the disavowed similarity between events on the British Isles and occupied Europe. Such dramatic polyphony conveys the fact that responsibility for Theresa's death is, like the newspaper itself, shared between islanders and Germans. The island authorities' "obsequious" (Pascal, "Introduction," 7) correspondence with the Germans about the orders is represented by means of the same technique of shared utterance:

2ND NARRATOR: I have the honour to be
THERESA: sir
SCULPHER: your obedient servant. (*Theresa*, 43)

This dialogue defamiliarizes the conventions of letter-writing by dividing such phrases between Theresa and their author Sculpher, and anticipates the Germans' delayed but chilling response. At the play's end, the Gestapo officer gives voice to an utterance that consists of a montage of documentary material (see Luckhurst, "The Case of Theresa," 258): "The Guernsey Police have been most helpful. In fact the island authorities—although they consider themselves British—have behaved like true servants of the Reich" (*Theresa*, 49). This repetition of Sculpher's word "servant" in a new and threatening context acts as a synecdoche for the play's theme, that the collusion with the Nazis' genocide in a British setting still goes unacknowledged. In *Theresa* the dramatic techniques of "collaborative" dialogue and alienating effects are directed at the audience. This is not simply for metafictional effect, designed to remind the reader of the aesthetic form of what they encounter, but to shock spectators out of their "apathetic amnesia" (Pascal, quoted in Luckhurst, "The Case of Theresa," 255) over British links to the events of the Holocaust, and what might have taken place in an occupied British mainland.

Conclusion: Aesthetic Choices

Both of these works about the occupation of the Channel Islands represent history using different aesthetic techniques and to disruptive effect. *The Book of Lies* purports to be constituted from an authentic document, that of Cathy's diary with its elaborate citations and inclusion of wartime material, yet the novel's plot centers on invention and deception. Incorporating her uncle's memoir into her own enables Cathy to convert wartime suffering into her personal alibi; the genre of historiography is imitated and satirized both within the text and in terms of its construction. In *Theresa*, the historical material that Pascal gathered—she describes herself copying archival documents in Guernsey "painstakingly" by hand ("Introduction," 7)—has been reimagined as experimental theater. The inseparability of aesthetic disruptiveness and the historical material it represents in both these texts is made clear when they are contrasted with other examples of late-twentieth-century fiction about the occupation, in which survival and redemption are prioritized over ethical uncertainty and death.

Despite the location of both *The Book of Lies* and *Theresa* in wartime events, neither incorporates unaltered the documentary evidence on which the plot depends. Such material is forced into dialogic relation with the fiction and, in Pascal's term, "dramatized" ("Introduction," 7). This is in contrast to, for instance, Libby Cone's novel *War on the Margins* (2009) about Marlene Zimmer, a Jewish woman in Jersey who survives the war in hiding. We are introduced to Marlene as she reads the "First Order" concerning the registration of Jews as it appears in the October 1940 edition of the local newspaper. This moment condenses the novel's method of representing its subject, since a fictional character is placed alongside a document that is reproduced unaltered. Indeed, where this material appears to be most dialogized, its documentary status is in fact preserved:

> The particulars to be provided upon registration are:
> 1. Surname
> 2. Christian name. [sic]
> 3. Date of birth.[27]

The "sic" included here seems to represent Marlene's viewpoint, and the very act of commentary appears to be an early example of her rebellion against official strictures. However, it is significant that the word's origin is not narratively identified, since it is a direct quotation from a historical source, Frederick Cohen's chapter on "The First Order Against the Jews," where the "sic" is his (Cohen, *The Jews in the Channel Islands*, 19). Annotation is incorporated into the novel along with the document on which it appears.

Both Horlock's novel and Pascal's play deconstruct the notion of a Manichean world of clearly distinguishable moral agents. The contrasting temptation to resolve the occupation's moral ambiguities is evident in Mary-Ann Shaffer's *The Guernsey Literary and Potato Peel Pie Society* (2008).[28] In this novel, the narrative trope of a transgressive romance between a local woman, Elizabeth McKenna, and one of the occupying soldiers, Christian Hellman, is redeemed by the sacrifice of the latter, who was sent back to Germany, and by Elizabeth's own heroic acts of resistance that resulted in deportation from Guernsey to Ravensbrück where she died.[29] Thus the moral ambiguity of fraternization is transformed not only into romantic love, but also into the virtue of resistance. The conclusions of Horlock's novel and Pascal's play eschew such reassurance. At the end of *The Book of Lies*, the last lines are ostensibly directed at Mrs. Rozier, but extend beyond the text's diegesis to address the reader too:

> I went and wrote [a book] just for you . . . It's got all the things you like best.
>
> It's even got a proper twist at the end.
> The twist is that you get to choose it.

The choice offered to Mrs. Rozier is one between concluding the story by allowing her daughter to leave Guernsey, or giving away Cathy's secret and being accused of murder in turn. The reader's choice, however, is entirely open ("you get to choose it"), as if the arbitrariness of the novel's fictional world had been laid bare, despite Cathy's insistence on historical determinism. In Pascal's play, ontological disruption of this kind takes a historicized form, since the audience is made to witness Theresa's final deportation. Although Pascal argues that Auschwitz is "impossible to stage," her play *The Dybbuk* of two years later uses the same elements of staging as *Theresa*, but takes them a step further. In contrast to Theresa standing still in a spotlight with the Gestapo officer behind her, while the audience hears trains and *The Blue Danube* as the scene fades to blackout (*Theresa*, 52), in *The Dybbuk*, a "*very slow blackout*" accompanies Mozart's Mass in C Minor and "cases, coats, hats" appear on stage, the "relics of those just murdered" (Pascal, *The Holocaust Trilogy*, 127). In both cases, a history that British audiences keep at a continent's distance has returned in dramatic form.

Notes

The epigraph is from Julia Pascal, *The Holocaust Trilogy: Theresa, A Dead Woman on Holiday, The Dybbuk* (London: Oberon, 2009). I am grateful to the following for their help in writing this article: Sandra Booer, David Fraser, Julia Pascal, Axel Stähler, and particularly Petra Rau.

1. Gillian Carr, "Occupation Heritage, Commemoration and Memory in Guernsey and Jersey," *History and Memory* 24, no. 1: 87–117, at 88–89.

2. In a reexamination of this stereotype, Paul Sanders documents the lives of "the Jersey Twenty," individuals who were deported from the Channel Islands for acts of defiance and did not return. Paul Sanders, *The Ultimate Sacrifice* (St. Helier: Jersey Heritage Trust, 1998).

3. Speech by Winston Churchill to the House of Commons, May 13, 1940. See Gillian Carr, "Examining the Memorialscape of Occupation and Liberation: A Case Study from the Channel Islands," *International Journal of Heritage Studies* 18, no. 2 (2012): 174–93, at 188.

4. Tony Kushner, "Loose Connections? Britain and the 'Final Solution,'" in *Britain and the Holocaust: Remembering and Representing Genocide*, ed. Caroline Sharples and Olaf Jensen (Basingstoke, Eng.: Palgrave, 2013): 51-67, at 53.

5. Philip Ballhache, "Foreword," in Sanders, *The Ultimate Sacrifice*, 1.

6. Hazel Knowles Smith, *The Changing Face of the Channel Islands Occupation: Record, Memory and Myth* (Basingstoke, Eng.: Palgrave, 2007), 210; see also Frederick Cohen, *The Jews in the Channel Islands during the German Occupation 1940–1945* (St. Helier: Jersey Heritage Trust, 2000), 12.

7. Julia Pascal, quoted in Mary Luckhurst, "The Case of Theresa: Guernsey, the Holocaust, and Theatre Censorship in the 1990s," in *Morality and Justice: The Challenge of European Theatre*, ed. Edward Batley and David Bradby (Amsterdam: Rodopi, 2001), 255–68, at 255.

8. Madeleine Bunting, *The Model Occupation: The Channel Islands Under German Rule, 1940–1945*, 2nd ed. (London: Pimlico, 1994).

9. Gavriel Rosenfeld, *The World Hitler Never Made: Alternate History and the Memory of Nazism* (Cambridge: Cambridge University Press, 2005), 82–83.

10. Luckhurst's article focuses on the refusal of the Guernsey authorities to grant Pascal a license to perform her play, which has never been staged in the Channel Islands.

The play was broadcast on Radio 4, retitled *The Road to Paradise*, in July 1996, and has thus reached audiences in Guernsey.

11. See Michael André Bernstein, *Foregone Conclusions: Against Apocalyptic History* (Berkeley: University of California Press, 2004).

12. Mary Horlock, *The Book of Lies* (Edinburgh: Canongate, 2012).

13. Mary Horlock, interview, http://www.youtube.com/watch?v=JSolxhe26dU.

14. Ford Madox Ford, *The Good Soldier* (Harmondsworth, Eng.: Penguin, [1915] 2007).

15. The phrase originates in a French context: see for instance Patrick Buisson on the "national shame" of relationships between French women and the occupying Germans in his *1940–45: Les Années Erotiques*, vols. 1 and 2 (Paris: Michel Albin, 2009), and is widely used of relationships that took place in the Channel Islands to imply ideological or pragmatic complicity or barter rather than genuine sentiment.

16. See also Victoria Stewart, *The Second World War in Contemporary British Fiction: Secret Histories* (Edinburgh: Edinburgh University Press, 2011), 100.

17. Christian House, review, *The Independent* (March 6, 2011).

18. Julia Pascal, "Introduction," in *The Holocaust Trilogy*, 7.

19. See Ulrike Behlau-Dengler, *Zakhor! Remembering the British-Jewish Experience in British-Jewish Drama after 1945* (Trier: Wissenschaftlicher Verlag Trier, 2011), 324.

20. Mark Jenkins, review, http://www.theatre-wales.co.uk/plays/review_archive.asp?playname=Theresa&company=Found%20%20Reality.

21. See Phyllis Lassner, *Anglo-Jewish Women Writing the Holocaust: Displaced Witnesses* (Basingstoke, Eng.: Palgrave, 2008), 162.

22. The song was meant as an "exasperated warning" against lenience in defeat but interpreted as sympathetic to the Germans, which led to its being banned by the BBC during the war. Sheridan Morley, *Noël Coward* (London: Haus, 2005), 80.

23. David Fraser, "The Jews of the Channel Islands, 1940–1945," talk delivered at the Leo Baeck Institute, London, March 2013.

24. Christopher Browning, drawing on Stanley Milgram's obedience experiments, *Ordinary Men: Reserve Police Battalion 101 and the Final Solution in Poland* (New York: Harper Perennial, 1998), 173. Thanks to Petra Rau for drawing my attention to the relevance of this concept here.

25. Julia Pascal, interview, http://www.genderforum.org/fileadmin/archiv/genderforum/anybody2/interview_pascal.html.

26. See the review by Lyn Gardner, *City Limits* (November 8–15, 1990).

27. Libby Cone, *War on the Margins* (London: Duckworth, 2009), 7.

28. Mary Ann Shaffer and Annie Barrows, *The Guernsey Literary and Potato Peel Pie Society* (London: Bloomsbury, 2010), 325.

29. The character of Elizabeth in Shaffer's *The Guernsey Literary and Potato Peel Pie Society*, and that of Pauline in Cone's *War on the Margins*, are based on versions of two historical figures: Alice Thaureux, whose death sentence for sheltering Nicolas Schmitz, her deserter German boyfriend, was commuted after an appeal by the bailiff, although Schmitz was shot (Roland Quintaine, Jersey Archive, personal correspondence, June 29, 2012); and Louisa Gould, who was sent to Ravensbrück where she was killed, for sheltering Feodor Burryiy, a Russian forced laborer (Knowles Smith, *Changing Face of the Channel Islands Occupation*, 53, 199).

MARGARET D. STETZ

Dress, Women's Holocaust Survivor Memoirs, and the "Thoughtful" Work of Linda Grant

> Writing and thinking about clothes is generally relegated to the fashion pages of newspapers . . . Fashion is lightweight, trivial, and obsession with appearance the sign of a second-rate mind . . . As if appearances don't matter when, most of the time, they are all we have to go on. Or sometimes all that is left in the ruins of a life.
>
> —LINDA GRANT, *The Thoughtful Dresser* (2009)

Reviewing *Sexual Violence against Jewish Women during the Holocaust*, a collection of essays published in 2010, Rochelle G. Ruthchild offers an observation as simple as it is shocking: "The Holocaust remains a largely male story, although women were probably the majority of its victims"; even now, "in most Holocaust scholarship women are an afterthought."[1] If it is true that women's stories seldom have served as the grounding for historical and theoretical meditations on the Holocaust phenomenon in general, then it is doubly true that women's Holocaust-related material culture has rarely been treated as a matter of consequence, except perhaps by female survivors themselves and their immediate families. How else can one account for the fact that, in 2013, the website of the Maltz Museum of Jewish Heritage in Cleveland, Ohio, could publicize the exhibition *Spots of Light: To Be a Woman in the Holocaust* by announcing, “A production of the Museums Division, Yad Vashem in Jerusalem, it is the first exhibition to focus exclusively on Jewish women and their experiences in the Holocaust”?[2] Nearly seventy years after the liberation of the concentration camps, it is clearly newsworthy to suggest that there were experiences unique to Jewish women and that the objects associated with them might be worth displaying and studying. Except in a rare exhibition such as this, evidence abounds, moreover, that the actual fabrics—that is, the pieces of cloth—so important in women’s daily lives have not been integrated into the metaphorical fabric of the Holocaust, any more than other items or systems of knowledge associated with the quotidian world of female-dominated domestic spaces have been welcomed into the main historical narrative. The argument that Linda Grant makes in her “Introduction” to Trudi Kanter’s Holocaust memoir, *Some Girls, Some Hats and Hitler*, “that fashion is more than surface, and that it says something about the times those who wear it live through,” even if the times in question encompass the Nazi genocide of the 1930s and 1940s, remains controversial.[3] Whenever and wherever one examines the Holocaust, to do so in terms of subjects identified particularly with women’s interests still seems to require special pleading.

In an article for the *New York Times* on April 27, 2011, for instance, Florence Fabricant, whose reports on restaurants often appear in the “Dining In, Dining Out” section of the newspaper, had a different topic to discuss: the publication of *Recipes Remembered: A Celebration of Survival*, a collection of recipes from Holocaust survivors, many of them former inmates of the death camp at Auschwitz. With its release timed to coincide with the May 1 commemoration of Holocaust Remembrance Day in the United States, this volume, compiled by June Feiss Hersh and published in association with New York’s Museum of Jewish Heritage, makes an explicit link between the experience of mass genocide and memories of Jewish life both before and after the Second World War—memories focused on food. Identity, its contributors insist, is deeply connected to food preparation. It is both an assumption that anthropologists would endorse and a statement that seems almost too obvious to require making. Who would not agree that to preserve and transmit such a history of cooking practices is a valuable effort?

Fabricant’s article, however, opens not with the expected celebration of this enterprise, but with a potential objection to it: “Recipe books based on the memories of Holocaust survivors might seem to trivialize the horror."[4] Behind this sentiment lies an expression of anxiety—a quite understandable anxiety, if we consider current debates over Holocaust representation, which have turned on deciding which sorts of representation are or are not appropriate, a topic taken up by scholars such as Alvin Rosenfeld in *The End of the Holocaust* (2011) and Ruth Franklin in *A Thousand Darknesses: Lies and Truth in Holocaust Fiction* (2011). Yet there is also another issue here: a broader question about whether matters particularly relevant to the daily lives, work, and interests of women are, by definition, innately "trivial" and thus unfit to be mentioned in the same breath as historical events of real consequence. Collecting and handing down recipes is something that, more often than not, women have done. For women, it has been both a form of necessary cultural labor and a source of personal pleasure. Therefore, to make a place for this gendered domestic concern in documenting the Holocaust is supposedly to risk being insufficiently serious, merely by introducing something associated with women.

Not surprisingly, we find similar objections and anxieties, as well as an implicit tone of apology or defensiveness, wherever there are attempts to represent Holocaust experience, either at firsthand or at secondhand, through the related issue of dress. Unlike an interest in food preparation, which at least has links to religious directives and prohibitions that, especially in Judaism, make it a necessary part of sacred rituals, an appreciation of dress has always been morally suspect. After all, at that most solemn moment in life, when one is grieving for the dead, traditional Jewish mourning practices require tearing one's garments and covering all the mirrors in the house. To care about how one looks is to mark oneself as an unserious person—to mark oneself, in fact, as a woman. This has been true across cultures and communities. Women, more than men, are required to pay attention to dress, yet also looked down upon for doing so. Daniel Miller captures this paradox nicely in his "Introduction" to *Clothing as Material Culture* (2005):

> In colloquial discussion of clothing, the principal problem has been precisely that the whole topic doesn't really matter. Since it is used as a covering or as a surface, clothing is easily characterized as intrinsically superficial . . . a slight, transient aspect that is

> shallow, more contrived, somehow less real and certainly less important. Politics as abstract and explicit debate is profound, while attention to forms such as clothing is trivial and self-indulgent. This denigration of surfaces has been part of the denigration of clothing and, by extension, of those said to be particularly interested in clothing, often seen as women.[5]

The British Jewish novelist and journalist Linda Grant (b. 1951) is, therefore, well aware that she treads on contested ground when self-consciously linking Holocaust experience with issues of fashion in *The Thoughtful Dresser: The Art of Adornment, the Pleasures of Shopping, and Why Clothes Matter* (2009). The narrative that holds together this collection of essays is Grant's brief recounting throughout of the life story of a Hungarian Jew named Catherine Hill, who was liberated from a concentration camp and who eventually settled in Canada, where she married and opened a high-end women's clothing store in Toronto. Arguing for "Why Clothes Matter," Grant asserts that clothes are important because they offer pleasure, and pleasure is both the antithesis of and the antidote to suffering. Catherine Hill's story—which includes an episode during her internment at Auschwitz-Birkenau when she tore a strip from the hem of her Nazi-issued striped uniform and tied it around her shaved head in a bow, to cover her baldness with something that reminded her of the existence of beauty and of her own former identity—is Grant's example of how "even for those of us who have not experienced the horror of the camps, the desire for luxury, for beautiful clothes, can be the revenge against poverty and neglect and cruelty" (*Thoughtful Dresser*, 196). Grant's volume begins with her reflections on seeing a woman's red high-heeled shoe amid "a great mountain of footwear" in a glass display case at the museum now at Auschwitz (*Thoughtful Dresser*, 3)—a sight that fuels her own empathetic efforts to imagine the personality and to recover the particular circumstances of its unidentified owner, who was murdered in a gas chamber. Thus, the shoe takes her to the borderline between history and fiction, between the woman who died and her own situation as a British Jewish writer.

With her novel *The Clothes on Their Backs* (2008), Grant had already entered explicitly into the world of fictionalized Holocaust representation. There the focus is on the tension between first- and second-generation Holocaust experience through the stories of an uncle and niece, both living in London in the 1970s, who are united in part by their shared attitudes toward clothing as a powerful means of self-definition. Through this narrative, with its equal emphasis on a male survivor's attention to issues of dress, Grant moves beyond the usual associations between concern with dress and women's culture alone—an association common in the Holocaust memoirs of women survivors, who have emphasized the importance of items of clothing while recording their personal histories.

Searching for links to her own life as a Jewish woman in present-day Britain, Grant turns to stories by an earlier generation of women who lived through the Holocaust, and she makes clear that she has found these connections in a common appreciation of fashion as a necessity, rather than as a luxury. This is a positive view of clothing that, according to Grant, too few men have felt comfortable in admitting. As she says with bitter comic irony in *The Thoughtful Dresser*,

> The purpose of this book is . . . to [give voice to] the ordinary mass of humanity who is interested in fashion and might, quite wrongly . . . fear that they are not going to be taken seriously. That in announcing this preoccupation they will have confessed that women are not really fully grown up; unlike our male counterparts, who have mature and adult preoccupations without which the human race could not survive, such as moving balls from one end of a grassy field to the other with the aid of the human foot. (*Thoughtful Dresser*, 13)

That Jewish women had recourse to this "preoccupation" for comfort and strength in extremis, amidst the darkest days of the Nazi genocide, helps to make the argument for her about clothes as possessing a "power" that is "elemental" (*Thoughtful Dresser*, 12).

Clothes in Women's Holocaust Memoirs

Even as they have talked about their relationships with clothing, however, some women who lived through the Holocaust have found it impossible to remain untouched by the assumption that to focus on such issues is a sign of superficiality and lack of serious intent. Thus we hear a note of self-deprecation enter the otherwise matter-of-fact voice of Gerda Weissmann Klein, a Holocaust survivor who became famous in 1996 as the subject of Kary Antholis's documentary, *One Survivor Remembers*, as she recalls in a filmed interview what she thought about, near the end of the war, during the Nazis' forced death march of women across Eastern Europe:

> "We didn't get anything to eat for days, literally. We were bitter cold and hungry . . . I was planning a party after the war. I had the dilemma for almost an entire day, if I should have a blue velvet dress or a red velvet dress. I couldn't resolve it. I really liked the color blue much better as a color, but I knew that red looked better on me. You could occupy your mind and hang your thoughts on trivia of that nature. They became very important, and this was how you passed the hours and forgot the hunger and the cold."[6]

Looking back, Klein's own way of labeling this episode, which involved imagining an opportunity in the future to dress up again, is to call it "trivia." At the same time, it is clear that, while she was on this forced march, there was nothing frivolous to her about such a topic; it allowed her to focus her mind beyond the present moment of extreme physical suffering and emotional anguish. Not only color but the materiality of texture—the idea of velvet as essential to her future party dress—took on tremendous importance and helped her to keep hold of her sense of self. The self she preserved through such musings was one that could still appreciate aesthetic experiences, as embodied by clothing, and one that could imagine someday enjoying them again. It is difficult to convey the degree of life-saving denial and resistance involved, for a young woman whose body had become skeletal through starvation and sickness, to think in terms of which color "looked better" on her.

Very different in character, however, is another of Gerda Weissman Klein's clothes-related memories, also captured on film. In contrast to the story of the imaginary party dress, we have her account of the actual pair of shoes that she wore throughout her ordeal—a pair of ski boots, which she put on when she was first taken from home and sent to a forced labor camp. Here, there is no talk of "trivia," only of survival made possible by a man's miraculous foresight. The boots have been sanctified for her through their association with paternal wisdom and authority, as it was her father who insisted that she wear them, just before she was separated from him forever: "When I last saw him in June, the very last day, practically in the last moment before he left . . . My father had [said . . .] 'Wear your skiing boots.'" She recalls objecting, pointing out the incongruity of ski boots in the summertime, then adds that she had obeyed purely out of respect for his wishes. In retrospect, she wonders how he could have known: "Those boots were really instrumental in saving my life on that march [in January]. I had ski shoes; some girls had sandals. We slept outside. The frost . . . I saw girls breaking off their toes like twigs."[7]

Interestingly, when Gerda Weissmann Klein published her memoir *All But My Life*, first in 1957 and then in an expanded edition in 1995, she included several references to the ski boots, which represented survival through her father's seemingly divine foresight.[8] But she did not mention the story of the two imaginary party dresses, which reflected her own brilliant strategy for keeping intact her identity, her spirit, and her will to go on living through a mental exercise closely linked to gender-specific concerns. What we see here is an instance of self-censorship—hardly the first or the last associated with women Holocaust survivors. Fearing that their particular experiences—especially those that were gender-based—somehow do not measure up and do not carry the weight of universal significance, many women have edited their memories and silenced themselves. That was certainly the conclusion reached by the historian Joan Ringelheim in her groundbreaking 1985 article for the U.S. feminist journal, *Signs*, titled "Women and the Holocaust: A Reconsideration of Research." There, she dared to raise the questions that no one had bothered to consider: "Were women's experiences during the Holocaust different from men's in some respects? Were there differences in work, relationships, roles, and in maintenance possibilities or capabilities—that is, in what a person did or tried to do simply to keep going, to make it from day to day?"[9] Because she was asking a new set of questions, the women whom she interviewed provided new answers—in some cases, disturbing ones that revealed forty years of self-silencing, especially on topics such as sexual violence. As Ringelheim put it,

> Although there are many stories about sexual abuse, they are not easy to come by. Some think it inappropriate to talk about these matters. . . . For others, it is simply too difficult and painful. Still others think it may be a trivial issue. One survivor told me . . . that it "was not important . . . except to me." She meant that it had no significance within the larger picture of the Holocaust. But why should ideas about the Holocaust as a whole exclude these women's experiences—exclude what is important to women—and thus make the judgment that women's experiences as women are trivial? (Ringelheim, "Women and the Holocaust," 745)

The impress of the feminist work that Ringelheim initiated in the 1980s helped to change not only how Holocaust scholars today define what is "important," but also what women survivors themselves have considered worth preserving, documenting, and sharing in their recent accounts. Thus a Hungarian-born survivor, Marika Roth, has used her 2011 memoir to report her rape in the immediate aftermath of the war, a sexual assault that she links to the necessity for shoes at a time of extreme privation. A teenager at the time, alone in Budapest with no family, she received a "tiny salary" that "only paid for my bed and a bit of food" for her work sewing trousers in a factory that made uniforms for Russian soldiers. Unable to afford shoes, which had become an expensive luxury, she kept her feet wrapped in newspaper and scraps of cloth, until another young woman introduced her to a tailor named Bela who, "grinning at me as if he were the cat and I the canary . . . promised me a brand-new pair of pretty custom-made shoes."[10] The outcome was a violent attack: "In a matter of minutes, I was robbed of my virginity in exchange for a pair of shoes that I purposely left behind once he let me go" (Roth, *All the Pretty Shoes*, 95).

Rape at every stage of the Holocaust, including the lawless and chaotic period immediately following the end of the war, was a common experience, though one not always talked about by women until decades after, if at all. What is remarkable about Marika Roth's memoir, however, is not merely that it contains such a story, but that it couches the event within a narrative deliberately and self-consciously structured throughout by the author's relationship to clothing. In later years, after emigrating to Canada, Roth would earn her living in Montreal as "a full-fledged fashion model with a diploma from WTMA [the Walter Thornton Modeling Agency]"; as she puts it, "With the aid of proper accessories, perfect posture, and makeup, one can easily be transformed into an attractive person [. . . and] so began the second major transition in my life" (*All the Pretty Shoes*, 150). As she looks back, items of dress become the links that give shape and coherence to the otherwise disconnected and fragmentary story of her Holocaust experience. It begins, for her, with memories of her mother: "I recalled the times the two of us walked arm-in-arm along the fashionable avenues, looking at all the pretty shoes and dresses in shop windows. Mother was opposed to buying ready-made clothes or shoes. To her it was just as inconceivable as wearing fake jewelry. People of class only wore real jewelry and tailor-made shoes and clothes" (*All the Pretty Shoes*, 5). But the central trauma of this narrative is the moment when, as a girl of twelve, she claims to have witnessed from a place of concealment under a bush near the Danube the murder of a group of Jews taken out of the "Swedish-protected housing complex[,] rounded up by the Arrow Cross execution brigade[,] and dragged away, regardless of their age or gender" (1). She writes, "While I could not see their faces, I could see their shoes well enough to recognize that these were shoes of good quality, belonging to the members of an affluent society. Yet regardless of their stature, there they stood, humbled and humiliated in the last moments of their lives [. . . before they were shot] point blank" (7). To emphasize the ironic continuities and the historical complexities of the roles that items of dress have played throughout her own story, Marika Roth titles her book *All the Pretty Shoes*.

Shoes function in prominent ways, too, in Mira Ryczke Kimmelman's *Echoes from the Holocaust: A Memoir* (1997), where they embody the gender-specific experiences of women, which sometimes were more nuanced and morally problematic than convention might allow us to recognize. Kimmelman tells of the forced march of prisoners from the camp at Auschwitz-Hindenburg in January 1945, as the Soviet army approached. Weak and feverish from typhus, she "dragged" herself along a "snow-covered highway": "Wearing the assigned wooden shoes, to which snow was sticking, every step took more of my strength." In danger of "stumbling and falling" and thus of being left on a road already "covered with the bodies of our friends and comrades,"[11] she was the beneficiary of an inexplicably chivalrous gesture, almost certainly motivated by the gender conditioning of an earlier time and place, from a man whose job it had been until then to work toward her extermination:

> One of the SS guards saw me struggling. He was an older man, a guard at the camp in Hindenburg from which we were evacuated. "Take my extra pair of boots. You will be able to walk better. You can return them to me once we get to Gleiwitz," he said. And he handed me the pair of leather military boots that had been hanging over his left shoulder.
>
> I had no time to think. Should I accept the boots or not? I took them. (Kimmelman, *Echoes from the Holocaust*, 75)

Given her debilitated and exhausted state, the boots eventually proved too heavy to allow her to lift her feet, and she had to abandon them, "but I always remembered that an SS guard tried to help me" (Kimmelman, *Echoes from the Holocaust*, 76).

Acts not merely of unexpected charity, but of self-sacrifice, have also been memorialized through women's stories involving clothes in general and gender-specific garments in particular, especially high-heeled shoes—not coincidentally, the objects with which Linda Grant begins her Holocaust-related meditations in *The Thoughtful Dresser*. For Lily Mazur Margules, one of the defining episodes of her own Holocaust experience was her aunt's life-saving gesture at the moment when her family was ordered to leave the Jewish ghetto of Vilna, Poland, in 1943:

> Rumblings in the crowd told us that the line to the right would live and to the left would not. Knowing my sister Rachel looked very young and small, my aunt removed her high heels and exchanged them with Rachel's shoes. Rachel now looked taller and older and along with me, was spared, but my Aunt Sonia was not. We were sent to the right, to live and she was sent to the left, to die.[12]

The efficacy of this measure depended upon the continued existence of a prewar gendered code of appearance, which had to be understood—and clearly was understood—by the Nazi soldiers who saw and judged both Margules's sister and aunt. Little girls did not wear high heels; only young women did. But high heels, too, were associated with women in the prime of life and thus with those who were most fit for hard labor. In giving up this signifier of youth for the sake of her niece, Margules's aunt lost her own chance at survival.

A single high-heeled shoe also figures as the central prop in a story about prisoner resistance at Auschwitz that has circulated for decades among survivors and that Kirsty Chatwood records, in its various incarnations, in "Schillinger and the Dancer: Representing Agency and Sexual Violence in Holocaust Testimonies" (2010), her study both of the incident itself and of the conflicting narratives surrounding it. In this tale, which has taken on a mythic quality in all of its versions, a beautiful woman (who has been identified variously as an actress and a dancer) allegedly was able to distract two SS guards on her arrival at the camp's undressing room by slowly removing her clothes in a provocative manner. Then, as one of the eyewitness accounts claims, "she grabbed her shoe and slammed its high heel violently" into the head of one of the guards: "At this moment the young woman flung herself at him and made a quick grab for his pistol."[13] As a result, she was able to shoot to death Josef Schillinger, one of the two Nazis, and to wound the other. Whether the detail about the hyper-feminine (and hyper-sexualized) shoe having served as a weapon is apocryphal or not, it is still significant as a narrative trope, giving an ironic edge to Linda Grant's observation in *The Thoughtful Dresser* that "proper shoes are fundamental to our survival" (*Thoughtful Dresser*, 156).

Narratives about clothing do not, however, involve only the most extraordinary circumstances alone, as Grant also suggests in both her nonfiction and fiction about dress. Bringing into view the unique relationships of women to clothing can alter our perspectives on women's quotidian experiences—including their Holocaust experiences—and affect how we read the narratives of those experiences, allowing us both to pay attention to and understand more fully what Joan Ringelheim has labeled the things "a person did or tried to do . . . from day to day," especially when that person was a woman. In her 1993 multimedia installation *Holocaust Project: From Darkness into Light*, the feminist artist Judy Chicago features a section called "Double Jeopardy." Its title comes from her realization, as she writes in the accompanying catalog, that women "have been omitted from most of the exhibitions on the Holocaust that we've seen. . . . The investigation I've done so far suggests that women were doubly victimized—as women *and* as Jews—but I want to discover if there were particular ways in which women suffered differently."[14] The first panel in "Double Jeopardy" is *Sewing Circle*, which depicts a group of three women hunched over their work, stitching. As Judy Chicago explains, "I definitely want to include an image of women sewing Jewish stars onto their family's clothing, maybe in a little quilting-bee format. Everyone has seen photos of Jews wearing stars, but little consideration has been given to those who sewed them on—another example of how women's experience has remained invisible" (Chicago, *Holocaust Project*, 127–28).

In a volume of essays titled *Broken Threads: The Destruction of the Jewish Fashion Industry in Germany and Austria* (2007), edited by Roberta S. Kremer, the contributors document the centrality of the Jewish community to the design, manufacture, sales, marketing, and consumption of clothing before the Holocaust, including the importance of Jewish women, such as Elsa Herzog, Ola Alsen, and Lieselotte Friedländer, as fashion journalists and graphic artists for magazines.[15] Part of the Nazi project focused on the deliberate destruction of this sphere of art and business, as well as on its appropriation and cleansing through "Aryanization." Ironically, "Many of the Jews forced out of the fashion industry were deported to ghettos, once mass deportations began in October 1941. There they worked endless hours under abhorrent conditions to produce clothing and shoes for Nazi officials and their wives."[16] And, of course, much of the clothing and jewelry of Jews about to be murdered in the gas chambers was collected and either sold or distributed in Germany.

Describing the forced labor to which she and other young women were assigned at a textile manufacturing plant, Gerda Weissmann Klein records, in *All But My Life*, another overlooked aspect of women's Holocaust experience. At Grünberg, in Silesia, Klein had to oversee the operation of machines that took bundles of used clothing formerly owned by Jews and "tore the raw materials to shreds," to be spun into new thread. As Klein writes,

> Deliveries of old clothes arrived daily from Auschwitz to be shredded and converted into yarn. A number of the girls who ran the shredding machines insisted that they had recognized their

> parents' clothes. . . . Once as I passed the shredder I thought I saw Mama's coat. I turned away, praying, then forced myself to look again. It was just a black coat. It could have been anybody's—hundreds of people wore black coats. (Klein, *All But My Life*, 176)

The intimacy of a daughter's connection to and memory of her mother's clothing here becomes an additional source of suffering, one particular to the gendered relationship between women and items of dress. But we cannot begin to comprehend all that is implicit in Klein's moment first of recognition, then of willful denial, unless we, too, focus on the horror of seeing her mother's fate embodied in the fate of a coat—that is, unless we appreciate how Klein reads that garment and unless we read it along with her, paying attention to the role of clothing as an important carrier of both individual and communal identity, rather than as trivia. As the anthropologist Emma Tarlo has pointed out, the "peculiar proximity to our bodies" of items of clothing "gives them a special potential for symbolic elaboration."[17] This is especially true when it comes to "perceptions of identity": "for clothes are frequently perceived as expressions and even extensions of the people who wear them" (Tarlo, *Clothing Matters*, 16). Jewish women's labor while working the shredding machines created, therefore, a *material* form of knowledge of the murders of individual family members that contributed to their own trauma as survivors.

An ability to master the art of fashioning clothes for others was also a way for some women to survive. In terms of the British legacy of the Holocaust, it proved, in a few rare cases, a ticket out of danger—a skill that allowed a lucky few to cross borders, flee persecution, and find employment in London. In her memoir *Some Girls, Some Hats and Hitler* (1984), Trudi Kanter describes her success as a leading millinery designer and businesswoman in prewar Vienna, with a hat salon and a workroom of her own. It was that success that enabled her to win permission from the Austrian authorities in 1938 to travel to England, ostensibly on a brief sales mission, even though she was a Jew: "I'm on a business trip, selling model hats in order to bring English pounds to Nazi Germany."[18] Of course, she was instead leaving her homeland forever and bringing her husband with her; later, she would manage to help her parents to escape, as well. With her talent for creating hats that were more stylish than the British market was used to seeing, she found work immediately and prospered, for "even with the war on, ladies were still wearing hats" (*Some Girls*, 234).

Linda Grant's "Thoughtful" Refashionings of Holocaust Stories

With its focus on memories of beautiful clothes worn by both men and women and expressions of longing for the lost world of extravagant hats—"A toque made entirely of violets. Large, floppy hats of black horsehair braid . . . covered in white cabbage roses" (Kanter, *Some Girls*, 63)—Trudi Kanter's memoir languished in obscurity after its publication in the mid-1980s. It was, however, reprinted at last on both sides of the Atlantic in 2012—fittingly, with an "Introduction" by Linda Grant, who could understand and explicate the sort of prejudice that such a tale had faced on its first appearance. As Grant puts the matter, *Some Girls, Some Hats and Hitler* had been the victim of "an instinctive shrinking away from accounts of the war which did not treat it with the seriousness and solemnity of historians." To readers accustomed to more traditional Holocaust narratives, Kanter "must have seemed too shallow . . . to be a sympathetic narrator of the life of the refugee" ("Introduction," in Kanter, *Some Girls*, xii), and the author and her husband were, therefore, easy to dismiss as merely "fashionable, trivial people" (xi). For Grant, on the contrary, Trudi Kanter represents a heroic figure: "successful, independent, smart and determined" and, in fact, "a heroine for the modern age" (xii). Her ability to flourish in the hat trade, first in Vienna and then in London, demonstrates, from Grant's perspective, a pragmatic and wholly admirable grasp of how to make the most of options that were limited not only by Kanter's identity as a Jew, but as a woman: "It was because fashion was (and still is) regarded as inconsequential that women were permitted to dominate it, and to have the autonomy and decision-making that was closed off in other businesses" (xii).

For similar reasons, Grant chooses as the real-life protagonist of *The Thoughtful Dresser* Katerina Deutsch, the Hungarian Jewish survivor of Auschwitz-Birkenau now known by the name of Catherine Hill, who remade herself, after the Second World War, into a Canadian dress shop owner specializing in designer labels. Grant celebrates Hill's almost miraculous self-transformation from her status as a victim of the Nazis' "dehumanizing" process, which included stripping her naked and shaving her head (*Thoughtful Dresser*, 196), and locates the reclamation of identity and of personal power at the moment when she returned from the concentration camp and rediscovered the joy of exercising individual will by clothing herself. Accompanied by her sole remaining family member, she

> went to the uncle's house and, as in a fairy tale, found gold hidden in the well in the garden, and with her share of the money Catherine bought herself new clothes. She was living by herself in a rooming house. Standing in front of the mirror, her hair just starting to grow, she looked at herself in a blouse she thought was beautiful after all the months of that striped and filthy burlap dress. Once again, pretty. (*Thoughtful Dresser*, 200)

After resettling in Canada, Catherine Hill extended to other women, through the medium of the high-end shop that she opened, the "therapeutic" function of "shopping for clothes" (*Thoughtful Dresser*, 203), which involves an aesthetic declaration of selfhood and also allows for the exercise of social aspiration. As Grant puts it, clothes are "more than what you put on"; they are "the means by which you situate . . . yourself in the present tense" (15).

Through the principle of dress as a vehicle for both literal and figurative *refashioning*, Grant makes a direct connection from Hill's post-Holocaust experience to her own situation as a British Jew and to the history of her family. The resemblances that she finds between the philosophy of Catherine Hill, a refugee remaking herself in a new environment, and the values espoused by her mother and father, "the children of Eastern European immigrants" (*Thoughtful Dresser*, 16) who entered Britain earlier in the twentieth century, come together explicitly in her discussion of dress and social relocation: "For as every immigrant knows, with the opportunity for complete reinvention, without a past, a history, in a strange land, how you look is what matters" (17). Here, Grant does not hesitate to reveal her own class background or to declare that she owes her "superior private education" at "a bluestocking school established in the nineteenth century . . . for the daughters of gentlemen" to the very ungentlemanly work that her father did in the beauty industry (14–15). Making no false equivalencies between her own life and those of Holocaust survivors such as Catherine Hill—indeed, announcing frankly that, to the contrary, "in my own life, thank God, there has been no such suffering" (5)—she nonetheless acknowledges that her own family of Jews who emigrated to Liverpool from the Ukraine sprang from roots in which privation was the norm: "You see, my grandparents actually were poor, it was not a temporary condition. And so they understood shopping more deeply than their shallow privileged grandchildren" (65). Despite their financial and cultural insecurity they, like the later generation of refugees who fled the Second World War, used dress to reframe their condition and "dressed defiantly above their station" (119), for "clothing was not just a disguise, though it could be; it also allowed the process of assimilation, in which they became Englishmen and -women, to take hold" (121). She herself absorbed from her family this lesson of how to assert through visual display the right to be treated not as a stigmatized outsider, but as a privileged insider: "You used clothes as a weapon, as armor, as a means of gaining respect in the eyes of a frequently hostile world" (120).

Throughout *The Thoughtful Dresser*, Linda Grant recurs to the first-person testimony of Catherine Hill who, after liberation from Auschwitz-Birkenau and transplantation to Canada, had to relearn "how to be free" (*Thoughtful Dresser*, 39) and to restore to herself a degree of psychic wholeness—something she achieved, in large part, thanks to her relationship with dress. While telling this story, Grant uses the various chapters of her book to ponder, in a serious and "thoughtful" manner, the more general question of the different powers of clothing, whether on the individual or the cultural level. But as the recorder of someone else's history, Grant must maintain a necessary distance from the central issue of Hill's Holocaust experience, which she can never fully imagine. Only once does her language suggest a problematic slippage, when she is writing about Hill's time at Auschwitz-Birkenau and about a moment when the women inmates stood naked and exposed: "Years after, Catherine would understand how clothes are such security for us" (196). Who is Grant's "us"? Is it all human beings? Is it women? Is it Jews? Is it anybody who has been victimized and humiliated? Can anyone who did not stand naked alongside Catherine Hill in a concentration camp, facing the malignant gaze of Nazi guards, inhabit this identity and "understand"?

If nonfiction raises uncomfortable and perhaps irresolvable issues around the dangers of appropriation, so too does fiction. Thus Linda

Grant has approached Holocaust representation in this genre, too, with respectful caution. In *The Clothes on Their Backs,* she presents an imaginary Holocaust survivor's experience, but makes it clear to her audience that she claims no inside knowledge of that experience by changing the subject's gender, using a male character who emigrated to London after the war. The story of his experience, moreover, comes to the reader already mediated and set at a double remove—through the recollection of a first-person dramatized female narrator who had, in turn, learned it by interviewing her late uncle many years earlier. This fictional uncle and niece, who have been estranged from one another for a variety of reasons, do manage to bond over their attraction to fashion: as the narrator says, "Like me, he had a taste for and an interest in flashy unusual clothes."[19] In the case of her uncle Sándor, this "taste" is a direct result of his suffering as a Hungarian Jew who had to endure the tortures of forced labor:

> A few months later [after his twenty-second birthday] he would march off to labour service in a suit which would not leave his back for a further four and a half years. During that time, he kept sane by picturing himself lounging on the gilded chairs of the Café Astoria, holding court with his girls, dressed in a fine suit. Whenever he slept and dreamed, that's how he saw himself, not a slave in rags. He thought of spats and tie-pins and cravats and Oxford bags and double-breasted jackets and turn-ups and leather brogues and embroidered braces and opera pumps. (*Clothes on Their Backs*, 167–68)

Few nonfiction narratives of Holocaust survival by men—particularly, by heterosexual men—recount such detailed compensatory fantasies centered on clothing. Dress, of course, has long been stigmatized as a feminine preoccupation and tabooed to masculinity. To admit, therefore, that one could preserve the core of one's identity by fixing attention upon items of apparel would be a shameful and unmanly confession for a man to make. Among the list of sources in the "Acknowledgments" that accompany her novel, Grant mentions no Holocaust memoirs by male authors. In search of equivalent statements in Holocaust testimonies, we must turn instead to accounts by women—for instance, to Gerda Weissman Klein's recollections of staying alive by keeping her thoughts on the velvet party dress that she would wear in the future. Such testimony serves to vindicate Linda Grant's angry protest, in *The Thoughtful Dresser*: "So I no longer take seriously . . . derisory accusations leveled against those who are interested in clothes. I certainly won't take it from those men who judge and condemn women for the various failures of our appearance while simultaneously barking that only feeble shallow creatures such as women would pay any attention to how they look" (10). Weissman's account of the life-saving pleasure—the only pleasure available to her—that she received from imagining herself in pretty clothes and of being looked at with admiration bears witness to mental strength, rather than feebleness.

Alvin H. Rosenfeld does not mention Linda Grant by name when, in *The End of the Holocaust* (2011), he condemns recent representations of the Holocaust, especially those in popular culture, on the grounds that they "work to undermine its gravity and render it a more familiar thing." For Rosenfeld, "The more successfully it [the Holocaust] enters the cultural mainstream, the more commonplace it becomes," so that "the mass murder of innocent people is trivialized."[20] But, as Linda Grant's nonfiction and fiction alike encourage us to recognize, classifications such as "trivia" and "gravity" are themselves gendered categories. Texts such as Grant's, which deal specifically with what is "familiar" to women, do not make the Holocaust "commonplace" and unimportant by looking at it through the lens of clothing and, in a sense, by domesticating it. Instead, they render the historical events all the more horrifying, by helping us to apprehend how viciously and deliberately Nazi genocide attacked the core of Jewish women's identities, how women themselves bore that destruction, and how some of them survived it, both during the war and afterwards, by dressing themselves in thought.

Notes

The epigraph is from Linda Grant, *The Thoughtful Dresser: The Art of Adornment, the Pleasures of Shopping, and Why Clothes Matter* (New York: Scribner, 2009), 10.

1. Rochelle G. Ruthchild, "The Gender of Survival," *Women's Review of Books* 28, no. 5 (September/October 2011): 10–11, at 11.

2. *Spots of Light: To Be a Woman in the Holocaust, March 19–June 9, 2013*, Maltz Museum of Jewish Heritage, http://www.maltzmuseum.org/happenings/special-exhibitions/spots-of-light/.

3. Linda Grant, "Introduction," in Trudi Kanter, *Some Girls, Some Hats and Hitler* (London: Virago, [1984] 2012), ix.

4. Florence Fabricant, "If Food Could Talk: Recipes with a Dark Heritage," *New York Times*, April 27, 2011, D3.

5. Daniel Miller, "Introduction," in *Clothing as Material Culture* (Oxford: Berg, 2005), 1–19, at 3.

6. *One Survivor Remembers*, DVD, directed by Kary Antholis (1996; Santa Monica, Calif.: Direct Cinema Limited, 2005).

7. Ibid.

8. Gerda Weissmann Klein, *All But My Life*, expanded edition (New York: Hill and Wang, 1995), 208.

9. Joan Ringelheim, "Women and the Holocaust: A Reconsideration of Research," *Signs: A Journal of Women in Culture and Society* 10, no. 4 (Summer 1985): 741–61, at 742.

10. Marika Roth, *All the Pretty Shoes: A Memoir of Survival and the Feminine Spirit* (Deadwood, Ore.: Wyatt-MacKenzie, 2011), 92–93.

11. Mira Ryczke Kimmelman, *Echoes from the Holocaust: A Memoir* (Knoxville: University of Tennessee Press, 1997), 75.

12. Lily Mazur Margules, "Lily Mazur Margules and Edward Margules," in *Recipes Remembered: A Celebration of Survival*, ed. June Feiss Hersh (New York: Ruder Finn, 2011), 108–10, at 109.

13. Kirsty Chatwood, "Schillinger and the Dancer: Representing Agency and Sexual Violence in Holocaust Testimonies," in *Sexual Violence against Jewish Women during the Holocaust*, ed. Sonja M. Hedgepeth and Rochelle G. Seidel (Waltham, Mass.: Brandeis University Press, 2010), 61–74, at 65.

14. Judy Chicago, *Holocaust Project: From Darkness into Light* (New York: Penguin, 1993), 124.

15. Ingrid Loschek, "Contributions of Jewish Fashion Designers in Berlin," in *Broken Threads: The Destruction of the Jewish Fashion Industry in Germany and Austria*, ed. Roberta S. Kremer (Oxford: Berg, 2007), 48–75, at 62.

16. Irene Guenther, "The Destruction of a Culture and an Industry," in *Broken Threads: The Destruction of the Jewish Fashion Industry in Germany and Austria*, ed. Roberta S. Kremer (Oxford: Berg, 2007), 77–97, at 94.

17. Emma Tarlo, *Clothing Matters: Dress and Identity in India* (Chicago: University of Chicago Press, 1996), 16.

18. Trudi Kanter, *Some Girls, Some Hats and Hitler* (London: Virago, [1984] 2012), 139.

19. Linda Grant, *The Clothes on Their Backs* (New York: Scribner, 2008), 167.

20. Alvin H. Rosenfeld, *The End of the Holocaust* (Bloomington: Indiana University Press, 2011), 11.

Contributors

Paula Derdiger is an assistant professor in the Department of English at the University of Minnesota Duluth, where she works on modern and contemporary British literature and culture. She has written articles on Colin MacInnes and Elizabeth Bowen, and her current research focuses on literature, film, and housing in postwar Britain.

Richard Farmer is a postdoctoral research associate at the University of East Anglia, and previously taught at University College London, where he was also a Leverhulme Early Career Fellow. He has published widely on British cinema and leisure culture, and is the author of *The Food Companions: Cinema and Consumption in Wartime Britain, 1939–45*.

Allan Hepburn is James McGill Professor of Twentieth-Century Literature at McGill University. In addition to *Intrigue: Espionage and Culture* and *Enchanted Objects: Visual Art in Contemporary Fiction*, he has published forty articles on various aspects of literature and culture. He edited three books of previously uncollected stories, essays, and broadcasts by Elizabeth Bowen. A fourth book, devoted to Bowen's reviews, is forthcoming from Northwestern University Press. He is currently writing a book about "Faith and British Culture, 1939–1962," as well as a book about Elizabeth Bowen's major fiction.

Elizabeth Maslen is a senior research fellow at the Institute of English Studies. Her books include *Doris Lessing* and *Political and Social Issues in British Women's Fiction, 1928–1968* as well as many essays on early modern writing and twentieth-century women writers such as Naomi Mitchison, Storm Jameson, and Rumer Godden. Her biography, *Life in the Writings of Storm Jameson*, was published by Northwestern University Press.

Michael Perfect is an assistant professor of English literature at Bilkent University in Ankara, Turkey. His main research and teaching interests are in twentieth- and twenty-first-century literature and culture. His book *Contemporary Fictions of Multiculturalism: Diversity and the Millennial London Novel* was published in 2014. He has also published journal articles and book chapters on contemporary British literature and postcolonial studies, and has taught at the University of Cambridge as well as in London.

Adam Piette is a professor of English literature at Sheffield University. He is the author of *Imagination at War: British Fiction and Poetry 1939–1945*, *Remembering and the Sound of Words: Mallarmé, Proust, Joyce, Beckett*, and *The Literary Cold War, 1945 to Vietnam*. He has also edited, with Mark Rawlinson, *The Edinburgh Companion to Twentieth-Century English and American War Literature*.

Gill Plain is a professor of English literature and popular culture at the University of St Andrews. She has research interests in war and representation, gender, national identity, and crime fiction. Her publications include *Women's Fiction of the Second World War*, *Twentieth-Century Crime Fiction: Gender, Sexuality and the Body*, and *John Mills and British Cinema: Masculinity, Identity and Nation*. She has edited, with Susan Sellers, *A History of Feminist Criticism* and, with Danielle Hipkins, *War-Torn Tales: Literature, Film and Gender in the Aftermath of World War II*. Her book *Literature of the 1940s: War, Postwar and "Peace"* was published by Edinburgh University Press.

Petra Rau is Senior Lecturer in Modern Literature at the University of East Anglia. Her research interests include literature about war and fascism, memory studies, Anglo-German cultural relations, and travel writing. She is the author of *English Modernism, National Identity and the Germans, 1890–1950* and *Our Nazis: Representations of Fascism in Contemporary Literature and Film* as well as the editor of *Conflict, Nationhood and Corporeality: Bodies-at-War*.

Margaret D. Stetz is Mae and Robert Carter Professor of Women's Studies and Professor of Humanities at the University of Delaware. Among her publications on fin-de-siècle literature and culture are *Facing the Late Victorians, Gender and the London Theatre, 1880–1920*, and *British Women's Comic Fiction, 1890–1990: Not Drowning, But Laughing*. She has also curated several major exhibitions on Victorian publishing history and art, and, with Bonnie B. C. Oh, edited a collection on gendered war experience, *Legacies of the Comfort Women of World War II*.

Victoria Stewart is a reader in the department of English at the University of Leicester. She is the author of *Women's Autobiography: War and Trauma*, *About O'Casey*, *Narratives of Memory: British Writing of the 1940s*, and *The Second World War in Contemporary British Fiction: Secret Histories*.

Eluned Summers-Bremner is Senior Lecturer in English at the University of Auckland, New Zealand. She is the author of *Insomnia: A Cultural History* and *Ian McEwan: Sex, Death and History*. Her current research focuses on a history of wandering and on a project funded by the Royal Society on responses to trauma in British novels and diaries of the Second World War.

Sue Vice is a professor of English literature at the University of Sheffield. She has published widely on Malcolm Lowry, literary theory, and Holocaust writing, notably *Holocaust Fiction*, *Children Writing the Holocaust*, and the British Film Institute companion to Claude Lanzmann's documentary *Shoah*. Her most recent book is *Textual Deceptions: False Memoirs and Literary Hoaxes in the Contemporary Era*.